The Olivet Discourse

A Reconstruction of the Text
From Matthew, Mark, and Luke

with Commentary

Sam A. Smith

Biblical Reader Communications

The Olivet Discourse: A Reconstruction of the Text From Matthew, Mark, and Luke, with Commentary

First print edition: January 2010, revised July 2013

Published by
Biblical Reader Communications (www.biblicalreader.com)
Raleigh, N.C.

In cooperation with **CreateSpace**

Scripture quotations taken from the *New American Standard Bible* ®, Copyright © 1960, 1962, 1963, 1968, 1971, 1972, 1973, 1975, 1977, 1995 by the Lockman Foundation. Used by permission. (www.Lockman.org) The "NASB," "NAS," "New American Standard Bible," and "New American Standard" trademarks are registered in the U.S. Patent and Trademark Office by the Lockman Foundation. Use of these trademarks requires the permission of the Lockman Foundation.

Scripture quotations taken from the HOLY BIBLE, NEW INTERNATIONAL VERSION ® Copyright © 1973, 1978, 1984 by International Bible Society. Used by permission of Zondervan Publishing House. All rights reserved. The "NIV" and "New International Version" trademarks are register in the United States Patent and Trademark Office by International Bible Society. Use of either trademark requires the permission of International Bible Society.

The Greek texts of Matthew, Mark, and Luke and all other citations of the Greek New Testament are from *The Greek New Testament*, Third Edition (UBS-3), published by the United Bible Societies.

The Greek New Testament, Third Edition, edited by Kurt Aland, Matthew Black, Carlo M. Martini, Bruce Metzger, and Allen Wikgren in cooperation with the Institute for New Testament Textual Research, Münster/Westphalia, © 1975 United Bible Societies. Used by permission.

Library of Congress Cataloging-in-Publication Data

Smith, Sam A.

The Olivet Discourse: a reconstruction of the text from Matthew,
   Mark, and Luke: with commentary / Sam A. Smith

Includes bibliographic references (p. 265-268).

ISBN: 9781449996659
        1449996655

1. Jesus Christ-Prophecies.   2. Bible. N.T. Gospels-Prophecies-Second Advent.
3. Second Advent-Biblical teaching.

BT370.S65 2010
226/ .077 22

Digital edition in PDF format published online by Biblical Reader Communications (www.biblicalreader.com)

For other books and papers by the author visit : www.biblicalreader.com

Contents

Illustrations, Tables, and Outline

Abbreviations

AV	Authorized Version (The King James Version of the Bible)
BAGD	*A Greek-English Lexicon of the New Testament and other Early Literature,* by W. Bauer, translated and adapted by W.F. Arndt and F. Wilbur Gingrich, and revised and augmented by F.W. Gingrich and F.W. Danker (2nd ed.; Chicago: University of Chicago Press, 1979)
BDB	*The New Brown-Driver-Briggs-Gesenius Hebrew and English Lexicon* (Hendrickson Publishers, 1979)
cf.	Confer (see these references)
cp.	Compare
ff.	And following verses ("f." for one verse)
GP	*Gospel Parallels: A Synopsis of the First Three Gospels,* ed. by Burton H. Throckmorton (an adaptation of Albert Huck's *Synopsis of the First Three Gospels* based on the 9th ed. of the English edition by Hans Leitzmann, 1936)
MS	Manuscript, pl. MSS
NASB	*The New American Standard Bible*
NIV	*The New International Bible*
RGGNT	*A Grammar of the Greek New Testament in the Light of Historical Research,* by A.T. Robertson (Nashville: Broadman Press, 1934)
SYNOP	*Synopsis of the Four Gospels: English Edition,* ed. by Kurt Aland (1st edition, United Bible Societies, 1982)
TDNT	*Theological Dictionary of the New Testament,* edited by G. Kittle and G. Friedrich; translated and edited by G.W. Bromiley (10 vols.; Grand Rapids: Eerdmans, 1964-76)
UBS-3	*The Greek New Testament,* 3rd Edition, ed. by Kurt Aland, Matthew Black, Carlo M. Martini, Bruce Metzger, and Allen Wikgren in cooperation with the Institute for New Testament Textual Research (New York: United Bible Societies, 1975)
UBS-4	*The Greek New Testament,* 4th Edition, ed. by Barbara Aland, Kurt Aland, Johannes Karavidopoulos, Carlo M. Martini, and Bruce Metzger in cooperation with the Institute for New Testament Textual Research (Stuttgart: Deutsche Bibelgesellschaft, 1993)
vv.	Verse range for multiple verses ("v." for one verse)

Transliteration of Greek into English

All Hebrew terms in this volume appear with an English transliteration, however, it was not practical to transliterate the Greek. Since in most cases Greek is pronounced as written, the reader will find the following guidelines useful in transliterating the Greek text into English characters for pronunciation.

Alphabet

α	a (as in "f<u>a</u>ther")	ν	n
β	b	ξ	x (as in e<u>x</u>it)
γ	g (as in "gone")	o	o (as in "t<u>o</u>p")
δ	d	π	p
ε	e (as in "n<u>e</u>t")	ϱ	r
ζ	z (as in "<u>z</u>one")	σ (ς)	s
η	ē (sounds like "m<u>a</u>te")	τ	t
0	th	υ	u (as in "<u>up</u>")
ι	i (sounds like "h<u>e</u>")	φ	ph
κ	k	χ	ch (as in "a<u>ch</u>e")
λ	l	ψ	ps (as in "<u>ps</u>ychology")
μ	m	ω	o (as in "<u>o</u>bey")

Irregularities

1. When γ appears before another γ, or a κ, ξ, or χ, the leading γ takes an "n" sound; thus γγ is pronounced "ng," and transliterated accordingly.
2. When ϱ appears as the first letter of a word it has a rough breathing mark (ῥ), and is written "rh."
3. ς and σ are the same letter; ς is the form used when it appears at the end of a word, but they are translated the same ("s").
4. A rough breathing mark (῾), not to be confused with the smooth breathing mark (᾿), or the accent (`), indicates an "h" sound; thus ὁ is transliterated "ho."
5. The *iota* subscript (as in ᾳ, or ῃ) has no effect on pronunciation or transliteration.

Diphthongs

The common Greek diphthongs are pronounced (but not transliterated) like the underlined letter(s) below:

αι, pronounced like "<u>ai</u>sle"	αυ, pronounced like "h<u>ow</u>"	υι, pronounced like "<u>we</u>"
ει, pronounced like "m<u>a</u>te"	ευ, pronounced like "f<u>eu</u>d"	
οι, pronounced like "<u>oi</u>l"	ου, pronounced like "m<u>oo</u>d"	

Accents

Greek has three accents, the acute (´), the circumflex (˜), and the grave (`). All polysyllabic words will have one accent found over a vowel or the second vowel of a diphthong. Stress should be placed on the accented syllable. When a breathing mark and an accent are over the same letter, the breathing mark is to the left of the accent, except that a circumflex accent appears above the breathing mark.

Punctuation

Greek as it appears in the printed Greek texts has four punctuation marks. The comma and the period are the same as in English. The question mark (;) looks like an English semicolon, and the Greek colon (·) is a raised dot.

Preface

This volume is both a reconstruction and interpretation of Christ's Olivet Discourse reported in Matthew 24-25, Mark 13, and Luke 21, as well as other portions of Matthew and Luke. Generally, commentaries on the gospels suffer from the following deficiency: they fail to reflect that the synoptic accounts (Matthew, Mark, and Luke) are highly condensed, and that it is only when the gospel material is reconstructed that some things come into proper perspective.[1] Regrettably, most commentaries treat the synoptic gospels, as well as John's gospel, individually. This volume takes a different approach. The text upon which the commentary is based is a compilation of all of the discourse material found in the synoptics. With that in mind, the reader can see that the parallel texts, which appear in both Greek and English in this volume, are the key to everything else. Since the author subscribes to the verbal inspiration of the original New Testament texts, there is no extended discussion of their development. The underlying assumption of this work is that the Holy Spirit gave recall to one or more of Jesus' disciples of the things he said, as promised in John 14:26; and that Matthew, Mark, and Luke drew upon that source material in compiling their gospels.[2] It seems likely from a comparison of the texts that Mark's account was produced first, and that Matthew and Luke likely had access to Mark's gospel, as well as the original source material that Mark had selectively used (and other material that Mark had not used).[3] Of course there is no

---

[1] Consider the fact that 31 percent of Luke's material is unique (307 words out of 980 words total—not counting isolated unique words, phrases or transitions). This means there is a considerable amount of discourse material that is found nowhere else. Over half of this material is found in Luke's main-body account (chapter 21); the remainder is dislocated in chapters 12 and 17. Not surprisingly, one of the major shortcomings in the interpretation of the Olivet Discourse is the failure to take some of this material into consideration.

[2] With the possible exception of Luke, we do not know the names of the actual authors of these books, since the books do not tell us. The names applied to these gospels come from a rather incomplete early church history. Recognizing that fact, we will refer to the authors of these holy and inspired scriptures as Matthew, Mark, and Luke.

[3] According to McKnight (Scott McKnight, *Interpreting the Synoptic Gospels*, Baker Book House, 1988, pp.35-40) the "Oxford Hypothesis" (also called the "Two/Four Source Hypothesis") is the dominant explanation of the synoptic phenomena. This view states that Matthew and Luke had access to Mark and at least one common source (generally referred to as "Q"), and possibly multiple common sources. It is true that wherever Matthew deviates from Mark, Luke follows Mark; and wherever Luke deviates from Mark, Matthew follows Mark with no cases where both Matthew and Luke deviate from Mark in the same place. (This can be seen in the parallel texts in this volume.) Of course the fact that there are approximately two hundred verses common to both Matthew's gospel and Luke's gospel that do not appear in Mark, many with strong verbal agreement, argues that Matthew and Luke had access to common source material other than Mark's gospel. Thus, the position favored here is that Mark was likely composed first, and that

particular reason why there could not have been multiple sources upon which the gospel writers drew, as long as we understand that they drew upon accurate information under divine inspiration.

Another problem found in many commentaries on the gospels is a failure to interpret within the framework of sound biblical eschatology; this is particularly important in interpreting this discourse, since it is entirely eschatological. As will be seen, this discourse is Jesus' extended answer to the disciples' question regarding the end of the age and his second coming (Mt. 24:1-4a). If we approach the text with an inadequate view of biblical eschatology, or worse, with a distorted view, we cannot hope to properly understand Jesus' statements. In this respect we are hampered by almost nineteen hundred years of "replacement theology" and "realized eschatology." The apostolic church was premillennial, and there can be no serious doubt that both the Old and New Testaments, at face value, present a premillennial picture of the kingdom of God.[4] As the church spread into a predominately Greek world the premillennial theology of both the Old and New Testaments increasingly came under attack, particularly after the destruction of Jerusalem in A.D. 70.[5] Owing to the ubiquitous influence of Platonism in its many forms, and to stoicism, and to gnosticism (a Platonized derivative of Christianity that almost overran the church in the second century), Christianity was quickly transformed from a Jewish centered religion, into a Grecianized, anticosmic religion. Naturally, premillennialism with its core belief being the return of Christ to establish the kingdom of God on earth and rule over the earth

---

Matthew and Luke were composed independently using Mark and an additional common source, or sources. None of this has any bearing on the inspiration of the texts of Matthew, Mark or Luke, since inspiration is an entirely distinct issue, and there is no reason why an inspired writer could not make use of source material (which seems to have been common, especially in the Old Testament).

[4] Premillennialism is the position that Christ will return prior to the establishment of the visible aspect of the kingdom of God on earth (*i.e.*, the millennium). Premillennialism stands in contrast to "realized eschatology" (amillennialism) which teaches that the kingdom in all of its aspects began with the early church and continues to the present day (spiritually), and postmillennialism, which takes a more literal view of the kingdom, but like amillennialism teaches that Christ will return at the conclusion rather than the beginning of the millennium. [The terms "amillennialism" and "postmillennialism" can be confusing, as both positions subscribe to the postmillennial return of Christ, and originally both positions were referred to as "postmillennialism." However, in recent times those who subscribe to "realized eschatology" (that the kingdom is now) are generally referred to as "amillennialists."] For a survey of these views see: Sam A. Smith, *What the Bible Says About the Future,* Second edition (Biblical Reader Communications, 2005, also available through the Internet at www.biblicalreader.com), pp.41-54.

[5] Rationalistic philosophy, which substitutes human reason for divine revelation, was already making inroads into the local churches by the time Paul wrote his letter to the Colossians in about A.D. 61 (cf. Col.2:8).

from Jerusalem, the capital of a restored and ascendant Israel, did not fit the prevailing mindset of the Grecianized church. First came replacement premillennialism—the idea that the Church[6] replaces Israel in the premillennial kingdom program.[7] Since replacement premillennialism required the spiritualization (*i.e.*, non-normal/non-objective interpretation) of the promises of God to Israel, it was only one small step away from the complete spiritualization of the kingdom program which followed quickly in the form of realized eschatology, or what is referred to today as "amillennialism." Realized eschatology took replacement premillennialism to the next logical step—not only the spiritualization of the promises to Israel as being fulfilled in and through the Church, but the spiritualization of the very nature of the kingdom itself.

By the third century, realized eschatology was firmly rooted, especially in the eastern churches, and some canons did not even include the book of Revelation because of its patent premillennialism.[8] By the close of the fifth century a general consensus on the spiritualization of eschatology, and especially a spiritualized view of the book of Revelation had largely obscured the premillennialism of both the gospels and the book of Revelation.[9] Thus, the rejection of the express and implicit teaching of the New

---

[6] References to the invisible Church, *i.e.* "the Body of Christ," are capitalized to distinguish them from general references to the visible church.

[7] Replacement premillennialism is first seen in Justin Martyr's *Dialogue With Trypho* (see chapters LXXX-LXXXI for Justin's view of premillennialism, and chapters CXIX-CXX for his view that the Church replaces Israel in the kingdom program). Justin's work dates to the mid-second century.

[8] Ostensibly the reasons given for denying the inspiration of Revelation involved objections that the book was impossible to interpret—and indeed it was to those who had rejected premillennialism, which is the framework upon which the book is built. Those in the early church who rejected premillennialism had a difficult enough job spiritualizing the kingdom from the gospels, though they took some comfort in Christ's statement in Luke 17:20 that "the arrival of the kingdom of God will not be observable," for such a statement taken out of its context can easily be distorted to imply that the kingdom program is to have no physical/material aspect. However, those who adopt such a position usually neglect Jesus' teaching in the same book that the kingdom of God will be inaugurated in connection with Christ's return (Lk. 21:31). Luke 21:31 reads: οὕτως καὶ ὑμεῖς, ὅταν ἴδητε ταῦτα γινόμενα, γινώσκετε ὅτι ἐγγύς ἐστιν ἡ βασιλεία τοῦ θεοῦ ("likewise, when you see these things happening, know that the kingdom of God is near"). Here, "these things" refers to the things Jesus had just described, things leading up to his second advent. Since the kingdom cannot be both realized (*i.e.*, present) and "near" at the same time (since "near" is anticipatory), Jesus' statement implied that the kingdom will begin in connection with, or soon after his second coming—precisely the picture given in Matthew 24:29-25:46 (especially 25:31).

[9] The first entirely spiritual (allegorized) interpretation of Revelation appears to have been developed by Tychonius (Tichonius), a North African Donatist who lived near the end of the fourth century. His *Commentary on the Apocalypse* was extant as late as the ninth century, but is now known only indirectly. Tichonius' principles of hermeneutics are preserved in Augustine's

Testament by the post-apostolic church eventually became Christian orthodoxy. It is a sad state of affairs when the principal task of interpreters is to explain why scripture does not mean what it says, and implies; yet this is precisely what the great bulk of the interpretation of the gospels and Revelation has done, at least as it relates to eschatological statements; and this is true in both the Catholic and the Reformed traditions.[10]

Another problem found in many commentaries is the failure to reflect the structure of the gospels, especially the structure of this discourse. There are a number of instances in the texts of this discourse where material has been dislocated, either by the author (as seems to be the case with Matthew 25:1-30, which as will be shown later was almost certainly spoken between 24:42 and verse 43), or post-compositionally (as is likely the case with Luke 17:31-33, which should precede, rather than follow Luke 17:22-30). Of course, the fact that sections of the Olivet Discourse in Luke are found within the context of the Sermon on the Mount has to be resolved, and that dislocated material has to be reconnected with the main body of the discourse. Obviously, a failure to reconstruct the text will have a significant impact on our understanding of what Jesus said, and regrettably that shortcoming is universal in the commentaries.

Finally, there are problems even among premillennial interpreters. Prior to the mid-nineteen hundreds both dispensational and covenantal premillennialists generally viewed Matthew 24:45-25:30 as pertaining to the Church at the end of the age.[11]

De Doctrina Christiana (III, 30-37; P.L., XXIV, 81-90). Augustine adapted Tichonius' hermeneutical principles in order to present a highly spiritualized view of virtually all biblical eschatology. The adoption of realized eschatology in the western churches was due largely to Augustine's influence.

[10] In light of this, it is understandable why Martin Luther questioned the canonicity of Revelation, and why John Calvin, who wrote commentaries on almost every other book of the New Testament, wrote no commentary on the book of Revelation.

[11] The term "rapture" (from the Latin "rapio," meaning "to snatch," or "to catch away"—a translation of the Greek term ἁρπάζω {harpazō} in 1 Thessalonians 4:7) designates the aspect of Christ's coming at which the Church will be caught away in new, glorified bodies (by the resurrection of the dead, and translation of the living). The term "rapture" is a theological term, and does not appear in the English translations of the New Testament; nevertheless, as pointed out, the underlying terminology is found in the Greek text of 1 Thessalonians 4:17. Dispensationalists teach that only the redeemed living between the arrival of the Holy Spirit at Pentecost (A.D. 33) and the rapture will be included in this event. Covenant premillennialists view all saved people as part of the Church. While dispensationalists almost universally believe that the rapture will occur before the wrath of God begins at the day of the LORD (variously placing the rapture from about two to seven years prior to the second coming), because of their more inclusive definition of the Church, covenantalists include the tribulation saints as part of the Church; and consequently, they teach that the rapture occurs at the second coming.

However, since the time of Henry C. Thiessen and Lewis Sperry Chafer in the mid-nineteen hundreds, and John F. Walvoord, Chafer's successor, pretribulationists have generally regarded this part of the text as pertaining to Israel at the close of the tribulation. Both views have resulted in significant problems for pretribulationists, and as will be shown, it is quite impossible that Matthew 25:36-25:30 could describe anything other than the rapture of the Church, a doctrine further developed by the Apostle Paul in 1 Corinthians 15:51-52 and 1 Thessalonians 4:13-18.[12] One of the fundamental principles of biblical hermeneutics is that the first mention of any truth is likely to contain information critical to the understanding of that truth elsewhere. Matthew 24:32-51 is the first mention of the rapture of the Church, and as such, it is the fountainhead of the dual appearance view (*i.e.*, that the future appearing of Christ will occur in two phases, the first involving the removal of the Church from the earth prior to the outpouring of divine wrath at the day of the LORD, and the second being the regal appearing that will conclude the tribulation period and result in the establishment of the millennial phase of the kingdom of God).[13, 14]

Clearly this work will not be without its own imperfections, limitations, and errors, albeit unintentional; however, it is a start—a start toward a more complete and eschatologically sound understanding of Jesus' final, and most complete pre-passion teaching about the future.

---

[12] Early pretribulationists viewed 24:36-44 as a description of the second coming and the parables in Matthew 24:45-25-30 as pertaining to the last days of the Church and its rapture. This was the view of J.N. Darby and William Kelly, and seems to have been the view of C.I. Scofield. A.C. Gaebelein and H.A. Ironside held to essentially the same view. However, in the early to mid-1900s Henry C. Thiessen and Lewis Sperry Chafer adopted the position that the Church is not in view at all, prophetically, in the Olivet Discourse; hence, according to this view all of the descriptions there of Christ's appearing must pertain to the second coming. The view of Thiessen and Chafer is mostly implied by the omission of Matthew 24:36-25:30 from their discussions of the rapture (see: H. C. Thiessen, "Will the Church Pass Through the Tribulation," *Bibliotheca Sacra*, vol.92, num.365, pp.39-54, and num.366, pp.187-205; also see: Lewis Sperry Chafer, *Systematic Theology*, vol.4, pp.374-378). It is not certain who originated this view, but it seems to have been the influence of Chafer, and later, John F. Walvoord that accounts for its pervasiveness in contemporary pretribulationism. As will be seen further along in this volume, both the original view of Darby, Kelly, and Scofield, and the view of Thiessen, Chafer, and Walvoord, have proved to be highly problematic both for pretribulationism and for the interpretation of the Olivet Discourse.

[13] The alternative to the dual appearance view is posttribulationism, which takes several forms (*i.e.*, premillennial posttribulationism and various forms of amillennial and postmillennial posttribulationism). All forms of posttribulationism are unitary views, in that they view the rapture and the second coming either as the same event, or occurring at the same time.

[14] In this volume, the second coming proper is referred to simply as "the second coming," or "the regal appearing."

Hermeneutics

It seems a rather strange circumstance that so many godly, capable, and scholarly interpreters in the history of the church have engaged in the "spiritualization" of scripture, which is required for the support of all forms of both replacement theology and realized eschatology. In fact, the process is virtually universal from the second century forward. It seems that it can only be explained on the basis of uncritically accepted theological suppositions. In other words, those who engage in spiritualization of scripture ultimately do so because their theology is inconsistent with the plain sense of the Bible, and assuming their theological assumptions to be correct, they see no reasonable alternative than to spiritualize statements that contradict that theology.

Of course, there is no way to know if an interpretation is correct unless one first knows that the interpretive process is correct. We could fill countless pages examining spiritualized interpretations and attempting to outline the faults; however, such a process would be pointless, for in spiritualized interpretation the only real interpretive mistakes are the technical mistakes of the underlying exegesis of the passage that is subsequently spiritualized. The reason for saying this is that the spiritualization itself is a post-exegetical step, for it cannot be elsewise; and that step is subject only to theological criticism. To put it another way: spiritualization, as it is actually practiced, and there are virtually unlimited examples in the commentaries, is the product of a two-step process. The first step is the normal, literal (objective) exegesis of a passage, for all competent interpreters must first seek to explain the language and circumstances of a passage. This is the objective step in the process, and it involves exposing what the passage actually says. On the validity of this step all competent interpreters should agree, regardless of theological disposition, otherwise there would be no need for a text at all. The fact that the objective step must underlie all biblical interpretation is the reason that interpreters of widely diverse theological perspectives, such as covenantalists and dispensationalists, often make use of shared hermeneutical principles, at least as they pertain to this initial step; and thus to some extent they can benefit from commentaries by interpreters from other theological perspectives, at least with respect to observations and conclusions regarding the objective meaning of the text. However, interpreters whose theological assumptions do not coincide with the objective meaning of a text take the process one step further. After determining the objective meaning, they then interpolate that meaning to represent something "spiritual" (*i.e.*, a truth in allegorical form).[1] Where, and to what degree such interpolation occurs is

---

[1] Spiritualized interpolation assigns to a passage an allegorical meaning that is purported to be more sublime (spiritual) than the literal (objective) meaning. Of course, such interpolation is highly subjective. Amillennialism is dependent upon this type of interpolation, since consistently normal/objective interpretation of scripture leads inexorably to premillennialism.

largely determined by the disposition and theological assumptions of the interpreter. Generally, spiritual interpolation occurs at points where the objective meaning is simply incompatible with the theological assumptions of the interpreter; and the degree of interpolation necessary is determined by the gap between the objective meaning and the interpreter's theology.[2] Of course it should be obvious that this adjunct to the interpretive process is not actually interpretation at all; it is merely a method of conforming scripture to the theological assumptions of the interpreter. Spiritualization arose in early Christianity primarily as a result of two related theological developments: "replacement theology" and "realized eschatology." Replacement theology developed in the early second century; it views the Church as replacing Israel in the kingdom of God. Thus according to replacement theology, because of Israel's rejection of Christ, all or most of the promises God made to Israel have been transferred to the Church.[3] Obviously, since most of the national, ethnic, and geopolitical aspects of the kingdom of God cannot be fulfilled literally to the Church, it became necessary to interpolate those aspects of the kingdom to have a spiritual meaning, which could be applied to the Church. The spiritualization of the kingdom program to the Church resulted first in what is called, "replacement premillennialism" (that the Church replaces Israel in a premillennial kingdom program); but replacement premillennialism is not entirely satisfactory because it is highly arbitrary in what is spiritualized.[4] It wasn't long before an entirely new theology developed, which theologians have since dubbed, "realized eschatology." Realized eschatology became popular in many of the eastern churches in the second and third centuries, but it did not find broad acceptance in the western churches until the fifth and sixth centuries. Realized eschatology maintains that not only were the promises to Israel transferred to the Church, but some or all of the prophecies of the end of the age have already been fulfilled.[5] There have been many refinements to both replacement theology and realized eschatology throughout church history. However, it is important to understand that spiritual interpolation is what undergirds all forms of both replacement theology and realized eschatology; and thus, where such

---

[2] Even many amillennialists, who themselves engage in spiritualization, are appalled at the degree of spiritualization evidenced in full preterism (the view that all eschatological prophecy was fulfilled by the conclusion of A.D. 70).

[3] Paul, in Romans 11, specifically warned the Roman church about falling into this error.

[4] Replacement premillennialism can be clearly seen in the mid-second century in Justin Martyr's *Dialogue With Trypho,* where chapters LXXX-LXXXI exhibit premillennialism and chapters CXIX-CXX and CXXXV exhibit replacement theology.

[5] Most amillennialists view only some of the prophecies of the end of the age as having been fulfilled (this position is called "partial preterism"), while others view all of the prophecies of the end of the age as having been fulfilled by the conclusion of A.D. 70 (referred to as, "full preterism").

doctrines are held, spiritualization is viewed as an accepted and even necessary adjunct to biblical interpretation.

If the spiritual interpolation of a text says something other than what the text actually says, then by what sound and defensible principles is that spiritual meaning to be determined? The answer is that there are no such principles, nor can there be; for if the meaning is something other than what the text objectively states, as determined by means of the conventional use of language, then any meaning assigned to the text can only be arbitrary. In reality, spiritualization is nothing more than a pretext for jettisoning the objective meaning of the text for the sake of prior theological assumptions.

Of the two major interpretive systems (dispensationalism and covenant theology) only dispensationalism subscribes to a consistently normal/objective interpretation of scripture. In other words, dispensationalism represents a truly exegetical method of interpretation. By "objective interpretation" dispensationalists do not mean that one should ignore figures of speech or various literary devices like symbols. Objective interpretation requires that these forms be understood according to the prevailing usage at the time they were written. Thus, the key to interpreting symbols is to ask the question, "How would they have been understood by the writer's contemporary target audience?"

A consistently normal/objective method of interpretation is superior for at least two reasons. First, it is the only method by which exegesis is possible. If we accept the fact that the Bible is God's communication to man and that God intends for man to understand that communication, we can only conceive of God as using human language in a rational and logical manner, according to prevailing usage. The reason is that this is the only way man could ever discern the intended meaning, because the rules of language apply only when language is being used in its normal, conventional sense. Second, scripture in general, and prophecy in particular, makes sense when interpreted normally/objectively. This is the method of interpretation that we depend upon for other areas of doctrine, including fulfilled prophecy, so it is only consistent to apply it to future prophecy as well. It is worth observing that prophecy that has been fulfilled has been fulfilled in a manner consistent with normal/objective interpretation. By what authority does the covenantal interpreter maintain that only future prophecy will be fulfilled according to a different pattern? [6]

The application of a dual (normal/allegorical) system of interpretation, as in covenant theology, results in inconsistencies. For example, it results in the first sixty-nine weeks of Daniel's seventy-weeks prophecy (Dan. 9:24-27) being interpreted literally

---

[6] Since fulfilled prophecy was future prophecy before it was fulfilled, how does one justify a dual hermeneutic in which fulfilled prophecy is interpreted objectively, but future prophecy is spiritualized?

but the last, or seventieth week, being understood non-literally. Or, in the case of Christ's advent, it requires a literal interpretation of the first advent of Christ and a non-literal interpretation of the events associated with the second coming, even though they may be contained within the same passage, (*e.g.*, Isa. 61:1-3). Once the decision is made to depart from a consistently normal/literal manner of interpretation, interpretation becomes merely the opinion of the interpreter.

The Structure of the Discourse

The material comprising the text of the Olivet Discourse comes from two types of sources within the synoptics: main-body accounts, as found in Matthew 24-25, Mark 13, and Luke 21; and sources disconnected from the main-body accounts, such as Matthew 10:17-23, Luke 12:35-46, and 17:22-37. While most commentators at least compare the main-body accounts, few acknowledge some of the disconnected portions as part of the same discourse, and none make any attempt to reconstruct the text.[1] There are numerous reasons for this, but likely the primary reason is the pervasive influence of redaction criticism in modern synoptic interpretation.[2] Redaction criticism views the differences in the synoptic accounts as owing primarily to the weaving of different, and often, incompatible (and hence uninspired) sources into the gospel accounts. At its core, redaction criticism is built on an evolutionary view of the development of the gospels; and regrettably, this view has been integrated into much of conservative New Testament interpretation. The author does not subscribe to the evolutionary view of the origin of the gospels. Instead, we will operate on the much simpler and more biblical assumption that the gospels were written early, certainly during the lifetime of Jesus' original disciples, and that just as Jesus promised (Jn. 14:26; 15:26-27; 16:13) the Spirit of God gave inspired recall to some of his disciples who recorded Jesus' teachings, and that those early and inspired sources served as the basis for the writing of the synoptic gospels. Of course, the gospel writers exercised some degree of freedom under the supervision of the Spirit of God in arranging and condensing the material. That the original sources of information were composed in Hebrew or Aramaic seems virtually certain (if Jesus spoke in one of these languages, why would the Holy Spirit have given recall in a different language?); and differences in the translation of these original sources into the Greek of the gospels is yet another explanation of the differences. Therefore, to account for the differences in the synoptic gospels we have at least four factors: 1) multiple early inspired sources, some of which undoubtedly included information not contained in other sources; 2) the measure of individual freedom the gospel writers were given under the supervision of the Holy Spirit to compose their accounts, both in regard to the arrangement and abridgement of the material; 3) the fact

---

[1] At the time of publication, the author is unaware of any major published attempt to present a complete and well-reasoned reconstruction of the entire text of the Olivet Discourse. Kurt Aland's *Synopsis of the Four Gospels* (United Bible Societies, 1984) attempts to compare the texts, but lacks details; and there is no attempt to reconstruct the reading of the text. The same is true of other volumes, such as, *Gospel Parallels: A Synopsis of the First Three Gospels,* edited by Burton H. Throckmorton (Thomas Nelson Publishers, 1957).

[2] For concise presentations of redaction criticism see McKnight's *Interpreting the Synoptic Gospels* (chapter 8) and, *What is Redaction Criticism?* by Norman Perrin, Philadelphia: Fortress Press, 1969.

that the source material was almost certainly translated from Hebrew or Aramaic; and, 4) the possibility of post-compositional rearrangement of some material. It is the author's belief that such a view of the origin of the synoptics answers far more questions than does redaction criticism, and that it permits us to have complete confidence in the text and its message, though undoubtedly, in order to get the complete message some reconstruction of the text will be necessary. The structural analysis presented in this volume is based on the belief that all of the eschatological teachings of Jesus that connect verbally and structurally to the main-body accounts in Matthew, Mark, and Luke are from the same discourse, and as will be presented, there is much evidence, both in terms of verbal agreement and contextual clues to support that assumption.

An overview of the structure of the discourse

[A complete structural arrangement of both the Greek and English texts is presented in the parallel texts beginning on page 41.]

Mark contains no dislocated material.

Matthew 24:1-42 is in sequence, except that verse 28 should be placed between verses 41 and 42, since Matthew 24:28 is parallel to Luke 17:37b and Matthew 24:41 is parallel to Luke 17:37a. (On the position of Luke 17:22-37, see the discussion below under, "Material disconnected from the main body.") Matthew 10:17-22 merges with 24:9-13 (cf. Mark 13:9-13 and Luke 21:12-19). Matthew 25:1-30 (the similitudes of the virgins and the stewards) falls between 24:42 and 24:43 to match with Mark 13:34-36 (also parallel to Luke 12:35-38). (Luke 12:35-38 matches to Mark 13:34-35, and Matthew 24:43-51 matches to Luke 12:39-46; placing Matthew 25:1-30 between 24:42 and 24:43.) Again, on the position of Luke 12:36-46 see the discussion below. Finally, Matthew 25:31-46 closes the discourse.

Luke 21:1-21 is in sequence. Luke 17:32 matches Matthew 24:17-18 and Mark 13:15-16, and Luke 21:22-24 matches Matthew 24:19-22 and Mark 13:17-18; thus, Luke 17:31-33 falls between Luke 21:21 and 21:22. Luke 21:22-24 follows Luke 17:31-33, as can be seen by the fact that it matches Matthew 24:19-21 and Mark 13:17-19. Luke 17:22-25 falls between Luke 21:24 and 21:25. (Luke 17:22-25 matches Matthew 24:23-27 and Mark 13:21-23, and Luke 21:25-33 matches Matthew 24:29-36 and Mark 13:24-32; thus Luke 17:22-25 falls between Luke 21:24 and 21:25.) Luke 21:25-33 is in sequence. Luke 17:26-30 and 34-37 fall between Luke 21:33 and 21:34.[3] Luke 21:34-36, which matches to Matthew

---

[3] Likely the material now contained in Luke 17:26-30 and verses 34-37 was moved from its original location in the main-body account to an earlier point in the book (chapter 17). Subsequently (but perhaps not far removed in time) the illustration of Lot's wife (Lk. 17:31-33) that came from earlier in the discourse was also moved and inserted after the illustration of Lot on the incorrect assumption that the illustrations of Lot and his wife should go together. Thus it

24:42 and Mark 13:33-36 is in sequence. Luke 12:35-46 follows 21:36 (Luke 12:35-38 matches Mark 13:34-36), which completes the discourse.

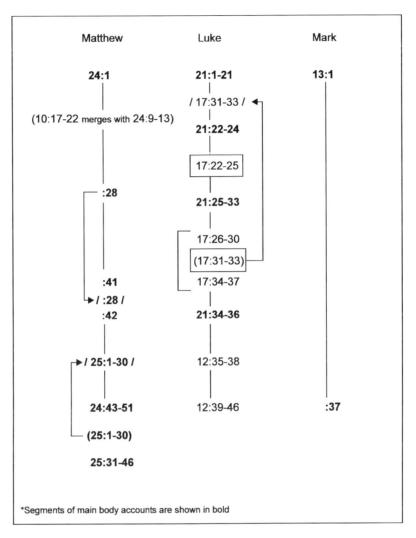

The Overall Structure of the Olivet Discourse

One additional problem remains in aligning Luke's account with Matthew and Mark. Luke employs a recursive structure, citing some events of the end of the age at 21:11b ("terrors and from heaven great signs") and then recursively describing events leading up to that point in verses 21:12-19. This requires Luke to introduce 21:12 with

---

seems likely that the material contained in Luke 17:26-37 was moved from the main-body account in a two-step process. That the illustrations of Lot and his wife do not belong in the same immediate context is discussed in the commentary.

the qualifying clause: "But before all these things." In order to align Luke with Matthew and Mark, this recursive structure can be unfolded by placing 21:11b after the recursion (*i.e.*, after 21:19), and by dropping the qualifying clause ("But before all these things") found in 21:12a. (See the illustration below.)

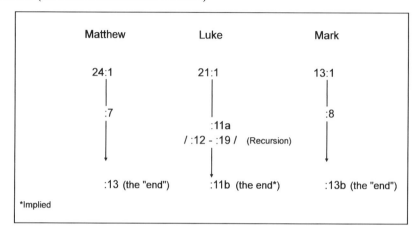

Unfolding the Recursive Structure of Luke 21:11-19

Material disconnected from the main body of the discourse (Matthew 10:17-23; Luke 12:35-46; and 17:22-37)

As is noted below, each of these sections correlates closely with material found in one or more of the main-body accounts of the discourse. In most cases the dislocated material correlates to material in the main-body account of another gospel, but is absent in the main-body account of the gospel in which it is found. In each of the four cases, Robertson regards these as sayings distinct from the Olivet Discourse.[4] Aland, at Matthew 10:17-23, refers the reader to statements in the main body of the Olivet Discourse accounts of Mark and Luke, but does not consider Matthew 10:17-23 to be parallel to the discourse. At Luke 12:35-48 he parallels verses 35-38 to Matthew 25:8-12.[5] However, Aland does view Luke 12:39-46 as parallel to Matthew 24:43-51, and Luke 17:22-37 as parallel to sections of Matthew 24.[6] *Gospel Parallels* shows Luke 12:39-40 as

---

[4] Interestingly, in all four cases Robertson does not mention that nearly identical material appears in the Olivet Discourse accounts of other gospels (A.T. Robertson, *A Harmony of the Gospels*, Harper and Brothers, 1922) for Matthew 10:17-23 see pp.80-81; for Luke 12:35-46 see pp.127-128; for Luke 17:22-37 see p.140.

[5] There is no verbal correlation between Luke 12:35-38 and Matthew 25:8-13, and only a very loose topical connection. Luke 12:35-38 is best seen as having been omitted in Matthew's account (between 24:42 and 43).

[6] Rather than moving Luke 17:32-33 to match with Matthew 24:17-18 (retaining Matthew's sequence), Aland moves Matthew 24:17-18 to match with the sequence of Luke 17:32-33 (Aland,

parallel to Matthew 24:42-44, Luke 12:42-46 as parallel to Matthew 24:45-51, Luke 17:23-24, and verse 37 as parallel to Matthew 24:26-28, and Luke 17:26-27 and verses 34-35 as parallel to Matthew 24:37-41.[7]

The general argument for including all of these sections as part of the Olivet Discourse, rather than as similar sayings at an earlier time, is the very close, and in some cases identical verbal correspondence with sections of discourse material found in other main-body accounts; and the fact that in each gospel where disconnected material is found, that material is also absent in that gospel's main-body account of the discourse.[8] The simplest and most reasonable explanation for this would seem to be that in each case a section of discourse material has been dislocated.

Matthew 24:45-51 and Luke 12:35-46

Most of Matthew 24:43-51 is nearly identical to Luke 12:35-46. However, Mark ends the discourse with the admonition to "watch" (Mk. 13:37), which falls between Matthew 24:44 and verse 45. Luke has the content of Matthew 24:45-51 in chapter 12, which would seem to place it at an earlier time, leading to the possibility that Matthew 24:45-51 might have been appended to the Olivet Discourse from an earlier discourse, and that the discourse in Matthew 24 should end after verse 44. However, arguing against this is the fact that Luke's gospel has significant chronological dislocations; and the material immediately prior to Luke 12 is Jesus' pronouncement of woes on the Pharisees (11:42-54), which in Matthew is recorded in chapter 23, and which by

---

Synopsis, p.203, sec.235). However, Luke's material is already dislocated from the main body of the discourse (chapter 21); thus, it is apparent that the Luke material must be moved to match with Matthew. That this is the correct solution is further confirmed by the fact that the illustration of Lot and the allusion to Lot's wife illustrate entirely different ideas that do not belong in the same immediate context (*i.e.*, one immediately following the other). The story of Lot, just as the preceding story of Noah, is used to illustrate the unexpectedness of the Lord's appearing, with its concomitant judgment, whereas the allusion to Lot's wife illustrates that those fleeing Jerusalem after the abomination is set up in the temple should flee quickly and not return to retrieve possessions—a subject discussed earlier in the discourse (cf. Mt. 24:15-22). It seems likely that the allusion to Lot's wife was moved in Luke's account (post-compositionally) to follow the illustration of Lot on the assumption that these go together, which is not the case.

[7] Throckmorton, *Gospel Parallels,* secs.218, 224, 225, 226. *GP* also shows Luke 19:12-27 as parallel to Matthew 25:14-30; however, in view of the many differences in the details of these analogical stories it seems unlikely that the Luke 19:12-27 material is from the Olivet Discourse.

[8] For instance, Matthew 10:17-23 is parallel to a portion of Mark's and Luke's main-body account, but, except for two verses (vv. 17 and 22b) is absent in Matthew's main-body account. Also, Luke 12:35-47 parallels a portion of Matthew's main-body account, but is absent from Luke's main-body account. Finally, Luke 17:22-37 parallels sections of both Matthew's and Mark's main-body accounts, but is absent in Luke's main-body account.

comparison with Mark's gospel can be established as having occurred on Tuesday of the passion week—the same day the Olivet Discourse was spoken. Thus, it seems reasonably certain that the content from Luke 12:35-46 is from the Olivet Discourse, and that it was moved to an earlier position in Luke's gospel (which tends to be more topical in arrangement).[9] The lack of textual variations in the existing manuscripts, the earliest of which date from the third century, suggests that the dislocation occurred very early. Somehow the moving of this material must have resulted in the moving of the account of the "woes" on the Pharisees to this earlier position in Luke (or *vice versa*). One might hypothesize that Jesus delivered the same material twice, accounting for why it is found in two settings. However, this is not a satisfactory hypothesis since it would require that immediately prior to both instances Jesus pronounced woes on the Pharisees; and it does not explain why, if this content were spoken on two occasions, it is missing from Luke's main-body account. The best explanation seems to be that this material was moved from its original location as part of Luke's main-body account, and spliced into an earlier setting in the book. The fact that this material does not fit with the theme of the other material in Luke 12 further supports this conclusion.[10, 11]

Matthew 10:17-23

Interestingly, Matthew 10:17-23 correlates more closely to both Mark and Luke than does the Matthew 24 account, which mostly contains material unique to verses 24:9-14, though there is close correspondence at 24:9b and 24:13 to the other accounts. The nearly identical verbal agreement between Matthew 10:17-23 and Mark's and Luke's main-body accounts leads one to believe that the material in Matthew 10:17-23 was originally in the Olivet Discourse, but subsequently moved to an earlier position in Matthew. Quite interestingly, in this case the moving of material was highly selective; some material was relocated while other material within the same immediate context

---

[9] Bock notes a parallel to the Olivet Discourse, but like others he suggests that Jesus may have given more than one eschatological discourse (Darrell Bock, *Luke,* vol.2, Grand Rapids: Baker Academic, 1996, p.1171); however, this would not explain why Luke also has Jesus' pronouncement of woes on the Pharisees (11:42-54) just prior to this eschatological section, as is also found in Matthew 23:1-39 just prior to Matthew's main-body account of the Olivet Discourse in chapters 24-25; neither does it take into consideration the points of contact with Mark's main-body account at Mark 13:34-35 (see the parallel texts). That Luke 12:35-46 comes from a prior eschatological discourse seems to be far less likely than that this section has somehow become disconnected from the main body of Luke's account.

[10] Luke 12:13-34 deals with divine providence, whereas verse 35 abruptly switches to stewardship.

[11] Additionally, διχοτομήσει (to "cut in two"), which appears in Luke 12:46, appears in only one other place in the NT—Matthew 24:51 (Matthew's main-body parallel to Luke 12:46)—supporting the view that Luke 12:35-46 is a displaced segment of the Olivet Discourse.

was left in place (24:10-12 and verse 14 were not moved, and verses 9 and 13 appear in both places). Also, by comparison of Matthew 10:1-35 with Luke 12:2-53, it can be determined that the material moved in Matthew from the main-body account to 10:17-23 was placed in the same immediate context of the material in Luke that was relocated to Luke 12:35-53 (note that Matthew 10:26-33 is parallel to Luke 12:2-9, and Matthew 10:34-35 is parallel to Luke 12:51-53). That Matthew 10:17-23 was originally a portion of the Olivet Discourse seems almost certain when one sees the connections to the other three accounts both in the illustration below and in the parallel texts.[12]

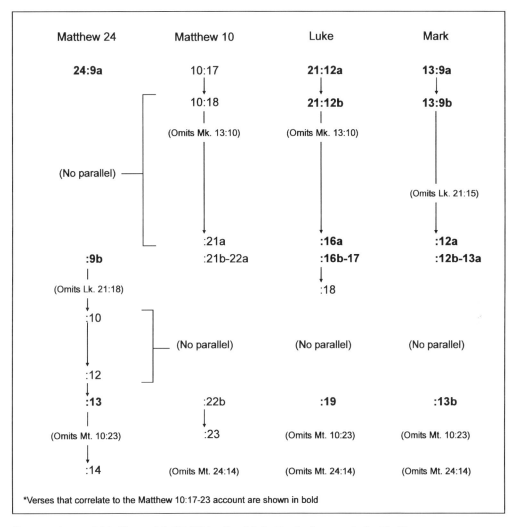

Comparison of Matthew 10:17-23 to the Main Body Accounts in Matthew, Luke, and Mark

[12] The parallel texts appear in "Reconstruction of the Discourse," beginning on page 41. Note also the summary table on page 29.

As can be seen from the comparison above, while all four accounts correlate in the introduction to this segment, the Matthew 24 account has no parallel to the material in Matthew 10:18-21a, or to Luke 21:12-16a and Mark 13:9-12a. In contrast, while all four accounts correlate to the material in Matthew 24:9b, the Matthew 10, Luke, and Mark accounts do not contain the material found in Matthew 24:10-12; but all four accounts correlate from Matthew 24:13 forward (with the exception that Matthew 10:23 and 24:14 are unique).[13]

Luke 12:47-53 (not included in the reconstructed text)

This material follows Luke 12:35-46, which is part of the Olivet Discourse. However, none of the gospels include any of these verses in their main-body accounts of the discourse. Verses 47-49 are unique to Luke 12; and the material in Luke 12:51-53 appears in Matthew 10:34-35, which closely follows the displaced Olivet material in 10:17-24. It is possible that this section might have a connection to the Olivet Discourse; however, there isn't sufficient evidence of such a connection to include it in the reconstructed text.

Luke 17:22-37

Both Lenski and Bock view this passage as similar to material in the Olivet Discourse, but spoken on an earlier occasion.[14] Geldenhuys takes the same view.[15] However, in Lange's commentary (Luke), Starbuck is confident that this material is a fragment from the Olivet Discourse.[16] As already noted above, Aland views Luke 17:22-37 as parallel to sections of Matthew 24.[17]

---

[13] Note also that Mark 13:10 and Luke 21:18 are unique.

[14] R.C.H. Lenski, *The Interpretation of St. Luke's Gospel,* Augsburg Publishing House, 1961, pp.883-891. Darrell L. Bock (*Luke*, vol.2, pp.1421-1423).

[15] Norval Geldenhuys, *Commentary on Luke* in the New International Commentary on the New Testament (William B. Eerdmans Publishing, 1951), p.445, note 12.

[16] Starbuck's bracketed note, inserted at Luke 17:31, states the following: "I do not see how any one can regard vss. 31-37 as anything else than a fragment of our Savior's subsequent prediction of the destruction of Jerusalem. It fits perfectly into that, while it is impossible to see any immediate applicableness here. It is doubtless inserted here as an element of the eschatological discourse of our Lord…." (C.C. Starbuck was the American Editor of the Luke volume of Lange's Commentary). See, J. P. Lange, *Luke,* in Lange's Commentary on the Holy Scriptures (Zondervan Publishing House, in an undated reprint of the American edition based on a translation from the German original by J.J. Van Oosterzee), p.267 at v.31.

[17] Aland, *Synopsis*, p.203 (sec. 235).

The Unity of the Discourse

The table below indicates the extent of precise agreement among all of the segments of the discourse. This extremely high level of verbal agreement argues strongly that these segments once formed a unified discourse.

Mt. 10	Mt. 24	Lk. 12	Lk. 17	Lk. 21	Mk. 13
	1a				1a
	2				2
	3a				3a
	3c			7b	3b
	4			8a	5
	5			8b	6
	6			9	7
	7			10	8a
	8				8b
17	9a			12a	9a
18				12b-13	9b
19					11a
20					11b
21					12
22a	9b			17	13a
22b	13			19	13b
	15a			20	14a
	15b				14b
	16			21	14c
	17		31a		15
	18		31b		16
	19			23a	17
	20				18
	21			23b	19
	22				20
	23				21
	24				22
	25				23
	27			24	
	29a				24
	29b			26b	25b
	30b			27	26
	31				27
	32a				28a
	32b			30	28b
	33			31	29
	34			32	30
	35			33	31
	36				32
	37		26		
	38b		27a		
	39a		27b		
	39b		30		
	41		35		
	/28/		37b		
	42a			36a	33a
	42b				33b
	43	39			
	44	40			
	45	42			
	46	43			
	47	44			
	48	45a			
	49	45b			
	50	46a			
	51	46b			

*Verses on the same horizontal line contain a substantial amount of text that is identical, or part of an equivalent expression (*i.e.*, verbal equivalency).

Verbal Matching Among the Olivet Discourse Accounts

As has been noted, modern scholarship tends to view the segments in Matthew 10, and Luke 12 and 17 as possibly being pieces of different eschatological discourses. There are several reasons for rejecting this theory. The first is the rather obvious fact that none of these segments are set within the context of an eschatological discourse. So far as can be determined from the gospel record there was only one such discourse. That is not to say that Jesus did not make occasional reference to future events, but rather that there is no indication that he gave more than one indepth discourse concerning future events. That such a discourse would have occurred only after his rejection near the end of his ministry seems quite reasonable. The main reason, however, for viewing these segments as a once unified discourse is the otherwise inexplicable verbal agreement between the accounts—agreement so close that the only way these segments could have come from different discourses would have been if Jesus read a transcript of a previous discourse, or quoted himself word-for-word, both of which seem unlikely.

Consider the following additional evidence supporting the inclusion of Matthew 10:17-23, Luke 12:35-38 and 39-46, and Luke 17:26-37 as part of the discourse. Of the 93 words in the Matthew 10:17-23 account that correspond to expressions in the main-body accounts of Matthew, Mark, and Luke, 88 of those words are identical or are part of verbally equivalent expressions such as two translators might legitimately translate from the same text (remember the original source material was almost certainly in Hebrew or Aramaic); and the five words that are different (the first five words of Matthew 10:17) are an alternate expression of the same statement in Mark 13:9. Matthew 10:17-23 also contains 36 words that have no corresponding expressions in the other accounts. Thus, in regard to the material in common, there is 95 percent verbal agreement between Matthew 10:17-23 and the main-body accounts of Matthew, Mark, and Luke.[18] While it cannot be ruled out that Jesus in his Olivet Discourse read from a script (or transcript), or that he precisely quoted a prior discourse from memory, such seems highly unlikely; the simplest explanation is that Matthew 10:17-23 is a dislocated piece of the Olivet Discourse. Consider also Luke 17:31-32. Of the 26 words that have corresponding expressions in Matthew and Mark, all 26 words are identical, or part of verbally equivalent expressions. Of the remaining 23 words in Luke 17:31-32, the first four words in verse 31 are a unique introduction and the remaining 19 words comprise verse 32, which is also unique to Luke. Thus, of the expressions common to Luke 17:31-32 and the main-body accounts in Matthew and Mark, there is a 100 percent verbal match. In Luke 17:26-37 (exclusive of verses 31-32, which were dealt with above), of the 68 words that have corresponding expressions in Matthew or Mark, all 68 words are identical or part of verbally equivalent expressions. There are an additional 56 words for which there are no corresponding expressions in Matthew or Mark (these consist of verses 28-29, 30, and 37a). Thus, of the expressions common to this segment and the main-body accounts in

---

[18] Word counts are based on the Greek text (UBS-3/4). See the parallel texts in this volume.

Matthew or Mark, there is a 100 percent verbal match. Finally, in regard to Luke 12:35-46, Mark 13:34-36 appears to be an abridgement of the longer statement in Luke 12:35-38 (Matthew does not include this); thus, one would not expect verbal agreement there. Of the remaining 135 words in Luke 12:39-46 for which there are corresponding expressions in Matthew or Mark, 131 of those words are identical or part of verbally equivalent expressions. (Luke 12:39-46 contains 19 words for which there are no parallel expressions in Matthew or Mark; they are: verse 41, and the first four words of verse 42). Thus, for the material that Luke 12:39-46 has in common with the main-body account in Matthew (Mark does not include this), 97 percent is identical or part of a verbally equivalent expression. It should also be noted that the level of verbal agreement between dislocated segments and the main-body accounts which they parallel is considerably greater than the average level of verbal agreement among the main-body accounts themselves.[19] This data, part of which is summarized in the table below, offers a strong argument that Matthew 10:17-23, Luke 12:35-46, and Luke 17:26-37 are dislocated portions of the Olivet Discourse, whereas redaction criticism, which is primarily focused on explaining differences, offers no explanation of these verbal consistencies.

	Words in parallel expressions	Words that are identical or in expressions verbally equivalent to the wording of a main body account	Level of verbal agreement with one of more main-body accounts
Matthew 10:17-23	93	88	95%
*Luke 12:35-38	36	0	0%
Luke 12:39-46	135	131	97%
Luke 17:26-37	94	94	100%

* Note that the substance of some of Luke 12:35-38 is presented in abridged form only in Mark 13:34-36; therefore, one would not expect verbal agreement.

Word counts are based on the Greek text (UBS-3). See the parallel texts.

Levels of Verbal Agreement Between Dislocated Portions and Main-Body Accounts of the Olivet Discourse

---

[19] The average level of verbal agreement between any main-body account and the other two main-body accounts is 74 percent. (This does not mean that on average 74 percent of the main-body text is identical or verbally equivalent to other accounts; it means that for those sections that have parallels in other accounts, on average 74 percent of that parallel material is identical or verbally equivalent to at least one other main-body account.) See the summary on the agreement of the main-body accounts on page 42.

Outline of the Discourse

I. The departure from the temple for the Mount of Olives   24:1-3

II. A prophetic overview of the coming tribulation   24:4-14

III. The period of great tribulation culminating in the regal appearing   24:15-31

IV. The dual nature of Christ's future appearing, and the imminent rapture of the Church   24:32-51

V. Similitudes illustrating the imminency of the rapture and the importance of continued faithfulness   25:1-30

VI. The disposition of the tribulation survivors   25:31-46

Introduction

The historical setting

The Olivet Discourse was spoken to a small group of Jesus' disciples on the Mount of Olives. The text is found in Matthew 24-25, Mark 13, and Luke 21 (along with portions of Matthew 10 and Luke 12, and 17); it is one of the two longest messages recorded in the gospels. As far as the text indicates, only four disciples—Peter, James, John, and Andrew—were present. It was delivered on Tuesday, just three days before Jesus was crucified on Friday.[1] Jesus had made his triumphal entry into Jerusalem just two days earlier, on Sunday; and had returned to Bethany, a small village about two miles southeast of Jerusalem. Monday, as he was on his way back to Jerusalem, he became hungry and finding a fig tree with no figs, he cursed it.[2] When he arrived at the temple, he cast out the merchants and the moneychangers. This led the Chief Priests and Scribes to renew their efforts to kill him (Mk. 11:12-19). That evening Jesus returned to Bethany, and on Tuesday he and his disciples set out again for Jerusalem, where along the way they saw the withered fig tree Jesus had cursed (Mk. 11:20-22). Seeing the fig tree occasioned Jesus' first recorded teaching that day—a lesson on faith as they walked along the road to Jerusalem (Mk. 11:20-24). Arriving at Jerusalem, Jesus entered the temple where the Priests, Scribes, and Elders were awaiting him to challenge his authority (Mk. 11:27-28). Jesus responded by asking them a question—whether John's baptism was from God or man. It was generally acknowledged that John had given testimony to the fact that Jesus is the Christ (Mk. 11:9-32, cf. Jn. 1:19-37; Mt. 3:1-17), and John was popularly regarded as a prophet (Mk. 11:32). When the leaders would not

---

[1] Mark 13:3 indicates that this was a private discourse. The sense of ἐπηρώτα αὐτὸν κατ᾽ ἰδίαν Πέτρος καὶ Ἰάκωβος καὶ Ἰωάννης καὶ Ἀνδρέας ("Peter and James and John and Andrew questioned him privately") seems to indicate that these four, and Jesus, were the only ones present. In any case, this was clearly a private discourse between teacher and disciples. As to the timing of this discourse, Mark's account is very helpful in pinpointing the day as Tuesday before the crucifixion. We know that Jesus was crucified on a Friday (the day before the Sabbath, cf. Mk 15:42; Lk. 23:54,56), which was also a Passover (Jn. 19:31), and Mark's account indicates the passage of days for this final week. [Jesus' cursing of the fig tree and his cleansing of the temple occurred the day after the triumphal entry (Mk. 11:1-19); some of Jesus' teachings (including the Olivet Discourse) occurred the following day (Mk. 11:20-13:37); Jesus' anointing by Mary, and Judas' arrangement to betray him occurred the next day (Mk. 14:1-11); the Passover supper and Jesus' betrayal and arrest occurred the next day (Mk. 14:12-72); the crucifixion occurred the following day—Friday (Mk. 15:1-47). Thus we simply have to count back three days from Friday, which places the Olivet Discourse on Tuesday.]

[2] The cursing of the fig tree on Monday, and the disciples' seeing the withered tree on Tuesday morning, was likely a preparatory analogy to Jesus' teaching on faithfulness in the Olivet Discourse delivered later the same day (cf. Mt. 24:45-25:30).

commit to an unambiguous answer, Jesus refused to respond to their question. Of course had the leaders affirmed that John was sent from God, that affirmation would have been an implicit acknowledgment of Jesus' identity as the Messiah. This occasioned the parable of the vineyard (Mk. 12:1-12) in which Jesus brought an indictment against the nation's leaders (Mk. 12:12). Some of them tried to entangle him with questions about taxation (Mk. 12:13-17) and the resurrection (Mk. 12:18-27), but Jesus refused to be trapped, and instead engaged them in a discussion of the deity of the Christ (Mk. 12:35-36)—a point the religious leaders had consistently rejected (Jn. 8:48-59; 10:22-39). He followed this with a pronouncement of woes upon the Scribes and Pharisees (Mt. 23:1-39) and then set out for the Mount of Olives.[3] As they were leaving the temple some of his disciples pointed out the grandeur of the structures, and Jesus replied that someday all those things would be destroyed. The disciples had a rudimentary knowledge of eschatology, and they quickly equated what Jesus said about the temple with the end of the age and Jesus' return to establish the kingdom.[4] Perhaps Jesus retreated to the Mount of Olives to pray, or rest. But as he sat on the Mount, Peter, James, John, and Andrew approached and questioned him privately, saying: "Teacher, tell us, when will these things be, and what will be the sign of your appearing and of the end of the age?"[5] This discourse is Jesus' answer to that question.

The text as it appears in the gospels of Matthew, Mark, and Luke

It is certainly providential that we have three parallel (synoptic) accounts of this discourse. It also seems beyond coincidence that this is the minimum number of accounts required for the resolution of apparent discrepancies in the texts. If we had only one account, our knowledge of the discourse would be incomplete. And, if we had only two accounts we would never be able to resolve many of the apparent discrepancies, for no two accounts are the same. This is, of course, the "synoptic problem," *i.e.*, how to account for both the similarities and differences in the synoptic gospels. However, because we have three accounts, we have a check wherever two accounts differ. Thus, by careful comparison of the three accounts it is possible to

---

[3] Mark does not record the woes pronounced upon the Pharisees. Matthew records it as having occurred on the same day as the Olivet Discourse (Mt. 23:1-36) and Luke records it in Luke 11:42-52; however, Luke's account is dislocated.

[4] Cf. Mt. 24:3. This may explain why the disciples asked Jesus after his resurrection if he was going to establish his kingdom at that time (Acts 1:6). In their minds he had already left and returned; this question demonstrates that at least up to that point in time, the disciples were still anticipating a visible (physical/political) kingdom as the fulfillment of biblical prophecy. Of course, they had been present when Jesus had said to the Pharisees that the arrival of the kingdom of God would not be observable (Lk. 17:21), but they knew that the kingdom was to have both an initial redemptive aspect, and a subsequent physical and political aspect.

[5] Cf. Mt. 24:1-3.

reconstruct a more complete record of this discourse than by working from one account alone; and interestingly, when we do so, we find that virtually every apparent discrepancy is resolved, as well as a great many previously vexing questions answered. Like most of the other gospel material, the Olivet Discourse, as spoken by Christ, was considerably longer than any of the abridged accounts contained in the gospels. Aside from John's acknowledgement that the accounts we know as "gospels" were abridged accounts of the life and teaching of Jesus (Jn. 20:25), it is easy to see from a simple comparison of the texts that each gospel leaves out a considerable amount of material contained in the others. This volume contains both a parallel arrangement of the Greek texts of all three gospel accounts of the discourse, and a parallel English translation of those texts.[6] It is not difficult to see, though it is clearer from the Greek, that each writer compressed his account. Here, as elsewhere in these gospels, compression is found in two forms. In many cases the gospel writers simply omitted material. Sometimes these omissions are individual words or phrases, but in many instances longer segments such as sentences, and even paragraphs were omitted. In other cases the gospel writers compressed their accounts by summarizing the material. In an abridged account each of these methods is perfectly legitimate; and this type of compression accounts for most of the differences between the three gospel reports. Actually, if we exclude the omissions and summaries, most of the material agrees perfectly, though there are numerous instances where verbal equivalency is found rather than strict verbal and syntactical agreement. But again, the gospels are clearly abridged accounts, and it is not necessary for abridged accounts to agree verbally, as long as one account does not contradict another. Undoubtedly compression in the gospels was of great practical importance since these documents were not written to be complete biographies, but abbreviated accounts preserving the key facts about Christ's birth, life, claims, teaching, death, and resurrection, in a form easily copied and distributed. Had longer, more detailed accounts been composed, it is doubtful that they could have been as quickly or as widely distributed.

Not only are the synoptic accounts condensed, it appears they were condensed largely from the same source material. That is to say that Matthew, Mark, and Luke's gospels appear to have been derived from a longer account of Jesus' life and teaching. Jesus had promised that he would send the Holy Spirit, and that the Spirit would bring to the disciples' remembrance all the things that Jesus had said (Jn. 14:26). It certainly seems possible that under the enablement of the Holy Spirit someone composed an account of Jesus' teachings, as Jesus had promised (Jn. 14:26), and that Matthew, Mark, and Luke, under the inspiration of the Holy Spirit, drew upon that source material, and

---

[6] The translations that appear in the English parallel texts are the author's translation.

possibly one another, in the composition of their gospels.[7] (In the case of the Olivet Discourse, if we assume that only Peter, James, John, and Andrew were present, Matthew, Mark, and Luke must have gotten their material from some source.) Of course, it is possible that the Holy Spirit supernaturally revealed the material to each of the gospel writers individually; however, there is no necessity to appeal to miracles when a simpler explanation will do. It seems plausible that some eyewitness was given the recall to write an accurate account of Jesus' teachings, just as Jesus had promised; but that document was not in a language or form, or of such a length so as to be broadly distributed.[8] It is possible that one gospel was composed first from this source material (sometimes referred to as the "Q" document), and then others were written using both that gospel and the source document.[9] This would account for the frequent, near perfect verbal agreement.[10] Of course one would not expect condensed material in one gospel to match verbally with material in another gospel.

---

[7] Though many theories have been offered, we do not know the order in which the gospels were written. The testimony of the early church fathers is that Matthew produced the first gospel; however, modern scholarship, based principally on comparisons of the gospels, tends to view Mark as having been composed first. Papias (c. pre-A.D. 70-155) wrote that Matthew "put together the oracles [of the Lord] in the Hebrew language, and each one interpreted them as best he could." Some have taken this to indicate that Matthew's gospel was originally composed in Hebrew or Aramaic. However, there is little evidence to support this claim and considerable evidence to the contrary. Possibly Papias was referring to Matthew as having written Jesus' teachings in Hebrew or Aramic, which he and others eventually used in the production of the Greek gospels. Regarding the date of composition of the synoptic gospels little is known; however, it seems most likely that they were all composed prior to A.D. 70.

[8] There is some indication in 2 Thessalonians 2 that Paul was familiar with the content of the Olivet Discourse at a time generally believed to have been prior to the writing of the gospels. Also, since Jesus undoubtedly spoke in Hebrew or Aramaic rather than Greek, it is possible that such a source document might have been recorded in Hebrew or Aramaic, and thus would have been less suitable for broad distribution in the Roman provinces to the west, where Greek was the language of commerce; after all, why would the Holy Spirit have given recall in a language other than the language, or languages Jesus spoke? Translation of the source material from Hebrew or Aramaic to Greek could also account for some minor variations between the Greek texts of the synoptics, as well as the presence of Aramaisms in some portions of the gospels.

[9] In New Testament scholarship "Q" (from the German word "quelle," meaning "source") is identified as the source of material common to Matthew and Luke that is not found in Mark; however, that does not mean that Mark was not familiar with, or did not make use of "Q."

[10] There has been much discussion as to whether Matthew's gospel was originally composed in a Semitic language (Hebrew or Aramaic) or Greek. Lenski's introduction to Matthew's gospel contains a summary of the arguments for and against a Hebrew or Aramaic original (R.C.H. Lenski, *The Interpretation of St. Matthew's Gospel*, Augsburg Publishing House, 1961, pp.11-18). Lenski concludes that the weight of evidence supports that Matthew's gospel was originally

Another interesting feature of this discourse discussed under "The Structure of the Discourse," is the fact that there are several instances where material has been moved from its original context (as part of the discourse) to some other location.[11] While this might appear somewhat confusing, the fact that we have three accounts with strong verbal agreement and numerous points of contact, makes the reconstruction of the more complete text of the discourse a rather straightforward process, and leaves only a few questions regarding the reading unanswered.

While most commentaries treat these accounts individually, with occasional comparisons made to the text of the other accounts, it is important that we first reconstruct as much of the original discourse as possible before attempting an interpretation. To illustrate this consider the following examples: Apart from reconstructing the text we would not know that the question asked in Luke 12:41 is answered in Mark 13:37, since Mark does not include the question and Luke 12:35-46 is disconnected from the discourse proper, the main-body of which appears in chapter 21. A check of the standard commentaries fails to yield even one commentator who makes this connection, yet once the material is properly placed in parallel and recombined, it is clear that Mark 13:37 is the answer to the question asked by Peter in Luke 12:41.[12] While

---

composed in Greek; however, Lenski's arguments do not preclude that the gospel writers, writing in Greek, might have drawn upon Hebrew or Aramaic source material.

[11] For example, according to Luke's account, the statement made in Matthew 24:28 should appear after verse 41, not after verse 27. Also, Luke 17:31-32 fits between Luke 21:22 and 21:23; and Luke 17:22-25 fits between Luke 21:24 and 21:25; and Luke 17:26-30 and verses 33-37 fit between Luke 21:33 and 21:34. Finally, Luke 12:35-46 should be appended to the end of Luke's account after 21:36. (See the parallel texts on page 42, and the structural diagram of the discourse on page 23.) Generally, the material in Luke's gospel is arranged more topically than historically; and we find material from the Olivet Discourse (Lk 12:35-46) and the Sermon on the Mount in the same passage (for examples see: Lk. 12:22-32 cf. Mt. 6:25-34; Lk. 12:33-34 cf. Mt. 6:19-21; Lk. 12:57-59 cp. Mt. 5:21-26), even though these messages were widely separated in time. In addition, in Matthew some of the Olivet Discourse material pertaining to future evangelism during the tribulation period (10:17-23) is placed within the context of the sending out of the disciples to preach (10:1-16)—an event that happened earlier in Jesus' ministry before his rejection by the leaders of Israel (Mt. 12:1-45). It is possible that some of these dislocations may represent a topical arrangement of material, and thus be original to the text; in other cases the dislocations have probably occurred post-compositionally, but early enough that they do not show up as textual variations in the extant manuscripts. Given the fact that the extant manuscripts, a few of which date to the late third and fourth centuries, do not show such variations, any such rearrangement of the text is presumed to be earlier—prior to the late third century.

[12] Most conservative interpreters view Luke 12:35-46 as an earlier discourse which just happens to have near one hundred percent verbal agreement with Matthew's ending of the Olivet Discourse (Mt. 24:43-51a). However, while it is possible that Jesus spoke the same material on two widely separated occasions (see Bock, *Luke*, vol.2, p.1171), if that were the case it would not account for

the connection of Mark 13:37 to Luke 12:41, pointed out above, appears to have only a relatively minor impact on interpretation, it serves to illustrate the need for a reconstructed text. Some of the dislocated material represents significant portions of material, which in some cases does have an impact on interpretation. Take for example the segment of material in which Lot's wife is mentioned (Lk. 17:32-33); it is only recorded in Luke's gospel, but it is misplaced within a larger section of dislocated material.[13] Aside from comparing Luke with both Matthew and Mark, we would not know that the section containing the reference to Lot's wife (Lk. 17:31-33) does not follow the illustration of Lot as indicated in Luke's gospel, but instead occurred much earlier in the discourse, and illustrates an entirely different point.[14] While there are several instances of dislocated material in this discourse, these two examples should be sufficient to point out the importance of working from a reconstructed text that takes into account all of the discourse material contained in Matthew, Mark, and Luke.

The text as it appears in the commentary

The reconstructed text that appears in this volume, and on which the commentary is based, has been derived from a comparison of the Olivet Discourse

---

why the same material is conspicuously absent from Luke's account of the Olivet Discourse in chapter 21. The solution to this riddle is that the material was moved to an earlier point within Luke's gospel—whether by Luke, out of topical considerations, or post-compositionally, is uncertain—but it seems clear that it was moved. Lenski fails to see that Luke 12:35-46 is from the Olivet Discourse and places it at the sending of the twelve and seventy, and as a result he fails to see that Mark 13:37 is the answer to the question posed in Luke 12:41 (Lenski, *Luke*, p.706, at v.41). Likewise in commenting on Mark 13:37, Lenski fails to see Jesus' statement there as the answer to the question in Luke 12:41 (R.C.H. Lenski, *The Interpretation of St. Mark's Gospel*, Augsburg Publishing House, 1964, p.595). Bock also fails to see the connection between the question in Luke 12:41 and the answer in Mark 13:37 (*Luke*, vol.2, pp.1177-1178). Geldenhuys, as well as others, make the same mistake, failing to see the connection of Luke 12:35-46 with the Olivet Discourse, and seeking to interpret those verses in connection with the adjoining material (Lk. 12:1-34), which is not its native context, for these segments were not spoken on the same occasion (see Geldenhuys, *Luke*, pp.362-365).

[13] In this instance we can determine by comparison with Matthew 24:17-18 that Luke 17:31-33 should appear before the material it follows (Lk. 17:22-30), all of which was taken from the Olivet Discourse (see, "The Structure of the Discourse," p.21).

[14] The illustration of Lot (Lk. 17:28-29) that appears after the illustration of Noah (Mt. 24:37-39 cf. Lk. 17:26-30) exemplifies how unexpected judgment will fall on the world at Christ's appearing; whereas the mention of Lot's wife is in regard to not returning to Jerusalem once the abomination is set up in the temple at the midpoint of the tribulation period. In this instance it appears that an early copyist moved the section containing mention of Lot's wife so that it would follow the illustration of Lot, but these illustrations were spoken in different contexts, and illustrate different truths.

material contained in Matthew, Mark, and Luke. The reader should consult the parallel texts tables in the following pages, which contain the Greek texts of all the Olivet Discourse material along with the author's reconstruction of the text and English translation. All of the Greek appearing in this volume, whether in tables, commentary, or notes, is accompanied by an English translation.[15] The reconstructed text is based on the following assumptions.

1. The entire biblical text, in the original autographs, is verbally inspired.

2. All the gospel accounts are of equal authority, regardless of the order of composition or any interdependency of one to the other.

3. Any apparent discrepancies are ultimately resolvable, whether a solution is apparent or not.

4. All the gospels are compressed accounts of the life and teachings of Christ.[16] Wherever material in one account is in substantial verbal agreement with another account (*i.e.*, it is not summarized or restated), the longer reading is regarded as the more complete statement, and the shorter reading is regarded as an abridgment. This applies equally to the omission of words, phrases, sentences and paragraphs, but only where the material has not been summarized.[17]

5. Material appearing outside of the immediate context of the main body of the Olivet Discourse in any account, which is in substantial verbal agreement with material found in the main body account of another gospel, is regarded

---

[15] I have elected not to transliterate Greek in this volume since that would be only marginally helpful for non-Greek readers, and a great hindrance for readers of Greek who are unaccustomed to seeing the text presented that way. For help in transliteration, see "Transliteration of Greek into English," on page 9.

[16] The degree of compression in the gospel accounts has long been recognized. John Calvin wrote: "Even our Savior's discourses, of which a summary is given by these three evangelists, ought to prevent everyone from treating their writings with contempt" (*Institutes of the Christian Religion*, trans. by Henry Beveridge, Peabody: Hendrickson Publishers, 2008, p.41 {Book 1, Chap. 8, sec. 11}.

[17] This is a departure from the usual position of modern critical scholarship, which holds that longer accounts are the product of textual evolution. While it is usually true that copies of biblical texts become longer as they are copied, here we are not concerned with transmission, but with original composition. If we assume the verbal inspiration of the original autographs of the gospels, then we cannot account for longer readings in some accounts on the basis of the evolution of the text. In fact, if we assume verbal inspiration, the order in which the manuscripts were produced has no effect on interpretation at all.

as Olivet Discourse material that has been dislocated (either compositionally, or post-compositionally).[18]

Because of the dominance that has been assigned to Matthew's account, both because of its place in the traditional canon and its relative completeness, it is particularly suited as the framework for organizing the reconstructed reading and its versification.[19] Any departure from Matthew's account is noted, and the reasons, if not obvious from the parallel texts, are stated. Generally, the reconstructed account is based on similarity of language and points of contact between accounts. However, the reconstruction of a few sections (*e.g.*, Matthew 24:9-13 and 24:15) present us with multiple options; in which case the one that seems to best fit with the flow of thought has been selected, and any alternatives are noted if they appear to have a significant impact on the interpretation of the passage.

---

[18] (As previously indicated, the main-body accounts are found in Matthew 24-25, Mark 13, and Luke 21.) The question arises as to whether some parallel material was repeated from earlier sermons. However, the fact that parallel material is found elsewhere in a gospel but missing from its native gospel's main-body account, strongly suggests that such material has been moved. In other words, the absence of such material in the main-body account of its native gospel seems significant. We should also weigh the likelihood of whether Jesus would have introduced detailed eschatological information so early in his ministry, especially instructions and warning in view of specific eschatological events. While this last point reduces to a matter of theological opinion, it seems most unlikely that these parallel materials are from an earlier sermon, especially from the Sermon on the Mount, where some of them are found (note especially Lk. 12:22-32 cf. Mt. 6:25-34, Lk. 12:33-34 cf. Mt. 6:19-21, Lk. 12:57-59 cf. Mt. 5:21-26). See the discussion of the unity of the discourse on pages 28-31.

[19] Luke's account of this discourse has several major sections of dislocated material, which makes it unsuitable as a frame of reference. Mark's account has no dislocated material, and would be the best suited from a purely structural point of view. However, it is shorter than the Matthew account and that presents problems in using it as a framework for a combined account. Given these factors, it seems best to use Matthew as the framework for reconstructing the text, even though this presents a minor problem in chapter 25 since much of that material (vv.1-30) was spoken earlier in the discourse, between 24:42 and 24:43.

Reconstruction of the Discourse

The Parallel Texts

This section contains four tables of text. Table 1 presents the Greek texts of the Olivet Discourse from Matthew, Mark, and Luke, along with a reconstructed Greek text and translation of the reconstructed text into English.[1] Since there is only one detailed account of the material found in Matthew 25, there is no need to reconstruct that portion of the discourse, consequently that material does not appear in Table 1. Table 2 contains an English translation of the material found in Table 1, and Table 3 contains the Greek text of Matthew 25 along with an English translation. Table 4 contains the English translation of the entire reconstructed text, along with the material found in Matthew 25, in a more convenient format. The English translations in these tables and in the commentary are the author's, unless otherwise indicated.

As can be seen from the parallel texts in Table 1, most of the material appearing in **bold** text is identical to parallel material in other accounts. In some instances, instead of identical wording, verbal equivalence is found. Verbal equivalence, as used here, means that any differences between the compared texts could reasonably be due to translational peculiarities. (It is highly likely that the original source material had to be translated from Hebrew or Aramaic.) If the differences in parallel material are greater than what one would expect from translational differences, then the materials, though parallel, are not considered to be verbally equivalent. For example: Matthew 24:5 and Mark 13:6 are not identical, but the statements are close enough that both could be legitimate translations of common source material; thus, they are considered to be verbally equivalent.

The point has been made earlier that these reports are not transcripts, and it is not necessary for reports to agree verbally (as long as they do not disagree in substance); the writers had significant freedom to summarize the material as they saw fit, under the guidance of the Holy Spirit. Nevertheless, it is interesting to note the high level of verbal agreement that exists among these accounts.

The following summary shows the verbal agreement found among the parallel sections of the main-body accounts.[2] This summary does not include the material covered in Matthew 25 (since there is no parallel to that material other than a brief

---

[1] Since Luke often bridges the gap between Matthew and Mark, it is convenient to switch the traditional order of Mark and Luke in the tables, placing Luke between Matthew and Mark.

[2] The two tables on the following page are based only on a comparison of parallel material. Unique material (*i.e.,* material appearing in only one account) was excluded, since there is no basis of comparison.

summary in Luke 12:35-38); and it does not include the material from Matthew 10:17-23, Luke 12:35-46, or Luke 17:26-37.

	Words contained in parallel expressions	Words that are identical or verbally equivalent to other accounts	Level of verbal agreement with other main-body accounts
Matthew 24	736	638	87%
Mark 13	563	391	69%
Luke 21	308	201	65%

* Material from dislocated sections is not reflected in this data.

This is a comparison of how the authors stated the material they reported in common; therefore, only words in parallel material are considered.

"Words contained in parallel expressions" include only words found in verbally equivalent expressions of a clause or more, not isolated unique words or phrases, or transitions.

Verbal Agreement Among Main-Body Accounts

The following is a summary of the agreement among parallel materials from all sources (including the dislocated segments).

	Words contained in parallel expressions	Words that are identical or verbally equivalent to other accounts	Level of verbal agreement with other accounts
Matthew	836	726	87 %
Mark	563	391	69%
Luke	619	434	70%

* Includes all discourse materials from the main-body accounts, as well as Matthew 10:17-23, Luke 12:35-46, and 17:26-37.

Verbal Agreement For All Sources (Including Dislocated Material)

Table 1: Parallel Greek Texts and Reconstructed Text

Translation	Reconstructed Text	Matthew 24	Luke	Mark
24:1-8 ¹And as Jesus was going forth from the temple, the disciples approached him to show him the temple buildings; and one of his disciples was saying to him, "Teacher, behold these great stones and these great buildings."	**24:1-8** ¹Καὶ ἐξελθὼν ὁ Ἰησοῦς ἀπὸ τοῦ ἱεροῦ ἐπορεύετο, καὶ προσῆλθον οἱ μαθηταὶ αὐτοῦ ἐπιδεῖξαι αὐτῷ τὰς οἰκοδομὰς τοῦ ἱεροῦ, < λέγει αὐτῷ εἰς τῶν μαθητῶν αὐτοῦ, Διδάσκαλε, ἴδε ποταποὶ λίθοι καὶ ποταπαὶ οἰκοδομαί >Mk. 13:1	**24:1-8** ¹Καὶ ἐξελθὼν ὁ Ἰησοῦς ἀπὸ τοῦ ἱεροῦ ἐπορεύετο, καὶ προσῆλθον οἱ μαθηταὶ αὐτοῦ ἐπιδεῖξαι αὐτῷ τὰς οἰκοδομὰς τοῦ ἱεροῦ·	**21:5-24** ⁵Καί τινων λεγόντων περὶ τοῦ ἱεροῦ, ὅτι λίθοις καλοῖς καὶ ἀναθήμασιν κεκόσμηται,	**13:1-37** ¹Καὶ ἐκπορευομένου αὐτοῦ ἐκ τοῦ ἱεροῦ λέγει αὐτῷ εἷς τῶν μαθητῶν αὐτοῦ, Διδάσκαλε, ἴδε ποταποὶ λίθοι καὶ ποταπαὶ οἰκοδομαί.
²And answering he said to them, "Do you not see all these things? Truly I tell you,	²ὁ δὲ ἀποκριθεὶς εἶπεν αὐτοῖς, Οὐ βλέπετε ταῦτα πάντα; ἀμὴν λέγω ὑμῖν,	²ὁ δὲ ἀποκριθεὶς εἶπεν αὐτοῖς, Οὐ βλέπετε ταῦτα πάντα; ἀμὴν λέγω ὑμῖν,	εἶπεν, ⁶Ταῦτα ἃ θεωρεῖτε, ἐλεύσονται ἡμέραι ἐν αἷς	²καὶ ὁ Ἰησοῦς εἶπεν αὐτῷ, Βλέπεις ταύτας τὰς μεγάλας οἰκοδομάς;
not even a stone will be left upon (another) stone that will not be torn down."	οὐ μὴ ἀφεθῇ ὧδε λίθος ἐπὶ λίθον ὃς οὐ καταλυθήσεται.	οὐ μὴ ἀφεθῇ ὧδε λίθος ἐπὶ λίθον ὃς οὐ καταλυθήσεται.	οὐκ ἀφεθήσεται λίθος ἐπὶ λίθῳ ὃς οὐ καταλυθήσεται.	οὐ μὴ ἀφεθῇ ὧδε λίθος ἐπὶ λίθον ὃς οὐ μὴ καταλυθῇ.
³And as he sat on the Mount of Olives, opposite the temple,	³Καθημένου δὲ αὐτοῦ ἐπὶ τοῦ Ὄρους τῶν Ἐλαιῶν, < κατέναντι τοῦ ἱεροῦ	³Καθημένου δὲ αὐτοῦ ἐπὶ τοῦ Ὄρους τῶν Ἐλαιῶν	⁷Ἐπηρώτησαν δὲ αὐτὸν	³Καὶ καθημένου αὐτοῦ εἰς τὸ Ὄρος τῶν Ἐλαιῶν κατέναντι τοῦ ἱεροῦ
Peter and James and John and Andrew questioned him privately,	ἐπηρώτα αὐτὸν κατ' ἰδίαν Πέτρος καὶ Ἰάκωβος καὶ Ἰωάννης καὶ Ἀνδρέας, >Mk. 13:3	προσῆλθον αὐτῷ οἱ μαθηταὶ κατ' ἰδίαν		ἐπηρώτα αὐτὸν κατ' ἰδίαν Πέτρος καὶ Ἰάκωβος καὶ Ἰωάννης καὶ Ἀνδρέας,
saying:	λέγοντες,	λέγοντες,	λέγοντες,	
"Teacher,	< Διδάσκαλε, >Lk. 21:7		Διδάσκαλε,	
"Tell us, when will these things be,	Εἰπὲ ἡμῖν πότε ταῦτα ἔσται,	Εἰπὲ ἡμῖν πότε ταῦτα ἔσται,	πότε οὖν ταῦτα ἔσται,	⁴Εἰπὸν ἡμῖν ... πότε ταῦτα ἔσται,

Translation	Reconstructed Text	Matthew 24	Luke	Mark
and what will be the sign of your appearing and of the end of the age?"	καὶ τί τὸ σημεῖον τῆς σῆς παρουσίας καὶ συντελείας τοῦ αἰῶνος.	καὶ τί τὸ σημεῖον τῆς σῆς παρουσίας καὶ συντελείας τοῦ αἰῶνος.	καὶ τί τὸ σημεῖον ὅταν μέλλῃ ταῦτα γίνεσθαι;	καὶ τί τὸ σημεῖον ὅταν μέλλῃ ταῦτα συντελεῖσθαι πάντα.
4And answering, Jesus said to them,	4καὶ ἀποκριθεὶς ὁ Ἰησοῦς εἶπεν αὐτοῖς,	4καὶ ἀποκριθεὶς ὁ Ἰησοῦς εἶπεν αὐτοῖς,	8ὁ δὲ εἶπεν,	5ὁ δὲ Ἰησοῦς ἤρξατο λέγειν αὐτοῖς,
"See that no one misleads you.	Βλέπετε μὴ ὑμᾶς πλανήσῃ:	Βλέπετε μὴ ὑμᾶς πλανήσῃ:	Βλέπετε μὴ πλανηθῆτε:	Βλέπετε μή τις ὑμᾶς πλανήσῃ:
5For many will come in my name saying,	5πολλοὶ γὰρ ἐλεύσονται ἐπὶ τῷ ὀνόματί μου λέγοντες,	5πολλοὶ γὰρ ἐλεύσονται ἐπὶ τῷ ὀνόματί μου λέγοντες,	πολλοὶ γὰρ ἐλεύσονται ἐπὶ τῷ ὀνόματί μου λέγοντες,	6πολλοὶ ἐλεύσονται ἐπὶ τῷ ὀνόματί μου λέγοντες ὅτι
'I am the Christ,' and 'The time is near,'	Ἐγώ εἰμι ὁ Χριστός, < καί, Ὁ καιρὸς ἤγγικεν > Lk. 21:8	Ἐγώ εἰμι ὁ Χριστός,	Ἐγώ εἰμι: καί, Ὁ καιρὸς ἤγγικεν:	Ἐγώ εἰμι,
and they will mislead many.	καὶ πολλοὺς πλανήσουσιν:	καὶ πολλοὺς πλανήσουσιν.		καὶ πολλοὺς πλανήσουσιν.
Do not follow them.	< μὴ πορευθῆτε ὀπίσω αὐτῶν. > Lk. 21:8		μὴ πορευθῆτε ὀπίσω αὐτῶν.	
6But you will hear of wars and threats of wars;	6μελλήσετε δὲ ἀκούειν πολέμους καὶ ἀκοὰς πολέμων:	6μελλήσετε δὲ ἀκούειν πολέμους καὶ ἀκοὰς πολέμων:	9ὅταν δὲ ἀκούσητε πολέμους καὶ ἀκαταστασίας,	7ὅταν δὲ ἀκούσητε πολέμους καὶ ἀκοὰς πολέμων,
see that you do not panic, for these things must happen first,	ὁρᾶτε, μὴ θροεῖσθε: δεῖ γὰρ γενέσθαι < πρῶτον, > Lk. 21:9	ὁρᾶτε, μὴ θροεῖσθε: δεῖ γὰρ γενέσθαι.	μὴ πτοηθῆτε: δεῖ γὰρ ταῦτα γενέσθαι πρῶτον,	μὴ θροεῖσθε: δεῖ γενέσθαι,
but it is not yet the end."	ἀλλ' οὔπω ἐστὶν τὸ τέλος.	ἀλλ' οὔπω ἐστὶν τὸ τέλος.	ἀλλ' οὐκ εὐθέως τὸ τέλος.	ἀλλ' οὔπω τὸ τέλος.
Then he said to them,	< Τότε ἔλεγεν αὐτοῖς, > Lk. 21:10		10Τότε ἔλεγεν αὐτοῖς,	
"For people will rise up against people and kingdom against kingdom,	7ἐγερθήσεται γὰρ ἔθνος ἐπὶ ἔθνος καὶ βασιλεία ἐπὶ βασιλείαν,	7ἐγερθήσεται γὰρ ἔθνος ἐπὶ ἔθνος καὶ βασιλεία ἐπὶ βασιλείαν,	Ἐγερθήσεται ἔθνος ἐπ' ἔθνος καὶ βασιλεία ἐπὶ βασιλείαν,	8ἐγερθήσεται γὰρ ἔθνος ἐπ' ἔθνος καὶ βασιλεία ἐπὶ βασιλείαν,

44

Translation	Reconstructed Text	Matthew 24	Luke	Mark	Matthew 10
and there will be famines and pestilences and great earthquakes in various places;	καὶ ἔσονται λιμοὶ < καὶ λοιμοί >Lk 21:11 καὶ σεισμοὶ < τε μεγάλοι >Lk 21:11 κατὰ τόπους;	καὶ ἔσονται λιμοὶ καὶ σεισμοὶ κατὰ τόπους;	11σεισμοί τε μεγάλοι καὶ κατὰ τόπους λιμοὶ καὶ λοιμοὶ ἔσονται,	ἔσονται σεισμοὶ κατὰ τόπους, ἔσονται λιμοί:	
8But all these things are merely the beginning of birth pains.	8πάντα δὲ ταῦτα ἀρχὴ ὠδίνων.	8πάντα δὲ ταῦτα ἀρχὴ ὠδίνων.	-----	ἀρχὴ ὠδίνων ταῦτα.	
			Luke 21:11b appears after Luke 21:19. This relocation is necessary in order to unfold Luke's recursive structure so this account can be merged with Matthew and Mark.		Matthew 10:17-23 [Parallel to Mt. 24:9-14] ------
9But beware of men,	9 < προσέχετε δὲ ἀπὸ τῶν ἀνθρώπων		-----	9βλέπετε δὲ ὑμεῖς ἑαυτούς;	17προσέχετε δὲ ἀπὸ τῶν ἀνθρώπων·
for they will hand you over to courts, and they will scourge you in their assemblies;	παραδώσουσιν γὰρ ὑμᾶς εἰς συνέδρια, καὶ ἐν ταῖς συναγωγαῖς αὐτῶν μαστιγώσουσιν ὑμᾶς;	9τότε παραδώσουσιν ὑμᾶς εἰς θλίψιν	12πρὸ δὲ τούτων πάντων ἐπιβαλοῦσιν ἐφ᾽ ὑμᾶς τὰς χεῖρας αὐτῶν καὶ διώξουσιν, παραδιδόντες εἰς τὰς συναγωγὰς καὶ φυλακάς,	παραδώσουσιν ὑμᾶς εἰς συνέδρια καὶ εἰς συναγωγὰς δαρήσεσθε	παραδώσουσιν γὰρ ὑμᾶς εἰς συνέδρια, καὶ ἐν ταῖς συναγωγαῖς αὐτῶν μαστιγώσουσιν ὑμᾶς;
and you will be brought before governors and kings for my sake,	καὶ ἐπὶ ἡγεμόνας δὲ καὶ βασιλεῖς ἀχθήσεσθε ἕνεκεν ἐμοῦ		ἀπαγομένους ἐπὶ βασιλεῖς καὶ ἡγεμόνας ἕνεκεν τοῦ ὀνόματός μου:	καὶ ἐπὶ ἡγεμόνων καὶ βασιλέων σταθήσεσθε ἕνεκεν ἐμοῦ	18καὶ ἐπὶ ἡγεμόνας δὲ καὶ βασιλεῖς ἀχθήσεσθε ἕνεκεν ἐμοῦ
for a testimony to them and to the nations.	εἰς μαρτύριον αὐτοῖς καὶ τοῖς ἔθνεσιν. >Mt. 10:17-18		13ἀποβήσεται ὑμῖν εἰς μαρτύριον.	εἰς μαρτύριον αὐτοῖς.	εἰς μαρτύριον αὐτοῖς καὶ τοῖς ἔθνεσιν.
And the gospel must first be proclaimed unto all the nations.	< καὶ εἰς πάντα τὰ ἔθνη πρῶτον δεῖ κηρυχθῆναι τὸ εὐαγγέλιον. >Mk. 13:10			10καὶ εἰς πάντα τὰ ἔθνη πρῶτον δεῖ κηρυχθῆναι τὸ εὐαγγέλιον.	

Translation	Reconstructed Text	Matthew 24	Luke	Mark	Matthew 10
But when they hand you over, do not be anxious how or what you should speak,	< ὅταν δὲ παραδῶσιν ὑμᾶς, μὴ μεριμνήσητε πῶς ἢ τί λαλήσητε:		14Θέτε οὖν ἐν ταῖς καρδίαις ὑμῶν μὴ προμελετᾶν ἀπολογηθῆναι,	11καὶ ὅταν ἄγωσιν ὑμᾶς παραδιδόντες, μὴ προμεριμνᾶτε τί λαλήσητε,	19ὅταν δὲ παραδῶσιν ὑμᾶς, μὴ μεριμνήσητε πῶς ἢ τί λαλήσητε:
for it will be given to you in that hour what you should say,	δοθήσεται γὰρ ὑμῖν ἐν ἐκείνῃ τῇ ὥρᾳ τί λαλήσητε; > Mt. 10:19			ἀλλ᾽ ὃ ἐὰν δοθῇ ὑμῖν ἐν ἐκείνῃ τῇ ὥρᾳ τοῦτο λαλεῖτε,	δοθήσεται γὰρ ὑμῖν ἐν ἐκείνῃ τῇ ὥρᾳ τί λαλήσητε;
for I will give you a mouth and wisdom, which none of the ones opposing you will be able to withstand or contradict;	< ἐγὼ γὰρ δώσω ὑμῖν στόμα καὶ σοφίαν ἧ οὐ δυνήσονται ἀντιστῆναι ἢ ἀντειπεῖν ἅπαντες οἱ ἀντικείμενοι ὑμῖν. > Lk. 21:15		15ἐγὼ γὰρ δώσω ὑμῖν στόμα καὶ σοφίαν ἧ οὐ δυνήσονται ἀντιστῆναι ἢ ἀντειπεῖν ἅπαντες οἱ ἀντικείμενοι ὑμῖν.		
for you are not the ones speaking, but the Spirit of your Father is speaking by you.	< οὐ γὰρ ὑμεῖς ἐστε οἱ λαλοῦντες ἀλλὰ τὸ πνεῦμα τοῦ πατρὸς ὑμῶν τὸ λαλοῦν ἐν ὑμῖν.			οὐ γάρ ἐστε ὑμεῖς οἱ λαλοῦντες ἀλλὰ τὸ πνεῦμα τὸ ἅγιον.	20οὐ γὰρ ὑμεῖς ἐστε οἱ λαλοῦντες ἀλλὰ τὸ πνεῦμα τοῦ πατρὸς ὑμῶν τὸ λαλοῦν ἐν ὑμῖν.
And brother will deliver up brother to death, and a father (will deliver up) a child, and children will rise up against parents	παραδώσει δὲ ἀδελφὸς ἀδελφὸν εἰς θάνατον καὶ πατὴρ τέκνον, καὶ ἐπαναστήσονται τέκνα ἐπὶ γονεῖς		16παραδοθήσεσθε δὲ καὶ ὑπὸ γονέων καὶ ἀδελφῶν καὶ συγγενῶν καὶ φίλων,	12καὶ παραδώσει ἀδελφὸς ἀδελφὸν εἰς θάνατον καὶ πατὴρ τέκνον, καὶ ἐπαναστήσονται τέκνα ἐπὶ γονεῖς	21παραδώσει δὲ ἀδελφὸς ἀδελφὸν εἰς θάνατον καὶ πατὴρ τέκνον, καὶ ἐπαναστήσονται τέκνα ἐπὶ γονεῖς
and kill them.	καὶ ἀποκτενοῦσιν ὑμᾶς,	καὶ ἀποκτενοῦσιν ὑμᾶς,	καὶ θανατώσουσιν ἐξ ὑμῶν,	καὶ θανατώσουσιν αὐτούς;	καὶ θανατώσουσιν αὐτούς.
And you will be hated by all on account of my name;	καὶ ἔσεσθε μισούμενοι ὑπὸ πάντων τῶν ἐθνῶν διὰ τὸ ὄνομά μου. > Mt. 10:20-22a	καὶ ἔσεσθε μισούμενοι ὑπὸ πάντων τῶν ἐθνῶν διὰ τὸ ὄνομά μου.	17καὶ ἔσεσθε μισούμενοι ὑπὸ πάντων διὰ τὸ ὄνομά μου.	13καὶ ἔσεσθε μισούμενοι ὑπὸ πάντων διὰ τὸ ὄνομά μου.	22καὶ ἔσεσθε μισούμενοι ὑπὸ πάντων διὰ τὸ ὄνομά μου:
yet not a hair of your head will perish.	< καὶ θρὶξ ἐκ τῆς κεφαλῆς ὑμῶν οὐ μὴ ἀπόληται. > Lk. 21:18		18καὶ θρὶξ ἐκ τῆς κεφαλῆς ὑμῶν οὐ μὴ ἀπόληται.		

46

Translation	Reconstructed Text	Matthew 24	Luke	Mark	Matthew 10
[10]And then many will be caused to fall away and betray one another and hate one another;	[10]καὶ τότε σκανδαλισθήσονται πολλοὶ καὶ ἀλλήλους παραδώσουσιν καὶ μισήσουσιν ἀλλήλους·	[10]καὶ τότε σκανδαλισθήσονται πολλοὶ καὶ ἀλλήλους παραδώσουσιν καὶ μισήσουσιν ἀλλήλους·			
[11]and many false prophets will arise and mislead many;	[11]καὶ πολλοὶ ψευδοπροφῆται ἐγερθήσονται καὶ πλανήσουσιν πολλούς·	[11]καὶ πολλοὶ ψευδοπροφῆται ἐγερθήσονται καὶ πλανήσουσιν πολλούς·			
[12]and because the iniquity will be increased, the love of many will grow cold.	[12]καὶ διὰ τὸ πληθυνθῆναι τὴν ἀνομίαν ψυγήσεται ἡ ἀγάπη τῶν πολλῶν.	[12]καὶ διὰ τὸ πληθυνθῆναι τὴν ἀνομίαν ψυγήσεται ἡ ἀγάπη τῶν πολλῶν.			
[13]But the one enduring to the end will be delivered.	[13]ὁ δὲ ὑπομείνας εἰς τέλος οὗτος σωθήσεται.	[13]ὁ δὲ ὑπομείνας εἰς τέλος οὗτος σωθήσεται.	[19]ἐν τῇ ὑπομονῇ ὑμῶν κτήσασθε τὰς ψυχὰς ὑμῶν.	ὁ δὲ ὑπομείνας εἰς τέλος οὗτος σωθήσεται.	ὁ δὲ ὑπομείνας εἰς τέλος οὗτος σωθήσεται.
But when they persecute you in one city, flee to another; for truly I say to you, you will certainly not finish (going through) the cities of Israel until the Son of Man comes."	< ὅταν δὲ διώκωσιν ὑμᾶς ἐν τῇ πόλει ταύτῃ, φεύγετε εἰς τὴν ἑτέραν· ἀμὴν γὰρ λέγω ὑμῖν, οὐ μὴ τελέσητε τὰς πόλεις τοῦ Ἰσραὴλ ἕως ἂν ἔλθῃ ὁ υἱὸς τοῦ ἀνθρώπου. > Μt. 10:23				[23]ὅταν δὲ διώκωσιν ὑμᾶς ἐν τῇ πόλει ταύτῃ, φεύγετε εἰς τὴν ἑτέραν· ἀμὴν γὰρ λέγω ὑμῖν, οὐ μὴ τελέσητε τὰς πόλεις τοῦ Ἰσραὴλ ἕως ἂν ἔλθῃ ὁ υἱὸς τοῦ ἀνθρώπου.
(And) there will be terrors and great signs from the heavens.	< φόβητρά τε καὶ ἀπ' οὐρανοῦ σημεῖα μεγάλα ἔσται. > Lk. 21:11b		[Inserted from 21:11b] φόβητρά τε καὶ ἀπ' οὐρανοῦ σημεῖα μεγάλα ἔσται.		
[14]And this gospel of the kingdom will be proclaimed in the whole inhabited world for a testimony to all nations, and then the end will come.	[14]καὶ κηρυχθήσεται τοῦτο τὸ εὐαγγέλιον τῆς βασιλείας ἐν ὅλῃ τῇ οἰκουμένῃ εἰς μαρτύριον πᾶσιν τοῖς ἔθνεσιν, καὶ τότε ἥξει τὸ τέλος.	[14]καὶ κηρυχθήσεται τοῦτο τὸ εὐαγγέλιον τῆς βασιλείας ἐν ὅλῃ τῇ οἰκουμένῃ εἰς μαρτύριον πᾶσιν τοῖς ἔθνεσιν, καὶ τότε ἥξει τὸ τέλος.			

Translation	Reconstructed Text	Matthew 24	Luke	Mark
¹⁵Therefore, when you see	¹⁵Ὅταν οὖν ἴδητε	¹⁵Ὅταν οὖν ἴδητε	²⁰Ὅταν δὲ ἴδητε	¹⁴Ὅταν δὲ ἴδητε
Jerusalem being surrounded by armies,	< κυκλουμένην ὑπὸ στρατοπέδων Ἰερουσαλήμ, >Lk. 21:20		κυκλουμένην ὑπὸ στρατοπέδων Ἰερουσαλήμ,	
{and} the abomination of desolation	{καὶ} τὸ βδέλυγμα τῆς ἐρημώσεως	τὸ βδέλυγμα τῆς ἐρημώσεως		τὸ βδέλυγμα τῆς ἐρημώσεως
spoken of through Daniel the prophet	τὸ ῥηθὲν διὰ Δανιὴλ τοῦ προφήτου	τὸ ῥηθὲν διὰ Δανιὴλ τοῦ προφήτου		
standing in the holy place	ἑστὸς ἐν τόπῳ ἁγίῳ,	ἑστὸς ἐν τόπῳ ἁγίῳ,		ἑστηκότα ὅπου οὐ δεῖ,
—let the reader understand—	ὁ ἀναγινώσκων νοείτω,	ὁ ἀναγινώσκων νοείτω,		ὁ ἀναγινώσκων νοείτω,
then know that its desolation has drawn near.	< τότε γνῶτε ὅτι ἤγγικεν ἡ ἐρήμωσις αὐτῆς. >Lk. 21:20		τότε γνῶτε ὅτι ἤγγικεν ἡ ἐρήμωσις αὐτῆς.	
¹⁶Then let those in Judea flee unto the mountains.	¹⁶τότε οἱ ἐν τῇ Ἰουδαίᾳ φευγέτωσαν εἰς τὰ ὄρη,	¹⁶τότε οἱ ἐν τῇ Ἰουδαίᾳ φευγέτωσαν εἰς τὰ ὄρη,	²¹τότε οἱ ἐν τῇ Ἰουδαίᾳ φευγέτωσαν εἰς τὰ ὄρη,	τότε οἱ ἐν τῇ Ἰουδαίᾳ φευγέτωσαν εἰς τὰ ὄρη,
			{21:21b overlaps with 17:31 below}	
			καὶ οἱ ἐν μέσῳ αὐτῆς ἐκχωρείτωσαν, καὶ οἱ ἐν ταῖς χώραις μὴ εἰσερχέσθωσαν εἰς αὐτήν,	
¹⁷In that day	17 < ἐν ἐκείνῃ τῇ ἡμέρᾳ >Lk. 17:31		17:31-32 {matches Mt. 24:17-18 and Mk. 13:15-16.}	
			³¹ἐν ἐκείνῃ τῇ ἡμέρᾳ	

Translation	Reconstructed Text	Matthew 24	Luke	Mark
let not the one on the roof go down to take the things out of his house,	ὁ ἐπὶ τοῦ δώματος μὴ καταβάτω ἆραι τὰ ἐκ τῆς οἰκίας αὐτοῦ,	17ὁ ἐπὶ τοῦ δώματος μὴ καταβάτω ἆραι τὰ ἐκ τῆς οἰκίας αὐτοῦ,	ὃς ἔσται ἐπὶ τοῦ δώματος καὶ τὰ σκεύη αὐτοῦ ἐν τῇ οἰκίᾳ, μὴ καταβάτω ἆραι αὐτά,	15ὁ [δὲ] ἐπὶ τοῦ δώματος μὴ καταβάτω μηδὲ εἰσελθάτω ἆραί τι ἐκ τῆς οἰκίας αὐτοῦ,
18and let not the one in the field turn back to retrieve his garment.	18καὶ ὁ ἐν τῷ ἀγρῷ μὴ ἐπιστρεψάτω ὀπίσω ἆραι τὸ ἱμάτιον αὐτοῦ.	18καὶ ὁ ἐν τῷ ἀγρῷ μὴ ἐπιστρεψάτω ὀπίσω ἆραι τὸ ἱμάτιον αὐτοῦ.	καὶ ὁ ἐν ἀγρῷ ὁμοίως μὴ ἐπιστρεψάτω εἰς τὰ ὀπίσω.	16καὶ ὁ εἰς τὸν ἀγρὸν μὴ ἐπιστρεψάτω εἰς τὰ ὀπίσω ἆραι τὸ ἱμάτιον αὐτοῦ.
Remember the wife of Lot.	< μνημονεύετε τῆς γυναικὸς Λώτ.		32μνημονεύετε τῆς γυναικὸς Λώτ.	
Whoever will seek to save his possessions will forfeit {his life}, but whoever will forfeit {his possessions} will save {his life}.	ὃς ἐὰν ζητήσῃ τὴν ψυχὴν αὐτοῦ περιποιήσασθαι ἀπολέσει αὐτήν, ὃς δ' ἂν ἀπολέσῃ ζῳογονήσει αὐτήν. >Lk.17:32,33		33ὃς ἐὰν ζητήσῃ τὴν ψυχὴν αὐτοῦ περιποιήσασθαι ἀπολέσει αὐτήν, ὃς δ' ἂν ἀπολέσῃ ζῳογονήσει αὐτήν. -------------	
Because these are the days of vengeance (in which) all (the things) having been written are to be fulfilled.	< ὅτι ἡμέραι ἐκδικήσεως αὗταί εἰσιν τοῦ πλησθῆναι πάντα τὰ γεγραμμένα. >Lk.21:22		21:22-24 / 22ὅτι ἡμέραι ἐκδικήσεως αὗταί εἰσιν τοῦ πλησθῆναι πάντα τὰ γεγραμμένα.	
19But woe to the ones who are pregnant and the ones nursing in those days.	19οὐαὶ δὲ ταῖς ἐν γαστρὶ ἐχούσαις καὶ ταῖς θηλαζούσαις ἐν ἐκείναις ταῖς ἡμέραις.	19οὐαὶ δὲ ταῖς ἐν γαστρὶ ἐχούσαις καὶ ταῖς θηλαζούσαις ταις ἡμέραις.	23οὐαὶ ταῖς ἐν γαστρὶ ἐχούσαις καὶ ταῖς θηλαζούσαις ἐν ἐκείναις ταῖς ἡμέραις·	17οὐαὶ δὲ ταῖς ἐν γαστρὶ ἐχούσαις καὶ ταῖς θηλαζούσαις ἐν ἐκείναις ταῖς ἡμέραις.
20But pray that your flight might not occur in winter, neither on a Sabbath;	20προσεύχεσθε δὲ ἵνα μὴ γένηται ἡ φυγὴ ὑμῶν χειμῶνος μηδὲ σαββάτῳ:	20προσεύχεσθε δὲ ἵνα μὴ γένηται ἡ φυγὴ ὑμῶν χειμῶνος μηδὲ σαββάτῳ:		18προσεύχεσθε δὲ ἵνα μὴ γένηται χειμῶνος·

Translation	Reconstructed Text	Matthew 24	Luke	Mark
²¹for then there will be great tribulation	²¹ἔσται γὰρ τότε θλῖψις μεγάλη	²¹ἔσται γὰρ τότε θλῖψις μεγάλη	ἔσται γὰρ ἀνάγκη μεγάλη	¹⁹ἔσονται γὰρ αἱ ἡμέραι ἐκεῖναι θλῖψις
upon the earth, and wrath to this people,	<ἐπὶ τῆς γῆς καὶ ὀργὴ τῷ λαῷ τούτῳ, > Lk 21:23		ἐπὶ τῆς γῆς καὶ ὀργὴ τῷ λαῷ τούτῳ,	
such as has neither occurred from the beginning of the world until now, nor will happen (again).	οἵα οὐ γέγονεν ἀπ' ἀρχῆς κόσμου ἕως τοῦ νῦν οὐδ' οὐ μὴ γένηται.	οἵα οὐ γέγονεν ἀπ' ἀρχῆς κόσμου ἕως τοῦ νῦν οὐδ' οὐ μὴ γένηται.		οἷα οὐ γέγονεν τοιαύτη ἀπ' ἀρχῆς κτίσεως ἣν ἔκτισεν ὁ θεὸς ἕως τοῦ νῦν καὶ οὐ μὴ γένηται.
And they will fall by the edge of the sword and will be led captive unto all nations, and Jerusalem will be trodden down by the nations until the times of the Gentiles are complete.	< καὶ πεσοῦνται στόματι μαχαίρης καὶ αἰχμαλωτισθήσονται εἰς τὰ ἔθνη πάντα, καὶ Ἰερουσαλὴμ ἔσται πατουμένη ὑπὸ ἐθνῶν, ἄχρι οὗ πληρωθῶσιν καιροὶ ἐθνῶν > Lk 21:24		²⁴καὶ πεσοῦνται στόματι μαχαίρης καὶ αἰχμαλωτισθήσονται εἰς τὰ ἔθνη πάντα, καὶ Ἰερουσαλὴμ ἔσται πατουμένη ὑπὸ ἐθνῶν, ἄχρι οὗ πληρωθῶσιν καιροὶ ἐθνῶν	
²²And except (for the fact that) those days will be cut short, no flesh would be delivered; but on account of the elect, those days will be cut short.	²²καὶ εἰ μὴ ἐκολοβώθησαν αἱ ἡμέραι ἐκεῖναι, οὐκ ἂν ἐσώθη πᾶσα σάρξ· διὰ δὲ τοὺς ἐκλεκτοὺς κολοβωθήσονται αἱ ἡμέραι ἐκεῖναι.	²²καὶ εἰ μὴ ἐκολοβώθησαν αἱ ἡμέραι ἐκεῖναι, οὐκ ἂν ἐσώθη πᾶσα σάρξ· διὰ δὲ τοὺς ἐκλεκτοὺς κολοβωθήσονται αἱ ἡμέραι ἐκεῖναι.		²⁰καὶ εἰ μὴ ἐκολόβωσεν κύριος τὰς ἡμέρας, οὐκ ἂν ἐσώθη πᾶσα σάρξ· ἀλλὰ διὰ τοὺς ἐκλεκτοὺς οὓς ἐξελέξατο ἐκολόβωσεν τὰς ἡμέρας.
			17:22-37	
			{Verses 20-21, below, are not part of the Olivet Discourse; however, they are included here to show Luke's thematic connection to verses 22-37.}	
			--------	
			²⁰Ἐπερωτηθεὶς δὲ ὑπὸ τῶν Φαρισαίων πότε ἔρχεται ἡ βασιλεία τοῦ θεοῦ ἀπεκρίθη αὐτοῖς καὶ εἶπεν, Οὐκ ἔρχεται ἡ βασιλεία τοῦ θεοῦ μετὰ παρατηρήσεως,	

Translation	Reconstructed Text	Matthew 24	Luke	Mark
²³Then if anyone says to you, 'Look, here [is] the Christ,' or: 'There [he is],' do not believe [it];	²³τότε ἐάν τις ὑμῖν εἴπῃ, Ἰδοὺ ὧδε ὁ Χριστός, ἤ, Ὧδε, μὴ πιστεύσητε:	²³τότε ἐάν τις ὑμῖν εἴπῃ, Ἰδοὺ ὧδε ὁ Χριστός, ἤ, Ὧδε, μὴ πιστεύσητε:	²¹οὐδὲ ἐροῦσιν, Ἰδοὺ ὧδε: ἤ, Ἐκεῖ: ἰδοὺ γὰρ ἡ βασιλεία τοῦ θεοῦ ἐντὸς ὑμῶν ἐστιν. -----	²¹καὶ τότε ἐάν τις ὑμῖν εἴπῃ, Ἴδε ὧδε ὁ Χριστός, Ἴδε ἐκεῖ, μὴ πιστεύετε:
²⁴for false christs and false prophets will be raised up and they will give great signs and miracles so as to deceive, if possible, even the elect.	²⁴ἐγερθήσονται γὰρ ψευδόχριστοι καὶ ψευδοπροφῆται, καὶ δώσουσιν σημεῖα μεγάλα καὶ τέρατα ὥστε πλανῆσαι, εἰ δυνατόν, καὶ τοὺς ἐκλεκτούς:	²⁴ἐγερθήσονται γὰρ ψευδόχριστοι καὶ ψευδοπροφῆται, καὶ δώσουσιν σημεῖα μεγάλα καὶ τέρατα ὥστε πλανῆσαι, εἰ δυνατόν, καὶ τοὺς ἐκλεκτούς:		²²ἐγερθήσονται γὰρ ψευδόχριστοι καὶ ψευδοπροφῆται καὶ δώσουσιν σημεῖα καὶ τέρατα πρὸς τὸ ἀποπλανᾶν, εἰ δυνατόν, τοὺς ἐκλεκτούς.
²⁵See, I have told you all these things before [they happen]."	²⁵ἰδοὺ προείρηκα ὑμῖν < πάντα. >Mk 13:23	²⁵ἰδοὺ προείρηκα ὑμῖν.		²³ὑμεῖς δὲ βλέπετε: προείρηκα ὑμῖν πάντα.
And he said to the disciples, "Days will come when you will long to see one of the days of the Son of Man and will not see [it].	< Εἶπεν δὲ πρὸς τοὺς μαθητάς, Ἐλεύσονται ἡμέραι ὅτε ἐπιθυμήσετε μίαν τῶν ἡμερῶν τοῦ υἱοῦ τοῦ ἀνθρώπου ἰδεῖν καὶ οὐκ ὄψεσθε. >Lk 17:22		²²Εἶπεν δὲ πρὸς τοὺς μαθητάς, Ἐλεύσονται ἡμέραι ὅτε ἐπιθυμήσετε μίαν τῶν ἡμερῶν τοῦ υἱοῦ τοῦ ἀνθρώπου ἰδεῖν καὶ οὐκ ὄψεσθε.	
²⁶Therefore, if they say to you: 'Look, he is in the desert,' [or] 'Look, [he is in] the inner chamber,' do not believe [them].	²⁶ἐὰν οὖν εἴπωσιν ὑμῖν, Ἰδοὺ ἐν τῇ ἐρήμῳ ἐστίν, μὴ ἐξέλθητε: Ἰδοὺ ἐν τοῖς ταμείοις, μὴ πιστεύσητε:	²⁶ἐὰν οὖν εἴπωσιν ὑμῖν, Ἰδοὺ ἐν τῇ ἐρήμῳ ἐστίν, μὴ ἐξέλθητε: Ἰδοὺ ἐν τοῖς ταμείοις, μὴ πιστεύσητε:	²³καὶ ἐροῦσιν ὑμῖν, Ἰδοὺ ἐκεῖ: [ἤ,] Ἰδοὺ ὧδε: μὴ ἀπέλθητε μηδὲ διώξητε.	
²⁷For just as the lightning flashes from the east and shines even unto the west, so will be the appearing of the Son of Man.	²⁷ὥσπερ γὰρ ἡ ἀστραπὴ ἐξέρχεται ἀπὸ ἀνατολῶν καὶ φαίνεται ἕως δυσμῶν, οὕτως ἔσται ἡ παρουσία τοῦ υἱοῦ τοῦ ἀνθρώπου.	²⁷ὥσπερ γὰρ ἡ ἀστραπὴ ἐξέρχεται ἀπὸ ἀνατολῶν καὶ φαίνεται ἕως δυσμῶν, οὕτως ἔσται ἡ παρουσία τοῦ υἱοῦ τοῦ ἀνθρώπου.	²⁴ὥσπερ γὰρ ἡ ἀστραπὴ ἀστράπτουσα ἐκ τῆς ὑπὸ τὸν οὐρανὸν εἰς τὴν ὑπ' οὐρανὸν λάμπει, οὕτως ἔσται ὁ υἱὸς τοῦ ἀνθρώπου [ἐν τῇ ἡμέρᾳ αὐτοῦ].	

Translation	Reconstructed Text	Matthew 24	Luke	Mark
But first it is necessary for him to suffer many things and to be rejected by this generation.	< πρῶτον δὲ δεῖ αὐτὸν πολλὰ παθεῖν καὶ ἀποδοκιμασθῆναι ἀπὸ τῆς γενεᾶς ταύτης. >Lk. 17:25		25πρῶτον δὲ δεῖ αὐτὸν πολλὰ παθεῖν καὶ ἀποδοκιμασθῆναι ἀπὸ τῆς γενεᾶς ταύτης.	
[Verse 28 appears after verse 41.]	[Verse 28 appears after verse 41.]	[Verse 28 appears after verse 41.]	21:25-33 [Resumed]	
29But immediately after the affliction of those days, the sun will be darkened, and the moon will not give its light,	29Εὐθέως δὲ μετὰ τὴν θλῖψιν τῶν ἡμερῶν ἐκείνων, ὁ ἥλιος σκοτισθήσεται, καὶ ἡ σελήνη οὐ δώσει τὸ φέγγος αὐτῆς,	29Εὐθέως δὲ μετὰ τὴν θλῖψιν τῶν ἡμερῶν ἐκείνων, ὁ ἥλιος σκοτισθήσεται, καὶ ἡ σελήνη οὐ δώσει τὸ φέγγος αὐτῆς,	25Καὶ ἔσονται σημεῖα ἐν ἡλίῳ καὶ σελήνῃ καὶ ἄστροις,	24Ἀλλὰ ἐν ἐκείναις ταῖς ἡμέραις μετὰ τὴν θλῖψιν ἐκείνην ὁ ἥλιος σκοτισθήσεται, καὶ ἡ σελήνη οὐ δώσει τὸ φέγγος αὐτῆς,
and the stars will fall from heaven,	καὶ οἱ ἀστέρες πεσοῦνται ἀπὸ τοῦ οὐρανοῦ,	καὶ οἱ ἀστέρες πεσοῦνται ἀπὸ τοῦ οὐρανοῦ,		25καὶ οἱ ἀστέρες ἔσονται ἐκ τοῦ οὐρανοῦ πίπτοντες,
and on earth there will be distress of nations powerless at the sound of the sea and surf,	< καὶ ἐπὶ τῆς γῆς συνοχὴ ἐθνῶν ἐν ἀπορίᾳ ἤχους θαλάσσης καὶ σάλου, >Lk. 21:25b		καὶ ἐπὶ τῆς γῆς συνοχὴ ἐθνῶν ἐν ἀπορίᾳ ἤχους θαλάσσης καὶ σάλου,	
[and] men collapsing from fear and [the] anticipation of the things coming upon the earth;	< ἀποψυχόντων ἀνθρώπων ἀπὸ φόβου καὶ προσδοκίας τῶν ἐπερχομένων τῇ οἰκουμένῃ, >Lk. 21:26		26ἀποψυχόντων ἀνθρώπων ἀπὸ φόβου καὶ προσδοκίας τῶν ἐπερχομένων τῇ οἰκουμένῃ,	
for the powers of the heavens will be shaken.	καὶ αἱ δυνάμεις τῶν οὐρανῶν σαλευθήσονται.	καὶ αἱ δυνάμεις τῶν οὐρανῶν σαλευθήσονται.	αἱ γὰρ δυνάμεις τῶν οὐρανῶν σαλευθήσονται.	καὶ αἱ δυνάμεις αἱ ἐν τοῖς οὐρανοῖς σαλευθήσονται.

Translation	Reconstructed Text	Matthew 24	Luke	Mark
30And then the sign of the Son of Man will appear in heaven, and all the peoples of the earth will mourn,	30καὶ τότε φανήσεται τὸ σημεῖον τοῦ υἱοῦ τοῦ ἀνθρώπου ἐν οὐρανῷ, καὶ τότε κόψονται πᾶσαι αἱ φυλαὶ τῆς γῆς	30καὶ τότε φανήσεται τὸ σημεῖον τοῦ υἱοῦ τοῦ ἀνθρώπου ἐν οὐρανῷ, καὶ τότε κόψονται πᾶσαι αἱ φυλαὶ τῆς γῆς		
and they will see the Son of Man coming on the clouds of heaven with great power and glory.	καὶ ὄψονται τὸν υἱὸν τοῦ ἀνθρώπου ἐρχόμενον ἐπὶ τῶν νεφελῶν τοῦ οὐρανοῦ μετὰ δυνάμεως < πολλῆς >Mk. 13:26 καὶ δόξης πολλῆς:	καὶ ὄψονται τὸν υἱὸν τοῦ ἀνθρώπου ἐρχόμενον ἐπὶ τῶν νεφελῶν τοῦ οὐρανοῦ μετὰ δυνάμεως καὶ δόξης πολλῆς:	27καὶ τότε ὄψονται τὸν υἱὸν τοῦ ἀνθρώπου ἐρχόμενον ἐν νεφέλῃ μετὰ δυνάμεως καὶ δόξης πολλῆς.	26καὶ τότε ὄψονται τὸν υἱὸν τοῦ ἀνθρώπου ἐρχόμενον ἐν νεφέλαις μετὰ δυνάμεως πολλῆς καὶ δόξης.
When these things begin to happen, raise yourself up and lift up your heads because your redemption draws near.	< ἀρχομένων δὲ τούτων γίνεσθαι ἀνακύψατε καὶ ἐπάρατε τὰς κεφαλὰς ὑμῶν, διότι ἐγγίζει ἡ ἀπολύτρωσις ὑμῶν. >Lk. 21:28		28ἀρχομένων δὲ τούτων γίνεσθαι ἀνακύψατε καὶ ἐπάρατε τὰς κεφαλὰς ὑμῶν, διότι ἐγγίζει ἡ ἀπολύτρωσις ὑμῶν.	
31And he will send forth his angels with a great trumpet, and they will gather his elect from out of the four winds, from one end of the heavens unto the other end.	31καὶ ἀποστελεῖ τοὺς ἀγγέλους αὐτοῦ μετὰ σάλπιγγος μεγάλης, καὶ ἐπισυνάξουσιν τοὺς ἐκλεκτοὺς αὐτοῦ ἐκ τῶν τεσσάρων ἀνέμων ἀπ' ἄκρων οὐρανῶν ἕως [τῶν] ἄκρων αὐτῶν.	31καὶ ἀποστελεῖ τοὺς ἀγγέλους αὐτοῦ μετὰ σάλπιγγος μεγάλης, καὶ ἐπισυνάξουσιν τοὺς ἐκλεκτοὺς αὐτοῦ ἐκ τῶν τεσσάρων ἀνέμων ἀπ' ἄκρων οὐρανῶν ἕως [τῶν] ἄκρων αὐτῶν.		27καὶ τότε ἀποστελεῖ τοὺς ἀγγέλους καὶ ἐπισυνάξει τοὺς ἐκλεκτοὺς [αὐτοῦ] ἐκ τῶν τεσσάρων ἀνέμων.
32Now learn the parable of the fig tree,	32Ἀπὸ δὲ τῆς συκῆς μάθετε τὴν παραβολήν:	32Ἀπὸ δὲ τῆς συκῆς μάθετε τὴν παραβολήν:	29Καὶ εἶπεν παραβολὴν αὐτοῖς: Ἴδετε τὴν συκῆν	28Ἀπὸ δὲ τῆς συκῆς μάθετε τὴν παραβολήν:
indeed all the trees:	< καὶ πάντα τὰ δένδρα: >Lk. 21:29b		καὶ πάντα τὰ δένδρα:	

53

Translation	Reconstructed Text	Matthew 24	Luke	Mark
When its branch becomes tender and it puts forth leaves, you know that summer is near;	ὅταν ἤδη ὁ κλάδος αὐτῆς γένηται ἁπαλὸς καὶ τὰ φύλλα ἐκφύῃ, γινώσκετε ὅτι ἐγγὺς τὸ θέρος;	ὅταν ἤδη ὁ κλάδος αὐτῆς γένηται ἁπαλὸς καὶ τὰ φύλλα ἐκφύῃ, γινώσκετε ὅτι ἐγγὺς τὸ θέρος;	³⁰ὅταν προβάλωσιν ἤδη, βλέποντες ἀφ' ἑαυτῶν γινώσκετε ὅτι ἤδη ἐγγὺς τὸ θέρος ἐστίν·	ὅταν ἤδη ὁ κλάδος αὐτῆς ἁπαλὸς γένηται καὶ ἐκφύῃ τὰ φύλλα, γινώσκετε ὅτι ἐγγὺς τὸ θέρος ἐστίν.
³³likewise when you see all these things, know that the kingdom of God is near at the doors.	³³οὕτως καὶ ὑμεῖς, ὅταν ἴδητε πάντα ταῦτα, γινώσκετε ὅτι ἐγγύς ἐστιν ἐπὶ θύραις < ἡ βασιλεία τοῦ θεοῦ. >Lk. 21:31	³³οὕτως καὶ ὑμεῖς, ὅταν ἴδητε πάντα ταῦτα, γινώσκετε ὅτι ἐγγύς ἐστιν ἐπὶ θύραις.	³¹οὕτως καὶ ὑμεῖς, ὅταν ἴδητε ταῦτα γινόμενα, γινώσκετε ὅτι ἐγγύς ἐστιν ἡ βασιλεία τοῦ θεοῦ.	²⁹οὕτως καὶ ὑμεῖς, ὅταν ἴδητε ταῦτα γινόμενα, γινώσκετε ὅτι ἐγγύς ἐστιν ἐπὶ θύραις.
³⁴Truly I say to you that this people will certainly not perish before all these things come to pass.	³⁴ἀμὴν λέγω ὑμῖν ὅτι οὐ μὴ παρέλθῃ ἡ γενεὰ αὕτη ἕως ἂν πάντα ταῦτα γένηται.	³⁴ἀμὴν λέγω ὑμῖν ὅτι οὐ μὴ παρέλθῃ ἡ γενεὰ αὕτη ἕως ἂν πάντα ταῦτα γένηται.	³²ἀμὴν λέγω ὑμῖν ὅτι οὐ μὴ παρέλθῃ ἡ γενεὰ αὕτη ἕως ἂν πάντα γένηται.	³⁰ἀμὴν λέγω ὑμῖν ὅτι οὐ μὴ παρέλθῃ ἡ γενεὰ αὕτη μέχρις οὗ ταῦτα πάντα γένηται.
³⁵Heaven and earth will pass away, but my words will never fail.	³⁵ὁ οὐρανὸς καὶ ἡ γῆ παρελεύσεται, οἱ δὲ λόγοι μου οὐ μὴ παρέλθωσιν.	³⁵ὁ οὐρανὸς καὶ ἡ γῆ παρελεύσεται, οἱ δὲ λόγοι μου οὐ μὴ παρέλθωσιν.	³³ὁ οὐρανὸς καὶ ἡ γῆ παρελεύσονται, οἱ δὲ λόγοι μου οὐ μὴ παρελεύσονται.	³¹ὁ οὐρανὸς καὶ ἡ γῆ παρελεύσονται, οἱ δὲ λόγοι μου οὐ μὴ παρελεύσονται.
³⁶But concerning that day and hour no one knows, neither the angels of the heavens nor the Son, only the Father.	³⁶Περὶ δὲ τῆς ἡμέρας ἐκείνης καὶ ὥρας οὐδεὶς οἶδεν, οὐδὲ οἱ ἄγγελοι τῶν οὐρανῶν οὐδὲ ὁ υἱός, εἰ μὴ ὁ πατὴρ μόνος.	³⁶Περὶ δὲ τῆς ἡμέρας ἐκείνης καὶ ὥρας οὐδεὶς οἶδεν, οὐδὲ οἱ ἄγγελοι τῶν οὐρανῶν οὐδὲ ὁ υἱός, εἰ μὴ ὁ πατὴρ μόνος.		³²Περὶ δὲ τῆς ἡμέρας ἐκείνης ἢ τῆς ὥρας οὐδεὶς οἶδεν, οὐδὲ οἱ ἄγγελοι ἐν οὐρανῷ οὐδὲ ὁ υἱός, εἰ μὴ ὁ πατήρ.
			------------ Luke 17:26-37	
³⁷For just as the days of Noah, so will be the appearing of the Son of Man.	³⁷ὥσπερ γὰρ αἱ ἡμέραι τοῦ Νῶε, οὕτως ἔσται ἡ παρουσία τοῦ υἱοῦ τοῦ ἀνθρώπου.	³⁷ὥσπερ γὰρ αἱ ἡμέραι τοῦ Νῶε, οὕτως ἔσται ἡ παρουσία τοῦ υἱοῦ τοῦ ἀνθρώπου.	²⁶καὶ καθὼς ἐγένετο ἐν ταῖς ἡμέραις Νῶε, οὕτως ἔσται καὶ ἐν ταῖς ἡμέραις τοῦ υἱοῦ τοῦ ἀνθρώπου:	
³⁸For as in the days before the flood	³⁸ὡς γὰρ ἦσαν ἐν ταῖς ἡμέραις [ἐκείναις] ταῖς πρὸ τοῦ κατακλυσμοῦ	³⁸ὡς γὰρ ἦσαν ἐν ταῖς ἡμέραις [ἐκείναις] ταῖς πρὸ τοῦ κατακλυσμοῦ		

Translation	Reconstructed Text	Matthew 24	Luke	Mark
they were eating and drinking, and marrying and giving in marriage, until the day Noah entered into the ark,	τρώγοντες καὶ πίνοντες, γαμοῦντες καὶ γαμίζοντες, ἄχρι ἧς ἡμέρας εἰσῆλθεν Νῶε εἰς τὴν κιβωτόν,	τρώγοντες καὶ πίνοντες, γαμοῦντες καὶ γαμίζοντες, ἄχρι ἧς ἡμέρας εἰσῆλθεν Νῶε εἰς τὴν κιβωτόν,	27ἤσθιον, ἔπινον, ἐγάμουν, ἐγαμίζοντο, ἄχρι ἧς ἡμέρας εἰσῆλθεν Νῶε εἰς τὴν κιβωτόν,	
39and knew not	39καὶ οὐκ ἔγνωσαν	39καὶ οὐκ ἔγνωσαν		
until the flood came and destroyed {them} all.	ἕως ἦλθεν ὁ κατακλυσμὸς καὶ ἦρεν ἅπαντας,	ἕως ἦλθεν ὁ κατακλυσμὸς καὶ ἦρεν ἅπαντας,	καὶ ἦλθεν ὁ κατακλυσμὸς καὶ ἀπώλεσεν πάντας.	
Likewise it was the same in the days of Lot; for they were	< ὁμοίως καθὼς ἐγένετο ἐν ταῖς ἡμέραις Λώτ· ἤσθιον,		28ὁμοίως καθὼς ἐγένετο ἐν ταῖς ἡμέραις Λώτ· ἤσθιον,	
eating, drinking, buying, selling, planting, {and} building;	ἔπινον, ἠγόραζον, ἐπώλουν, ἐφύτευον, ᾠκοδόμουν·		ἔπινον, ἠγόραζον, ἐπώλουν, ἐφύτευον, ᾠκοδόμουν·	
but the day Lot went out from Sodom, it rained fire and brimstone from heaven and destroyed {them} all.	δὲ ἡμέρᾳ ἐξῆλθεν Λὼτ ἀπὸ Σοδόμων, ἔβρεξεν πῦρ καὶ θεῖον ἀπ᾽ οὐρανοῦ καὶ ἀπώλεσεν πάντας. >Lk.17:28-29		29ᾗ δὲ ἡμέρᾳ ἐξῆλθεν Λὼτ ἀπὸ Σοδόμων, ἔβρεξεν πῦρ καὶ θεῖον ἀπ᾽ οὐρανοῦ καὶ ἀπώλεσεν πάντας.	
It will be the same {when} the Son of Man appears.	οὕτως ἔσται [καὶ] ἡ παρουσία τοῦ υἱοῦ τοῦ ἀνθρώπου.	οὕτως ἔσται [καὶ] ἡ παρουσία τοῦ υἱοῦ τοῦ ἀνθρώπου.	30κατὰ τὰ αὐτὰ ἔσται ᾗ ἡμέρᾳ ὁ υἱὸς τοῦ ἀνθρώπου ἀποκαλύπτεται.	
			------- {Verses 31-33 are dislocated in Luke; they match Matthew 24:16-18, above. -------	

Translation	Reconstructed Text	Matthew 24	Luke	Mark
I tell you in that night there will be two men in one bed, and one will be taken and the other left;	< Λέγω ὑμῖν, ταύτῃ τῇ νυκτὶ ἔσονται δύο ἐπὶ κλίνης μιᾶς, ὁ εἷς παραλημφθήσεται καὶ ὁ ἕτερος ἀφεθήσεται: > Lk.17:34		34Λέγω ὑμῖν, ταύτῃ τῇ νυκτὶ ἔσονται δύο ἐπὶ κλίνης μιᾶς, ὁ εἷς παραλημφθήσεται καὶ ὁ ἕτερος ἀφεθήσεται:	
40there will be two men in the field, one will be taken and one left;	40τότε δύο ἔσονται ἐν τῷ ἀγρῷ, εἷς παραλαμβάνεται καὶ εἷς ἀφίεται:	40τότε δύο ἔσονται ἐν τῷ ἀγρῷ, εἷς παραλαμβάνεται καὶ εἷς ἀφίεται:		
41two women will be grinding at the mill, one will be taken and one left."	41δύο ἀλήθουσαι ἐν τῷ μύλῳ, μία παραλαμβάνεται καὶ μία ἀφίεται.	41δύο ἀλήθουσαι ἐν τῷ μύλῳ, μία παραλαμβάνεται καὶ μία ἀφίεται.	35ἔσονται δύο ἀλήθουσαι ἐπὶ τὸ αὐτό, ἡ μία παραλημφθήσεται ἡ δὲ ἑτέρα ἀφεθήσεται.	
			----- {Verse 36 does not appear in the Greek text; it was inserted into the AV from Mt. 24:40.} -----	
And answering they said to him: "Where, Lord?"	< καὶ ἀποκριθέντες λέγουσιν αὐτῷ, Ποῦ, κύριε;		37καὶ ἀποκριθέντες λέγουσιν αὐτῷ, Ποῦ, κύριε;	
And he said to them:	ὁ δὲ εἶπεν αὐτοῖς, > Lk.17:37		ὁ δὲ εἶπεν αὐτοῖς,	
------- 24:28 inserted here	------- 24:28 inserted here	------- 24:28 inserted here		
{Matthew 24:28 has been placed here to match Luke 17:37b.}				
[28]"Wherever the carcass is, there the birds will be gathered.	28ὅπου ἐὰν ᾖ τὸ πτῶμα, ἐκεῖ συναχθήσονται οἱ ἀετοί.	28ὅπου ἐὰν ᾖ τὸ πτῶμα, ἐκεῖ συναχθήσονται οἱ ἀετοί.	Ὅπου τὸ σῶμα, ἐκεῖ καὶ οἱ ἀετοὶ ἐπισυναχθήσονται.	
-------	-------	-------		

Translation	Reconstructed Text	Matthew 24	Luke	Mark
But take heed to yourselves lest your hearts be weighted down in stupor and intoxication, and the cares of this life, and that day slip up on you unexpectedly	< Προσέχετε δὲ ἑαυτοῖς μήποτε βαρηθῶσιν ὑμῶν αἱ καρδίαι ἐν κραιπάλῃ καὶ μέθῃ καὶ μερίμναις βιωτικαῖς, καὶ ἐπιστῇ ἐφ' ὑμᾶς αἰφνίδιος ἡ ἡμέρα ἐκείνη		**21:34-36** [Resumed] 34Προσέχετε δὲ ἑαυτοῖς μήποτε βαρηθῶσιν ὑμῶν αἱ καρδίαι ἐν κραιπάλῃ καὶ μέθῃ καὶ μερίμναις βιωτικαῖς, καὶ ἐπιστῇ ἐφ' ὑμᾶς αἰφνίδιος ἡ ἡμέρα ἐκείνη	
like a trap. For it will come upon all those dwelling upon the whole face of the earth.	ὡς παγίς, ἐπεισελεύσεται γὰρ ἐπὶ πάντας τοὺς καθημένους ἐπὶ πρόσωπον πάσης τῆς γῆς. >Lk 21:34-35		35ὡς παγίς, ἐπεισελεύσεται γὰρ ἐπὶ πάντας τοὺς καθημένους ἐπὶ πρόσωπον πάσης τῆς γῆς	
				33βλέπετε ἀγρυπνεῖτε:
42Therefore watch,	42γρηγορεῖτε οὖν,	42γρηγορεῖτε οὖν,	36ἀγρυπνεῖτε δὲ	
at all times petitioning (God) that you might be qualified to escape all these things that are about to happen, and stand before the Son of Man,	< ἐν παντὶ καιρῷ δεόμενοι ἵνα κατισχύσητε ἐκφυγεῖν ταῦτα πάντα τὰ μέλλοντα γίνεσθαι, καὶ σταθῆναι ἔμπροσθεν τοῦ υἱοῦ τοῦ ἀνθρώπου. >Lk 21:36		ἐν παντὶ καιρῷ δεόμενοι ἵνα κατισχύσητε ἐκφυγεῖν ταῦτα πάντα τὰ μέλλοντα γίνεσθαι, καὶ σταθῆναι ἔμπροσθεν τοῦ υἱοῦ τοῦ ἀνθρώπου.	
because you do not know which day your Lord is coming."	ὅτι οὐκ οἴδατε ποία ἡμέρα ὁ κύριος ὑμῶν ἔρχεται.	ὅτι οὐκ οἴδατε ποία ἡμέρα ὁ κύριος ὑμῶν ἔρχεται.		οὐκ οἴδατε γὰρ πότε ὁ καιρός ἐστιν.

Translation	Reconstructed Text	Matthew 24	Luke	Mark
------- {Matthew 25:1-30 belongs here}	------- {Matthew 25:1-30 belongs here}	------- {Matthew 25:1-30 belongs here}	**12:35-46** ³⁵Ἔστωσαν ὑμῶν αἱ ὀσφύες περιεζωσμέναι καὶ οἱ λύχνοι καιόμενοι, ³⁶καὶ ὑμεῖς ὅμοιοι ἀνθρώποις προσδεχομένοις τὸν κύριον ἑαυτῶν πότε ἀναλύσῃ ἐκ τῶν γάμων, ἵνα ἐλθόντος καὶ κρούσαντος εὐθέως ἀνοίξωσιν αὐτῷ. ³⁷μακάριοι οἱ δοῦλοι ἐκεῖνοι, οὓς ἐλθὼν ὁ κύριος εὑρήσει γρηγοροῦντας· ἀμὴν λέγω ὑμῖν ὅτι περιζώσεται καὶ ἀνακλινεῖ αὐτοὺς καὶ παρελθὼν διακονήσει αὐτοῖς. ³⁸κἂν ἐν τῇ δευτέρᾳ κἂν ἐν τῇ τρίτῃ φυλακῇ ἔλθῃ καὶ εὕρῃ οὕτως, μακάριοί εἰσιν ἐκεῖνοι. {In Luke's account the following material from chapter 12 is presented in combination with material from the Sermon on the Mount—illustrating Luke's thematic arrangement (see, Lk. 12:22-32 cp. Mt. 6:25-34; Lk. 12:33-34 cp. Mt. 6:19-21; Lk. 12:57-59 cp. Mt. 5:21-26).}	³⁴ὡς ἄνθρωπος ἀπόδημος ἀφεὶς τὴν οἰκίαν αὐτοῦ καὶ δοὺς τοῖς δούλοις αὐτοῦ τὴν ἐξουσίαν, ἑκάστῳ τὸ ἔργον αὐτοῦ, καὶ τῷ θυρωρῷ ἐνετείλατο ἵνα γρηγορῇ. ³⁵γρηγορεῖτε οὖν, οὐκ οἴδατε γὰρ πότε ὁ κύριος τῆς οἰκίας ἔρχεται, ἢ ὀψὲ ἢ μεσονύκτιον ἢ ἀλεκτοροφωνίας ἢ πρωΐ, ³⁶μὴ ἐλθὼν ἐξαίφνης εὕρῃ] ὑμᾶς καθεύδοντας.
-------	-------	-------		

58

Translation	Reconstructed Text	Matthew 24	Luke	Mark
[43]But you know that if the master of the house knew in which watch the thief was coming, he would have been vigilant and (would) not have allowed his house to be broken through.	[43]ἐκεῖνο δὲ γινώσκετε ὅτι εἰ ᾔδει ὁ οἰκοδεσπότης ποίᾳ φυλακῇ ὁ κλέπτης ἔρχεται, ἐγρηγόρησεν ἂν καὶ οὐκ ἂν εἴασεν διορυχθῆναι τὴν οἰκίαν αὐτοῦ.	[43]ἐκεῖνο δὲ γινώσκετε ὅτι εἰ ᾔδει ὁ οἰκοδεσπότης ποίᾳ φυλακῇ ὁ κλέπτης ἔρχεται, ἐγρηγόρησεν ἂν καὶ οὐκ ἂν εἴασεν διορυχθῆναι τὴν οἰκίαν αὐτοῦ.	[39]τοῦτο δὲ γινώσκετε ὅτι εἰ ᾔδει ὁ οἰκοδεσπότης ποίᾳ ὥρᾳ ὁ κλέπτης ἔρχεται, οὐκ ἂν ἀφῆκεν διορυχθῆναι τὸν οἶκον αὐτοῦ.	
[44]Because of this you also be ready, because the Son of Man will come at an hour you do not anticipate."	[44]διὰ τοῦτο καὶ ὑμεῖς γίνεσθε ἕτοιμοι, ὅτι ᾗ οὐ δοκεῖτε ὥρᾳ ὁ υἱὸς τοῦ ἀνθρώπου ἔρχεται.	[44]διὰ τοῦτο καὶ ὑμεῖς γίνεσθε ἕτοιμοι, ὅτι ᾗ οὐ δοκεῖτε ὥρᾳ ὁ υἱὸς τοῦ ἀνθρώπου ἔρχεται.	[40]καὶ ὑμεῖς γίνεσθε ἕτοιμοι, ὅτι ᾗ ὥρᾳ οὐ δοκεῖτε ὁ υἱὸς τοῦ ἀνθρώπου ἔρχεται.	
But Peter said, "Lord, are you speaking this parable (only) to us, or to everyone?"	< Εἶπεν δὲ ὁ Πέτρος, Κύριε, πρὸς ἡμᾶς τὴν παραβολὴν ταύτην λέγεις ἢ καὶ πρὸς πάντας; >Lk.1241		[41]Εἶπεν δὲ ὁ Πέτρος, Κύριε, πρὸς ἡμᾶς τὴν παραβολὴν ταύτην λέγεις ἢ καὶ πρὸς πάντας;	
(And Jesus said,) "What I say to you, I say to all: Watch!"	< ὃ δὲ ὑμῖν λέγω, πᾶσιν λέγω, γρηγορεῖτε. >Mk.1337			[37]ὃ δὲ ὑμῖν λέγω, πᾶσιν λέγω, γρηγορεῖτε.

				[End of Mark's account]
[45]And the Lord said,			[42]καὶ εἶπεν ὁ κύριος,	
"Who then is the faithful and prudent servant whom the lord appointed over his household to give them food at the proper time?	[45]Τίς ἄρα ἐστὶν ὁ πιστὸς δοῦλος καὶ φρόνιμος ὃν κατέστησεν ὁ κύριος ἐπὶ τῆς οἰκετείας αὐτοῦ τοῦ δοῦναι αὐτοῖς τὴν τροφὴν ἐν καιρῷ;	[45]Τίς ἄρα ἐστὶν ὁ πιστὸς δοῦλος καὶ φρόνιμος ὃν κατέστησεν ὁ κύριος ἐπὶ τῆς οἰκετείας αὐτοῦ τοῦ δοῦναι αὐτοῖς τὴν τροφὴν ἐν καιρῷ;	Τίς ἄρα ἐστὶν ὁ πιστὸς οἰκονόμος ὁ φρόνιμος, ὃν καταστήσει ὁ κύριος ἐπὶ τῆς θεραπείας αὐτοῦ τοῦ διδόναι ἐν καιρῷ [τὸ] σιτομέτριον;	
[46]Blessed (is) the servant whom his lord (at his) coming finds so doing.	[46]μακάριος ὁ δοῦλος ἐκεῖνος ὃν ἐλθὼν ὁ κύριος αὐτοῦ εὑρήσει οὕτως ποιοῦντα:	[46]μακάριος ὁ δοῦλος ἐκεῖνος ὃν ἐλθὼν ὁ κύριος αὐτοῦ εὑρήσει οὕτως ποιοῦντα·	[43]μακάριος ὁ δοῦλος ἐκεῖνος, ὃν ἐλθὼν ὁ κύριος αὐτοῦ εὑρήσει ποιοῦντα οὕτως·	
[47]Truly I say to you that he will appoint him over all his possessions.	[47]ἀμὴν λέγω ὑμῖν ὅτι ἐπὶ πᾶσιν τοῖς ὑπάρχουσιν αὐτοῦ καταστήσει αὐτόν.	[47]ἀμὴν λέγω ὑμῖν ὅτι ἐπὶ πᾶσιν τοῖς ὑπάρχουσιν αὐτοῦ καταστήσει αὐτόν.	[44]ἀληθῶς λέγω ὑμῖν ὅτι ἐπὶ πᾶσιν τοῖς ὑπάρχουσιν αὐτοῦ καταστήσει αὐτόν.	

Translation	Reconstructed Text	Matthew 24	Luke
⁴⁸But if that wicked servant says in his heart: 'My lord delays,'	⁴⁸ἐὰν δὲ εἴπῃ ὁ κακὸς δοῦλος ἐκεῖνος ἐν τῇ καρδίᾳ αὐτοῦ, Χρονίζει μου ὁ κύριος,	⁴⁸ἐὰν δὲ εἴπῃ ὁ κακὸς δοῦλος ἐκεῖνος ἐν τῇ καρδίᾳ αὐτοῦ, Χρονίζει μου ὁ κύριος,	⁴⁵ἐὰν δὲ εἴπῃ ὁ δοῦλος ἐκεῖνος ἐν τῇ καρδίᾳ αὐτοῦ, Χρονίζει ὁ κύριός μου ἔρχεσθαι,
⁴⁹and begins to abuse his fellow servants, and eats and drinks with drunkards,	⁴⁹καὶ ἄρξηται τύπτειν τοὺς συνδούλους αὐτοῦ, ἐσθίῃ δὲ καὶ πίνῃ μετὰ τῶν μεθυόντων,	⁴⁹καὶ ἄρξηται τύπτειν τοὺς συνδούλους αὐτοῦ, ἐσθίῃ δὲ καὶ πίνῃ μετὰ τῶν μεθυόντων,	καὶ ἄρξηται τύπτειν τοὺς παῖδας καὶ τὰς παιδίσκας, ἐσθίειν τε καὶ πίνειν καὶ μεθύσκεσθαι,
⁵⁰the lord of that servant will come on a day in which he does not expect and at an hour he does not know,	⁵⁰ἥξει ὁ κύριος τοῦ δούλου ἐκείνου ἐν ἡμέρᾳ ᾗ οὐ προσδοκᾷ καὶ ἐν ὥρᾳ ᾗ οὐ γινώσκει,	⁵⁰ἥξει ὁ κύριος τοῦ δούλου ἐκείνου ἐν ἡμέρᾳ ᾗ οὐ προσδοκᾷ καὶ ἐν ὥρᾳ ᾗ οὐ γινώσκει,	⁴⁶ἥξει ὁ κύριος τοῦ δούλου ἐκείνου ἐν ἡμέρᾳ ᾗ οὐ προσδοκᾷ καὶ ἐν ὥρᾳ ᾗ οὐ γινώσκει,
⁵¹and will severely punish him, and relegate [him] his lot with the hypocrites;	⁵¹καὶ διχοτομήσει αὐτὸν καὶ τὸ μέρος αὐτοῦ μετὰ τῶν ὑποκριτῶν θήσει·	⁵¹καὶ διχοτομήσει αὐτὸν καὶ τὸ μέρος αὐτοῦ μετὰ τῶν ὑποκριτῶν θήσει·	καὶ διχοτομήσει αὐτὸν καὶ τὸ μέρος αὐτοῦ μετὰ τῶν ἀπίστων θήσει.
there will be wailing and gnashing of teeth.	ἐκεῖ ἔσται ὁ κλαυθμὸς καὶ ὁ βρυγμὸς τῶν ὀδόντων.	ἐκεῖ ἔσται ὁ κλαυθμὸς καὶ ὁ βρυγμὸς τῶν ὀδόντων.	

Table 2: Parallel English Texts

Translation of the Reconstructed Text	Matthew 24	Luke	Mark	
(As shown in the previous table.)				
24:1-8 ¹And as Jesus was going forth from the temple, the disciples approached him to show him the temple buildings; and one of his disciples was saying to him, "Teacher, behold these great stones, and these great buildings."	24:1-8 ¹And as Jesus was going forth from the temple, the disciples approached him to show him the buildings of the temple.	21:5-24 ⁵As some were speaking about the temple, what beautiful stones and dedicated things (with which) it had been adorned,	13:1-37 ¹And as he was going out of the temple one of his disciples was saying to him: "Teacher, behold what kind of stones and what kind of buildings."	
²And answering he said to them, "Do you not see all these things? Truly I tell you,	²And answering he said to them, "Do you see all these (things)? Truly I tell you,	(and) he said: "(Concerning) these things you gaze upon, days will come in which	²And Jesus said to him: "(Do) you see these great buildings?	
not even a stone will be left upon (another) stone that will not be torn down."	not even a stone will be left upon (another) stone which will not be torn down."	there will not be a stone left upon (another) stone which will not be torn down."	There shall certainly not be left a stone upon a stone which will not be torn down."	
³And as he sat on the Mount of Olives, opposite the temple,	³And as he sat on the Mount of Olives		³And as he sat upon the Mount of Olives opposite the temple,	
Peter and James and John and Andrew questioned him privately,	the disciples approached him privately	⁷And they questioned him	Peter and James and John and Andrew questioned him privately,	
saying: "Teacher,	saying:	saying: "Teacher,	(saying):	

Reconstructed Text	Matthew 24	Luke	Mark
"Tell us, when will these things be,	"Tell us, when will these (things) be,	when will these (things) be?	"Tell us, when these (things) will be,
and what will be the sign of your appearing and of the end of the age?"	and what (will be) the sign of your appearing and of the completion of the age?"	And what will be the sign when these things are about to happen?"	and what (will be) the sign when all these (things) are about to be accomplished."
4 And answering, Jesus said to them,	4 And Jesus answering said to them,	8 But he said:	5 And Jesus began to say to them:
"See that no one misleads you.	"See that no one misleads you.	"Beware lest you be led astray;	"See that no one misleads you.
5 For many will come in my name saying	5 For many will come in my name saying:	for many will come in my name, saying:	Many will come in my name saying,
'I am the Christ,'	'I am the Christ,'	'I am (he),'	'I am (he),'
and 'The time is near;'		and: 'The time is near;'	
and will mislead many.	and will mislead many.		and will mislead many.
Do not follow them.		do not follow after them.	
6 But you will hear of wars and threats of wars;	6 But you will hear of wars and threats of wars;	9 And when you hear of wars and conflicts,	7 But when you hear of wars and instabilities (with the potential) of wars,
see that you do not panic, for these things must happen first,	see that you are not frightened, for (these things) must happen,	do not be frightened; for these (things) must happen first,	do not be frightened; (these things) must happen,
but it is not yet the end."	but it is not yet the end.	but the end does not follow immediately."	but (it is) not yet the end.
7 Then he said to them,		10 Then he said to them,	

Reconstructed Text	Matthew 24	Luke	Mark	Matthew 10:17-23 [Parallel to Mt. 24:9-14]
"For people will rise up against people and kingdom against kingdom,	7"For people will rise up against people and kingdom against kingdom,	10"People will be raised up against people and kingdom against kingdom,	8"For people will rise up against people and kingdom against kingdom.	
and there will be famines and pestilences and great earthquakes in various places;	and there will be famines and earthquakes in various places;	11and there will be great earthquakes and in various places pestilences and famines.	There will be earthquakes (and) in various places, there will be famines;	
8But all these things are merely the beginning of birth pains.	8But all these (things) are (merely) (the) beginning of birth pains.		these (things) are (the) beginning of birth pains.	
		Luke 21:11b appears after Luke 21:19. This relocation is necessary in order to unfold Luke's recursive structure so this account can be merged with Matthew and Mark.		- - - - - - - - - - -
9But beware of men,	9Then they will deliver you unto affliction	12But before all these (things) they will lay their hands on you and persecute (you), handing (you) over unto the courts and assemblies and prisons,	9But see (to) yourselves;	17But beware of men;
for they will hand you over to courts, and they will scourge you in their assemblies;			(for) they will hand you over to courts and in (their) assemblies you will be beaten,	for they will hand you over to courts, and they will scourge you in their assemblies;
and you will be brought before governors and kings for my sake,		and you will be led away before kings and governors for my name's sake,	and you will stand before governors and kings for my sake,	18and you will be brought before governors and kings for my sake,
for a testimony to them and to the nations.		13[for] it will result (in) you (being) a testimony.	for a testimony to them.	for a testimony to them and to the nations.

Reconstructed Text	Matthew 24	Luke	Mark	Matthew 10
And the gospel must first be proclaimed unto all the nations.			10And the gospel must first be proclaimed unto all the nations.	
But when they hand you over, do not be anxious how or what you should speak;		14Therefore resolve in your hearts not to prepare to defend yourselves;	11And when they take you, handing you over, do not be anxious beforehand {concerning} what you {should} say,	19But when they hand you over, do not be anxious how or what you should speak;
for it will be given to you in that hour what you should say;			but whatever is given to you in that hour, this speak,	for it will be given to you in that hour what you should say;
for I will give you a mouth and wisdom, which none of the ones opposing you will be able to withstand or contradict;		15for I will give you a mouth and wisdom, which none of the ones opposing you will be able to withstand or contradict.		
for you are not the ones speaking, but the Spirit of your Father is speaking by you.			for you are not the {ones} speaking but the Holy Spirit.	20for you are not the ones speaking, but the Spirit of your Father is speaking by you.
And brother will deliver up brother to death, and a father {will deliver up} a child, and children will rise up against parents		16And you will also be betrayed by parents and brothers and relatives and friends,	12And brother will hand over brother to death and a father a child, and children will rise up against parents	21And brother will deliver up brother to death, and father {will deliver up} child, and children will rise up against parents
and kill them.	and will kill you,	and they will put some of you to death,	and put them to death;	and put them to death.
And you will be hated by all on account of my name;	and you will be hated by all the nations on account of my name.	17and you will be hated by all men on account of my name.	13and you will be hated by all men on account of my name;	22And you will be hated by all men on account of my name;
yet not a hair of your head will perish.		18Yet not a hair of your head will perish.		

Reconstructed Text	Mathew 24	Luke	Mark	Matthew 10
[10]And then many will be caused to fall away and betray one another and hate one another;	[10]And then many will be caused to fall away and betray one another and hate one another;			
[11]and many false prophets will arise and mislead many;	[11]and many false prophets will arise and mislead many;			
[12]and because the iniquity will be increased, the love of many will grow cold.	[12]and because lawlessness will be increased, the love of many will grow cold.			
[13]But the one enduring to the end will be delivered.	[13]But the one enduring to the end will be delivered.	[19]You must preserve your lives by your endurance.	but the one who endures to the end will be delivered.	but the one who endures to the end will be delivered.
But when they persecute you in one city, flee to another; for truly I say to you, you will certainly not finish (going through) the cities of Israel until the Son of Man comes."				[23]But when they persecute you in this city, flee to another; for truly I say to you, you will (certainly) not finish (going through) the cities of Israel until the Son of Man comes."
(And) there will be terrors and great signs from the heavens.		[Inserted from 21:11b] --------- There will be terrors and from heaven great signs. ---------		---------
[14]And this gospel of the kingdom will be proclaimed in the whole inhabited world for a testimony to all nations, and then the end will come.	[14]And this gospel of the kingdom will be proclaimed in the whole inhabited world for a testimony to all nations, and then the end will come.			

Reconstructed Text	Matthew 24	Luke	Mark
[15]Therefore, when you see	[15]Therefore when you see	[20]But when you see	[14]But when you see
Jerusalem being surrounded by armies,		Jerusalem being surrounded by encampments (of armies),	
(and) the abomination of desolation	the abomination of desolation		the abomination of desolation
spoken of through Daniel the prophet	having been spoken (of) through Daniel the prophet		
standing in the holy place	standing in the holy place,		standing where it ought not,
—let the reader understand—	let the one reading (this) understand.		let the one reading this understand,
then know that its desolation has drawn near.		then you know that its desolation has drawn near.	
[16]Then let those in Judea flee unto the mountains.	[16]Then let those in Judea flee unto the mountains,	[21]Then let those in Judea flee unto the mountains,	then let those in Judea flee unto the mountains;
		------- (21:21b overlaps with 17:31 below)}	
		and let those in the midst (of Jerusalem) get out of (the city), and let those in the suburbs not come into it, -------	

Reconstructed Text	Matthew 24	Luke	Mark
		-------------	-------------
		17 31-32 [Matches Mt. 24:17-18 and Mk. 13:15-16]	
[17]In that day		[31]In that day	
let not the one on the roof go down to take the things out of his house,	[17][and] let not the one on the roof go down to take the [things] out of his house,	the one who is one the roof and his possessions in the house, let him not come down to take them,	[15]let not the one on the roof come down nor enter to take anything out of his house,
[18]and let not the one in the field turn back to retrieve his garment.	[18]and let not the one in the field turn back to retrieve his garment.	and likewise the one in the field must not turn back [to retrieve] the things [left] behind.	[16]and let not the one in the field turn back to retrieve his garment.
Remember the wife of Lot.		[32]Remember the wife of Lot.	
Whoever will seek to save his possessions will forfeit [his life], but whoever will forfeit [his possessions] will save [his life].		[33]Whoever will seek to save his possessions will forfeit [his life], but whoever will forfeit [his possessions], will save [his life].	

		21-22-24 [Resumed]	
Because these are the days of vengeance [in which] all [the things] having been written are to be fulfilled.		[22]Because these are the days of vengeance [in which] all [the things] having been written are to be fulfilled.	
[19]But woe to the ones who are pregnant and the ones nursing in those days.	[19]But woe to the ones who are pregnant and to the ones nursing in those days.	[23]Woe to the ones who are pregnant and to the ones nursing in those days;	[17]But woe to the ones who are pregnant and to the ones nursing in those days.

Reconstructed Text	Matthew 24	Luke	Mark
20But pray that your flight might not occur in winter, neither on a Sabbath;	20But pray that your flight might not happen in winter nor on a Sabbath;		18But pray that it might not happen in winter;
21for then there will be great tribulation	21for then there will be great tribulation,	For there will be great distress	19for those days will be (days) of tribulation
upon the earth, and wrath to this people,		upon the earth and wrath to this people,	
such as has neither occurred from the beginning of the world until now, nor will happen (again).	such as has neither occurred from the beginning of the world until now, nor ever could happen (again).		of such a kind the likes of which has not occurred from the beginning of (the) creation which God created until now and will certainly never be (again).
And they will fall by the edge of the sword and will be led captive unto all nations, and Jerusalem will be trodden down by the nations until the times of the Gentiles are complete.		24 And they will fall by the edge of the sword and will be led captive unto all nations, and Jerusalem will be trodden down by the nations until the times of the Gentiles are complete.	
22And except (for the fact that) those days will be cut short, no flesh would be delivered; but on account of the elect, those days will be cut short.	22 And except (for the fact that) those days will be cut short, no flesh would be delivered; but on account of the elect, those days will be cut short		20And unless (the) Lord shorten those days, of all flesh none would be delivered; but on account of the elect whom he chose he (will) shorten these days.

Reconstructed Text	Matthew 24	Luke	Mark
		17:22-25 [Luke 17:20-21 is not a part of the Olivet Discourse; however, it has been included here to show Luke's thematic connection to verses 22-37, which are derived from the Olivet Discourse.] —————— [20]And having been questioned by the Pharisees [as to] when the kingdom of God is coming, he answered them and said: "The arrival of the kingdom of God [will] not be observable, [21]neither will they say: 'See, here [it is],' or 'See, there [it is];' for behold, the kingdom of God is in your midst." ——————	
[23]Then if anyone says to you, 'Look, here [is] the Christ,' or: 'There [he is],' do not believe [it];	[23]Then if anyone says to you, 'Look, here [is] the Christ,' or: 'There [he is],' do not believe [it];		[21]And then if anyone says to you: 'Look, here [is] the Christ, [or] 'Look, there [he is],' do not believe [them];
[24]for false christs and false prophets will be raised up and they will give great signs and miracles so as to deceive, if possible, even the elect.	[24]for false christs will be raised up and they will give great signs and miracles so as to deceive, if possible, even the elect.		[22]for false christs and false prophets will be raised up and will perform signs and miracles in order to lead astray, if possible, even the elect.
[25]See, I have told you all these things before [they happen]."	[25]I have told you before .		[23]But see, I have told you all these things before [they happen].

69

Reconstructed Text	Matthew 24	Luke	Mark
And he said to the disciples, "Days will come when you will long to see one of the days of the Son of Man and will not see {it}.		22And he said to the disciples, "Days will come when you will long to see one of the days of the Son of Man and will not see {it}.	
26Therefore, if they say to you: 'Look, he is in the desert,' do not go out {there}; {or} 'Look, {he is in} the inner chamber,' do not believe {them}.	26Therefore, if they say to you: 'Look, he is in the desert,' do not go out {there}; {or} 'Look, {he is in} the inner chamber,' do not believe {them}.	23And they will say to you, 'Look, there {he is},' {or} 'Look, here {he is}.' Do not go forth {to them}, neither follow after them.	
27For just as the lightning flashes from the east and shines even unto the west, so will be the appearing of the Son of Man.	27For just as the lightning flashes from the east and shines even unto the west, so will be the appearing of the Son of Man.	24For just as the lightning flashing out of one part of the sky shines unto the other part of the sky, so it will in the day of the Son of Man.	
But first it is necessary for him to suffer many things and to be rejected by this generation.		25But first it is necessary for him to suffer many things and to be rejected by this generation.	
{Verse 28 appears after verse 41.}	{Verse 28 appears after verse 41.}	21:25-33 {Resumed}	
29But immediately after the affliction of those days, the sun will be darkened, and the moon will not give its light,	29But immediately after the affliction of those days, the sun will be darkened, and the moon will not give its light,	25And there will be signs in {the} sun and moon and stars,	24But in those days after the affliction, the sun will be darkened, and the moon will not give its light,
and the stars will fall from heaven,	and the stars will fall from heaven,		25and the stars will be falling from heaven,

70

Reconstructed Text	Matthew 24	Luke	Mark
and on earth there will be distress of nations powerless at the sound of the sea and surf,		and on earth distress of nations powerless (at) the sound of the sea and surf,	
(and) men collapsing from fear and (the) anticipation of the things coming upon the earth;		26(and) men collapsing from fear and (the) anticipation of the things coming upon the earth;	
for the powers of the heavens will be shaken.	and the powers of the heavens will be shaken.	for the powers of the heavens will be shaken.	and the powers in the heavens will be shaken.
30And then the sign of the Son of Man will appear in heaven, and all the peoples of the earth will mourn	30And then the sign of the Son of Man will appear in heaven, and all the peoples of the earth will mourn		
and they will see the Son of Man coming on the clouds of heaven with great power and glory.	and they will see the Son of Man coming on the clouds of heaven with power and great glory;	27And then they will see the Son of Man coming in a cloud with power and great glory.	26And then they will see the Son of Man coming in (the) clouds with great power and glory.
When these things begin to happen, raise yourself up and lift up your heads because your redemption draws near.		28When these things begin to happen raise yourselves up and lift up your heads because your redemption draws near."	
31And he will send forth his angels with a great trumpet, and they will gather his elect from out of the four winds, from one end of the heavens unto the other end.	31and he will send forth his angels with a great trumpet, and they will gather his elect from out of the four winds, from one end of the heavens unto the other end.		27And then he will send forth the angels and they will gather together his elect from the four winds, from the furthermost end of the earth to the furthermost end of heaven.

Reconstructed Text	Matthew 24	Luke	Mark
		29And he told them a parable (saying):	
32Now learn the parable of the fig tree,	32Now learn the parable of the fig tree:	"Look (at) the fig tree	28Now learn the parable of the fig tree:
indeed all the trees:		indeed all the trees;	
When its branch becomes tender and it puts forth leaves, you know that summer is near;	When its branch becomes tender and it puts forth leaves, you know that summer is near;	30When they put forth leaves, you know, seeing it yourselves, that the summer is near;	When its branch becomes tender and it puts forth leaves, you know that summer is near;
33likewise when you see all these things, know that the kingdom of God is near at the doors.	33likewise when you see all (these things), know that it is near at the doors.	31likewise when you see these (things) happening, know that the kingdom of God is near.	29likewise when you see these (things) happening, know that it is near at the doors.
34Truly I say to you that this people will certainly not perish before all these things come to pass.	34Truly I say to you that this people (shall) certainly not perish before all these things come to pass.	32Truly I say to you that this people (shall) certainly not perish before all these things come to pass.	30Truly I say to you that this people (shall) certainly not perish before all these things come to pass.
35Heaven and earth will pass away, but my words will never fail.	35Heaven and earth will pass away, but my words will never fail.	33Heaven and earth will pass away, but my words will never fail.	31Heaven and earth will pass away, but my words will never fail.
36But concerning that day and hour no one knows, neither the angels of the heavens nor the Son, only the Father.	36But concerning that day and hour no one knows, neither the angels of the heavens nor the Son; (no one knows) except the Father only.		32But concerning that day or hour no one knows, neither the angels of heaven nor the Son; (no one knows) except the Father.
		Luke 17:26-37	
37For just as the days of Noah, so will be the appearing of the Son of Man.	37For just as the days of Noah, so will be the appearing of the Son of Man.	26And just as it was in the days of Noah, so also it will be in the days of the Son of Man;	

Reconstructed Text	Matthew 24	Luke	Mark
38For as in the days before the flood	38For as in the days before the flood		
they were eating and drinking, and marrying and giving in marriage, until the day Noah entered into the ark,	they were eating and drinking, and marrying and giving in marriage, until the day Noah entered into the ark,	27they were eating, drinking, marrying, (and) being given in marriage, until the day Noah entered the ark,	
39and knew not	39and knew not		
until the flood came and destroyed (them) all.	until the flood came and took (them) all,	and the flood came and destroyed (them) all.	
Likewise it was the same in the days of Lot; for they were eating, drinking, buying, selling, planting, (and) building;		28Likewise as it was in the days of Lot; they were eating, drinking, buying, selling, planting, (and) building;	
but the day Lot went out from Sodom, it rained fire and brimstone from heaven and destroyed (them) all.		29but on the day Lot went out from Sodom, it rained fire and brimstone from heaven and destroyed (them) all.	
It will be the same (when) the Son of Man appears.	so will be the appearing of the Son of Man.	30It will be just the same in the day the Son of Man is revealed.	
		------- (Verses 31-33 are dislocated in Luke; they match Matthew 24 16-18, above) -------	
I tell you in that night there will be two men in one bed, and one will be taken and the other left;		34I tell you, in that night there will be two men (lying) upon one bed, one will be taken and the other will be left;	

Reconstructed Text	Matthew 24	Luke	Mark
[40]there will be two men in the field, one will be taken and one left;	[40]Then there will be two [men] in the field, one will be taken and one left;		
[41]two women will be grinding at the mill, one will be taken and one left."	[41]two [women] will be grinding at the mill, one will be taken and one left.	[35]there will be two women grinding at the same place, one will be taken but the other left."	
		[Verse 36 does not appear in the Greek text; it was inserted into the AV from Mt. 24:40.]	
And answering they said to him, "Where, Lord?"		[37]And replying they said to him, "Where, Lord?"	
And he said to them,		And he said to them,	
‑‑‑‑‑‑‑‑‑‑	‑‑‑‑‑‑‑‑‑‑		
24:28 inserted here	24:28 inserted here		
	[Matthew 24:28 has been placed here to match Luke 17:37b.]		
[28]"Wherever the carcass is, there the birds will be gathered.	[28]Wherever the carcass is, there the birds will be gathered.	"Where the body [is], even there the birds will be gathered together.	
‑‑‑‑‑‑‑‑‑‑	‑‑‑‑‑‑‑‑‑‑		
But take heed to yourselves lest your hearts be weighted down in stupor and intoxication, and the cares of this life, and that day slip up on you unexpectedly		21:34-36 [Resumed] [34]But take heed to yourselves lest your hearts be weighted down in stupor and intoxication and anxieties of this life, and that day should slip up on you unexpectedly	

74

Reconstructed Text	Matthew 24	Luke	Mark
like a trap. For it will come upon all those dwelling upon the whole face of the earth.		35Like a trap; for it will come upon all those dwelling upon the whole face of the earth.	
42Therefore watch,	42Therefore watch,	36But be watchful (and)	33Look, be vigilant,
at all times petitioning (God) that you might be qualified to escape all these things that are about to happen, and stand before the Son of Man,		at all times petitioning (God) that you might be qualified to escape all these things that are about to happen, and stand before the Son of Man.	
because you do not know which day your Lord is coming."	because you do not know which day your Lord is coming.		for you do not know when the time is.
-------- [Matthew 25:1-30 belongs here]	-------- [Matthew 25:1-30 belongs here]	**12:35-46** 35Let your loins be girded and (your) lamps burning;	
		36and (be) like men awaiting their lord, when he returns from the wedding celebrations, and knocking they might immediately open (the door) to him.	34It is like a man on a trip leaving his house and giving his servants fiduciary authority (over his holdings), to each his own task, and he commanded the doorkeeper that he should watch.
		37Blessed (are) those servants, whom the lord will find watching (when) he comes;	

Reconstructed Text	Matthew 24	Luke	Mark
		truly I say to you, that he will gird himself and cause them to recline (at the table) and will come along beside (them) and serve them.	
			[35]Watch therefore, for you do not know when the lord of the house comes, either at evening or at midnight or at the cock (crowing), or at dawn;
		[38]And if he comes in the second watch, or in the third and finds (it) so, blessed are those servants.	
			[36]lest coming unexpectedly he find you sleeping.
---------	---------	[In Luke's account the following material is presented in combination with material from the Sermon on the Mount—illustrating Luke's thematic arrangement (see, Lk. 12:22-32 cp. Mt. 6:25-34; Lk. 12:33-34 cp. Mt. 6:19-21; Lk. 12:57-59 cp. Mt. 5:21-26).]	
[43]But you know that if the master of the house knew in which watch the thief was coming, he would have been vigilant and (would) not have allowed his house to be broken through.	[43]But you know that if the master of the house knew in which watch the thief was coming, he would have been vigilant and (would) not have allowed his house to be broken through.	[39]But know this: that if the master of the house had known in what hour the thief (would) come, he would not have allowed his house to be broken through.	
[44]Because of this you also be ready, because the Son of Man will come at an hour you do not anticipate."	[44]On account of this you also be ready, because the Son of Man will come at an hour you do not anticipate.	[40]And you be prepared, because the Son of Man will come at an hour you do not anticipate."	

Reconstructed Text	Matthew 24	Luke	Mark
But Peter said, "Lord, are you speaking this parable (only) to us, or to everyone?"		[41]But Peter said: "Lord, are you speaking this parable (only) to us, or to everyone?"	
(And Jesus said,) "What I say to you, I say to all: Watch!"			[37]What I say to you, I say to all: Watch!
[45]And the Lord said,		[42]And the Lord said:	------- (End of Mark's account)
"Who then is the faithful and prudent servant whom the lord appointed over his household to give them food at the proper time?	[45]Who then is the faithful and prudent servant whom the lord appointed over his household to give them food at the proper time?	"Who then is the faithful (and) prudent steward, whom the lord will appoint over his attendants to give (them) their portion of food at the proper time?	
[46]Blessed (is) the servant whom his lord (at his) coming finds so doing.	[46]Blessed (is) the servant whom his lord (at his) coming finds so doing.	[43]Blessed (is) the servant whom his lord (at his) coming will find so doing.	
[47]Truly I say to you that he will appoint him over all his possessions.	[47]Truly I say to you that he will appoint him over all his possessions.	[44]Truly I tell you that he will appoint him over all his possessions.	
[48]But if that wicked servant says in his heart: 'My lord delays,'	[48]But if that wicked servant says in his heart: 'My lord delays,'	[45]But if that servant says in his heart, 'My lord delays to come,'	
[49]and begins to abuse his fellow servants, and eats and drinks with drunkards,	[49]and begins to abuse his fellow servants, and eats and drinks with drunkards,	and (he) begins to abuse the men servants and the maidservants, (and) both to eat and drink and to become drunk,	

Reconstructed Text	Matthew 24	Luke
[50]the lord of that servant will come on a day in which he does not expect and at an hour he does not know,	the lord of that servant will come on a day in which he does not expect and at an hour he does not know,	[46]the lord of that servant will come on a day in which he does not expect and at an hour he does not know,
[51]and will severely punish him, and relegate (him) his lot with the hypocrites;	[51]and will severely punish him, and relegate (him) his lot with the hypocrites;	and will severely punish him, and relegate (him) his lot with the unbelievers."
there will be wailing and gnashing of teeth.	there will be wailing and gnashing of teeth.	

Table 3: Greek and English Text of Matthew 25

Matthew 25	Matthew 25
[1]"Then will the kingdom of the heavens be likened to ten virgins, who taking their lamps, went forth to meet the bridegroom,	[1]Τότε ὁμοιωθήσεται ἡ βασιλεία τῶν οὐρανῶν δέκα παρθένοις, αἵτινες λαβοῦσαι τὰς λαμπάδας ἑαυτῶν ἐξῆλθον εἰς ὑπάντησιν τοῦ νυμφίου.
[2]but five of them were foolish and five prudent.	[2]πέντε δὲ ἐξ αὐτῶν ἦσαν μωραὶ καὶ πέντε φρόνιμοι.
[3]For the foolish taking their lamps did not take oil with them,	[3]αἱ γὰρ μωραὶ λαβοῦσαι τὰς λαμπάδας αὐτῶν οὐκ ἔλαβον μεθ' ἑαυτῶν ἔλαιον·
[4]but the prudent took oil in vessels (along) with their lamps.	[4]αἱ δὲ φρόνιμοι ἔλαβον ἔλαιον ἐν τοῖς ἀγγείοις μετὰ τῶν λαμπάδων ἑαυτῶν.
[5]And while the bridegroom was delaying they all slumbered and slept.	[5]χρονίζοντος δὲ τοῦ νυμφίου ἐνύσταξαν πᾶσαι καὶ ἐκάθευδον.
[6]But in the middle of the night there had been a cry, 'See, the bridegroom, come out to meet [him].'	[6]μέσης δὲ νυκτὸς κραυγὴ γέγονεν, Ἰδοὺ ὁ νυμφίος, ἐξέρχεσθε εἰς ἀπάντησιν.
[7]Then all those virgins were awakened and trimmed their lamps.	[7]τότε ἠγέρθησαν πᾶσαι αἱ παρθένοι ἐκεῖναι καὶ ἐκόσμησαν τὰς λαμπάδας ἑαυτῶν.

Matthew 25	Matthew 25
8And the foolish said to the prudent, 'Give us some of your oil, because our lamps are going out.'	8αἱ δὲ μωραὶ ταῖς φρονίμοις εἶπαν, Δότε ἡμῖν ἐκ τοῦ ἐλαίου ὑμῶν, ὅτι αἱ λαμπάδες ἡμῶν σβέννυνται.
9But the prudent answered saying, 'No, lest we not have enough (for) us and you; rather go to the merchants and buy for yourselves.'	9ἀπεκρίθησαν δὲ αἱ φρόνιμοι λέγουσαι, Μήποτε οὐ μὴ ἀρκέσῃ ἡμῖν καὶ ὑμῖν· πορεύεσθε μᾶλλον πρὸς τοὺς πωλοῦντας καὶ ἀγοράσατε ἑαυταῖς.
10But (as they were) going away to buy, the bridegroom came, and those ready went in with him to the wedding celebration, and the door was shut.	10ἀπερχομένων δὲ αὐτῶν ἀγοράσαι ἦλθεν ὁ νυμφίος, καὶ αἱ ἕτοιμοι εἰσῆλθον μετ' αὐτοῦ εἰς τοὺς γάμους, καὶ ἐκλείσθη ἡ θύρα.
11Then later the remaining virgins came also saying, 'Lord, Lord, open (the door) for us.'	11ὕστερον δὲ ἔρχονται καὶ αἱ λοιπαὶ παρθένοι λέγουσαι, Κύριε κύριε, ἄνοιξον ἡμῖν.
12But answering he said, 'Truly I say to you, I do not know you.'	12ὁ δὲ ἀποκριθεὶς εἶπεν, Ἀμὴν λέγω ὑμῖν, οὐκ οἶδα ὑμᾶς.
13Watch therefore, because you do not know the day or the hour.	13Γρηγορεῖτε οὖν, ὅτι οὐκ οἴδατε τὴν ἡμέραν οὐδὲ τὴν ὥραν.
14For (it is) like a man going on a journey who called his own servants and entrusted his possessions to them,	14Ὥσπερ γὰρ ἄνθρωπος ἀποδημῶν ἐκάλεσεν τοὺς ἰδίους δούλους καὶ παρέδωκεν αὐτοῖς τὰ ὑπάρχοντα αὐτοῦ,

Matthew 25	Matthew 25
15and to one he gave five talents, and to another, two, and to another, one, to each according to his own ability, and he departed.	15καὶ ᾧ μὲν ἔδωκεν πέντε τάλαντα, ᾧ δὲ δύο, ᾧ δὲ ἕν, ἑκάστῳ κατὰ τὴν ἰδίαν δύναμιν, καὶ ἀπεδήμησεν.
16The one receiving the five talents immediately went (and) traded with them and earned another five.	16εὐθέως πορευθεὶς ὁ τὰ πέντε τάλαντα λαβὼν ἠργάσατο ἐν αὐτοῖς καὶ ἐκέρδησεν ἄλλα πέντε·
17Similarly the one (receiving) two (talents) earned another two.	17ὡσαύτως ὁ τὰ δύο ἐκέρδησεν ἄλλα δύο.
18But the one (receiving) one (talent) went (and) dug (into) (the) ground and hid his master's money.	18ὁ δὲ τὸ ἓν λαβὼν ἀπελθὼν ὤρυξεν γῆν καὶ ἔκρυψεν τὸ ἀργύριον τοῦ κυρίου αὐτοῦ.
19Then after a long time the lord of those servants came and settled with each of them.	19μετὰ δὲ πολὺν χρόνον ἔρχεται ὁ κύριος τῶν δούλων ἐκείνων καὶ συναίρει λόγον μετ' αὐτῶν.
20And approaching (him) the one who had received the five talents brought another five talents saying, 'Lord, you entrusted five talents to me; see, I have earned another five talents.'	20καὶ προσελθὼν ὁ τὰ πέντε τάλαντα λαβὼν προσήνεγκεν ἄλλα πέντε τάλαντα λέγων, Κύριε, πέντε τάλαντά μοι παρέδωκας· ἴδε ἄλλα πέντε τάλαντα ἐκέρδησα.
21His lord said to him, 'Well done, good and faithful servant; you were faithful over a few things, I will appoint you over many things; enter into the joy of your lord.'	21ἔφη αὐτῷ ὁ κύριος αὐτοῦ, Εὖ, δοῦλε ἀγαθὲ καὶ πιστέ, ἐπὶ ὀλίγα ἧς πιστός, ἐπὶ πολλῶν σε καταστήσω· εἴσελθε εἰς τὴν χαρὰν τοῦ κυρίου σου.

Matthew 25	Matthew 25
22Also approaching, the one {having received} the two talents said, 'You entrusted to me two talents; see I have earned another two talents.'	22προσελθών [δὲ] καὶ ὁ τα δύο τάλαντα εἶπεν, Κύριε, δύο τάλαντά μοι παρέδωκας· ἴδε ἄλλα δύο τάλαντα ἐκέρδησα.
23His lord said to him, 'Well done, good and faithful servant; you were faithful over a few things, I will appoint you over many things; enter into the joy of your lord.	23ἔφη αὐτῷ ὁ κύριος αὐτοῦ, Εὖ, δοῦλε ἀγαθὲ καὶ πιστέ, ἐπὶ ὀλίγα ἦς πιστός, ἐπὶ πολλῶν σε καταστήσω· εἴσελθε εἰς τὴν χαρὰν τοῦ κυρίου σου.
24And also approaching, the one {having received} the one talent said, 'Lord, I knew that you are a demanding man, reaping where you did not sow, and gathering where you did not scatter;	24προσελθών δὲ καὶ ὁ τὸ ἓν τάλαντον εἰληφὼς εἶπεν, Κύριε, ἔγνων σε ὅτι σκληρὸς εἶ ἄνθρωπος, θερίζων ὅπου οὐκ ἔσπειρας καὶ συνάγων ὅθεν οὐ διεσκόρπισας;
25and departing in fear I hid your talent in the ground; see, you have what is yours.'	25καὶ φοβηθεὶς ἀπελθὼν ἔκρυψα τὸ τάλαντόν σου ἐν τῇ γῇ· ἴδε ἔχεις τὸ σόν.
26And answering, his lord said to him: '{So,} you wicked and lazy servant; you knew that I reap where I do not sow, and I gather where I do not scatter?	26ἀποκριθεὶς δὲ ὁ κύριος αὐτοῦ εἶπεν αὐτῷ, Πονηρὲ δοῦλε καὶ ὀκνηρέ, ᾔδεις ὅτι θερίζω ὅπου οὐκ ἔσπειρα καὶ συνάγω ὅθεν οὐ διεσκόρπισα;
27Therefore, you ought to have deposited my money with the bankers, and at my coming I would have received it with interest.	27ἔδει σε οὖν βαλεῖν τὰ ἀργυριά μου τοῖς τραπεζίταις, καὶ ἐλθὼν ἐγὼ ἐκομισάμην ἂν τὸ ἐμὸν σὺν τόκῳ.

Matthew 25	Matthew 25
²⁸ἄρατε οὖν ἀπ᾽ αὐτοῦ τὸ τάλαντον καὶ δότε τῷ ἔχοντι τὰ δέκα τάλαντα·	²⁸Therefore take the talent from him and give it to the one having the ten talents;
²⁹τῷ γὰρ ἔχοντι παντὶ δοθήσεται καὶ περισσευθήσεται· τοῦ δὲ μὴ ἔχοντος καὶ ὃ ἔχει ἀρθήσεται ἀπ᾽ αὐτοῦ.	²⁹for to everyone who has [more] will be given, and he will have an abundance; but from the one who does not have even what he has will be taken from him.
³⁰καὶ τὸν ἀχρεῖον δοῦλον ἐκβάλετε εἰς τὸ σκότος τὸ ἐξώτερον· ἐκεῖ ἔσται ὁ κλαυθμὸς καὶ ὁ βρυγμὸς τῶν ὀδόντων.	³⁰And cast out the useless servant into the outer darkness; [where] there will be wailing and gnashing of teeth.'
³¹Ὅταν δὲ ἔλθῃ ὁ υἱὸς τοῦ ἀνθρώπου ἐν τῇ δόξῃ αὐτοῦ καὶ πάντες οἱ ἄγγελοι μετ᾽ αὐτοῦ, τότε καθίσει ἐπὶ θρόνου δόξης αὐτοῦ·	³¹But when the Son of Man comes in his glory and all the angels with him, then he will sit on his glorious throne;
³²καὶ συναχθήσονται ἔμπροσθεν αὐτοῦ πάντα τὰ ἔθνη, καὶ ἀφορίσει αὐτοὺς ἀπ᾽ ἀλλήλων, ὥσπερ ὁ ποιμὴν ἀφορίζει τὰ πρόβατα ἀπὸ τῶν ἐρίφων,	³²And all the nations will be gathered before him, and he will separate them from one another, as the shepherd separates the sheep from the goats;
³³καὶ στήσει τὰ μὲν πρόβατα ἐκ δεξιῶν αὐτοῦ τὰ δὲ ἐρίφια ἐξ εὐωνύμων.	³³and he will set the sheep on his right, but the goats on the left.

Matthew 25	Matthew 25
34Then the King will say to the ones on his right, 'Come, those blessed of my Father, inherit the kingdom prepared for you from the foundation of the world.	34τότε ἐρεῖ ὁ βασιλεὺς τοῖς ἐκ δεξιῶν αὐτοῦ, Δεῦτε, οἱ εὐλογημένοι τοῦ πατρός μου, κληρονομήσατε τὴν ἡτοιμασμένην ὑμῖν βασιλείαν ἀπὸ καταβολῆς κόσμου·
35For I was hungry and you gave me {something} to eat; I was thirsty and you gave me {something} to drink; I was a stranger and you took me in,	35ἐπείνασα γὰρ καὶ ἐδώκατέ μοι φαγεῖν, ἐδίψησα καὶ ἐποτίσατέ με, ξένος ἤμην καὶ συνηγάγετέ με,
36naked and you clothed me, sick and you visited me. I was in prison and you came to me.'	36γυμνὸς καὶ περιεβάλετέ με, ἠσθένησα καὶ ἐπεσκέψασθέ με, ἐν φυλακῇ ἤμην καὶ ἤλθατε πρός με.
37Then the righteous will answer him saying, 'Lord, when did we see you hungering and feed {you}, or thirsty and give you drink?	37τότε ἀποκριθήσονται αὐτῷ οἱ δίκαιοι λέγοντες, Κύριε, πότε σε εἴδομεν πεινῶντα καὶ ἐθρέψαμεν, ἢ διψῶντα καὶ ἐποτίσαμεν;
38And when did we see you a stranger and take {you} in, or naked and clothe {you}?	38πότε δέ σε εἴδομεν ξένον καὶ συνηγάγομεν, ἢ γυμνὸν καὶ περιεβάλομεν;
39And when did we see you sick or in prison and come to {visit} you?'	39πότε δέ σε εἴδομεν ἀσθενοῦντα ἢ ἐν φυλακῇ καὶ ἤλθομεν πρός σε;
40And answering the King will say to them, 'Truly I tell you, inasmuch as you did it to one of the least of these my brethren, you did it to me.'	40καὶ ἀποκριθεὶς ὁ βασιλεὺς ἐρεῖ αὐτοῖς, Ἀμὴν λέγω ὑμῖν, ἐφ' ὅσον ἐποιήσατε ἑνὶ τούτων τῶν ἀδελφῶν μου τῶν ἐλαχίστων, ἐμοὶ ἐποιήσατε.

Matthew 25	Matthew 25
[41]"Then he will also say to the ones on the left, 'Depart from me accursed ones into the eternal fire prepared for the Devil and his angels;	[41]Τότε ἐρεῖ καὶ τοῖς ἐξ εὐωνύμων, Πορεύεσθε ἀπ' ἐμοῦ [οἱ] κατηραμένοι εἰς τὸ πῦρ τὸ αἰώνιον τὸ ἡτοιμασμένον τῷ διαβόλῳ καὶ τοῖς ἀγγέλοις αὐτοῦ·
[42]For I hungered and you did not give me (anything) to eat, I thirsted and you did not give me anything to drink.	[42]ἐπείνασα γὰρ καὶ οὐκ ἐδώκατέ μοι φαγεῖν, ἐδίψησα καὶ οὐκ ἐποτίσατέ με,
[43]I was a stranger (and) you did not take me in, naked and you did not clothe me, sick and in prison and you did not visit me.'	[43]ξένος ἤμην καὶ οὐ συνηγάγετέ με, γυμνὸς καὶ οὐ περιεβάλετέ με, ἀσθενὴς καὶ ἐν φυλακῇ καὶ οὐκ ἐπεσκέψασθέ με.
[44]Then they also will answer saying, "Lord, when did we see you hungering or thirsting or a stranger or naked or sick or in prison and did not minister to you?'	[44]τότε ἀποκριθήσονται καὶ αὐτοὶ λέγοντες, Κύριε, πότε σε εἴδομεν πεινῶντα ἢ διψῶντα ἢ ξένον ἢ γυμνὸν ἢ ἀσθενῆ ἢ ἐν φυλακῇ καὶ οὐ διηκονήσαμέν σοι;
[45]Then he will answer them saying, 'Truly I say to you, inasmuch as you did it not to one of the least of these, neither did you do it to me.'	[45]τότε ἀποκριθήσεται αὐτοῖς λέγων, Ἀμὴν λέγω ὑμῖν, ἐφ' ὅσον οὐκ ἐποιήσατε ἑνὶ τούτων τῶν ἐλαχίστων, οὐδὲ ἐμοὶ ἐποιήσατε.
[46]And these will go away into eternal punishment, but the righteous into eternal life."	[46]καὶ ἀπελεύσονται οὗτοι εἰς κόλασιν αἰώνιον, οἱ δὲ δίκαιοι εἰς ζωὴν αἰώνιον.

Table 4: The Reconstructed Text of the Discourse

The reconstructed text is presented in a more readable form below. The versification is aligned with Matthew's gospel. Since this text is derived from a comparison of all three synoptic accounts, it is longer than any individual account. While the versification is based on the Matthew 24-25 account, the reader should keep in mind that some of the material is not actually contained in Matthew's account, and in some cases the material in Matthew 24-25 has been superseded by more detailed material from one of the other accounts; thus, a citation to Matthew 24:13, for example, and to 24:13 [in the reconstructed text] will not read the same.[3]

Chapter 24

1   And as Jesus was going forth from the temple, the disciples approached him to show him the temple buildings; and one of his disciples was saying to him, "Teacher, behold these great stones and these great buildings."

2   And answering he said to them, "Do you not see all these things? Truly I tell you, not even a stone will be left upon {another} stone that will not be torn down."

3   And as he sat on the Mount of Olives, opposite the temple, Peter and James and John and Andrew questioned him privately, saying: "Teacher, tell us, when will these things be, and what will be the sign of your appearing and the end of the age?"

4   And answering, Jesus said to them, "See that no one misleads you.

5   For many will come in my name saying 'I am the Christ,' and 'The time is near;' and they will deceive many. Do not follow them.

6   But you will hear of wars and threats of wars; see that you do not panic, for these things must happen first, but it is not yet the end."

---

[3] For information on the reconstruction of the text see, "The Structure of the Discourse," p.21, parallel texts, and the textual notes, which are part of the commentary.

7   Then he said to them, "For people will rise up against people, and kingdom against kingdom, and there will be famines and pestilences and great earthquakes in various places;

8   but all these things are {merely the} beginning of birth pains.

9   But beware of men, for they will hand you over to courts, and they will scourge you in their assemblies; and you will be brought before governors and kings for my sake, for a testimony to them and to the nations. And the gospel must first be proclaimed unto all the nations. But when they hand you over, do not be anxious how or what you should speak, for it will be given to you in that hour what you should say, for I will give you a mouth and wisdom, which none of the ones opposing you will be able to withstand or contradict; for you are not the ones speaking, but the Spirit of your Father is speaking by you. And brother will deliver up brother to death, and a father {will deliver up} a child, and children will rise up against parents and kill them. And you will be hated by all on account of my name; yet not a hair of your head will perish.

10 And then many will be caused to fall away and betray one another and hate one another;

11 and many false prophets will arise and mislead many;

12 and because the iniquity will be increased, the love of many will grow cold.

13 but the one enduring to the end will be delivered. But when they persecute you in one city, flee to another; for truly I say to you, you will certainly not finish {going through} the cities of Israel until the Son of

Man comes. {And} there will be terrors, and great signs from heaven.[4]

14   And this gospel of the kingdom will be proclaimed in the whole inhabited world for a testimony to all nations, and then the end will come.

15   Therefore, when you see Jerusalem surrounded by armies {and} the abomination of desolation spoken of through Daniel the prophet standing in the holy place—let the reader understand—then know that its desolation has drawn near.

16   Then let those in Judea flee unto the mountains.

17   In that day, let not the one on the roof go down to take the things out of his house,

18   and let not the one in the field turn back to retrieve his garment. Remember the wife of Lot. Whoever will seek to save his possessions will forfeit {his life}, but whoever will forfeit {his possessions}, will save {his life}. Because these are the days of vengeance {in which} all {the things} having been written are to be fulfilled.

19   But woe to the ones who are pregnant and to the ones nursing in those days.

20   But pray that your flight might not occur in winter neither on a Sabbath;

21   for then there will be great tribulation upon the earth, and wrath to this people, such as has neither occurred from the beginning of the world until now, nor will ever happen {again}. And they will fall by the edge of the sword and will be led captive unto all the nations, and Jerusalem will be trodden down by the Gentiles until the times of the Gentiles are completed.

---

[4] This statement from Luke 21:11b has been moved here in order to unfold the recursive structure found in Luke 21:11-18 so that the material from Luke can be merged with Matthew and Mark, which do not employ a recursive structure. This issue is discussed under "The Structure of the Discourse" on pages 23-24, and in the commentary at 24:7-8.

22 And except {for the fact that} those days will be cut short, no flesh would be delivered; but on account of the elect, those days will be cut short.

23 Then if anyone says to you, 'Look, here {is} the Christ,' or: 'There {he is},' do not believe {it};

24 for false christs and false prophets will be raised up and they will give great signs and miracles so as to deceive, if possible, even the elect.

25 See, I have told you all these things before {they happen}." And he said to the disciples, "Days will come when you will long to see one of the days of the Son of Man and will not see {it}.

26 Therefore, if they say to you, 'Look, he is in the desert,' do not go out {there}; {or} 'Look, {he is in} the inner chamber,' do not believe {them}.

27 For just as the lightning flashes from the east and shines even unto the west, so will be the appearing of the Son of Man. But first it is necessary for him to suffer many things and to be rejected by this generation.

28 >Omit<[5]

29 But immediately after the tribulation of those days, the sun will be darkened, and the moon will not give its light, and the stars will fall from heaven, and on earth {there will be} distress of nations powerless at the sound of the sea and surf, {and} men collapsing from fear and {the} anticipation of the things coming upon the earth; for the powers of the heavens will be shaken.

30 And then the sign of the Son of Man will appear in heaven, and all the peoples of the earth will mourn, and they will see the Son of Man coming on the

---

[5] Verse 28 appears after verse 41. Matthew 24:41 matches to Luke 17:35, thus Matthew 24:28, which matches Luke 17:37 should appear after Matthew 24:41. The dislocation appears to be original and is due to the way Matthew and Luke selected and edited material from their common source. (See the parallel texts.)

clouds of heaven with great power and glory. When these things begin to happen, raise yourselves up and lift up your heads because your redemption draws near.

31   And he will send forth his angels with a great trumpet, and they will gather his elect from out of the four winds, from one end of the heavens to the other.

32   Now learn the parable of the fig tree, indeed all the trees: When its branch becomes tender and it puts forth leaves, you know that summer is near;

33   likewise when you see all these things, know that the kingdom of God is near at the doors.

34   Truly I say to you that this people will certainly not perish before all these things come to pass.

35   Heaven and earth will pass away, but my words will never fail.

36   But concerning that day and hour no one knows, neither the angels of the heavens nor the Son, only the Father.

37   For just as the days of Noah, so will be the appearing of the Son of Man.

38   For as in the days before the flood they were eating and drinking, and marrying and being given in marriage, until the day Noah entered into the ark,

39   and knew not until the flood came and destroyed {them} all. Likewise, it was the same in the days of Lot; they were eating, drinking, buying, selling, planting, {and} building; but {the} day Lot went out from Sodom, it rained fire and brimstone from heaven and destroyed {them} all. It will be the same {when} the Son of man appears. I tell you, in that night there will be two men in one bed and one will be taken and the other left.

40   Then there will be two men in the field, one will be taken and one left;

41   two women will be grinding at the mill, one will be taken and one left." And answering they said: "Where, Lord?" And he said to them: "Where the carcass {is}, there the eagles will be gathered. But take heed to yourselves lest your hearts be weighted down in stupor and intoxication, and the anxieties of this life, and that day should slip up on you unexpectedly like a trap; for it will come upon all those dwelling upon the whole face of the earth.

42   Watch therefore, always petitioning {God} that you might be qualified to escape all these things that are about to happen, and stand before the Son of Man, because you do not know which day your Lord is coming."

{Matthew 25:1-30 belongs here}

----

[43][6]

"But you know that if the master of the house knew in which watch the thief was coming, he would have been vigilant and {would} not have allowed his house to be broken through.

44   Because of this you also be ready, because the Son of Man will come at an hour you do not anticipate." But Peter said, "Lord, are you speaking this parable {only} to us, or to everyone?" {And the Lord said,} "What I say to you, I say to all: Watch!"

45   And the Lord said, "Who then is the faithful and prudent servant whom the lord appointed over his household to give them food at the proper time?

[6] Verse 43 parallels Luke 12:39, and since Luke 12:35-38 summarizes the two parables in Matthew 25:1-30 (the parables of the virgins and the stewards), Matthew 24:43 was spoken after those parables. It appears that Matthew moved these parables to a later point in the discourse where they could be reported in greater detail, whereas Luke chose to report them in their original sequence in summary form.

46 Blessed {is} the servant whom his lord {at his} coming finds so doing.

47 Truly I say to you that he will appoint him over all his possessions.

48 But if that wicked servant says in his heart: 'My lord delays,'

49 and begins to abuse his fellow servants, and eats and drinks with drunkards,

50 the lord of that servant will come on a day in which he does not expect and at an hour he does not know,

51 and will severely punish him, and relegate {him} his lot with the hypocrites; there will be wailing and gnashing of teeth.

Chapter 25

1 Then will the kingdom of the heavens be likened to ten virgins, who taking their lamps went forth to meet the bridegroom,

2 but five of them were foolish and five prudent.

3 For the foolish taking their lamps did not take oil with them,

4 but the prudent took oil in vessels {along} with their lamps.

5 And while the bridegroom was delaying they all grew weary and slept.

6 But in the middle of the night there had been a cry, 'See, the bridegroom, come out to meet {him}.'

7 Then all those virgins were awakened and trimmed their lamps.

8 And the foolish said to the prudent, 'Give us some of your oil, because our lamps are going out.'

9 But the prudent answered saying, 'No, lest we not have enough {for} us and you; rather go to the merchants and buy for yourselves.'

10   But {as they were} going away to buy, the bridegroom came, and those ready went in with him to the wedding celebration, and the door was shut.

11   Then later the remaining virgins came also saying, 'Lord, Lord, open {the door} for us.'

12   But answering he said, 'Truly I say to you, I do not know you.'

13   Watch therefore, because you do not know the day or the hour.

14   For {it is} like a man going on a journey who called his own servants and entrusted his possessions to them,

15   and to one he gave five talents, and to another, two, and to another, one, to each according to his own ability, and he departed.

16   The one receiving the five talents immediately went {and} traded with them and earned another five.

17   Similarly the one {receiving} two {talents} earned another two.

18   But the one {receiving} one {talent} went {and} dug {into} {the} ground and hid his master's money.

19   Then after a long time the lord of those servants came and settled with each of them.

20   And approaching {him} the one who had received the five talents brought another five talents saying, 'Lord, you entrusted five talents to me; see, I have earned another five talents.'

21   His lord said to him, 'Well done, good and faithful servant; you were faithful over a few things, I will appoint you over many things; enter into the joy of your lord.'

22   Also approaching, the one {having received} the two talents said, 'You entrusted to me two talents; see I have earned another two talents.'

23 His lord said to him, 'Well done, good and faithful servant; you were faithful over a few things, I will appoint you over many things; enter into the joy of your lord.'

24 And also approaching, the one {having received} the one talent said, 'Lord, I knew that you are a demanding man, reaping where you did not sow, and gathering where you did not scatter;

25 and departing in fear I hid your talent in the ground; see, you have what is yours.'

26 And answering, his lord said to him: '{You} wicked and lazy servant; {so} you knew that I reap where I do not sow, and I gather where I do not scatter?

27 Therefore, you ought to have deposited my money with the bankers, and at my coming I would have received it with interest.

28 Therefore take the talent from him and give it to the one having the ten talents;

29 for to everyone who has {more} will be given, and he will have an abundance; but from the one who does not have even what he has will be taken from him.

30 And cast out the useless servant into the outer darkness; {where} there will be wailing and gnashing of teeth.'

31 But when the Son of Man comes in his glory and all the angels with him, then he will sit on his glorious throne;

32 And all the nations will be gathered before him, and he will separate them from one another, as the shepherd separates the sheep from the goats;

33 and he will set the sheep on his right, but the goats on the left.

34 Then the King will say to the ones on his right, 'Come, those blessed of my Father, inherit the kingdom prepared for you from the foundation of the world.

35   For I was hungry and you gave me {something} to eat; I was thirsty and you gave me {something} to drink; I was a stranger and you took me in,

36   naked and you clothed me, sick and you visited me; I was in prison and you came to me.'

37   Then the righteous will answer him saying, 'Lord, when did we see you hungering and feed {you}, or thirsty and give you drink?

38   And when did we see you a stranger and take {you} in, or naked and clothe {you}?

39   And when did we see you sick or in prison and come to {visit} you?'

40   And answering the King will say to them, 'Truly I tell you, inasmuch as you did it to one of the least of these my brethren, you did it to me.'

41   Then he will also say to the ones on the left, 'Depart from me accursed ones into the eternal fire prepared for the devil and his angels;

42   For I hungered and you did not give me {anything} to eat, I thirsted and you did not give me anything to drink.

43   I was a stranger {and} you did not take me in, naked and you did not clothe me, sick and in prison and you did not visit me.'

44   Then they also will answer saying, 'Lord, when did we see you hungering or thirsting or a stranger or naked or sick or in prison and did not minister to you?'

45   Then he will answer them saying, 'Truly I say to you, inasmuch as you did it not to one of the least of these, neither did you do it to me.'

46   And these will go away into eternal punishment, but the righteous into eternal life."

24:1-3 Commentary

Outline

    I.   **The departure from the temple for the Mount of Olives 24:1-3**

    II.   A prophetic overview of the coming tribulation 24:4-14

    III. The period of great tribulation culminating in the regal appearing 24:15-31

    IV. The dual nature of Christ's future appearing, and the imminent rapture of the Church 24:32-51

    V.   Similitudes illustrating the imminency of the rapture and the importance of continued faithfulness 25:1-30

    VI. The disposition of the tribulation survivors 25:31-46

After confronting the leaders of each of the major parties (the Herodians cf. Mt. 22:15-22, the Sadducees cf. Mt. 22:23-33, and the Pharisees cf. Mt. 22:34-46), and pronouncing woes upon the Pharisees (Mt. 23:1-36)—for they of all people should have seen the truth—Jesus lamented over Jerusalem (Mt. 23:37-39) and left the temple for the last time.

> **[1] And as Jesus was going forth from the temple, the disciples approached him to show him the temple buildings; and one of his disciples was saying to him, "Teacher, behold these great stones and these great buildings."**

> **[2] And answering he said to them, "Do you not see all these things? Truly I tell you, not even a stone will be left upon another stone that will not be torn down."**

> **[3] And as he sat on the Mount of Olives, opposite the temple, Peter and James and John and Andrew questioned him privately, saying: "Teacher, tell us, when will these things be, and what will be the sign of your appearing and the end of the age?"**

———

Exegetical and Textual Notes

v.1:   Mark (13:1) reads: …λέγει αὐτῷ εἷς τῶν μαθητῶν αὐτοῦ, Διδάσκαλε, ἴδε ποταποὶ λίθοι καὶ ποταπαὶ οἰκοδομαί ("…one of his disciples was saying to him, 'Teacher, behold {these} great buildings'"). Mark (13:1b) reads: ἴδε ποταποὶ λίθοι καὶ ποταπαὶ οἰκοδομαί ("behold what kind of stones and what kind of building." Ποταποὶ ("what kind") here is used as an expression of admiration.

v.2a   Mark reads: ταύτας τὰς μεγάλας οἰκοδομάς ("these great buildings"). Note the double negative, οὐ μὴ ("not even"), in Matthew and Mark.

v.3   Possibly Jesus had gone up alone to some location on the Mount to pray and these four disciples approached him. Mark (13:3) reads: ἐπηρώτα αὐτὸν κατ' ἰδίαν Πέτρος καὶ Ἰάκωβος καὶ Ἰωάννης καὶ Ἀνδρέας ("Peter and James and John and Andrew approached and questioned him privately") and seems to indicate that only these four disciples were present, though it is possible that others were nearby and only these disciples questioned Jesus. Mark adds: κατέναντι τοῦ ἱεροῦ ("opposite the temple"). Perhaps the significance of this statement is that the temple and its eastern gate were visible across the valley as Jesus spoke. The question refers to the completion of a specific "age" *i.e.*, the present interregnal age (καὶ συντελείας τοῦ αἰῶνος = "and the completion of the age"), not "the end of the world" as in the AV. Mark reads: συντελεῖσθαι πάντα, "the completion of all {these things}."

———

It was Tuesday, just three days before his crucifixion that Jesus departed from the temple for the last time. He would never again set foot in that temple.[1] His public ministry was now complete. The nation and its leaders had rejected him and were even then in the process of seeking the means of his death. There would be no more sermons to throngs of people, no more overtures to the nation, no more disputes with religious leaders. All that remained were a few final details. Later in the day he would speak privately to some of his disciples on the Mount of Olives overlooking the temple; and sometime in the evening he would return to Bethany, a couple of miles down the road, where he probably rested and prayed the next day in preparation for the ordeal he knew was soon to come. It would only be a short time now. This was the calm before the storm. There wasn't much time left, just enough to reach out to one more lost soul (Mk. 12:28-34), and to be anointed by Mary as he reclined at dinner with his friend Lazarus in the house of Simon, the leper (Mk. 14:1-9). On Thursday he would celebrate the Passover with his disciples, and later that evening Judas would deliver him to be arrested in the Garden of Gethsemane, adjacent to the Mount of Olives where he and his disciples were now headed.

As Jesus and the disciples were leaving the temple, one of the disciples commented on the grandeur of the temple structures (Mk. 13:1), and Jesus told them that the great edifice would be destroyed to such an extent that not even one stone would be left upon another.[2] Such trivial thoughts about the temple structure reveal that Jesus'

_____

[1] The first temple is called "Solomon's temple"; it was destroyed in 586 B.C. The temple of Jesus' day was the second temple (originally built in 516 B.C., and rebuilt beginning sometime around 19 B.C.; it was still under construction when Jesus delievered this discourse). There are two temples that will be built in the future: the third temple (the tribulation temple) in which will be fulfilled the prophecy of the abomination in Daniel 9:27, and a fourth temple—the millennial temple.

[2] Apparently this question was asked by one disciple (Mk. 13:1), but attributed to the group (Mt. 24:1). In Jesus' response, he referred not to the mount upon which the temple was built, but to the structures to which the disciple referred –the temple with its porticoes and courts. Just as Jesus

disciples had not yet comprehended what was about to happen, or its implications, both for them and for the nation of Israel. Jesus had already told the disciples that he would die.[3] Had they understood the prophecy of the seventy weeks in Daniel 9:24-27, they should have been aware that this temple, Israel's second temple, was doomed to destruction after Messiah's death, for that prophecy clearly states that after the Messiah is "cut off" (Dan. 9:26), the city (Jerusalem) and the sanctuary would be destroyed.[4]

Arriving at the Mount of Olives, just across the Kiddron Valley, east of the temple, Jesus sat down by himself.[5] Very possibly the temple was visible from where Jesus sat.[6] But his solitude was soon interrupted. Mark (13:3) tells us that Peter, James, John, and Andrew approached Jesus privately to question him.[7] Whether any of the other disciples were nearby, or whether they had been sent on various errands is not

---

said, those structures were completely dismantled and cast into the valley below by the Romans in A.D. 70. Today, not one of the original stones of the temple structure or porticoes is to be found on the temple mount.

[3] Cf. Mt. 9:15; 12:40; 16:4,21; 17:9,22-23; 20:18-19; 21:38-39; Jn. 2:19-22; 3:14; 6:51; 8:20-21,28; 10:11,15,17-18; 12:3-7,22-24,31-35.

[4] The prophecy of Daniel 9:24-27 is critical in understanding this discourse, and Jesus specifically directs his listeners to this prophecy and admonishes them to understand it (Mt. 24:15; Mk. 13:14). Regrettably, due to the early and continuing influence of both replacement theology and realized eschatology in both Catholic and Reformed traditions, most interpreters have a distorted view of the meaning and significance of the prophetic content of the book of Daniel, especially the prophecy of the 70 weeks. Most, in their efforts to either dismiss or to spiritualize Israel's promises to the Church, have taken the view that this prophecy, including the seventieth week (v.27), was either largely or completely fulfilled either in the intertestamental age or when the Romans destroyed Jerusalem in A.D. 70. However, assuming the verbal inspiration of scripture, that interpretation cannot be correct, since the prophecy clearly indicates that the seventieth week comes after the destruction of the second temple (the temple of Jesus' day) during the period of a third temple, which as yet, has not been built. How could the coming Roman Prince (the Antichrist) put a stop to the offerings in the temple in the middle of the seventieth week (v.27) if the temple is destroyed before the seventieth week begins (v.26) unless a third temple is built? Because this prophecy is of such importance in understanding the Olivet Discourse, a discussion of Daniel 9:24-27 is included in the Appendices beginning at page 201.

[5] Matthew 24:3 says that "the disciples approached him" indicating that perhaps Jesus had sat down in a place to rest, or to pray apart from the disciples.

[6] Mark adds: κατέναντι τοῦ ἱεροῦ ("opposite the temple"). Perhaps the significance of this statement is that the temple and its eastern gate, elsewhere associated with Messiah's return, was in view as Jesus spoke.

[7] Mark (13:3) is the only account that tells us specifically who was present and questioned Jesus. Both Matthew (24:3) and Mark (13:3) indicate that these disciples approached Jesus κατ' ἰδίαν ("by themselves," or "alone"). Lenski thinks that all twelve disciples were present, but the text does not support this (Lenski, *Matthew*, p.928).

known. In any case, the text indicates that only Jesus and these four disciples were present.[8] A burning question had developed among some of the disciples. Undoubtedly Jesus' remark about the temple either evoked this question, or had caused a long-standing issue to resurface. And so they approached and asked him: "Teacher, tell us, when will these things be, and what will be the sign of your appearing and of the end of the age?" It was late in the day, and it is possible that as Jesus spoke the disciples could see the sun setting on the temple in the background. Although the remainder of the discourse is an extended answer to this question, the question itself merits scrutiny, because it reveals a number of things about the disciples' interests and state of knowledge. First, we notice that it is a two-part question, and that the second part has two parts of its own.[9] The first part of the question, "when will these things be?" deals with Christ's prior statement concerning the destruction of the temple. The second part of the question deals with how they might know when this event is near at hand, *i.e.*, what signs will precede the event. Interestingly, the disciples had already equated the destruction of the temple with Jesus' return and the end of the interregnal age.[10] This assumption was only partly correct. The disciples were right in thinking that Jesus was speaking apocalyptically in reference to the destruction of the temple; thus it seemed to them to be reasonable to lump the destruction of the temple, Christ's return, and the end of the age together, which we may assume they thought to be much nearer than has proven to be the case. In the prophecy of the 70 weeks (Dan. 9:24-27) the death of Messiah and the destruction of Jerusalem and the temple are said to occur after the 69th week. As Jesus indicated in Matthew 24:15, a knowledge of the book of Daniel, especially the prophecy of the 70 weeks, is essential in order to understand his statements.

The disciples had asked a question, the answer to which they, and every Jew schooled in the Scriptures should have known, that the sign of the impending destruction of the temple was the death of Messiah (Dan. 9:26)—the very thing Jesus had been predicting. If the disciples had understood the prophecy of the 70 weeks recorded in Daniel, they would also have known that the destruction of the second temple (the

---

[8] Of this group, Peter, James, and John seem to have formed the inner core of Jesus' disciples, as we also see them with him at his transfiguration (Mt. 17:1-3). The fact that Matthew (24:3) refers to those who approached as "the disciples" (οἱ μαθηταὶ) does not mean that all of the twelve were present. Peter, James, John, and Andrew were "the disciples" that approached Jesus.

[9] The full question must be reconstructed from a comparison of the three accounts. Matthew leaves out the part of the question contained in Mark and Luke regarding the sign when "these things are about to happen," and Mark and Luke leave out the part of the question that addresses Christ's appearing and the end of the age.

[10] The clause, καὶ συντελείας τοῦ αἰῶνος ("and the completion of the age"), does not refer to "the end of the world" as translated in the AV, but to the completion of the present interregnal age, which falls between the first and second advents of Christ.

temple of Jesus' day) would not occur in connection with Jesus' second coming, it must happen before that, for according to Daniel, the second temple is to be destroyed after Messiah is "cut off" and another temple, the third temple, must be built in which the abomination will occur (Dan. 9:26-27). Thus, Jesus gave no answer as to when the temple would be destroyed, or what sign, or signs would precede that event; it had already been revealed. He simply referred the disciples to Daniel (Mt. 24:15).[11] However, Jesus did answer the question as to what signs will precede his coming and the end of the age. In fact, that answer takes up most of the substance of this discourse, at least from 24:4 through 25:31.

---

[11] The temple of Jesus' day was the second temple, built in 516 B.C. A complete renovation was begun by Herod the Great beginning sometime around 19 B.C. Although the temple structure itself was replaced in the renovation, it is still referred to as "the second temple" because the sacrifices never stopped throughout the rebuilding process. It is sometimes referred to as "Herod's temple." It was destroyed in A.D. 70 by the Romans in accordance with the prophecy in Daniel 9:26. According to the prophecy of the 70 weeks (Dan. 9:24-27) the third temple must be built before the end of the age and the return of Christ.

24:4-14 Commentary

  Part of the question Jesus' disciples had asked (24:3) pertained to the signs that would precede his return and the end of the age. He now begins to answer that question. While we do not want to read content from other portions of scripture into this text, it is important to understand the text within the broader biblical context. Jesus challenged his listeners to understand what he was saying in the light of what had been previously revealed, especially the book of Daniel (Mt. 24:15). The period of history just prior to the establishment of the kingdom of God on earth is commonly referred to as "the tribulation," though it is not given a formal name in Scripture.[1] The tribulation

---

[1] The term "tribulation" (θλῖψις) appears in several places in this passage as a description of the character of this period, but not as a title. That the tribulation period immediately precedes the establishment of the visible aspect of the kingdom of God is attested by the fact that every passage of scripture mentioning either the tribulation period or the visible kingdom of God on earth in relation to the regal appearing of Christ, views Christ's appearing as the conclusion of the tribulation, or alternatively, as the inception of the millennial aspect of the kingdom (Zech. 14:1-11; Mt. 24:29-31; Rev. 19:11-20:6, see also: Isa. 35:4-10; 61:2b-3; Joel 3:9-21; Zech. 2:6-10). In fact, many passages in discussing the tribulation and the visible aspect of the kingdom simply view the tribulation as an immediate prelude to the establishment of the kingdom (Isa. 1:24-2:4; 24:1-25:12; 34:1-35:10; Joel 2:1-32; Zech. 12:1-13:9). In spiritualized interpretation the regal appearing and the inception of the millennial aspect of the kingdom are often viewed as having been fulfilled at Christ's first advent (or, in connection with his resurrection and succeeding events). However, such a view requires either that the tribulation prophecies be seen as fulfilled in the intertestamental period, which is clearly at odds with Jesus' futurist teaching in this passage (and the book of Revelation), or that the order of the prophesied events be rearranged from the order universally found in scripture (tribulation > regal advent > kingdom) to some other order that places the regal advent prior to the tribulation. The general amillennial position (regal advent > kingdom > tribulation) can be broken down as follows: regal advent > k{tribulation}ingdom [Full Preterism], regal advent > kingdo{tribulation}m [Partial Preterism], or

period that Jesus described in Matthew 24:4-14 corresponds to the 70th week in the prophecy of the 70 weeks found in Daniel 9:24-27, as is apparent from the reference to the abomination in the temple (Mt. 24:15 and Mk. 13:14 cf. Dan. 9:27).[2] A common assumption made by many interpreters is that the tribulation is synonymous with the day of the LORD.[3] However, the prophecy of the 70 weeks does not indicate what portion of the 70th week is concurrent with the day of the LORD, though it is apparent from other scripture, particularly the book of Revelation, that the day of the LORD begins at some point during the tribulation period.[4]

There are several views as to the identification of the period concerning which Jesus spoke in verses 4-14. These views are illustrated below.

Views		The Church-age	The Tribulation
	1	v.4 ⟶ v.14	v.15 ⟶ v.31
	2	v.4 ⟶ v.8	v.9 ⟶ v.31
	3		v.4 ⟶ v.14 v.15 ⟶ v.31
	4		v.4 ⟶ v.8 v.9 ⟶ v.14
			v.15 ⟶ v.31

Comparison of Views on the Chronological Structure of Matthew 24:4-31

r{*kingdom*}egal advent > tribulation [Ideal Preterism]; and postmillennialism can be represented as: regal advent > tribulation > kingdom, or, regal advent > kingdo{*tribulation*}m. Only premillennialism reflects the biblical order, placing the tribulation prior to the regal appearing.

[2] In the prophecy of the 70 weeks each "week" is a unit of seven prophetic years (360 days each). The 490 prophetic years begin with a decree to rebuild and restore Jerusalem and extend to the establishment of the millennial aspect of the kingdom of God. The last week, or seven-year period, is the seven years of tribulation immediately preceding the establishment of the millennial aspect of the kingdom of God. The present Church age, which is a parenthesis to the prophetic program for Israel, falls between the 69th week of the prophecy (which ended just prior to Jesus' crucifixion) and before the beginning of the 70th week. See, "Daniel 9:24-27: The Prophecy of the 70 Weeks," beginning on page 201.

[3] The day of the LORD follows "the times of the Gentiles." It begins sometime during the tribulation period with divine judgments preparatory to the second coming and transitions into a time of great blessing during the kingdom.

[4] For arguments that the day of the LORD begins sometime during the second half of the tribulation see, "The chronology of the tribulation" beginning on p.242; also see, "A major problem with pretribulationism's central thesis," beginning on p.262.

The views include: 1) that verses 4-14 refer to the Church age, and verses 15-31 refer to the second half of the tribulation; 2) that verses 4-8 refer to the Church age, and verses 9-31 refer to the second half of the tribulation; 3) that verses 4-14 refer to the first half of the tribulation, and verses 15-31 refer to the second half; 4) that verses 4-8 are a general survey of the first half of the tribulation, and verses 9-14 are a general survey of the second half of the tribulation, with verses 15-31 being a recursion back to the midpoint to add additional information concerning the second half of the period. The first view, if correct, would mean that the passage omits any reference to the events of the first half of the tribulation, which would be odd since Revelation indicates that there are a number of events that occur early in the tribulation period, and those events (the first four seals, cf. Rev. 6:1-8) correspond both in substance and in sequence to those listed in Matthew 24:4-8 (*i.e.*, threat of war, war, famine, and death by pestilence). The second view, like the first, places some events into the Church age that properly belong in the first half of the tribulation (again, based upon comparison with Revelation 6:1-6). The third view seems better than the first two, but is still problematic in that verses 13-14 refer to the end of the period, rather than the time just prior to the midpoint. The fourth view is preferable because it has none of the shortcomings associated with the other three views, and the literary structure of the passage seems to support this view.[5] The exposition given here is based upon this last view.[6]

Since the Olivet Discourse is completely occupied with the tribulation and the interlude between the tribulation and the beginning of the millennial aspect of the kingdom, it is important that the reader survey the biblical teaching on this topic; for all that goes before serves as the antecedent theology to this discourse, and all that comes after, especially the extended discussion of the tribulation in the book of Revelation, elucidates the truths contained here.[7]

[4] And answering, Jesus said to them, "See that no one misleads you."

---

[5] Note the prominent transition between verses 8 and 9, where verse 8 ends with the summary statement: "But all these things…" (*i.e.* the things listed in verses 4-7) are merely "…the beginning of birth pains." Also, it should be clear from Daniel 9:27 (the prophecy of the 70 "weeks") that the abomination referred to in verse 15 begins the second half of the tribulation period; that fact, and the additional fact that verses 13-14 advance to "the end" (the only "end" referred to in the passage is the end of the tribulation period) leads to the conclusion that verses 15-31 must be recursive, jumping back to the midpoint.

[6] The recognition that 24:15-31 is chronologically recursive to 24:4-14 is critical to the interpretation of this portion of the passage. Verse 15 begins at the midpoint (cf. Dan. 9:27), and verses 9-10 describe the same events as verses 16-20 describe recursively; this permits us to see that the abomination referenced in verse 15 precedes, and likely precipitates the persecution and resultant apostasy described in verses 9-10.

[7] For a discussion of the biblical teaching on the tribulation period see, "The Character and Chronology of the Tribulation" in the Appendices.

[5] "For many will come in my name saying 'I am the Christ,' and 'The time is near;' and they will deceive many. Do not follow them."

Exegetical and Textual Notes:

v.4   The first clause is purely introductory to Jesus' statement, and each writer expresses the introduction differently. The second clause in Matthew (24:4) and Mark (13:5) are identical, but Luke (21:8) is slightly compressed in that it omits τις ὑμᾶς ("anyone you"), which of course is implied; thus the statements are verbally equivalent. It is important to recognize that this discourse is not addressed to the world; it is addressed to believers in Christ (or at least those who profess belief), and there is a strict "you" (believers), "they" (the unbelieving world) dichotomy throughout the discourse (for examples see: 24:4,6,9,15,20,23,25), though it is not always evident in the English translation since the pronominal root attached to the verb is not expressed where a specific subject is named (as in 24:7,10,11,24).

v.5   Mt. 24:5 and Mk. 13:5 are virtually identical, except that Matthew uses Ἐγώ εἰμι ὁ Χριστός ("I am the Christ") rather than Mark's Ἐγώ εἰμι ("I am {he}") with the implied pronoun; but Luke adds two additional clauses, and omits one clause found in Matthew and Mark (see the parallel texts). After, "for many will come in my name saying, 'I am {he},'" Luke adds "...and 'the time is near;' do not follow them." Luke omits the interposing clause: καὶ πολλοὺς πλανήσουσιν ("and will mislead many"). [πλανήσουσιν, from πλανάω, meaning, "to cause one to stray," *BAGD*, p.665.] Thus, this portion of the verse must be reconstructed to get the full statement. The sentence only flows properly by placing the indicative clauses as given in the reconstruction above, and splitting off Luke's final imperative clause as a separate sentence. Undoubtedly the imperative is the final statement of the verse. If we reversed the order of the indicative clauses, the structure would be unworkable since the deception referred to in, "they will deceive many" (the result) proceeds from the dual claim of Messiahship and that "the time is near," and the claims must precede their result.

With verse 4 Jesus begins his answer to the disciples' question asked in the previous verse. Of course, there have already been many in history that have claimed to be the Messiah—by which most mean that they are the Christ of the New Testament, either returned or re-incarnate. However, the false christs to which Jesus here refers will come on the scene early in the tribulation period, for it is the first item he mentions. The first half of the tribulation will be a time of great messianic expectation on the part of the Jewish people; for the third temple will be built either before the period begins, or more likely, early in the first half of the period.[8] The rebuilding of the temple and the re-

---

[8] Daniel 9:27 indicates that the third temple must be in operation by the midpoint of the tribulation, since the Prince to come (known in Revelation as "the first beast," and elsewhere in the New Testament as "the Antichrist") will cause the sacrifices to be stopped and desecrate the

implementation of the sacrificial system in Jewish worship is no small thing. When it occurs it will be one of the most significant events in history. From a purely secular point of view the very thought of such a thing must seem far removed from reality. But it will happen, and it will have a profound impact on the Jewish consciousness of their place in history, particularly as it relates to Jewish eschatological expectations. Even now in the literature of Jewish groups preparing for the rebuilding of the temple, the assumption on the part of some is that when the temple is rebuilt, Messiah will come. It is within this context that the false christs to which Jesus referred will arise; they will ride in on a wave of messianic euphoria.[9] Jesus gives some insight into the magnitude of this deception when he says, "many will come in my name saying, 'I am the Christ.'" As to the reception given to these false christs, he adds, "they will deceive many." It is likely that the coming deception of which Jesus spoke will eclipse anything of the sort that has been seen; and yet it will be eclipsed by an even greater deception when the Antichrist is finally revealed.

---

temple at the midpoint of the period (cf. 2 Thess. 2:4; Rev. 13:1-10). It is important to recall, as has already been pointed out, that this could not have been fulfilled historically, since it must occur in the third temple, which has not yet been built. Thus, the view held by some preterists that the abomination prophesied in Daniel 9:27 was fulfilled when Antiochus IV (Epiphanes), eighth ruler of the Selucid dynasty desecrated the temple in 167 B.C. by offering a pig on the altar, could not be correct; neither could the view of other preterists be correct that the Roman desecration of the second temple in A.D. 70 fulfilled the prophecy. Concerning the building of the third temple, it seems possible, perhaps even likely, that since the breaking of the covenant in the middle of Daniel's 70th week is associated with the cessation of the sacrifices in the temple (Dan. 9:27), that it is this very covenant made at the beginning of the tribulation between the Antichrist and Israel (Dan.9:27) that will provide for the rebuilding of the temple.

[9] Some view the re-implementation of the sacrificial system as theologically regressive, and therefore problematic. But it is only problematic to those who have spiritualized the promises God made to Israel, and in the process tainted Christianity with replacement theology, realized eschatology, and a profusion of other spiritual rubbish offered as biblical interpretation. With respect to the tribulation temple, we must remember that this temple will be built in unbelief, as Israel's conversion occurs sometime in the second half of the period. With respect to a millennial temple, while not directly related to the present discussion, there seems to be no soteriological reason why the re-implementation of memorial sacrifices, and elements of the ceremonial law, as pertaining to worship, would be problematic; for even under the Law, salvation was by grace alone. As the Old Testament sacrifices pointed forward to Christ and his work of atonement, so the millennial sacrifices will point back to the same. [In an interesting twist of theology, covenantalists who object to the re-implementation of sacrificial worship do so on dispensational grounds, making a sharp theological distinction in pre-cross and post-cross worship. However, while the cross certainly marks a dispensational transition, since salvation has always been by grace there is no reason why memorial sacrificial worship in the future should be problematic; for even the sacrifices offered under the Law only pointed the worshiper to Christ.]

[6] "But you will hear of wars and threats of wars;

Exegetical and Textual Notes

v.6a Matthew and Mark have μελλήσετε δὲ ἀκούειν πολέμους καὶ ἀκοὰς πολέμων ("but you will begin to hear of wars and reports of wars"), whereas Luke uses ἀκαταστασίας ("instabilities") in the place of ἀκοὰς πολέμων ("reports of wars"). [ἀκούειν is from the root ἀκούω, "to hear"; and ἀκοὰς is from the root ἀκοή, a "report" or "rumor," see *BAGD*, pp.30-31.] Luke's reading may help to understand the nuance of Matthew's and Mark's ἀκοὰς πολέμων ("reports of war"). To say, "you will hear of wars and reports of wars" would seem redundant; however, Luke's ἀκαταστασίας [from ἀκαταστασία, "political turmoil," *TDNT*, vol.3, p.446] in place of Matthew's and Mark's ἀκοὰς πολέμων probably indicates both open war and the kind of international instabilities that could break into open war. Thus, we could translate ἀκούειν πολέμους καὶ ἀκοὰς πολέμων, as "war and threats of war." This will not be an isolated conflict between neighboring states, but a large-scale war, with some nations being at war and others on the brink of war.

 Lenski refers to μελλήσετε δὲ ἀκούειν ("but you will be about to hear") as indicating that the disciples were soon to hear of these wars, as if Jesus were referring to events to be fulfilled within the lifetime of the disciples (Lenski, *Matthew*, p.930). However, there is no necessity for thinking that Jesus was referring to near events; he said only that the disciples (representative of believers living just prior to the end of the age) would hear of such wars and threats of wars in close conjunction with the coming of the false christs (cf. v.5) who will emerge at the outset of the tribulation period.

 With this verse we enter upon a segment (vv.6-14) that is closely paralleled by the first five seals of Revelation, and since scripture is its own best interpreter, we must take Revelation into account in trying to understand the larger picture of what Jesus was describing here in summary form.[10]

---

[10] One might argue that this discourse cannot be properly interpreted in the light of the book of Revelation, since the book of Revelation, as a subsequent revelation, must be interpreted in light of this discourse. And it is true that a prior revelation is determinative, whereas subsequent revelation is dependent. (Proponents of replacement theology and realized eschatology often reverse this relationship, particularly in regard to the relationship between OT eschatology and the NT gospels.) However, while the understanding of subsequent revelation is built upon the objective truth of prior revelation, which cannot be contradicted without denying verbal inspiration, subsequent revelation may inform the reader of details and relationships not previously revealed or apparent.

Jesus gave no details concerning these wars and threats of wars. However, we know from Revelation 6:1-4 that the first two seals represent political conquest and war.[11] We also learn from Daniel 2:1-45 (the account of Nebuchadnezzar's dream of the statue) and Daniel 7:1-28 (the account of Daniel's vision of the beasts), as well as Daniel 9:27 (the description of the seventieth "week" of the 70 weeks prophecy), that a latter day form of Daniel's fourth world empire will exist as a potent international power just prior to and during the tribulation period.[12] According to the objective (normal) interpretation of the prophecies in Daniel, that Empire corresponds to the Roman Empire (the four empires are: Babylon, Medo-Persia, Greece, and Rome). Thus, according to Daniel, a confederation of nations or peoples having some historical connection to the Roman Empire will exist in the days prior to and during the tribulation period. We are also told the leader of that confederation will make a covenant with Israel (9:27). While the substance of this covenant is not stated in Daniel (Daniel 9:27 is the only mention of the covenant), it might be some sort of regional security agreement, and possibly, it might provide for the rebuilding of the Jewish

---

[11]Revelation 6:1-20 is organized according to seven seals, seven trumpets, and seven bowls. The seals are movements within the tribulation period, not judgments. If the seals, as well as the trumpets and bowls represent divine judgment, then the entire tribulation period would be characterized by divine wrath, and the rapture of the Church would then need to be pretribulational (since the Church is not destined to wrath, but to the obtaining of salvation, *via* the rapture, 2 Thess. 5:13-5:11, esp. v.9). However, the problem with this reasoning is that Revelation nowhere indicates that all of the seals represent divine wrath. In fact, Revelation does not mention divine wrath until 6:15-17, after the events of the sixth seal have passed. There is an additional problem in viewing all of the seals as divine wrath. The fifth seal (Rev. 6:9-11) involves the martyrdom of many saints living at that time. How could the persecution and death of these faithful saints be attributed directly to divine wrath? If all of the seals represent divine wrath, then the fifth seal must also represent divine wrath; yet Revelation pictures the major event during the time of the fifth seal as an evil to be punished by a future, but soon outpouring of divine wrath (6:11 cf. 8:1-6). The fact that these martyrs are pictured in Heaven under the altar, making lamentation to God (6:9-11), and asking how long he will restrain his judgment and avenging of their blood upon the world, is indicative that the deaths of these saints can in no way be attributable to God's justice in the execution of wrath upon sin. God responds that they should wait a little while for the answer to their petition for judgment and vengeance (6:11). The events of the seventh seal (the sequence of trumpet and bowl judgments) are plainly indicated to be in response to the prayers of the saints from under the heavenly altar (8:1-6 cf. 16:4-7 and 19:2); they are also the only components of the tribulation period that are explicitly designated as divine wrath (Rev. 15:1; 16:1). Thus, it is not without significance that the first mention of divine wrath in this book occurs just prior to the opening of the seventh seal (6:17). Given this information it is difficult to sustain the case that all of the seals represent divine wrath.

[12] For a discussion of these passages see, *What the Bible says About the Future*, Second edition, by the author, pp.101-110, and the discussion of the 70 weeks prophecy in the Appendices of this volume.

temple. It is this covenant that begins the 70th week of Daniel 9:27 (the tribulation period). Three and a half years after making the covenant the Roman Prince, referred to in Revelation as, "the first beast" (13:2-13), and elsewhere as, "the Antichrist" (1 John 2:18,22; 4:1-3, and 2 John 7), will break this treaty and desecrate the rebuilt temple, putting a stop to the daily sacrifices (Dan. 9:27). Since this person will emerge as a virtual world dictator by the middle of the tribulation period, a certain amount of geopolitical reorganization with its associated conflict is to be expected. It is most likely this large-scale international turmoil to which Jesus here referred as, "wars and threats of wars."

> **see that you do not panic; for these things must happen first, but it is not yet the end."**

———

Exegetical and Textual Notes

v.6b   Luke (21:9) reads μὴ πτοηθῆτε ("you should not be terrified")—passive subjunctive; whereas Matthew and Mark read, μὴ θροεῖσθε ("not to be disturbed") ["frightened," *BAGD*, p.364]. The idea seems to be what is expressed in 2 Thessalonians 2:2, where Paul, in a more verbose phrase says, εἰς τὸ μὴ ταχέως σαλευθῆναι ὑμᾶς ἀπὸ τοῦ νοὸς μηδὲ θροεῖσθαι ("not suddenly frightened out of your minds"). While Paul's statement was made in a completely different context concerning his contemporaries in Thessalonica, it amplifies the idea behind μὴ θροεῖσθε, which represents a sudden, mind-numbing panic. Quite interestingly the Thessalonian Christians experienced their panic because they incorrectly thought themselves to be in that very period of which Jesus spoke prophetically in this discourse. Undoubtedly the generation of Christians living at the time these events begin will be tempted to succumb to sudden, paralyzing fear.

Luke (21:9) includes ταῦτα ("these things"), and adds, πρῶτον ("first").

The meaning of Matthew's ἀλλ' οὔπω ἐστὶν τὸ τέλος ("but the end is not yet") and Mark's similar statement (minus the verb) is clarified in Luke, which reads: ἀλλ' οὐκ εὐθέως τὸ τέλος—"but the end {does} not {follow} immediately." That is to say, the conclusion of the age at Christ's return does not immediately follow the events just described; other things must happen before the end comes—things of which Christ will speak in the following verses. The wars and threats of war are not simply a general description of the end of the age, but a specific set of events that will occur early within a larger set of events, *i.e.*, they represent only the beginning, not the sum total of this period of tribulation.

———

We should bear in mind that the tribulation is to be global, in fact, cosmic in scope (Mt. 24:14,21,30; 25:31-46; Rev. 6:4,8,10,12-17; 8:1-9:21; 12:7-12; 16:1-21; 19:17-21) and it will affect human life, geopolitics, the earth's environment, economics, religion, and eventually result in divine judgment largely in response to the world's brutal treatment of believers during the period (Rev. 6:9-11 cf. 8:1-5), many of whom will be martyred (Mt. 24:9,15-22; Rev. 6:9-11). For those who will be present to see these calamitous events, and especially for those who understand the significance and what the progression of the period holds in store, it will be an incredibly frightful time (see 24:29 cf. Lk. 21:26). Jesus' admonition is, "see that you do not panic."[13]

Why are believers not to panic? Because, "these things must happen first" (Lk. 21:9), *i.e.*, before the end of this age and the beginning of the kingdom reign of Messiah—which kingdom is the grand hope of all who understand and believe the irrevocable promises of God made to Abraham, and to his descendants who believe (Rom. 4:13; 11:11-36, esp. v.28-29).[14]

Of course, these things—the false messiahs and international turmoil and war—do not signal that the completion of the age is imminent, only that it is approaching; for there are additional signs that must be fulfilled before the end of the age actually arrives.

> **[7] Then he said to them, "For people will rise up against people, and kingdom against kingdom, and there will be famines and pestilences and great earthquakes in various places."**

———

Exegetical and Textual Notes

v.7   The opening phrase: τότε ἔλεγεν αὐτοῖς ("then he said to them…"), is found only in Luke 21:10.

ἔθνος designates a people bound by some racial, social, religious, or geographical commonality, distinguishing them as "a people," "clan," or "tribe." Although ἔθνος might otherwise be translated "nation," since nations are specifically referred to by βασιλεία ἐπὶ βασιλείαν ("kingdom against kingdom") it seems best to understand the reference to ἔθνος as "people," rather than "kingdoms." The connotation seems to be that as the conflict of the period intensifies an ethnic and religious element will become manifest. That this conflict will include a religious dimension is confirmed in Matthew 24:9, since believers, particularly Jewish believers, will experience severe persecution during this time.

Luke (21:11) reads, σεισμοί τε μεγάλοι ("great earthquakes"). It is not necessary to think of σεισμός as a natural (geological) earthquake. The term does not specify a cause, only an effect—a significant shaking of the earth.

———

[13] The level to which this panic will rise is seen most clearly in Luke 21:26, further along in the discourse (see the comments on 24:29).

[14] Based upon the Abrahamic covenant (Gen. 12:6-7; 13:14-17; 15:1-21;17:1-14; 22:15-18; cf. Ps. 105:10; Rom. 4:13; 11:11-32, esp. vv.28-29), and expansions upon that covenant in the land covenant (Deut. 29:1-30:20), the Davidic covenant (2 Sam. 7:12-16, cf. Ps. 89:28-37; Jer. 33:25-26), and the prediction of the new covenant (Jer. 31:31-34, cf. Mt. 26:28), God's unconditional and unalterable promises to Israel are for a literal earthly kingdom with Messiah ruling upon the throne of David, in which the regenerated descendants of Abraham will live in a perpetual state of blessing and fellowship with God. The blessings of God to the Gentiles result from the overflow of God's blessings to Israel (Rom. 11:18)—precisely the opposite position of replacement theology and realized eschatology. Such a picture is compatible only with premillennialism.

Luke (21:11) adds, καὶ λοιμοὶ ("and pestilences").

Luke (21:11) adds, φόβητρά τε καὶ ἀπ' οὐρανοῦ σημεῖα μεγάλα ἔσται ("and {there will be} terrors and great signs from heaven") [φόβητρά from φόβητρον, meaning, "dreadful portent," *BAGD*, p.863].

———

The false christs, wars, and international upheaval mentioned in verse 6 are only the beginning of the final phase of the tribulation. Not wanting to unduly alarm the disciples, Jesus introduced the tribulation at first only generally, and somewhat vaguely. Now the subject has been broached and the disciples are better prepared to hear the rest of what he has to say. Not only is the tribulation to be a time of international conflict, but that conflict will have a strong ethnic component (in the broader sense of the term). Literally, "people" will be at war with "people." Ethnic wars are always ugly, and this period in history is going to be terrible beyond anything that has ever happened. Though I do not wish to imply any insensitivity to people of Jewish heritage, even the holocaust, as horrible as it was, will pale in comparison to what is to come.[15]

The text does not indicate that the ensuing famines, earthquakes, and pestilences (Lk. 21:11) are entirely the result of these wars.[16] Though in view of ever-increasing globalization where food, energy, and various natural resources come through the "global pipeline," war could certainly precipitate famine and other human disasters. We should note that the text does not indicate that the things described here (early in the tribulation) will affect everyone on earth to the same degree. The events during the first half of the tribulation will be regional, *i.e.*, "in various places," although they certainly could exert an indirect global influence.[17]

Luke 21:11 (parallel to Matthew 24:7) is the only account that includes, "and there will be terrors, and great signs from heaven," which, as we know from elsewhere

———

[15] A note to Jewish readers: I am not unaware that some Jews resent the futurist position that there is to be an even greater holocaust in the future. They suppose that acceptance of the inevitability of such a holocaust might make it more tolerable to Christians. I would urge my Jewish friends to read the Hebrew Scriptures to which I have provided abundant references. This teaching did not originate in Gentile Christian theology. It is based on the objective (normal) interpretation of the Jewish Scriptures, and of the teachings of Jesus—a Jew. What Jesus described here will happen. And while Christians, at least those who reject replacement theology, do view it as inevitable, they also recognize it for what it is—evil. The Jew will find no greater friend among Gentiles than the premillennial Christian. Indeed, it is the teaching of Jesus in this very discourse that those Gentiles who survive the tribulation period will be judged, in part, on the basis of their compassion toward persecuted Jews during the tribulation period (Mt. 25:31-46).
[16] Only Luke (21:11) includes: καὶ λοιμοὶ ("and pestilences").
[17] κατὰ τόπους ("according to places," cf. v.7), in all three accounts, indicates the regional nature of the events at this stage of the tribulation.

occur near the end of the tribulation.[18] Why Luke chose to structure his account so as to include this material at this point is unknown, but it forces his subsequent description of the great persecution (Lk. 21:12-18) to be stated recursively, placing the persecution between the two clauses forming Luke 21:11.[19] While it is perfectly acceptable for the account to be reported in this way, it is unlikely to have been the way the discourse was delivered by Christ.[20] Thus, if our goal is to reconstruct the flow of the text as closely as possible to Jesus' actual delivery, it is necessary to "unfold" the recursive structure of

---

[18] Cf. Isa.13:10; Joel 2:10; 3:15-16; Rev. 6:12-17; 8:1-13.

[19] Note the introductory phase, πρὸ δὲ τούτων πάντων ("But before all these {things}"), which Luke uses to introduce the recursive section (vv.12-18). This phrase is not needed in Matthew and Mark.

[20] The reason is that in the actual delivery, the clause in Luke 21:11b (regarding "terrors" and "great signs from heaven") would not have preceded the declaration in Matthew 24:8 and Mark 13:8b that "all these things are merely the beginning of birth pains," because the "beginning of birth pains" refers only to the events of the first half of the tribulation, prior to the great persecution; the "terrors" and "great signs from heaven" occur late in the second half of the tribulation, long after the beginning of the persecution at the midpoint of the period (Mt. 24:15-21 cf. Dan. 9:27). In Luke's account, the placing of the 21:11b clause (describing events late in the period) prior to the description of the persecution (which begins near the middle of the period), and then referring to the persecution recursively, is purely stylistic (see the parallel text). If we unfold this structure Luke's account is compatible with Matthew and Mark. Though the difference in Luke's structure is only stylistic, it proves useful since a comparison of the two formats at this point (the linear in Matthew and Mark, and the recursive in Luke) yields an important observation: the persecution described in Luke 21:12-19 (which is parallel to Matthew 24:9-14 and Mark 13:9-13) falls between the "famines," "earthquakes," and "pestilences" in 21:11a, and the "terrors" and "great signs from heaven" in 21:11b. This is evident since, if the persecution preceded the "famines" and "earthquakes," Matthew and Mark would need a recursive introduction in describing the persecution too (which they lack). And if the "terrors" and "great signs from heaven" did not come after the persecution, Luke would not have used such an introduction before describing the persecution. Thus it is apparent that the Luke 21:11b clause refers to events after the onset of persecution, and hence, after the "beginning of birth pains." In our reconstructed text, Luke 21:11b has been moved to the end of Luke's description of the persecution (after Luke 21:19), in order to unfold the recursive structure so that it can be merged with Matthew and Mark. Precisely where this clause best fits in relation to the material in Matthew 24:14 (which Luke omits) is debatable, but it seems reasonable to place it before, "and then the end will come," though we would not want to base any theological conclusions solely on that placement. This is the only verse in the reconstructed text that needs to be moved out of its native (original) location, but the move is necessary, and certain to be closer to Jesus' actual delivery than what is found in Luke's report.

Luke's account. This requires that Luke 21:11b be moved to a point after 21:19 (at the end of 24:13 in the reconstructed text).[21]

We must bear in mind that the gospel accounts are not transcripts; they are reports, or accounts of the discourse. While some material is quoted, some is summarized, and some is partially or entirely omitted; and the general structure of the presentation varies by account.[22]

[8] "But all these things are merely the beginning of birth pains."

———

Exegetical and Textual Notes

v.8   Luke does not include this.

The idea behind ἀρχὴ ὠδίνων ("{the} beginning of labor pains") is that what has been described so far is only preliminary to what is yet to come.

Because Luke concludes the previous verse with events late in the tribulation (*i.e.,* "terrors" and "great signs from heaven," cf. 21:11b) after the mention of "famines," "earthquakes," and "pestilences" (21:11a), he does not follow up with this statement concluding the first half of the tribulation, as do Mathew and Mark.

———

The figure, "beginning of birth pains," seems quite appropriate for the first half of the tribulation.[23] Just as labor pains increase in both frequency and intensity as labor proceeds, so the affliction of this period will increase in frequency and intensity as it progresses. And as the main event in labor comes at the end of the process, so the main event of the tribulation—the end of the age and the return of the Lord—will occur at the end. How much of the tribulation represents divine judgment is not indicated in this discourse; however, Revelation indicates that the trumpet and bowl sequences are divine judgment; as has been observed, such does not appear to be the case with the seals, which are best understood as time periods within the tribulation.[24] The cascading effect of these events as the end of the period draws near can best be observed from Revelation, which explores the individual elements of the tribulation period in greater detail.

———

[21] Here we see one of the benefits of working from a harmonized account. If we had failed to harmonize the text we would be stuck with a serious and irresolvable conflict of information resulting from Luke's unique structure.

[22] See, "The Structure of the Discourse," p.21.

[23] The metaphor of birth pains as applied to the tribulation is reminiscent of Isaiah 26:17-27:1, which pictures Israel in the tribulation just prior to the kingdom age (27:2-6).

[24] They should be thought of as "chapters" in the book that John saw in Heaven (Rev. 5:1-2), each having its own specific content concerning the tribulation period.

[9] "But beware of men; for they will hand you over to courts, and they will scourge you in their assemblies, and you will be brought before governors and kings for my sake, for a testimony to them and to the nations. And the gospel must first be proclaimed unto all the nations."

———

Exegetical and Textual Notes

v.9   Matthew 10:17-23 is parallel to 24:9-13 (see the parallel texts and the discussion of Matthew 10:17-23 under, "The Structure of the Discourse"). This section has four parallel accounts (see the illustration on page 27). However, both Matthew accounts contain unique material; Matthew 10:17-21 is a detailed account of what is summarized in Matthew 24:9 (Matthew 10:17-21 is virtually identical to Mark 13:9-12). Matthew 24:10-12 is unique with respect to all three synoptics. Matthew 10:21-23 mentions the betrayal of brothers by brothers, children by fathers, parents by children (as do Mark and Luke), whereas the Matthew 24:10-13 account mentions betrayal only generally. Matthew 24:9-14 is unique in mentioning apostasy, false prophets, and lawlessness. The Matthew accounts (Mt. 10.17-22b and 24:9-13) and Mark (13:9-13b) all end with the identical wording, ὁ δὲ ὑπομείνας εἰς τέλος οὗτος σωθήσεται ("but the one enduring to the end will be delivered"); whereas Luke (21:19) ends with: ἐν τῇ ὑπομονῇ ὑμῶν κτήσασθε τὰς ψυχὰς ὑμῶν ("you must preserve your lives by your endurance"). Obviously Matthew chose to present two accounts (one in chapter 10 and one in chapter 24), each focusing on different details. All of these accounts are abridgements of a more detailed discourse than what is presented in any one account, and the text poses no real contradictions, only alternative abridgements and summarizations of the source material.

Matthew's abbreviated summary in chapter 24 has no introductory phrase; however, the more extended account in chapter 10 has: προσέχετε δὲ ἀπὸ τῶν ἀνθρώπων ("but beware of men"), whereas Mark (13:9) has: βλέπετε δὲ ὑμεῖς ἑαυτούς ("but see to yourselves").

On the use of συνέδρια ("courts") see *TDNT*, pp.860-871 and *BAGD*, pp.782-783; and on the use of συναγωγαῖς ("synagogues") see *TDNT*, pp.798-843 and *BAGD*, p.786. While these terms are generally applied to Jewish courts and synagogues in both Jewish and Christian literature, the idea is that these bodies have a cultic (religious) element or orientation, and can certainly refer to non-Jewish religious authorities of various levels. The fact that these courts will exact capital punishment in the form a beheading (Rev. 20:4), a practice for which there is no precedence in Judaism, would seem to indicate that Jewish courts are not particularly in view.

———

    [Note that here we leave out Luke's recursive introduction, "Before all these things," since in our reconstruction we have reversed Luke's recursive structure in order to integrate it with Matthew and Mark.[25]]

───────────────

[25] All three accounts have a recursive structure beginning at 24:15; however, since all three accounts employ the same structure there, it poses no problem for reconstructing the text.

In his initial survey of the tribulation, Jesus concluded the events of the first half of the tribulation with verse 8, referring to it as, "the beginning of birth pains." At verse 9 he begins his initial survey of the events of the second half of the tribulation, focusing primarily on the great persecution of Jewish believers.[26] It is important to recognize that, like the Old Testament prophecies concerning the tribulation, this discourse evidences a distinctly Jewish orientation; whereas the book of Revelation, written to the Church, is written from a more universal perspective.

Jesus begins with an abrupt warning: "But beware of men." The reason is explicit: "for they will hand you over to courts, and they will scourge you in their assemblies, and will kill you, and you will be hated by all nations because of my name." The reference to "courts" refers to religiously constituted courts. These councils will have the power to scourge and kill Christians—similar to the persecution of Jewish Christians in the early days of the Church (Acts 9:2; 22:5).[27] These Jewish believers will be "hated by all nations." In fact, the conversion of many Jews during the period may be cast negatively as a subversive, destabilizing influence, both by unbelieving Jews and by unbelieving Gentiles.[28] This persecution is specific to Christians, since Jesus said they will be hated "because of my name."

Christians worldwide will be arrested and brought before high government officials (referred to here as "governors" and "kings"). While it would be easy to see only the ugly side of persecution, for it is indeed ugly, Jesus said that it will result in a testimony to these officials, and that leaves open the possibility that some will come to faith in Christ as a result of their contact with these persecuted believers. It is a difficult lesson to accept in one's personal experience, but God's sovereignty extends even to the persecution and mistreatment of his children.[29]

"And the gospel must first be proclaimed unto all the nations" is found only in Mark 13:10, and at first glance seems explanatory rather than adjunctive; however, if that were the case, one would expect a postpositive particle ("for") rather than the conjunction "and," and the conjunction is well attested. Perhaps this statement was split off from a larger statement as part of the abridgement in the original composition of

---

[26] Lenski, in typical amillennial form, applies all of this to the Church (Lenski, *Matthew*, p.932).

[27] The fact that this persecution is viewed from the Jewish perspective does not mean that persecution during the tribulation will be directed only against Jewish Christians (cf. Rev. 13:11-18), only that the focus here is Jewish.

[28] Matthew 24:9 reads, ἔσεσθε μισούμενοι ὑπὸ πάντων τῶν ἐθνῶν ("you will be hated by all the nations").

[29] Rev. 9:9-11, esp. v.11.

Mark; it could be a summation of Matthew 24:14.[30] Perhaps Mark condensed the material found in Matthew 24:14 and placed it here to connect the persecution with the worldwide proclamation of the gospel.[31] In any case, the substance of the statement is the same: the gospel will be proclaimed worldwide before the end of the age comes, and one of the principal means through which that will be accomplished is the testimony of persecuted believers. Perhaps the contemplation of this truth will help to make that time more bearable. Believers must never lose sight of the truth that God is always sovereign, even in allowing their mistreatment. Such a statement must seem absurd to the existential mind that processes life in terms of personal experience, but the eternal salvation of even one soul outweighs any temporary suffering.

> **"But when they hand you over, do not be anxious how or what you should speak, for it will be given to you in that hour what you should say, for I will give you a mouth and wisdom, which none of the ones opposing you will be able to withstand or contradict; for you are not the ones speaking, but the Spirit of your Father is speaking by you. And brother will deliver up brother to death, and a father will deliver up a child, and children will rise up against parents and kill them. And you will be hated by all on account of my name;**

Exegetical and Textual Notes

v.9b This is mostly from Matthew 10:19-22a, since Matthew 24:9 provides only a summary. Matthew 10:19-22a is virtually identical to Mark 13:11-13, and parallels the summarization in Luke 21:14-17. Note that the closing statement, "And you will be hated by all on account of my name" in Matthew 10:22, 24:9b, Mark 13:13a, and Luke 21:17, is nearly identical, except that Matthew 24:9 inserts, τῶν ἐθνῶν ("the nations") after πάντων ("all").

ἐγὼ γὰρ δώσω ὑμῖν στόμα καὶ σοφίαν ᾗ οὐ δυνήσονται ἀντιστῆναι ἢ ἀντειπεῖν ἅπαντες οἱ ἀντικείμενοι ὑμῖν ("for I will give you a mouth and wisdom, which none of the ones opposing you will be able to withstand or contradict") is inserted from Luke 21:15. This statement is unique to Luke.

ἐν ὑμῖν ("by you") is instrumental; hence τὸ λαλοῦν ἐν ὑμῖν is "the one speaking *by* [or, *through*] you."

Matthew 10:20 reads, τὸ πνεῦμα τοῦ πατρὸς ὑμῶν ("the Spirit of your Father"); Mark 13:11 reads: τὸ πνεῦμα τὸ ἅγιον ("the Holy Spirit").

---

[30] The fact that Mark has no parallel to Matthew 24:14 would be consistent with the notion that Mark 13:10 is a summation of Matthew 24:14, and relocated. Here Luke does not help, since it has no parallel to either Matthew 24:14 or Mark 13:10.

[31] This is not meant to imply the priority of Matthew over Mark, only that in the source material used in Mark 13:10 has been more highly abridged than in Matthew 24:14.

The believers, having been delivered to persecution, are not to be apprehensive about how they ought to defend themselves. The Holy Spirit will speak by them at the appropriate time.[32] The extent to which the Holy Spirit will enable these believers is seen from Luke 21:15: "for I will give you a mouth and wisdom, which none of the ones opposing you will be able to withstand or contradict."

The description at this point gives a window into the severity of this persecution, and the pressure that is going to be brought upon believers. Members of their own families will betray them, even unto death. They will become the objects of such intense hatred that Jesus said they will be hated by all the nations on account of his name.

yet not a hair of your head will perish."

———

Exegetical and Textual Notes

v.9c   Only Luke 21:18 includes this clause .

———

This statement seems perplexing at first. How is it that believers will be delivered up to death, but not a hair of their head will perish? Of course those who allegorize prophecy have no shortage of imaginations about what this might mean, but our interpretive method is objective, not subjective. The solution would seem to be that Jesus is speaking both about believers in general (*i.e.*, some of whom will be killed) and a particular group, a subset of believers, who will be divinely protected for the remainder of the period. The existence of just such a group is described in Revelation 7:1-8 (cf. 14:1-5). They are referred to as the 144,000 "bond servants of God," and it appears that the seal on their foreheads protects them not only from the power of the Antichrist, but also from the plagues to come during the time of the seventh seal (cf. Rev. 7:1-8).[33]

———

[32] ἐν ὑμῖν should be understood not as "*in* you" (locative), but "*by* you" (instrumental). The present participles λαλοῦντες and λαλοῦν ("speaking") are periphrastic futures. Luke 21:17 constructs a tight periphrastic future (ἔσεσθε μισούμενοι = "you will be *being* hated"); however, in Matthew 10:19-20 the construction is more drawn out since the future verb δοθήσεται (v. 19) controls the tense of the participles that follow in verse 20 (δοθήσεται γὰρ ὑμῖν ἐν ἐκείνῃ τῇ ὥρᾳ τί λαλήσητε; οὐ γὰρ ὑμεῖς ἐστε οἱ λαλοῦντες ἀλλὰ τὸ πνεῦμα τοῦ πατρὸς ὑμῶν τὸ λαλοῦν ἐν ὑμῖν = "for it will be given [future tense] to you in that hour what you should say [aorist subjunctive]; for you are [present tense—*i.e.*, at that time in the future] not the ones speaking [present participle—masculine (*i.e.*, the disciples)], but the Spirit of your Father {is} the one speaking [present participle—neuter (*i.e.*, the Spirit)] by you."

[33] The fact that they are sealed at this point, between the sixth and seventh seals, may add support to the notion that divine wrath is limited to the time of the seventh seal. (See, "The Character and Chronology of the Tribulation" in the Appendices.)

[10] "And then many will be caused to fall away and betray one another and hate one another;

[11] and many false prophets will arise and mislead many;

[12] and because the iniquity will be increased, the love of many will grow cold."

———

Exegetical and Textual Notes

vv.10-12 This statement is found only in the Matthew 24 account; however, the statement immediately following (Mt. 24:13) is found in all three accounts, as well as Matthew 10:22b.

σκανδαλισθήσονται ("will be made to fall away") is future passive.

τὴν ἀνομίαν ("the iniquity") is not iniquity in general, but a particular iniquity.

———

In verse 10 Jesus referred to the apostasy that will take place in connection with the persecution following the revealing of the Antichrist in the temple.[34] Here we are

———

[34]Paul refers to this apostasy in 2 Thessalonians 2:1-12, where he tells the Thessalonians that the day of the Lord will not come "until the apostasy comes first" (v.3). It is almost certain that Paul had in mind the particular apostasy mentioned by Christ in Matthew 24:10, and concerning which the Thessalonians had been taught on a prior occasion. Note the strong connection between Matthew 24:9-22 and 2 Thessalonians 2:1-9. Of the eight features of the tribulation given in Matthew 24:9-31, Paul specifically mentions six in 2 Thessalonians 2:1-9: the abomination, vv.3-5 cf. Mt. 24:15; the apostasy, v.3 cf. Mt. 24:10; spiritual deception, vv.10-12 cf. Mt. 24:11; lawlessness, vv.3,7 cf. Mt. 24:12; deceiving signs and wonders, v.9 cf. Mt. 24:24; and the second coming, v.8 cf. Mt. 24:29-31. (These six characteristics are mentioned together only in two locations in the NT: the Olivet Discourse and in 2 Thessalonians 2:1-9.) Note that due to the recursive structure of Matthew 24:15-31, which jumps back to the midpoint of the tribulation, the apostasy mentioned in 24:10 actually occurs after the abomination described in verse 15, likely in connection with the persecution described in verses 16-22. (See the discussion of the chronology of Matthew 24 beginning on page 245.) In 2 Thessalonians 2:1-4, when Paul says the day of the Lord will not begin until the apostasy occurs first and the man of lawlessness is "revealed," he refers to "the apostasy" (ἡ ἀποστασία, v.3a), which occurs in connection with the revealing of the Antichrist (καὶ ἀποκαλυφθῇ ὁ ἄνθρωπος τῆς ἀνομίας, "even the man of lawlessness is revealed," v.3b) in the temple (ὥστε αὐτὸν εἰς τὸν ναὸν τοῦ θεοῦ καθίσαι, "such that he seats himself in the temple of God," v.4). That description clearly mirrors Jesus' description in Matthew 24:9-22. (Note that 2 Thessalonians 2:3-4 comprises one sentence, and the revealing and the apostasy are closely connected.) One important observation that results from the connection between Matthew 24:9-31 and 2 Thessalonians 2:1-12 is that Paul indicates the day of the Lord cannot precede the revealing of the Antichrist in the temple and the subsequent apostasy. Thus,

told that the severity of this persecution will cause many to fall away from their association with Christians and Christianity. Such falling away is not an indication of the loss of salvation, but the lack of it (1 Jn. 2:18-19). There are many who associate themselves with Christianity for reasons other than genuine faith in Christ.[35] This has been a persistent problem in the body of faith from the beginning (as Jesus predicted in the parables of Matthew 13), and it will continue until the cost of profession becomes too high for any but those who have forsaken all to follow Christ. Once the severe persecution begins at the midpoint of the tribulation, false and shallow profession of faith in Christ will greatly diminish, for it will carry a heavy price that only true believers will be willing to bear. This persecution will, like the purest water, wash clean the professing body. Having apostatized, those false brethren will betray others, and their betrayal will turn to hatred of anyone who clings to the faith. Ruthless and oppressive regimes often find willing accomplices among the defectors of those whom they oppress, and that will be the case with the coming Antichrist; he will have innumerable informants, likely counting among them a great many religious leaders. Obviously this will necessitate that the true worship of God go underground, and communities of believers will need to be small to avoid detection, as is the case even now in countries where there is state sponsored persecution of Christianity.

Jesus described false christs in the first half of the tribulation. However, once the Antichrist makes his own claim to deity at the midpoint of the period (2 Thess. 2:3-4) it is likely that thereafter there will be few competing claims. Nevertheless, spiritual deception will arise from false prophets, and many will be misled. In the days to come, as in the present, the lack of grounding in the Scriptures will leave many exposed to spiritual deception.

The iniquity to which Jesus referred is not simply moral laxness.[36] It is likely "the iniquity" associated with the rise of the Antichrist ("the man of *the* iniquity," cf. 2 Thess.

---

the inference from Paul's teaching is that the day of the Lord cannot begin until sometime in the second half of the tribulation, since the abomination occurs at the midpoint. This observation has profound implications for rapture theology, since one of the principal arguments for pretribulationism (*i.e.,* the wrath argument) rests upon the assumption that the entire tribulation is divine wrath. See "Rapture Theology," beginning on page 251 in the Appendices.

[35] For a discussion of the New Testament teaching on personal apostasy see: "The Biblical Doctrine of Personal Apostasy" by the author (Internet paper: www. biblicalreader.com/btr).

[36] τὴν ἀνομίαν, is translated "iniquity" in the AV, and "lawlessness" in the NASB. However, this is not general moral lawlessness, but "*the* iniquity," *i.e.,* the iniquity of global defection from the true God, as evidenced by the nearly universal acceptance of the false religion of the Antichrist (2 Thess. 2:6-12, esp. v.7, cf. Rev. 13-18, esp. vv.4-8). Paul clearly associated the Antichrist with "the iniquity" in calling him, ὁ ἄνθρωπος τῆς ἀνομίας ("the man of *the* iniquity") in 2 Thessalonians 2:3 (cf. v.8). As Paul penned his letter he stated, "the mystery of *the* iniquity" (τῆς ἀνομίας) is "now operative" (ἤδη ἐνεργεῖται), though restrained from its full manifestation

2:3,8), which will reach its zenith shortly after the midpoint of the period, once the world's long hidden agenda of substituting Antichrist for the true God breaks into the open with the revealing of the Antichrist in the temple.[37] This agenda has been in place for many millennia. When and where it began is debatable, but it is epitomized in "the times of the Gentiles," which began with Babylon and will culminate with the kingdom of the Antichrist (Dan. 2:1-45; 7:1-28).[38] Both in past ages and in the present, the manifestation of this iniquity has been restrained (2 Thess. 2:6-8).[39] But there is coming a time when the restrainer will depart, and the man of the iniquity (the Antichrist) will be revealed.[40] Jesus said that as the iniquity grows greater in power and influence, "the love of many will grow cold."[41] This love is not the love of Christ, for the love of Christ is a characteristic of true faith. This is the compassion of one human being toward another that compels one to act in the interest of another, even at considerable personal risk and sacrifice.[42] The sudden onset of severe persecution will be blistering. Belief will be forced underground, and few will be willing to come to the aid of the persecuted.

> **[13] "But the one enduring to the end will be delivered.**
>
> **But when they persecute you in one city, flee to another; for truly I say to you, you will certainly not finish going through the cities of Israel until the Son of Man comes."**

(v.7). There is a power operative in the world that tends toward iniquity in general and "the iniquity" in particular. Since its terminus is the regal advent of Christ (2 Thess. 2:8), which is also the conclusion of the "times of the Gentiles," it would not be unreasonable to think that the two are related (see: Lk. 21:24 cf. Dan. 2:1-45; 7:1-28).

[37] Due to the recursive structure of verses 15-31, with respect to tribulation chronology, verse 12 describes an event that follows the abomination in the temple (v.15). See "The Character and Chronology of the Tribulation" in the Appendices.

[38] "The times of the Gentiles" is specifically mentioned in this discourse in Luke's account (Lk. 21:24).

[39] In 2 Thessalonians 2:6 Paul says, καὶ νῦν τὸ κατέχον οἴδατε ("and now you know what restrains"). The restrainer, however, is not identified.

[40] He is to be revealed in his time (εἰς τὸ ἀποκαλυφθῆναι αὐτὸν ἐν τῷ ἑαυτοῦ καιρῷ) "for to be revealed in his own time"), cf. 2 Thessalonians 2:6. There has been much speculation regarding both the identity of the restrainer and what the reference to "comes out of the midst" (ἐκ μέσου γένηται) means; γένηται is subjunctive aorist and indicates the departure of the restrainer will occur suddenly. Some pretribulationists suggest that this could coincide with the removal of the Church at the rapture; however, such an interpretation is purely speculative.

[41] διὰ (with the accusative determiner τὸ) is causal. It is on account of the increase of the iniquity that the love of many will grow cold.

[42] ἀγάπη is the kind of love that motivates one to make a great personal sacrifice for another.

v.13a With respect to the first sentence, Matthew 24:13b and Mark (13:13b) are identical; Luke reads: ἐν τῇ ὑπομονῇ ὑμῶν κτήσασθε τὰς ψυχὰς ὑμῶν ("you must preserve your lives by your endurance").

v.13b The second sentence is inserted from Matthew 10:23, which concludes the Matthew 10 parallel account. Only the Matthew 10 segment includes this sentence.

The reference is not to eternal salvation, but to physical deliverance at the time of the second coming (Zech. 14:4-8). Luke puts this in the imperative (*i.e.*, you *must* preserve your lives by your endurance"). [43]

The second sentence (13b) is recorded only in Matthew 10:23, and refers to the persecution of Jewish believers during the tribulation. The promise Jesus made here is that even in Israel where the persecution will be the most severe, believers will find places of refuge. Revelation 12:1-6 indicates that some will flee to a place prepared by God in the desert, where he will protect them and provide for their needs for the remainder of the period. Many believers in Israel will flee to the desert, but the evangelists will do their work in the cities of Israel, fleeing from one city to the next as the need arises. Obviously the believers in the cities will need help from those who will be sympathetic, since they will be cut off from the economic system sometime early in the second half of the period, and unable to buy and sell (Rev. 13:11-18).[44]

"{And} there will be terrors, and great signs from heaven."

Exegetical and Textual Notes

v.13c This is inserted from Luke 21:11b in order to adjust for Luke's recursive structure in 21:11-19. Only Luke employs a recursive structure here, concluding 21:11 with the signs of the end of the age, and then recursively addressing the intervening events leading up to that point (vv. 12-19). Thus, in Luke 21:11-19, chronologically verses 12-18 fall between 21:11a and 21:11b. This is evident from a comparison with the Matthew and Mark accounts, and from the introductory phrase Luke employs in verse 12 (πρὸ δὲ τούτων πάντων = "but before all these things"), which is not found in either of the Matthew accounts or Mark. In order to merge these accounts, the recursive structure in Luke must be "unfolded," which requires placing 21:11b after the intervening events (vv.12-18). Luke 21:11b could be placed anywhere prior to the end of Matthew 24:14 which concludes the general survey of the tribulation. It would fit

[43] κτήσασθε ("preserve") is imperative.
[44] The economic isolation of believers during the tribulation will likely be global, though Revelation (13:11-18) does not indicate its extent. However, as was said before, the perspective of this discourse is Jewish.

after Luke 21:18, putting it immediately prior to Matthew 24:13 (Mt. 10:22b-23), or after Luke 21:19 (as in our reconstructed text), putting it immediately prior to Matthew 24:14. However, placing it after Luke 21:18 and merging it into the reconstructed text at that point would seem to interrupt the flow of Matthew 24:9-13, which is focused on the social dimension of the tribulation rather than the physical dimension that Luke 21:11b addresses. Thus, it seems best to place Luke 21:11b after Luke 21:19, and merge it into the reconstructed text immediately prior to 24:14, though alternative placements are certainly possible. (See the parallel texts beginning on page 43, and "The Structure of the Discourse," beginning on page 21.)

———

This statement comes from Luke 21:11b; it has been moved to this point (after Luke 21:19) in order to unfold Luke's recursive structure in verses 11-19 to match the linear structure of Matthew and Mark (Mt. 24:9-14; Mk. 13:9-13) so the three accounts can be merged. These "terrors" and "great signs from heaven" refer to the events of the sixth and seventh seals (Rev. 6:12-17; 8:1-13, cf. Is. 13:9-10; 24:19-23)—discussed in more detail at verse 29.

[14] "And this gospel of the kingdom will be proclaimed in the whole inhabited world for a testimony to all nations, and then the end will come."

———

Exegetical and Textual Notes

v.14   Only Matthew includes this.

τέλος ("end"—with or without the article, cf. Mt. 24:6,14; 10:22; Lk. 21:13) in this discourse refers to the end of the age and the regal appearing of Christ (note the original question in Matthew 24:3). The "end" is not the entire seven-year period of tribulation, but only the conclusion, as indicated in Matthew 24:6-14.

———

The tribulation will be the greatest period of evangelism in history. Jesus said the gospel will be proclaimed "in all the world." This is an amazing statement when we consider that when the rapture of the Church occurs, every believer will be removed from the earth, and the body of faith on earth will have to begin again. Rebuilding the community of faith and reaching the whole world with the gospel in less than seven years staggers the imagination. Not only will Christianity have to be reconstituted in terms of numbers, but also in terms of leadership and the understanding of biblical theology; and this will have to be accomplished amidst great spiritual deception, and eventually, persecution. It is incumbent on the Church to facilitate this by leaving behind a body of sound doctrine and biblical interpretation. Sadly, the spiritualized interpretations of those who have adopted replacement theology and realized eschatology will only serve to confuse the tribulation believers. But God will not leave his elect as orphans; he will pour out his Spirit on them, and their sons and daughters will prophesy, and their old men will dream dreams, and their young men will see visions (Joel 2:28-32). Once the worldwide proclamation of the gospel is complete, the way will be clear for the return of Christ and the end of the present age. The inclusion of the phrase, "for a testimony to all nations," probably indicates that the testimony of the persecuted believers will be the major means of this evangelism (cf. Mt. 10:17-18; Mk. 13:9-10; Lk. 21:12-13).

With this statement, Jesus concludes his initial survey of basic facts regarding the tribulation. Beginning with verse 15 he launches into a second round of discussion concerning the second half of the period, but this time the focus is practical: what believers should immediately do when the second half begins.

24:15-31 Commentary

While Jesus does not use the term, "the day of the Lord," it is employed in the Old Testament to describe God's final dealing with the nations, to punish them for their disobedience and to prepare the way for the establishment of the messianic kingdom on earth. Once the day of the Lord begins, "the times of the Gentiles" will be quickly brought to a conclusion.[1]

Verse 15 begins at the midpoint of the tribulation period.[2] Thus having given a general description of the entire seven-year period (vv.4-14), Jesus now returns to the midpoint in order to give special attention to certain features. This is the half of the tribulation during which the day of the Lord will begin. That is not to say that the day of the Lord begins precisely at the midpoint, but that it begins sometime during the second half of the tribulation.[3]

---

[1] The principal Old Testament passages describing the day of the Lord are: Isaiah 13:1-16; Joel 1-3; and Zephaniah 1:1-8. The prophecies of the day of the Lord are often presented in the context of historic judgments, which from the modern perspective have been fulfilled. This has led some to conclude that the term "the day of the Lord" is simply a generic term for judgment and does not refer to a future judgment in connection with the appearing of Christ. However, this conclusion is incorrect for two reasons. First, careful attention to the details of these prophecies reveals that the near prophecy is typological of the day of the Lord. Second, the New Testament writers clearly indicate the day of the Lord to be a discrete, future, eschatological event (1 Thess. 5:1-11; 2 Thess. 2:1-17; 2 Pet. 3:1-18).

[2] According to Daniel 9:27 the abomination in the temple marks the midpoint of the tribulation period.

[3] Evidence has already been presented that places the beginning of the day of the Lord after the apostasy that will occur after the abomination and subsequent persecution. See the footnote at 24:10; also see "The Character and Chronology of the Tribulation" (pp.221-249) and the discussion of 2 Thessalonians 2:1-9 under "Rapture Theology" in the Appendices (pp.262-264).

[15] "Therefore, when you see Jerusalem surrounded by armies, and the abomination of desolation spoken of through Daniel the prophet standing in the holy place—let the reader understand—then know that its desolation has drawn near."

Exegetical and Textual Notes

v.15   "When you see Jerusalem surrounded by armies," is inserted from Luke 21:20a. It is apparent that Matthew 24:15 (cf. Mark 13:14) and Luke 21:20 were abridged from a longer statement.

ἐστὸς ("standing") is a perfect participle from ἵστημι, meaning, "to place," "confirm," or "establish," _BAGD_, p.238 (ἀφίστημι, the reversal of the root idea, means to "apostatize," or "to fall away"); hence, the idea is that not only will the abomination be physically set in place in the temple, but its presence will represent the establishment of a new religious institution (_i.e._, the worship of the Antichrist).

Matthew reads, ἐστὸς ἐν τόπῳ ἁγίῳ ("standing in the Holy Place"), Mark reads, ἑστηκότα ὅπου οὐ δεῖ ("standing where it should not be"). It is unclear whether Matthew and Mark are simply paraphrasing the same thought (_i.e._, "standing in the holy place" and "where it should not be" being two ways of saying the same thing—Mark being more vague), or whether each is making an incomplete quotation of source material, requiring us to append one statement to the other (_i.e._, "standing in the holy place, where it should not be"). The translation given here assumes the former, that Matthew and Mark simply stated the same thing differently, and follows the more precise statement in Matthew.

Only Matthew includes, τὸ ῥηθὲν διὰ Δανιὴλ τοῦ προφήτου ("the one spoken of through Daniel the prophet").

The first clause, "But when you see Jerusalem being surrounded by military encampments," is found only in Luke's account at 21:20a.[4] This invasion is described in Joel 1-3, Ezekiel 38-39, and Zechariah 12:2-14:8.[5] It will involve a gathering of military

---

[4] _The New Scofield Reference Bible_ (p.1114, footnote 1) expresses the view that Luke 21:20 refers not to a future invasion of Israel, but to the A.D. 70 invasion by the Romans, whereas Matthew 24:15 and Mark 13:14 refer to the tribulation invasion. However, that view seems highly unlikely since Luke 21:20 is clearly parallel to Matthew 24:15 and Mark 13:14 (see the parallel texts).

[5] It is common for the book of Joel to be interpreted as a historical invasion of locusts described in apocalyptic language. However, it would be far more correct to view Joel as entirely apocalyptic and the locust plague being merely the occasion of a prophetic analogy to the coming day of the LORD. While the analogy of the locust plague is mentioned twice (in 1:4-12 and 2:25), the day of the LORD is mentioned six times, and in all three chapters of the book. This prophesied invasion of the land of Israel will occur just prior to the day of the LORD, and it will result in the land becoming desolate (1:8-20), and being destroyed (2:1-17); but the LORD will deliver his land and people (2:18-27), and pour out his Spirit on all mankind (2:28-29). He will display wonders in the sky and on the earth (blood, fire, and columns of smoke, cf. 2:30), and the sun will be turned to

forces in the land of Israel and a siege of Judah and Jerusalem beginning at the midpoint of the tribulation. [6] This siege will continue throughout the remainder of the period, until

---

darkness and the moon into blood (2:31). Then the injustices done to Israel will be rectified (3:1-21). Of course, very little of this could have much substantive connection to an actual locust plague. If there were an actual plague that Joel had in mind, it was little more than an occasion for illustrating the greater truth of the day of the LORD.

[6] Among premillennialists the two-invasion theory has been popular. According to this view the invasion described in Ezekiel 38-39 is not to be identified with the invasion of Israel by the Antichrist at the midpoint of the tribulation period (Joel 1-3; Zechariah 12:2-9); rather, it is a distinct invasion of Israel, possibly in the first half of the tribulation. [On this view see, *The Ryrie Study Bible* note on Ezekiel 38:1; or for variations of the two-invasion theory see, *The Prophecy of Ezekiel*, by Charles L. Feinberg, Moody Press, 1972, p.218.] The basis of the two-invasion theory is that the invaders in Ezekiel's prophecy seem to be nations distinct from the Revived Roman Empire of the Antichrist. However, there are numerous problems with the two-invasion theory. First, there is no singular prophecy that clearly pictures two distinct invasions associated with the approach of the day of the LORD. Secondly, in all three of the major descriptions of an invasion of Israel during the tribulation (Joel 1-3; Ezek. 38-39; and Zech. 12:2-14:8), the deliverance of God is said to be accompanied by spiritual renewal on the part of Israel (Joel 2:18-32, esp. vv.27-29; 3:17; Ezek. 39:22; Zech. 12:10-13), including the outpouring of the Spirit (Joel 2:28-29; Ezek. 39:29; Zech. 12:10). This would seem to identify all three descriptions as the same invasion. Third, while the two-invasion theory requires the Ezekiel 38-39 invasion to be unique, the invasion in Ezekiel is specifically said in 38:17 to be the same invasion prophesied by the former prophets. However, the only prior prophecies of such an invasion are in Joel and Isaiah. (Isaiah 5:26-30 appears to be a condensed description of the invasion described earlier by Joel, cf. Joel 1:6; 2:1-11; and it is uncertain if Isaiah 29:1-8 is eschatological or historical.) Thus, the case that the Ezekiel prophecy refers to a distinct invasion is specifically contradicted by the prophecy itself. Fourth, in Joel's description he says, "There has never been anything like it, nor will there be again after it to many generations (Joel 2:2)," which simply does not fit with a two-invasion theory, since that theory requires two devastating invasions of Israel within a period of only a few years at most. Fifth, in all three of the major descriptions, the conclusion of the war results in the permanent restoration of Israel (Joel 2:18-27; 3:18-21; Ezek. 39:25-29; Zech. 14:8-21) and the establishment of the kingdom (Joel 2:18-3:21; Ezek. 39:21-29; Zech. 14:8-21). Sixth, the condition of the land of Israel at the time of the invasion by the Antichrist ("like the garden of Eden," cf. Joel 2:3) could hardly be so if a prior invasion of such proportions as described in Ezekiel 38-39 (cf. 38:17-23; 39:9-16) had occurred at most, only a few years earlier. Seventh, the language of Revelation 19:17-18, which describes the final battle of Armageddon, is in substance virtually identical to Ezekiel 39:17-20 (cf. 39:4). [Armageddon is an extension of the invasion by the Antichrist at the midpoint of the tribulation. The Antichrist's invasion will result in the siege of Judah and a portion of Jerusalem (Zech. 12:2-3), with the Antichrist having control of the temple area (Dan. 9:27; Zech.14:2; Mt. 24:15). However, Israel will be divinely protected and the Antichrist will be unable to take control of the entire city and Judea. This siege will last until the final campaign (Armageddon) just prior to the end of the period, when, at Israel's most desperate hour, Christ will return to defend his people and defeat the armies of the Antichrist. Thus, the battle of

the final battle—the battle of Armageddon—is fought at the end and the Antichrist and his armies are defeated.[7]

The abomination of which Jesus here speaks is mentioned in only two other passages of scripture—Daniel 9:27 and 2 Thessalonians 2:1-4.[8] Recall that the event

---

Armageddon at the end of the period is simply an extension of the invasion and siege that begins at the midpoint.] The remaining problem is how to reconcile the list of nations opposing Israel in Ezekiel 38-39 (Magog, Rosh, Meshech, Tubal, Persia [Iran], Ethiopia [Sudan], Put [Libya], Gomer, and Beth-togarmah) with the kingdom of the Antichrist (the Revived Roman Empire). One of the major problems of the two-invasion theory is that proponents have never been able to resolve the identification of "Gog of the land of Magog" (Ezek. 38:1-6,14,16,18; 39:1,11). However, the Genesis record specifically lists Gomer, Magog, Tubal, Meshech, and Togarmah (all listed in the Ezekiel 38-39 invasion as participants, cf. 38:1-6) as descendants of Japheth, from whom the Europeans descended as they migrated westward in the direction of the Mediterranean coastlands and ultimately toward the Atlantic coast of Europe (Gen. 10:5). Thus, it seems quite reasonable to associate the invasion in Ezekiel 38-39 with the invasion of Israel by the Antichrist (leader of the Revived Roman Empire—originally, predominately of Japhetic descent), which occurs at the midpoint of the tribulation. In this case the reference to "Gog" could be understood as a reference to the Antichrist. If this view is correct, there is no prophesied invasion of Israel anytime during the first half of the tribulation prior to the invasion by the armies of the Antichrist at the midpoint. It is important to keep in mind that the battle of Armageddon, which takes place just prior to the regal appearing, is the culmination of a conflict that begins at the midpoint of the tribulation.

[7] The battle of Armageddon is described in Revelation 19:11-21 and in Zechariah 14:1-8, and in both of these accounts it is closely associated with the regal appearing of Christ.

[8] Some amillennialists attempt to connect the abomination of desolation spoken of in Matthew 24:15 to the abomination of desolation prophesied in Daniel 11:31, or to some similar event future to the time this discourse was given, while avoiding any connection to the abomination of desolation prophesied in Daniel 9:24-27 (e.g., Lenski, *Matthew*, pp.937-938). The reason is that Daniel 9:24-27 presents a picture of the future that is compatible only with premillennialism. (Only premillennialists view the building of the third temple as a prerequisite to the end of the age—amillennialists view the second coming as imminent; and only premillennialists believe that the abomination referred to by Christ is a future event.) Nevertheless it is clear that in 24:15 Jesus referred directly to the Daniel 9:24-27 prophecy. Daniel 9:26-27 is a messianic prophecy, and it predicts the approximate time of Messiah's rejection and death, and the subsequent destruction of Jerusalem and the second temple, as well as the abomination of desolation near the end of the age in the third temple yet to be built. Other than avoidance, there are two basic approaches taken by amillennialists to deal with this problem. The principal approach is to connect Matthew 24:15 to the abomination prophesied in Daniel 11:31 instead of the one prophesied in Daniel 9:27 (e.g., Lenski). However, from a purely exegetical standpoint there should be no doubt that Jesus was referring to the Daniel 9:24-27 prophecy. [The event to which Jesus pointed was future, but the Daniel 11:31 prophecy was completely fulfilled in 167 B.C. by Antiochus IV. On the other hand, the Daniel 9:24-27 prophecy is directly connected to the coming of Messiah and his

marking the beginning of the seventieth week (the tribulation) is the making of a covenant between "the Prince" (the Antichrist) and Israel. Daniel 9:27 states that in the middle of the 70th week (3½ years into the period) the covenant will be broken as the Antichrist invades Israel and takes control of the temple, stopping the sacrifices and offerings, and making the temple desolate—with respect to the worship of the true God—until he is destroyed at the appearing of Christ (Dan. 9:27, cf. Rev. 19:11-21). Paul expands on this topic and tells us that the Antichrist (whom he refers to as, "the man of lawlessness") opposes and exalts himself above every so-called god or object of worship, so that he takes his seat in the temple of God, displaying himself as being God" (2 Thess. 2:4). To this, Revelation adds that a second "beast" (the head of the state-sanctioned apostate religion of the tribulation) will cause an image to be made to the beast (the Antichrist). Through some means this image will appear to be alive (Rev. 13:14-15).

---

rejection and death, and the subsequent destruction of Jerusalem and the temple, and the eventual end of the age prior to the time in which all of the promises would be fulfilled. Thus, Daniel 9:24-27 is highly relevant to the central discussion in the Olivet Discourse, whereas Daniel 11:31 is not.] The other amillennial approach is an interpretation of Daniel 9:24-27 that views the covenant maker in verse 27 as the Messiah, instead of the Roman Prince (the Antichrist). This was the view of E.W. Hengstenberg and is also the view of many amillennialists today. Such a view ostensibly allows the amillennial interpreter to claim fulfillment of verse 27 in the making of the new covenant by Christ. However, the view that the Messiah is the covenant maker in verse 27 is highly problematic. C.F. Keil rejects the arguments for the view put forth by Hengstenberg on the grounds they are "destitute of validity" (C.F. Keil, *Biblical Commentary on the Book of Daniel*, translated from German by M.G. Easton, in Volume 9, of the Commentary on the Old Testament by C.F. Keil and F. Delitzsch, William B. Eerdmans Publishing, 1980, p.367.) Also, such a view requires an alternative view of the structure of Daniel's 70 weeks. For example, K. Riddlebarger describes the structure of the 70 weeks not as strict chronology, but as a reflection of the sabbath-jubilee pattern of sevens found in Leviticus 25 (Kim Riddlebarger, *A Case for Amillennialism: Understanding the End Times*, Baker Books, 2003, pp.149-156). However, such a view requires the 70th week to encompass the entire Church age, whereas Daniel 12:11, in referring back to 9:27, specifically states that from the abomination of desolation to the end (the second half of the 70th "week") is 1290 days, or 3 ½ years, making the entire 70th week 7 years long, not the entire Church age as this amillennial interpretation requires. Riddlebarger attempts to show New Testament support for this view by claiming that John interpreted the 70th week as symbolic of the Church age in Revelation 12:14. However, Revelation 12:14 was spoken in relation to Israel ("the woman who gave birth to the male child"—the Messiah), not the Church; and the time, times, and half a time (3 ½) is specifically stated in the immediate context to be 1260 days (12:6). Thus, Revelation does not support a symbolic view of the length of the 70th week. Of course it ought to be evident from the opening statement of the prophecy that it cannot be applied to the Church, for in Daniel 9:24, Gabriel specifically stated that the time is "for your people [the Jews] and your holy city [Jerusalem]."

Jesus' reference to the abomination "standing in the holy place" refers to this image being set up (or dedicated) in the temple sanctuary.[9]

The final clause, "then know that its devastation is near," is not indicative, but imperative. The believers are to recognize from these two signs (the presence of surrounding armies and the abomination standing in the temple) that the desolation of Jerusalem is near. During the second half of the period, Jerusalem will be at least partially under the control of the Antichrist. The remainder of the city and much of Judea will be under siege (Zech. 12:2-3). The situation will be somewhat analogous to that of West Berlin in modern times, except vastly more perilous.

[16] "Then let those in Judea flee unto the mountains.

[17] In that day, let not the one on the roof go down to take the things out of his house,

[18] and let not the one in the field turn back to retrieve his garment.

Remember the wife of Lot. Whoever will seek to save his possessions will forfeit {his life}, but whoever will forfeit {his possessions}, will save {his life}."

––––––

Exegetical and Textual Notes

vv.16-18a These verses are verbally equivalent in all three synoptics

v.18b   The allusion to Lot's wife and the sentence that follows it are inserted from Luke 17:32-33. In Luke's account, Luke 17:28-33 appears between the reference to Noah (Lk. 17:26-27) and the

––––––

[9] "The abomination of desolation" (τὸ βδέλυγμα τῆς ἐρημώσεως) is neuter and likely refers to an object. In the phrase ἑστὸς ἐν τόπῳ ἁγίῳ ("standing in the holy place") ἑστὸς ("standing") is a perfect participle from ἵστημι, meaning "to confirm," or "to establish." (Ἀφίστημι—the opposite—means to "apostatize," or "to fall away.") Thus, it seems that the abomination is to be "set up" or "established" in the temple in such a way as to represent a shift to a fundamentally different form of religion—the religion of the Antichrist. Perhaps the image referred to in Revelation 13:14-15 is the object that will be set up; though as Paul points out, the Antichrist himself will appear personally, likely at the outset, and possibly periodically through the remainder of the tribulation. Note the similar language in Daniel 12:11—*i.e.*, "set up," which implies that the abomination is an object, not just an act. Of course no such object was set up in the temple during the Roman conquest in A.D. 70, the temple was simply destroyed. The lack of an object (image) being set up by the Romans prior to the A.D. 70 destruction of the temple argues that the event referenced in Daniel 12:11, which refers back to 9:27, was not fulfilled by the A.D. 70 destruction of the temple, but pertains to the future. Also, the abomination described in Daniel 9:27 is to take place in the third temple, which has not yet been built. According to the prophecy, the abomination in the temple (v.27) occurs after the destruction of the second temple (v.26); thus necessitating the construction of a third temple for the fulfillment of the 70th week.

examples of the one taken and the other left (Lk. 17:34-36). However, the material in Luke 17:31-33 is dislocated and should appear earlier in the discourse to match Matthew 24:17-18 and Mark 13:15-16. Apparently the Luke 17:31-33 material, which includes the allusion to Lot's wife, was moved down in Luke's account to follow the illustration of Lot (17:28-30) on the incorrect assumption that the two illustrations belong together. However, the two illustrations were made in entirely difference contexts. The reference to Lot's wife illustrates a point being made in relation to the intensity of the persecution that will begin immediately after the midpoint of the tribulation period and parallels Matthew 24:17-18; whereas the rescue of Lot (Lk. 17:28-29) is used to illustrate the imminency of the Lord's appearing and matches Matthew 24:39b. (The arrangement of the Luke 17:22-35 material is best seen from the parallel texts.)

The statement appended from Luke 17:33 reads: ὃς ἐὰν ζητήσῃ τὴν ψυχὴν αὐτοῦ περιποιήσασθαι ἀπολέσει αὐτήν, ὃς δ' ἂν ἀπολέσῃ ζῳογονήσει αὐτήν ("whoever will seek to save his life {i.e., his financial life, or his possessions} will forfeit, but whoever will forfeit will save his life"). In the first clause, ὃς ἐὰν ζητήσῃ τὴν ψυχὴν αὐτοῦ περιποιήσασθαι ἀπολέσει αὐτήν ("whoever will seek to save his life possessions will forfeit") indicates the thing one seeks to save is not merely his life, but his material possessions (περιποίησις, ["save"] meaning, "to retain what one has acquired," is an economic term, *BAGD*, p.650, pertaining to material things). In the second clause, ὃς δ' ἂν ἀπολέσῃ ζῳογονήσει αὐτήν ("but whoever will forfeit will save his life") we find ζῳογονήσει (from ζῳογονονέω {"to save"}, meaning to preserve one's life). These clauses are mirror images; the second clause tells what is forfeited in the first clause (one's physical life), and the first clause tells what is forfeited in the second (one's possessions). The idea seems to be that to seek to save one's possessions is to forfeit {one's life}, and to forfeit {one's possessions} is to save one's physical life.

The siege of Jerusalem and Judea will occur suddenly, and when it happens, those in Judea are to flee to the mountains and those in Jerusalem are to immediately forsake all and flee the city; those in the environs of the city are not to seek to enter it for any reason.[10] Failure to act in all haste will result in almost certain death (Lk. 17:31-33, cf.

[10] Many amillennialists find the fulfillment of this prophecy in the invasion of Jerusalem in A.D. 70 by the Romans under Titus. However, the particulars do not fit. The invasion described here will occur so suddenly that residents of Jerusalem are warned to flee immediately, leaving all of their possessions and even their clothes. At the time of the A.D. 70 invasion by Titus, the city of Jerusalem had been engulfed in an intense, internal civil war for some time prior to the arrival of the Romans. As to the scope of this conflict, Josephus records that factions were using siege works and mechanized weapons within the city walls. (There were walled and fortified enclaves within the city; among them were the temple complex and the Fortress of Antonio.) During this internal conflict the stores of grain within the city were largely destroyed, many innocent citizens and worshipers at the temple were killed, and according to Josephus (*The Wars of the Jews,* Book 5, chapters 1-2) residents of the city were unable to leave, being prevented by the warring factions long before the arrival of the Romans. Thus, if this passage were intended as a warning to those living in the environs of Jerusalem to flee in advance of the approaching Roman Army, it would

Zech. 14:2; Lk. 21:24). Jesus emphasized that when the event described in verse 15 happens, time will be critical. When the siege begins, the enemy will seek to kill, capture, or trap as many as possible (cf. Zech 14:2). Mark indicates that the one on the roof should not delay to take even a single item out of his house; he is to abandon all and flee.[11] There will be no time to collect one's belongings, not even one's only garment.[12] In ancient times the laborer's clothes were his most important possession, as seen from the fact that on occasion they were used as collateral for debt. Jesus said that on this coming day, the one having left his garment, even his only garment in the city, is not to return for it. There is simply no circumstance that could justify returning to the city; all thought must be for immediate flight. Those who flee, forsaking all, will have the best opportunity for survival.

Jesus drew on a ready illustration—Lot's wife.[13] Lot's wife perished in the conflagration of Sodom because she looked (*i.e.*, turned) back to the city under

---

be a hollow warning, since such a flight would actually have needed to take place prior to the outbreak of civil war. One might argue that verse 15 refers to the civil war in advance of the Roman invasion, but if that were the case then the description given would be awry, for Matthew 24:15 (cf. Lk. 21:20 and Mk. 13:14) is clear that the armies referred to will be in the process of surrounding the city, while at the same time the abomination will be set up in the temple. Neither the Roman invasion of A.D. 70, nor the preceding civil war matches this description. Of course, according to the prophecy of the 70 weeks in Daniel 9:24-27, it is the third temple, not the second temple, in which the abomination will take place (see "Daniel 9:24-27—The Prophecy of the 70 Weeks" in the Appendices). Thus, the amillennial explanation does not fit the particulars of either the Scriptures or history.

[11] Mark (13:14) reads: …τι ἐκ τῆς οἰκίας αὐτοῦ ("…to take *anything* out of his house").

[12] Note that ἱμάτιον ("garment") is singular in both Matthew and Mark. Luke (17:31) reads: τὰ ὀπίσω ("the {things} left behind"), which is not contradictory, but less specific than Matthew and Mark.

[13] The insertion of Luke 21:32-33 (the reference to Lot's wife) is the most complex structural issue in reconstructing this discourse. According to Luke's account, as we have it, the reference to Lot's wife (vv.31-33) falls immediately after the illustration of Lot (vv.28-30), and the illustration of Lot falls between Matthew 24:37-39 (the reference to the flood) and Matthew 24:40-41 (the illustrations of one taken and another left). The problem is that the material pertaining to Lot's wife does not fit between Matthew 24:39 and 24:40; it clearly corresponds to an earlier segment of the discourse found in Matthew 24:17-18 (cf. Mark 13:15-16). Apparently the reference to Lot's wife was moved (perhaps post-compositionally) so as to connect it with the illustration of Lot himself. However, Jesus' references to Lot and to Lot's wife were made in different contexts, and thus one could not immediately follow the other. The reference to Lot's wife illustrates the intensity of the persecution that will begin immediately at the midpoint of the tribulation period (Mt. 24:15-21); whereas the rescue of Lot and the unexpected destruction of Sodom illustrate the imminency of the Lord's appearing (Lk. 17:36 cf. Mt. 24:37—where the context is clearly the coming of the Son of Man). Thus the material recorded in Luke 17:31-33 could not have followed

destruction (Gen. 19:23-26). Perhaps she intended to retrieve some valuable object left behind, we do not know; but we do know the result. Failure to follow the instructions she was given cost Lot's wife her life. Even so, when Jerusalem is surround by armies and the abomination stands in the temple, the one who delays flight in order to save his possessions will forfeit his life, but the one who forfeits his possessions will save his life.

> **"Because these are the days of vengeance in which all the things having been written are to be fulfilled."**

Exegetical and Textual Notes

v.18c   This statement is found only in Luke 21:22. [The next verse (Lk. 21:23) is parallel to Matthew 24:19 and Mark 13:17.]

The Jewish listeners would have been familiar with the Old Testament teaching regarding the day of the LORD, and they should have immediately understood the significance of Jesus' statement. Immediate flight, forsaking all one's material possessions will be necessary at that time because the presence of armies surrounding Jerusalem and the abomination standing in the temple will signal the approach of the day of the LORD, during which the dreadful prophecies of divine wrath will come to pass.[14]

> **[19] "But woe to the ones who are pregnant and to the ones nursing in those days.**
>
> **[20] But pray that your flight might not happen in winter neither on a Sabbath;**

---

the material in Luke 17:28-30 as delivered by Jesus, rather it parallels Matthew 24:17-18 and Mark 13:15-16, spoken earlier (see: "The Structure of the Discourse," p.21).

[14] This is not to say that the day of the LORD begins at the midpoint of the period. In view of Paul's statement in 2 Thessalonians 2:1-4 that the day of the LORD will not come until the apostasy associated with the revealing of the Antichrist in the temple occurs first (see the note at 24:10), it seems likely that the phrase ὅτι ἡμέραι ἐκδικήσεως αὐταί εἰσιν ("because these are days of vengeance") refers to the day of the LORD as being imminent rather than actual. It should be observed that contrary to the position of replacement theology and realized eschatology, Jesus expected a literal, physical fulfillment of Old Testament eschatological prophecy as seen by his literal (and physical) prescription: Flee for your lives! (Which would hardly seem appropriate if those prophecies are to be interpolated allegorically.) It is instructive to note that Luke 21:22 reads: "all the things having been written are to be fulfilled." From this statement we can infer that Jesus believed all eschatological prophecy would be fulfilled literally enough to justify drastic and concrete actions at specified events.

[21] for then there will be great tribulation upon the earth and wrath to this people, such as has neither occurred from the beginning of the world until now, nor will ever happen {again}.

And they will fall by the edge of the sword and will be led captive unto all the nations, and Jerusalem will be trodden down by the Gentiles until the times of the Gentiles are completed."

———

Exegetical and Textual Notes

v.19   All three synoptics are virtually identical on this verse.

v.20   Luke omits this. Matthew adds, μηδὲ σαββάτῳ ("neither a Sabbath")

v.21a   Only Luke (21:23b) includes: ἐπὶ τῆς γῆς καὶ ὀργὴ τῷ λαῷ τούτῳ ("...upon the earth and wrath to this people...").

ουδ' οὐ μὴ is an intensification of a double negative (οὐ μὴ). There is no grammatical equivalent in English. The word "ever" has been inserted in the translation in the place of "never," since the double negative would not be proper in English.

v.21b   Found only in Luke (21:24).

———

The difficulty of this period of persecution and flight is going to be particularly hard on those with special circumstances. It will also be far more difficult if the necessity of flight occurs in winter when the weather might be severe, or on a Sabbath when their flight might be more easily detected. The believers are told to pray that these events will not happen at a time where circumstances would make their flight more difficult.[15]

With verse 21 Jesus picks up after a brief excursus in verses 19-20: "For then there will be great affliction (tribulation)."[16] Only Luke records the longer form of the statement, which includes "upon the earth and wrath to this people." This great "tribulation," from which the name of the period is derived, will fall upon the whole earth, not just upon Israel. Not only will this period include affliction (*i.e.*, greatly distressing circumstances), but it will also include the additional element of divine

———

[15] προσεύχεσθε δὲ ("but pray") is present imperative; ἵνα ("so that," or "in order that") is a resultant particle, indicating that the result (*i.e.*, the flight not occurring at an inopportune time) could be affected by prayer. This entire clause is in the subjunctive mood, indicating that the outcome is contingent. Only Matthew includes μηδὲ σαββάτῳ ("neither on a Sabbath").

[16] The excursus in verses 19-20 slightly obscures the meaning of "for then," which harkens back to verse 18. Jesus was not saying that there will be great affliction only if this event occurs in winter or on the Sabbath, but that there will be great affliction "at that time" (not "in that case") and the believers should pray that the circumstances of flight will favor their survival.

wrath.[17] The phrase "to this people," likely refers to the Jewish people living in unbelief at that time, prior to the conversion of the nation.[18] The affliction of this period will exceed anything that has occurred since the creation, including the flood, or anything that will ever happen in the future. [19]

The last sentence (in v.21b): "And they will fall by the edge of the sword and will be led captive unto all the nations, and Jerusalem will be trodden down by the Gentiles until the times of the Gentiles are completed," is found only in Luke 21:24. Again we see that Jesus' treatment of the tribulation is centered on the Jewish people and nation. Those referred to (some who will fall by "the edge of the sword" and others who will be

---

[17] There are reasons to believe that divine wrath will be confined to the trumpets and bowls of the seventh seal. There is no evidence that the seals of Revelation are, by nature, judgments. Rather, the seals appear to be simply movements (*i.e.*, periods) within the tribulation, which individually may or may not contain divine wrath. Revelation does not mention divine wrath until 6:15-17, which is after the events of the sixth seal are past. The events contained in the seventh seal (the trumpets and the bowls) are specifically indicated to be divine wrath (Rev. 15:1; 16:1). Thus, it is not without significance that the first mention of divine wrath in Revelation occurs just prior to the opening of the seventh seal (6:17). That being the case, it is possible that divine wrath is confined to the time of the seventh seal. [Note the momentous transition at the opening of the seventh seal (Heaven is silent for about half an hour, cf. Rev. 8:1). Also note how Revelation segregates the first six seals, all of which are covered together in chapter six, from the seventh seal, which is covered from chapters eight through nineteen. Of course, one cannot be dogmatic on this point. Prior to the mid-twentieth century it was generally accepted among premillennialists that the day of the LORD would be confined to the time immediately prior to the second coming (see *The Scofield Reference Bible*, 1917 ed., p.1349, footnote 1; and Lewis Sperry Chafer's *Systematic Theology,* vol. IV pp.11, 383, 398; and vol. VII, p.110). Extending the period of divine wrath to cover the entire seven years of tribulation only became popular in the mid-twentieth century as an additional proof for the pretribulational rapture theory; and proponents have been unable to offer convincing biblical or theological support for characterizing the entire period as wrath. In fact, such a position is flatly contradicted by Paul in 2 Thessalonians 2:1-8, though we only know from that passage that the day of the LORD begins sometime in the second half of the tribulation. For additional discussion of the significance of 2 Thessalonians 2:1-8 in regard to the beginning of the day of the LORD, see in the Appendices "The Character and Chronology of the Tribulation" beginning on page 221, and the discussion of 2 Thessalonians 2:1-9 under "Rapture Theology" on page 262.]

[18] While individual Jews may be converted throughout the period, the conversion of the nation will culminate in connection with God's deliverance of his people at the end of the period (Zech. 12:10-13:9 cf. 14:1-8).

[19] As previously noted, οὐδ' οὐ μὴ is an intensification of the double negative (οὐ μὴ). There is no grammatical equivalent in English. The idea is rendered in English as, "nor ever could" (subjunctive). Jesus does not say that the destruction to the earth will be greater than at the flood, but that the human suffering implied by θλῖψις ("affliction") will be unparalleled in all of human history, past and future. Cf. Daniel 12:1.

"led captive unto all nations") are the Jews referred to previously in this verse as "this people." The reason for immediate flight, forsaking all of one's possessions, is that those who do not escape in great haste will be killed or captured. The assault on Jerusalem will result in at least a portion of the city, including the temple, falling under the control of the Antichrist. This control will last until the times of the Gentiles are completed (at the end of the period).[20] "The times of the Gentiles" is a reference to the period of time described in the book of Daniel that extends from the Neo-Babylon Empire under Nebuchadnezzar II to the destruction of the latter form of the Roman Empire (referred to as "the Revived Roman Empire") under the Antichrist.[21] During the final phase of the times of the Gentiles, the temple and the city will be "trodden down" (subjugated) by the Gentiles for forty-two months (Rev. 11:2).[22] This period, equal to three and a half years, extends from the time of the abomination in the temple (Rev. 13:5-6 cf. Dan. 9:27 and 2 Thess. 2:1-4) to the end of the period (Dan. 12:11); it also corresponds to the period of Israel's flight and exile during the second half of the tribulation (Rev. 12:5), the period during which the two witnesses of Revelation will prophesy (Rev. 11:3), and the severe persecution of believers described in this discourse and in the books of Daniel and Revelation (Dan. 7:25; Rev. 6:9-11; 13:6-18).

> **[22] "And except for the fact that those days will be cut short, no flesh would be delivered; but on account of the elect, those days will be cut short."**

The affliction of this period upon mankind and the earth will be so severe that were it not for the fact that God will abruptly cut the period short, no one would survive.[23] The cutting short of those days does not mean that the prophetic timetable as

---

[20] See the discussion at 24:12.

[21] $\pi\lambda\eta\rho\omega\theta\tilde{\omega}\sigma\iota\nu$ ("brought to an end"—subjunctive aorist passive) indicates that the times of the Gentiles will be brought to an end decisively (at the time of Christ's return, see Matthew 24:30-31 cf. Zechariah 14:1-21). This period is delineated in Nebuchadnezzar's dream (Dan. 2:1-45) and Daniel's vision (Dan. 7:1-28). For a discussion of those passages see: "The Character and Chronology of the Tribulation" in the Appendices (p.251).

[22] $\pi\alpha\tau\sigma\nu\mu\acute{\epsilon}\nu\eta$ ("trodden down") is a present participle. The idea is that Jerusalem will "be *being* trodden" down (*i.e.*, continually) from the time the city is captured until the times of the Gentiles are completed at the conclusion of the period.

[23] The affliction arises from three sources: the activity of the Antichrist and the world powers aligned with him (Rev. 6:1-11), the activity of Satan and the demons (Rev. 9:13-21; 12:7-17), and the wrath of God upon the world for its rebellion (Rev. 8:1-9:21; 15:1-16:21). The term "cut short" ($\dot{\epsilon}\kappa o\lambda o\beta\acute{\omega}\theta\eta\sigma\alpha\nu$) does not mean that the seven-year period (as prophesied in Daniel 9:27) will be shortened to less than the prophesied duration. Rather, what Jesus indicated is that the period will not be allowed to continue beyond the specified time; it will be brought to an abrupt halt at his appearing (cf. v.31). [Translational note: The AV translates $\kappa\alpha\grave{\iota}$ $\epsilon\grave{\iota}$ $\mu\grave{\eta}$ $\dot{\epsilon}\kappa o\lambda o\beta\acute{\omega}\theta\eta\sigma\alpha\nu$ $\alpha\acute{\iota}$ $\dot{\eta}\mu\acute{\epsilon}\rho\alpha\iota$ $\dot{\epsilon}\kappa\epsilon\tilde{\iota}\nu\alpha\iota$, "and except those days should be shortened," in the subjunctive mood; and the

revealed in scripture will be shortened, but that those days will be abruptly brought to a halt so as not to allow the complete extermination of mankind.

The deliverance refers to physical deliverance (we might say, "rescue") at the return of Christ, for God will not allow the complete destruction of his elect.[24]

> **[23] "Then if anyone says to you, 'Look, here is the Christ,' or: 'There he is,' do not believe it;**
>
> **[24] for false christs and false prophets will be raised up and they will give great signs and wonders so as to deceive, if possible, even the elect.**
>
> **[25] See, I have told you all these things before {they happen}." And he said to the disciples, "Days will come when you will long to see one of the days of the Son of Man and will not see it."**

———

Exegetical and Textual Notes

v.23-24   These verses are virtually identical in Matthew and Mark (13:21-22), but do not appear in Luke.

v.25a   The first sentence is virtually identical in Matthew and Mark (13:23), but does not appear in Luke. Mark adds, πάντα ("all").

v.25b   The second sentence of verse 25 is found only in Luke (17:22).

———

Once Israel has fled to the place where they will be protected from the reach of the Antichrist (Rev. 12:6,13-17), they will hear reports that Messiah, or a prophet has

---

NASB translates it, "unless those days had been cut short," reflecting a past tense. However, the expression is neither subjunctive nor past tense. Εἰ μὴ (Lit. "if not," translated, "except") is indicative, as can be seen from the aorist, passive, indicative verb (ἐκολοβώθησαν = "to be brought to an end") and expresses what is, or will be, not simply what could or should be. Although ἐκολοβώθησαν is aorist, the tense is controlled by the future verb ἔσται ("will be") in the previous statement (note the conjunction at the beginning of verse 22), and the context indicates that it refers to a future action (note that κολοβωθήσονται, used further along in the verse, is a future passive). Thus the aorist here is indicative of the type of action (punctiliar) rather than the tense of the action. Hence, the days referred to will be cut short "abruptly." When we reflect the proper mode, tense, and voice it seems better to translate the phrase: "except {for the fact that} those days will be {abruptly} cut short."]

[24] κολοβωθήσονται ("will be cut short") is future passive—the punctiliar nature of the action already having been established earlier in the verse by ἐκολοβώθησαν ("to be brought to an end"—aorist passive).

come.[25] These "messiahs" and "prophets" will be empowered to perform great signs and wonders (*i.e.*, "miracles"), but they will be deceivers, and their deception will be directed at the elect.[26] Since the deception is to be directed toward believers, we may safely assume that these false christs will pretend to be the true historical Jesus.

The believers are not to fall prey to these deceptions. They have been forewarned, and this warning is of crucial importance. Since these "christs" claim to be the historic Jesus, they acknowledge by their claim that the historic Jesus is the Christ, and thus in so doing they invalidate their own claim, since the historic Jesus has already warned his followers that those who will appear in this manner in the future, claiming to be him, will be liars. Only Luke (17:22) includes the second statement in this verse. This will be a particularly difficult test for the Jewish elect, since they will long for this affliction to be over and to see even one of the days of the Son of Man, when he offered himself to their nation. [27]

> **[26] "Therefore, if they say to you: 'Behold he is in the desert,' do not go out there; or 'Behold he is in the inner chamber,' do not believe them.**
>
> **[27] For just as the lightning flashes from the east and shines even unto the west, so will be the appearing of the Son of Man. But first it is necessary for him to suffer many things and to be rejected by this generation."**

———

Exegetical and Textual Notes

v.26-27 Mark does not include this material.

> In verse 27 the regal appearing is in view. Luke (17:24) reads: ὥσπερ γὰρ ἡ ἀστραπὴ ἀστράπτουσα ἐκ τῆς ὑπὸ τὸν οὐρανὸν εἰς τὴν ὑπ' οὐρανὸν λάμπει, οὕτως ἔσται ὁ υἱὸς τοῦ ἀνθρώπου ("For as the lightning flashing out of the one part of the sky shines unto the other part of the sky, so it will be in the day of the Son of Man"). The idea is that just as lightning flashes in one part of the sky and can be seen a long way off in another part of the sky, so Christ's coming will be apparent for all to see.

———

[25] ἐγερθήσονται ("will be raised up") is passive, as in the AV and NASB. These false christs do not arise of their own accord; they are the product of the powers of darkness and empowered by them to perform great signs.

[26] εἰ δυνατόν ("if possible") is indicative, not subjunctive. It does not pose a hypothetical (*i.e.*, whether or not it might be possible to deceive the elect), but rather states the goal of these false christs and false prophets—to deceive the elect. Matthew reads: ὥστε πλανῆσαι ("so as to deceive"), and Mark reads: πρὸς τὸ ἀποπλανᾶν ("for to lead astray").

[27] The second statement in verse 25 ("And he said to the disciples, 'Days will come when you will long to see one of the days of the Son of Man and will not see it'") is inserted from Luke 17:22.

The elect are not to be deceived by claims that Christ is "in the desert," or "in the inner chamber" (*i.e.*, in some secret place). His appearing will not be secretive; it will be as conspicuous as lightning that flashes and lights up not just a portion of the sky, but the whole sky (cf. Rev. 19:11-16). [28] The second statement (v.27b) appears only in Luke 17:25. Jesus will indeed return, but first he must suffer "many things" (injustice, ill-treatment, dishonor, humiliation, the guilt of mankind's sin, divine wrath, separation from the Father, and death), and be rejected by his own people (cf. Jn. 1:11).

[28] Verse 28 appears after 24:41.

[29] "But immediately after the tribulation of those days the sun will be darkened, and the moon will not give its light, and the stars will fall from heaven,

and on earth {there will be} distress of nations powerless at the sound of the sea and surf, {and} men collapsing from fear and {the} anticipation of the things coming upon the earth, for the powers of the heavens will be shaken."

Exegetical and Textual Notes

v.28 Verse 28 is dislocated in Matthew. In the reconstructed text it appears after 24:41. Note Matthew 24:28 is parallel to Luke 17:37b, and Matthew 24:41 is parallel to Luke 17:37a; this places Matthew 24:28 after Matthew 24:41. (See the parallel texts.)

v.29a Luke is abbreviated. Matthew and Mark are nearly identical, except that Mark has ἔσονται ..πίπτοντες ("will be..falling"—future deponent verb + present participle) instead of πεσοῦνται ("will fall"—simple future); Mark seems to indicate this activity will be spread over time.

v.29b This is found only in Luke (21:25b).

With the exception of the last clause (see below), the statement in verse 29b is found only in Luke (21:25b-26). It gives the reaction of the nations to the circumstances just described. [29] They will be in anguish, not knowing what to do or where to turn. [30]

---

[28] This verse has been used to denounce the doctrine of the rapture as unbiblical; however, the rapture (1 Thess. 4:13-17; I Cor. 15:51-53) is not in view in this verse; the only thing in view here is the second coming, at which Christ will judge the nations and establish the visible aspect of his kingdom on earth.

[29] Those who wish to limit the scope of the tribulation (principally posttribulationists) often state that τῆς γῆς ("the earth") in this prophecy, and similar expressions in passages such as Revelation 8:7, refer not to the whole earth, but to "the land," *i.e.*, Israel. However, if we translate

They will have no recourse to deal with the circumstances in which they find themselves.[31] The events described here will occur "immediately after the tribulation of those days." We should not think that Jesus here uses the term "tribulation" as a title for the period. He simply refers to the afflictions previously mentioned in verses 4-28. The events described in verse 29, while occurring on the heels of what was described in verses 4-28, are also part of the seven-year period of tribulation. They, along with the return of the Lord (v.30), form the concluding movement of the period. This will be a swift progression of events. Once the sequence of catastrophic judgments begins, the end will not be far off.[32]

The description of the sun becoming dark and the moon not giving its light at the day of the LORD is an Old Testament eschatological theme. Far from "reinterpreting" (i.e., "redefining") the eschatology of the Old Testament, Jesus, in this final discourse reaffirmed the normal/objective meaning of the Old Testament eschatological prophecies. So far in this discourse there has been no indication that Jesus intended for his statements to be taken any way other than literally (objectively). Further along he will employ parables to illustrate some points, but those are only illustrations of truth, not truth in allegorical form. It is notable that up to this point in the discourse, Jesus has employed neither symbolic nor figurative language. In fact, in his reference to the abomination in the book of Daniel (24:15), Jesus sternly warned his listeners that when they see the abomination (i.e., literally, see it standing in the holy place) they are to take certain swift and decisive measures, or forfeit their lives. This is not the literature of allegory. Everything that Jesus said here is consistent only with a normal/objective interpretation of the Old Testament. Those who subscribe to replacement theology and

---

ἐπὶ τῆς γῆς συνοχὴ ἐθνῶν, "upon the land, distress of nations," it does not make sense; nor would it fit with the statements already made earlier in this verse, or the broader context of eschatological prophecy found in Isaiah 13:10; Joel 2:10; 3:15; Amos 5:20; 8:9; Zeph. 1:15, and Rev. 6:12-17. The tribulation cannot be limited in scope to a regional phenomenon.

[30] συνοχὴ literally means "a narrow place." The metaphorical use signifies to be in "straits," i.e., having no place to turn, or "without hope."

[31] ἐν ἀπορίᾳ in Luke 21:25 (translated "perplexity" in both the AV and the NASB) literally means, to be "without a way"—not quizzical, as implied by "perplexity," but rather, "powerless," or "hopeless," i.e., without a way to solve the problem.

[32] The sequence of events immediately prior to the end is as follows: 1) The celestial and terrestrial judgments (Mt. 24:29; Rev. 6:12-17; 8:1-9:21 and 14:14-18:24). 2) The final proclamation of the gospel to the world. [This final proclamation may be associated directly with the sign of Christ in the sky. Note that 24:13b-14 (in the reconstructed text) indicates that the final proclamation of the gospel will occur either in connection with, or after the "terrors" and "great signs from heaven," and Zech. 12:9-13:9 seems to place the conversion of Israel at their most desperate hour, just prior to Messiah's appearing (Zech. 14:1-8).] 3) The return of Christ (Mt. 24:30).

realized eschatology will find no justification for the allegorical interpretation of prophecy in Jesus' words here.

In his description of the tribulation, Jesus drew heavily on Old Testament eschatological themes. That the sun and moon will be darkened at the day of the LORD was first mentioned in Joel 2:30-31 and 3:15, and then repeated in Isaiah 13:10. Isaiah also says that men will be terrified at the day of the LORD (13:7-8), and that the earth will be "shaken" (Isa. 13:13; 24:18-20). Even Jesus' previous allusions to "birth pains" (24:8) and "a day of vengeance" are found in Isaiah 7:8 and 34:8 respectively. Jesus was familiar with the Old Testament eschatological prophecies, and he understood and employed them according to their normal/objective meaning; and in so doing he encouraged his followers to do the same.[33]

Joel 2:10 says that the earth will "quake" and the heavens will "tremble;" and Isaiah 34:4 states that the sky will be "rolled up like a scroll" and "all their hosts will also wither away." (Note the similar language of Revelation 6:12-14.) Not only does the Old Testament speak of such things, but some New Testament passages indicate that this age will end in a series of devastating astrophysical catastrophes immediately prior to the coming of the Lord. Revelation gives the most precise picture. According to Revelation, the sixth seal (Rev. 6:12-17) involves the earth being struck by an object, or objects, from space (6:12-17). The impact will cause a great earthquake; dust and debris will obscure the light of the sun and moon, and matter glowing white hot will streak through the atmosphere. Revelation says that the sky will be blown apart "like a scroll when it is rolled up" (Rev. 6:14 cf. Isa. 34:4). So great will be the impact that every mountain and island will be moved out of their places.[34] The book of Revelation also describes four

---

[33] It should be pointed out that when Jesus made reference to the abomination in the book of Daniel, he did not tell his listeners to wait for replacement theology, or realized eschatology, or Augustine, or covenant theology to explain that the prophecy does not mean what it actually (objectively) says. He simply directed them to the book of Daniel, and said, "Let the reader understand." Of course, if, as some have insisted, the Old Testament eschatological prophecies cannot be properly understood by the normal/objective hermeneutic, such an admonition could hardly have been more than a cruel joke.

[34] Modern science has greatly aided our appreciation of Revelation 6:12-17. There can be little doubt that this is the description of an object from space, perhaps an asteroid, small comet, or fragment of such colliding with the earth. The details given, though set in phenomenological speech (as they appeared to John in his vision) correspond closely with contemporary scientific observations, especially the well-documented Shoemaker-Levy Comet impact on Jupiter in July, 1994. Note the details from Revelation 6:12-17: 1) A large shockwave ("a great earthquake"); 2) obscuration of the atmosphere ("the sun became black as sackcloth made of hair, and the whole moon became like blood"); 3) debris falling through the atmosphere in a meteoric display ("the stars of the sky fell to the earth"); 4) a blast-hole in the atmosphere arching upward from the impact site ("the sky was split apart like a scroll when it is rolled up"); 5) effects of the shock

successive events immediately after the sixth seal; they are the first four trumpets that occur during the time of the seventh seal. The first trumpet (Rev. 8:7) is described as "hail [ice] and fire mixed with blood."[35] The result will be the burning of a third of the surface of the earth. At the second trumpet (Rev. 8:8-9) "something like a great mountain burning with fire was thrown into the sea" and a third of the sea life on earth and a third of the ships are destroyed.[36] The third trumpet (Rev. 8:10-11) is described, phenomenologically, as a "great star" falling from heaven that will poison a third of the earth's fresh water, causing many to die. At the fourth trumpet (Rev. 8:12-13) the light from the sun, moon, and stars will be decreased.[37] Likely the "terrors" and "great signs from heaven"(24:13 in the reconstructed text—cf. Luke 21:11b) is a general reference to this entire set of events, whereas Jesus' statement here, in verse 29, seems to refer specifically to the same event as described in the fourth trumpet of Revelation.

The nations of the world will be in distress because of their inability to cope with these judgments (v.29b).[38] Of course, this is precisely the result God intends to bring

---

wave ("every mountain and island were moved out of their places"). That the event described in the sixth seal is astrophysical is further supported by two additional observations from the passage: 1) The response of those who dwell on the earth is to hide in caves and the rocks of the mountains (v.16). This would not be a typical response for a geophysical event, such as an earthquake. 2) This event immediately precedes the first four trumpets (Rev. 8:7-13), which are all clearly described as astrophysical in nature. Note the report of the Shoemaker-Levy impact on Jupiter in 1994, as recorded in *Astronomy* (October 1995, pp. 36-37). "After fragments of the Comet S-L 9 exploded in Jupiter's atmosphere they produced huge fireballs of hot gas and dust that rose high above the planet's clouds. Because Jupiter's atmosphere was literally blown away from above the impact site, hot gas and dust were funneled up to altitudes of 3,500 km…for about 20 minutes after each impact, the dust-laden plumes fell back into the atmosphere, reentering with a horrendous release of energy. The heat from the reentry was so intense it was easily detected from earth…On Jupiter, large, black dust clouds remained clearly visible at each impact site for weeks, suspended in the stratosphere. Even more than a year after the impacts, not all the dust has settled back into the deep atmosphere. These bruises have substantially reduced the amount of sunlight that reaches Jupiter's lower cloud tops."

[35] This is an interesting description in view of the fact that comets are composed of ice, but explode with thermonuclear-like force when colliding with a planet (Again, note the description of the Shoemaker-Levy Comet impact on Jupiter in 1994). The reference to "blood" is indicative of the devastating effect on people and animals.

[36] John did not say that he saw a mountain thrown into the sea; he said that he saw something "like" a mountain—that is, a mountain-size object, but not anything he recognized.

[37] This event will cause a third of the sunlight to be blocked from reaching the earth and will also affect moonlight and starlight (cf. Joel 2:10,30-31; 3:15; Isa. 13:10; Amos 5:20).

[38] συνοχὴ ἐθνῶν ("distress of nations"); ἐν ἀπορίᾳ ("powerless," literally, "in a narrow place," *i.e.*, having nowhere to turn). The idea being that the nations will be in distress because they have no way of dealing with this situation. No missile defense system, or other marvel of human

about. Mankind in its rebellion under the leadership of the Antichrist will seek to finally, and formally assert its independence from God. It will be the ultimate expression of secularism (or should we say, "post-secularism"), such that man himself (or at least, "a man") will be enthroned as God (2 Thess. 2:3-4 cf. vv.10-12). Such may be the very nature of "*the* iniquity" referred to earlier in the discourse (v.12).[39] While the modern age is often identified with such transformations as "the Industrial Age," "the Scientific Age," "the Space Age," "the Information Age," *etc.*, by far the most ominous transition has occurred quietly. Humanity has now arrived at what might be termed, "the Secular Age." From the earliest history of mankind until fairly recently, men might have argued over which religion was right, but most believed in some religion and acknowledged both the existence of a higher power and the preeminence of that higher power over human affairs; today that is not the case. Secularism has finally taken root and finds expression in a variety of forms. Most notably, it has taken root universally in the western world, which no longer regards government as subject to God (or "religion," as they call it), but rather, government is viewed as being subject only to human reason, and man is regarded as the ultimate authority. Whether there will yet be a revival of true religion we cannot say, but a day is coming in which mankind will be ready to accept humanity itself, as expressed through science, technology, and world government, as the true object of worship. This will represent the ultimate rebellion against God—
a rebellion the seeds of which were sown long ago in the region of the world that later became Babylon. At that time a man named Nimrod sought to unite humanity in rebellion against God (Gen. 10:8-11:9). Ever since, there have been many who have followed in Nimrod's footsteps; they are the leaders of the world's great empires. They have sought to unite mankind and impose a new world order in which religion is little more than the handmaiden of secularism. However, in their delusions of human grandeur, men refuse to accept the fact that independence from their eternal Creator can lead only to swift and certain destruction; for nature is not our "mother" as is so commonly proclaimed. Only God can impart and sustain life, and man cannot survive, much less flourish, without God's continual providence. Sinful men are blinded to their true condition: that they are poor, and weak, and corrupt. In his haughtiness, man imagines himself to be the master of his own destiny, and it is inevitable that he will someday, perhaps soon, reach the point where he beats his breast and declares himself—through his proxy, the Antichrist—to be his own God, (Dan. 7:25; 11:36-39 cf. 2 Thess. 2:3-4); but he will be brought low by the very forces over which he claims to have gained mastery (Isa. 2:10-22; 13:11).

---

engineering will protect earth from what is coming, and the ability of both governments and science will be completely overwhelmed.

[39] See the note on "the iniquity" at 24:12.

The oceans will be greatly disturbed. Men will be terrified, so much so that some will drop dead with fright as they anticipate what they think is earth's final destruction. But will they repent? Will they turn to God and worship him? No, even after all this, we are told: "The rest of mankind, who were not killed by these plagues, did not repent of the works of their hands, so as not to worship demons, and the idols of gold and of silver and of brass and of stone and of wood, which can neither see nor hear nor walk; and they did not repent of their murders nor of their sorceries nor of their immorality nor of their thefts" (Rev. 9:20-21 [NASB] cf. Rev. 16:9,11,21).

The degree to which the earth is to be impacted during this time will be staggering. Isaiah 13:6-13 says: "Wail, for the day of the LORD is near! It will come as destruction from the Almighty. Therefore all hands will fall limp, and every man's heart will melt. They will be terrified, pains and anguish will take hold of them; they will writhe like a woman in labor, they will look at one another in astonishment, their faces aflame. Behold, the day of the LORD is coming, cruel, with fury and burning anger, to make the land desolation; and He will exterminate its sinners from it. For the stars of heaven and their constellations will not flash forth their light; the sun will be dark when it rises and the moon will not shed its light. Thus I will punish the world for its evil and the wicked for their iniquity; I will also put an end to the arrogance of the proud and abase the haughtiness of the ruthless. I will make mortal man scarcer than pure gold and mankind than the gold of Ophir. Therefore I will make the heavens tremble, and the earth will be shaken from its place at the fury of the LORD of hosts in the day of His burning anger."[40] [NASB] Again, Isaiah 24:17-20 says: "Terror and pit and snare confront you, O inhabitant of the earth. Then it will be that he who flees the report of disaster will fall into the pit, and he who climbs out of the pit will be caught in the snare; for the windows above are opened, and the foundations of the earth shake. The earth is broken asunder, the earth is split through, the earth is shaken violently. The earth reels to and fro like a drunkard and it totters like a shack, for its transgression is heavy upon it, and it will fall, never to rise again." [NASB] [41]

While this may seem to be a very pessimistic outlook for the future, God hints at the possibility of protection for his elect, both Jew and Gentile. Zephaniah 2:1-3 says:

---

[40] The scope of the term הָאָרֶץ [ha'arets, cf. BDB, pp.75b-76] (translated "the land" in the AV, NASB and NIV in Isaiah 13:9b and 13a) is defined in verse 11 by תֵּבֵל [tebel, cf. BDB, p.385b], rendered "world" in all three translations. Contextually, הָאָרֶץ, as used in this passage, refers not to a localized event, but to a global, even celestial phenomenon. Note that all three versions translate הָאָרֶץ as "the earth" in verse 13, because only a planetary scope fits the sense. The picture seems to be that the judgment will fall on the whole earth, devastating much of its surface.

[41] The idea is not that the earth will be completely destroyed, but that this rebellion will be thoroughly crushed. There will, of course, be another rebellion at the end of the millennium, cf. Rev. 20:7-9. Nevertheless, there will never be a repeat of "the times of the Gentiles."

"Gather yourselves together, yes, gather O nation without shame, before the decree takes effect—the day passes like the chaff—before the burning anger of the LORD comes upon you, before the day of the LORD's anger comes upon you. Seek the LORD, all you humble of the earth who have carried out his ordinances; seek righteousness, see humility. Perhaps you will be hidden in the day of the LORD's anger." [NASB]

> **[30] "And then the sign of the Son of Man will appear in heaven, and all the peoples of the earth will mourn, and they will see the Son of Man coming on the clouds of heaven with great power and glory.**
>
> **When these things begin to happen, raise yourselves up and lift up your heads because your redemption draws near."**

——

Exegetical and Textual Notes

v.30a   The first sentence of the verse appears only in Matthew.

v.30b   The second sentence of the verse appears only in Luke (21:28).

——

We must bear in mind that while the catastrophic events described in the previous verse will be occurring, Israel will still be in a state of siege by the Antichrist and his armies. On the heels of such devastation on the earth, Christ will come. But first, his "sign" will appear in heaven.[42] We are not told the nature of this sign, but it will unmistakably signal to those on the earth that the return of the historic Christ of the New Testament is imminent. Perhaps the two prophets, prior to their deaths, will prophesy this event and prepare the people of the earth for this sign (Rev. 11:3-13). In any case, the sign, whatever it may be, will appear; and those on earth will clearly understand its meaning. This may be the very moment described in Zechariah 12:8-14, in which we are told that God will set about to destroy the nations that have come against Jerusalem, and pour out on the inhabitants of Jerusalem the Spirit of grace and supplication, so that they will look on him whom they have pierced, and mourn as one who mourns for an only son.

Jesus here gave only the barest of details concerning his return. He said that it will be preceded by a sign, that his descent will be visible for all to see, and that he will return in great power and glory. Zechariah 14:1-8 and Revelation 19:11-20:4 fill in the details of the regal appearance of Christ. When those details, along with Matthew 24:30 are put together, the following picture emerges. 1) The sign of Christ will appear in the

---

[42] The reference here is to the physical heaven; else it could hardly be a sign to men on earth.

sky (Mt. 24:29). 2) The world will see Christ returning (Mt. 24:30).[43] 3) This sight will provoke a bitter lament on the part of the rebellious world (Mt. 24:30), but great mourning on the part of elect Israel, who will recognize that the Jesus whom they rejected at his first appearance is indeed the true Messiah of Israel (Zech. 12:10-13:9). 4) Christ will descend upon the Mount of Olives (Zech. 14:4). 5) He will go forth to destroy the armies of the Antichrist (Zech. 14:1-3). 6) The Antichrist and his false prophet will be seized and thrown into the Lake of Fire (Rev. 19:19-20). 7) The armies that have gathered against Jerusalem will be destroyed (Rev. 19:21, cf. 2 Thess. 2:8; Zech. 14:12; Isa. 11:4) with great carnage (Rev. 14:19-20). 8) The saved and the unsaved will be gathered into their respective groups by angels (Mt. 24:31, cf. 13:40,49-50).[44] 9) Satan will be bound and confined in the Abyss (Rev. 20:1-3), undoubtedly along with his host of fallen angels.

We need, for a moment, to put ourselves in the place of the elect having endured the tribulation up to this late point. Much of the world's population will have perished, and the outlook for holding out much longer will seem bleak at best. It is amidst this great strain of endurance (24:13) that Jesus offers hope (v.30b): "When you see these things begin to happen, stand on your feet and look heavenward, for your deliverance is at hand."

[31] "And he will send forth his angels with a great trumpet, and they will gather his elect from out of the four winds, from one end of the heavens unto the other end."

_____

Exegetical and Textual Notes

v.31   Luke omits this.

Matthew and Mark summarize the last part of the verse differently. Matthew reads: ἀπ' ἄκρων οὐρανῶν ἕως [τῶν] ἄκρων αὐτῶν ("from one end of {the} heavens unto {the} other

---

[43] Unlike the rapture of the Church, which will occur suddenly, almost instantaneously, and without warning, the regal appearance of Christ at his second coming will be an event that all the people of the world will both anticipate and observe as it unfolds.

[44] At this point in time there will be few people remaining on earth (Isa. 13:12). According to Revelation 6:8, a fourth of mankind will perish in the first half of the period (assuming that the first four seals of Revelation occur prior to the midpoint of the tribulation—see "The Character and Chronology of the Tribulation," in the Appendices). We are not told how many will die during the fifth through the seventh seals, but one third of mankind perishes under the seventh trumpet alone (Rev. 9:15), and that is but one of thirteen judgments occurring in the time of the seventh seal. Thus, the implication is that the world's population will be reduced to a fraction of what it was at the beginning of the period.

end of them"); Marks reads: ἀπ' ἄκρου γῆς ἕως ἄκρου οὐρανοῦ ("from one end of {the} earth unto the end of {the} heavens").

———

At his appearing, Jesus will send forth his angels to gather his elect from every part of the earth, wherever they may be found. The significance of the great trumpet is not stated.[45] For millennia trumpets rallied armies. Whether there is a deeper significance we cannot say. Paul mentions "the last trumpet" in 1 Corinthians 15:52 in connection with the rapture of the Church, and some have been tempted to equate these two, implying a posttribulational rapture. However, there is no reason to believe that Paul was referring to the trumpet mentioned here by Christ, especially since it appears that these trumpets are sounded at different times and for different purposes.[46]

Jesus' description here is brief. He previously referred to the gathering at the end of the age in his parables of the kingdom of Heaven (Mt. 13:1-52). In the parable of the wheat and the tares (Mt. 13:24-30) and its interpretation (Mt. 13:34-43) he said that at the end of the age he would send forth his angels to gather out the tares (the unrighteous). Likewise in the parable of the dragnet (Mt. 13:47-48) and its interpretation (Mt. 13:49-50), he indicated the same—that the wicked will be taken out from among the righteous and cast into the furnace of fire. However, those descriptions are but bare summaries. The account of the judgment of the nations in Matthew 25:31-46 gives a more detailed picture revealing that the nations will be gathered before Christ and subsequently separated into their respective camps (the righteous and the unrighteous). Thus, at Jesus' appearing he will gather the nations, both the righteous and the wicked (though only the righteous are mentioned in 24:31), and he will separate them one from the

---

[45] The phrase: "with a great trumpet," appears only in Matthew.

[46] Paul's statement in 1 Corinthians 15:52 reads: ἐν ἀτόμῳ, ἐν ῥιπῇ ὀφθαλμοῦ, ἐν τῇ ἐσχάτῃ σάλπιγγι· σαλπίσει γάρ, καὶ οἱ νεκροὶ ἐγερθήσονται ἄφθαρτοι, καὶ ἡμεῖς ἀλλαγησόμεθα ("in a moment, in the glance of an eye, at the last trumpet; for it will sound, and the dead will be raised incorruptible, and we will be changed"). It might be argued that since Paul refers to "the" trumpet, he had in mind the trumpet previously mentioned by Christ in the Olivet Discourse (Mt. 24:31); however, that is not the case. In the Greek text of 1 Corinthians 15:52, the word "trumpet" occurs only once in this verse ("at the last trumpet"). (The second reference to "the trumpet" found in most English translations, including the AV and NASB, is a translation of σαλπίσει, a verb indicating a "sounding" of a trumpet; thus the second reference to "the trumpet" found in most English translations does not appear in the Greek text.) The definite article appears only once in connection with the word "trumpet" (ἐν τῇ ἐσχάτῃ σάλπιγγι = "at the last trumpet"), and in that instance it was necessary for Paul to employ the definite article since he specified the trumpet as the "last" trumpet (contextually, the last trumpet for the Church), thus by the addition of the qualifying word ἐσχάτῃ ("last") making this trumpet definite. Hence, we can make no connection between Paul's statement in 1 Corinthians 15:52 and Jesus' mention of "a great trumpet" (Mt. 24:31) in connection with his appearing.

other, with the righteous entering the kingdom and the unrighteous being cast out (cf. 25:31-46).

The second coming, which is described in 24:29-31, should not be confused with Christ's appearance at the rapture, described in 24:32-42. In view of this, the interpretation that 24:31-51 refers to the wicked being selectively taken in judgment at the second coming, leaving the righteous to go into the kingdom, would be difficult to sustain, since 24:29-31 and 24:36-44 clearly do not describe the same event.[47] Additionally, it should be apparent that 24:32-42 could not refer to the separation of the wicked from the righteous at the second coming, since the scenario described in 24:36-41 indicates that life will be proceeding in a normal fashion, with people eating, drinking, buying, selling, planting, and building, completely unaware right up to the instance of the disappearance. This is hardly compatible with the scenario at the second coming. Thus, is seems impossible that 24:36-42 could have been spoken in reference to the second coming as held by both covenantalists and a great many dispensational pretribulationists.[48]

---

[47] This is discussed more fully in the next chapter.
[48] See the footnotes on pages 15 and 155-157 concerning Matthew 24:36-25:30.

24:32-51 Commentary

Outline

In verses 4-31 Jesus describes the signs that will precede the end of the interregnal age.[1] With the description of his second coming in verse 31 he temporarily suspends discussion of the forward progression of future events. He will resume that progression in 25:31-46, concluding with the judgment of the nations, which will occur between the second coming and the establishment of the millennial kingdom.[2]

[32] "Now learn the parable of the fig tree, indeed all the trees: When its branch becomes tender and it puts forth leaves, you know that summer is near;

---

[1] The interregnal age should not be confused with the Church age, though there is considerable overlap. The interregnal age extends from the ascension of Christ to the regal appearing (the second coming). The Church age extends from Pentecost A.D. 33 to the rapture of the Church sometime prior to the regal appearing. The parables of the kingdom of Heaven given in Matthew 13 pertain to the interregnal age. Although there is overlap of the interregnal age and the Church age, it is important to keep the distinction in mind. We should also keep in mind that the kingdom of Heaven encompasses both the Church and those believing in Christ after the rapture of the Church.

[2] The millennial aspect of the kingdom is the first phase of the visible kingdom of God on earth. One might wonder why the kingdom of God would unfold in two phases (a millennial phase and then an eternal phase). The answer is that the visible kingdom begins before the final judgment on sin, and certain aspects of the kingdom cannot be brought about until all evil is finally dealt with (Rev. 20:11-22:21). Interestingly, this is one of the few eschatological points upon which amillennialists, postmillennialists, and premillenialists generally agree, though they have vastly different conceptions of the nature of the millennium.

Exegetical and Textual Notes

v.32   Luke 21:29 includes: καὶ πάντα τὰ δένδρα ("and all the trees"). Some interpretations of this parable have focused on some property specific to the fig tree, or its historical significance. However, the text clearly indicates that the meaning is not to be found in any property or special significance of the fig tree. The characteristic to which Jesus points can be found in trees in general.

    Matthew 24:32 and Mark 13:28 are virtually identical. Luke 21:29 does not follow Matthew and Mark.

Here in 24:32-25:30 Jesus deals with the question of when the things under discussion will happen, and how the question of "when" relates to his followers. This is in many respects the most challenging section of the discourse, interpretively. Jesus began with a parable. Perhaps there was a fig tree nearby as he spoke. He might have pointed to, or glanced at the tree, but the parable is not specific to fig trees or their unique properties or significance; in fact every tree generally illustrates this point: new growth portends the growth season.

[33] likewise when you see all these things, know that the kingdom of God is near at the doors."

Exegetical and Textual Notes

v.33   All three synoptics are virtually identical, except that Luke (21:31) has, γινώσκετε ὅτι ἐγγύς ἐστιν ἡ βασιλεία τοῦ θεοῦ ("know that the kingdom of God is near") instead of, γινώσκετε ὅτι ἐγγύς ἐστιν ἐπὶ θύραις ("know that summer is near") as found in Matthew and Mark.

The parable pertains to the original question in 24:3: "when will these things be, and what will be the sign of your appearing and of the completion of the age?" Contextually, "these things" refers to the things just mentioned in the immediate context. While signs may not tell specifically when the kingdom will begin, they can reliably predict that it is near. The emergence of tender new growth and foliage on tree branches is a sure indication that the growth season is about to resume. True, it is a gross estimation; trees emerging from dormancy don't suddenly burst out with new foliage an exact number of days before summer begins, but they are reliable predictors that winter is coming to a close and that summer approaches. Likewise, there is to be a period of eschatological dormancy, in which it will appear that nothing is happening; and then, after that long winter, tender shoots will appear, and finally foliage, tiny at first, will emerge.[3] Trees are not clocks, one does not use a tree to tell time, but they are good indicators of when a change of season is near.

When the things that Jesus has outlined happen, it will be possible to ascertain that the kingdom of God is near.[4] The aspect of the kingdom to which Jesus refers is the theocratic aspect, in which he will personally and visibly rule the world (the beginning of which is described in this very discourse, cf. 25:31-46). Of course this cannot be both realized and imminent at the same time. Thus, while the redemptive aspect of the kingdom has been active since the first advent of Christ, in anticipation of the theocratic rule, the messianic kingdom will not be inaugurated until after Christ returns (cf. Mt. 25:31).

> **[34] "Truly I say to you that this people will certainly not perish before all these things come to pass."**

_____

Exegetical and Textual Notes

v.34   Matthew, Mark, and Luke are virtually identical.

γενεὰ is usually translated "generation"; however, since it refers to a people of common ancestry—in this case, the Jews—it is here translated, "people." The term can be used of a family descended from a common ancestor, and hence, "a race" of people (*BAGD*, p.154).

ἕως ("before," or "until") in Matthew's reading, and μέχρι in Mark is best translated "before," *i.e.,* "this people will certainly not perish *before* all these things come to pass." Otherwise, if we use the term "until," that might imply a terminus—*i.e.,* that they will survive only until such a point, which is not implied here.

πάντα ταῦτα ("all these things") refers to the things Jesus has said pertaining to the course of the tribulation.

_____

_____

[3] It is the misunderstanding of this very thing, the period of eschatological dormancy, that gave rise to realized eschatology; for when the millennial aspect of the kingdom did not arrive as anticipated, the church of the second through the sixth centuries simply assumed the Scriptures must mean something other than what they actually said, and they began weaving elaborate allegorical interpretations of biblical prophecy.

[4] Luke 21:31 reads: οὕτως καὶ ὑμεῖς, ὅταν ἴδητε ταῦτα γινόμενα, γινώσκετε ὅτι ἐγγύς ἐστιν ἡ βασιλεία τοῦ θεοῦ ("Likewise you, when you see these things happening, know that the kingdom of God is near"). While the redemptive aspect of the kingdom of God began with Christ's earthly ministry (Lk. 17:20), it will be the end of the age and Christ's return that will usher in the theocratic aspect of the kingdom of God (first manifested in the millennium, then in eternity). Since the kingdom cannot be both present and imminent at the same time, Luke 21:31 has implications both for covenantalism and for progressive dispensationalism, both of which incorrectly view the theocratic kingdom as having already been inaugurated.

This statement has been variously interpreted. Some have applied it to the generation of Jesus' day and found fulfillment in the presumption that this generation did indeed live to see the kingdom of God realized in a spiritual or allegorical sense, or perhaps in some partial sense. However, neither of these views is satisfactory, since in both cases this would require the kingdom to precede the signs—exactly the opposite of the point that Jesus just made in 24:33 (that the signs will precede the kingdom).[5] Another problem is that the generation of Jesus' day did not actually live to see "all these things" come to pass; for they did not live to see the day of the LORD, or the second coming of Christ, which would have to be included in "all these things."[6] Another interpretation is that the future generation that sees these signs will be the generation that will see the coming of the Lord and his kingdom. This interpretation is certainly possible, though its revelatory significance would be questionable, since that fact should already have been apparent from Daniel 9:27. It is very important to note that Jesus appears to be giving a firm assurance, rather than simply stating a fact.[7] In view of the promissory nature of this statement (see v.35 below), it seems best to understand this as a promise to believing Jews that they, as a people, will not perish before all these things, including their deliverance at the return of Christ, are fulfilled (cf. Zech. 14:1-8). We should bear in mind the practical importance of such a promise. During the tribulation the Antichrist will attempt to destroy the Jewish nation and people, especially believing Jews, in order to preempt God's plan for redeemed Israel (Rev. 12:13-17). In the tribulation during the intense struggle for survival, this promise will prove to be of inestimable practical value; they are to endure (24:13) with the knowledge that they, as a people, will make it to the end.[8]

---

[5] In the amillennial conception the signs were largely fulfilled in the experiences of the early church and in the destruction of the temple in A.D. 70, even though such a view is inconsistent with the prophecy of the 70 weeks in Daniel 9:24-27.

[6] Full preterists have tried to make a connection between Christ's resurrection and the second coming, or events associated with the destruction of the temple in A.D. 70. However, any such connection is impossible for the following reasons. 1) He did not come on the clouds of heaven and send forth his angels to gather the righteous and the unrighteous together for judgment. 2) The book of Revelation, almost certainly written after A.D. 70, declares the regal appearing of Christ to be at future event (Rev. 19:11-21).

[7] Note the introduction to the statement: ἀμὴν λέγω ὑμῖν ("truly I say to you"), usually signifying a promise. Also note 24:35, which reinforces the idea that Jesus is issuing a firm assurance.

[8] If we understand γενεὰ to refer to a people rather than simply a generation (on this usage see, *BAGD*, p.154), Jesus would be saying that "this people," the Jewish people, will certainly not perish, but that they will survive unto his appearing, even though Satan will make every effort to destroy them in order to prevent the promises of God from being fulfilled. Satan knows that the *de facto* extension of his dominion since the cross will be over once Messiah appears to exercise

[35] "Heaven and earth will pass away, but my words will never fail."

Exegetical and Textual Notes

v.35   "Never" is οὐ μή, a double (intensive) negative.

Matthew, Mark and Luke are virtually identical. Matthew has παρέλθωσιν, [middle deponent, singular] ("fail"), whereas Mark and Luke have the middle deponent, plural, παρελεύσονται. The reason for the difference is not clear. One would expect the plural, since in all three accounts λόγοι μου ("my words") is plural. Possibly the reading in Matthew arose as a very early variation.

Jesus did not say that "God's" words would never fail; he said, "my words will never fail"—an implicit claim to deity. The peace that attends this promise is inseparably linked to faith in Jesus' identity as Messiah-God. This certainly seems to reinforce the promissory nature of the preceding statement made in verse 34. Believing Jews will be hard pressed, especially toward the end of the tribulation period. The promise given in these verses will undoubtedly give hope to believing Jews living at the most perilous hour of human history.

[36] "But concerning that day and hour no one knows, neither the angels of the heavens nor the Son, only the Father."

Exegetical and Textual Notes

v.36   Luke does not include this statement. Matthew and Mark are nearly identical, except that Matthew appends μόνος ("only") to the last clause, and Mark has τῆς ὥρας ("the hour"), whereas Matthew has simply ὥρας ("hour")—both are equivalent here since "that day and hour" can only be definite.

The original question that occasioned this discourse was: "When will these things be, and what will be the sign of your appearing and of the end of the age?"[9] In responding to this question, Jesus first answered the second part of the question concerning signs that would indicate the nearness of his appearing and the end of the age (vv.4-31). Here he turned his attention to the first part of the question, the matter of timing. Perhaps the reason Jesus dealt with the precursory events first was because that

---

his right to the throne of David, and to fulfill the promises of God to the Jewish nation, and through them, to the entire world. Indeed, the scroll described in Revelation 5:1-14 (cf. Rev. 11:15-18) may be viewed as Satan's eviction order, and though it has not yet been executed, it will be when Christ returns.

[9] Cf. 24:3.

was the simplest to explain; and like the good teacher he was, Jesus moved from the simple to the complex. The question of timing is far more complex for a number of reasons. First, the interregnal period between Jesus' ascension and regal appearing is of indefinite duration, and the approach of the regal appearing and the end of the age can only be adduced as one sees the signs that are proximate to the end of the age (*i.e.*, the things mentioned in 24:4-30). Second, as Jesus is about to reveal in verses 32-42, his appearing is not to be a singular event, as the disciples undoubtedly would have supposed. Rather, it is to be a dual event involving two appearings separated in time: a sudden, unexpected, and virtually instantaneous appearing during a time when life on earth could be characterized as normal, or ordinary; and the other, a protracted, public, and predictable appearing—at least it will be predictable once the abomination occurs in the third temple—preceded by an unmistakable sign, at the peek of a cataclysmic global judgment (24:21).[10] These two appearings are referred to respectively as "the rapture," and "the regal appearing" (or "second coming").[11] The dual nature of Christ's appearing is relevant to the question of timing, since the two appearings cannot occur at the same time. Therefore, it would have been impossible for Jesus to address the question of when he would appear without introducing the dual nature of his appearing. The importance of recognizing that Jesus taught a dual appearing cannot be emphasized strongly enough. This is the first mention of a sudden, unexpected appearing in scripture; and owing to the progressive nature of biblical revelation, the first mention of any new truth often contains information critical to the understanding of subsequent statements related to that truth. One of the reasons that the doctrine of the rapture is now largely ignored at the theological level is because pretribulationists failed to recognize that this passage

---

[10] Daniel 12:11 indicates that once the abomination occurs in the temple, there will be 1290 days, but Daniel does not specify what event occurs at the conclusion of the 1290 days. Revelation 12:6 indicates the length of the second half of the period to be 1260 days. (Possibly the longer figure in Daniel 12:11 refers to an unspecified event 30 days after the second coming.) That the abomination must occur in the third temple is evident from Daniel 9:24-27. At the time of the writing of the book of Daniel (c. 530 B.C.), the first temple (Solomon's temple) had already been destroyed in 587/586 B.C., by the Babylonians. The prophecy of the 70 weeks indicates that a second temple would be destroyed after Messiah's death, between the 69th and 70th weeks. Thus, in order for the abomination to occur in the temple at the midpoint of the 70th week, a third temple must be in operation by the midpoint of the tribulation. (See, "The Character and Chronology of the Tribulation" in the Appendices.)

[11] The "regal appearing" in which Christ will return to the earth to establish the visible, physical, and political aspect of his kingdom is commonly referred to as, "the second coming." The term "second coming" does not appear in the Bible; however, the general term, "appearing" ($\pi\alpha\rho\sigma\upsilon\sigma\acute{\iota}\alpha$, cf. v.37) is used in this discourse and elsewhere, and can refer to either the rapture or the regal appearing, or to Christ's coming generally, encompassing both events (which may be viewed as discrete phases of the same general event, occurring at different times).

(24:36-25:30) describes the rapture.[12] Thus Chafer and most post-Chafer pretribulationists have been forced to argue the doctrine of the imminency of the rapture regressively.[13]

---

[12] Pretribulationism underwent a subtle, yet significant transformation in the first half of the twentieth century. The earlier pretribulationism of J.N. Darby and C.I. Scofield began to be replaced by the pretribulationism of Henry C. Thiessen and Lewis Sperry Chafer, and later John F. Walvoord (see the footnote on page 15). The dividing line between these two forms of pretribulationism centers on the interpretation of Matthew 24:45-25:30. Earlier pretribulationists, while viewing Matthew 24:36-44 as describing the second coming, generally viewed Matthew 24:45-25:30 as a description of the latter Church age, culminating with the rapture. Consequently, they saw support in the Olivet Discourse for the imminency of the rapture. The newer form of pretribulationism differed on this point; proponents insisted that not only did 24:36-44 describe the second coming, but that the descriptions and illustrations given in 25:45-25:30 (*i.e.,* the wise servant in 24:45-51, the virgins in 25:1-13, and the servants in 25:14-30) pictured Israel awaiting the second coming, thus removing the Church and the rapture entirely from the scope of the discourse. While the new pretribulationists held strongly to the doctrine of the imminency of the rapture, they were forced to conclude that this discourse offers no support for that doctrine, since given their interpretation of Matthew 24:36-25:30, the rapture is not in view. (The earlier pretribulationists could at least point to 24:45-25:30 as support for imminency.) The latter form of pretribulationism is mostly implied in the writings of Thiessen and Chafer, and was later formally defended by Walvoord (*Matthew,* Moody Press, 1974, pp.193-195). Its presence in Pentecost's influential *Things to Come* (Zondervan Publishing House, 1958) is mainly implicit (note p.281, and the complete absence of any reference to Matthew 24:36-25:30 in connection to the rapture; also see pp.193-218). The significance of this shift in interpretation is impossible to overstate. Why did the new pretribulationists extend the description of the second coming all the way to 25:30? One reason is purely exegetical: they correctly understood the connection between 24:36-44 and the three illustrations following in 24:45-25:30—a point the earlier pretribulationists had failed to recognize. The other reason is both historical and theological. The new pretribulationists were deeply concerned about the advance of posttribulationism and partial rapturism, both of which drew support from arguments that viewed 24:36-25:30 as pertaining to the rapture. The correct solution to the exegetical problem would have been to recognize that all of 24:36-25:30 pertains to the rapture, but that was an uncomfortable solution since it would have acknowledged a discussion of the rapture on the heels of a discussion of the tribulation and the second coming. In the end, they opted to regard this entire section as pertaining to the second coming. Since most of the commentaries (having been written by amillennialists) supported such a view, and since the original pretribulationists had already taken the initial step in this direction by viewing 24:36-44 as the second coming, it was a convenient solution. Unfortunately, eliminating the rapture entirely from the Olivet Discourse had unintended consequences. The new pretribulationists failed to recognize the primacy of Matthew 24:36-25:30 (or at the very least, 24:45-25:30) to the doctrine of the rapture; for both the particularity of the rapture as an event distinct from the regal appearing, and the doctrine of the imminency of the rapture, are contingent upon Matthew 24:36-25:30. Thus, by arguing that the entire passage pertains to the

second coming proper, proponents inadvertently threw out any remaining support for the particularity and the imminency of the rapture. This crucial error has resulted in the virtual demise of pretribulationism in theology, at least at the scholarly level. However, this error didn't just jeopardize pretribulationism, it jeopardized all dual appearance views, that is, any view other than the unitary view of posttribulationism—which sees the rapture and the second coming as the same event. (Interestingly, it may have been the tension between imminency and non-imminency in this very discourse that gave rise to modern pretribulationism in the mid-1800s.) The new pretribulational solution also resulted in another significant problem: Matthew 24:36-25:30 is explicit in teaching the imminency of the appearing it describes. Thus, if one claims that the passage pertains to the second coming, they must conclude that the second coming will be imminent at such a time as described in the passage (*i.e.*, when people are going about the ordinary activities of life, unaware that they are in imminent danger of impending global judgment). Clearly, given the prophesied conditions of the tribulation period just prior to the second coming, such an interpretation is impossible from the standpoint of a normal/objective hermeneutic. Nevertheless, this is the interpretation offered by the new pretribulationists (for examples see: Chafer's *Systematic Theology*, vol.4, p.367; and vol.5, pp.129-140; and John F. Walvoord, *The Blessed Hope and the Tribulation*, Zondervan Publishing House, 1975, pp.22-24). If one denies that Matthew 24:36-25:30 describes the rapture, an enormous problem results, since Matthew 24:36-25:30 contains the only explicit biblical support for imminency. This is particularly problematic since other avenues for proving the imminency of the rapture, whether historical or deductive, have been inconclusive at best. Pentecost's book, *Things to Come*, which since its publication in 1958 has been considered the *sine qua non* of dispensational eschatology, is a classic example of the new pretribulational quandary regarding support for imminency (see pages 168-169, 180-181, 202-204). Pentecost cites several New Testament passages in support of imminency (Jn. 14:2-3; 1 Cor. 1:7; Philp. 3:20-21; 1 Thess. 1:9-10; 4:16-17; 5:5-9; Tit. 2:13; Jam. 5:8-9; Rev. 3:10; 22:17-22 [sic]). However, upon examination none of these passages directly supports the doctrine. Pentecost does not expound any of these passages; the weight of his evidence falls heaviest on the beliefs of the early church, for which he quotes from *2 Clement* and the *Didache* (pp.168-169). However, when the contexts of these two quotations are examined it is apparent that they were both based on statements made in Matthew 24:36-25:30—which Pentecost and all of the new pretribulationists reject as pertaining to the rapture. The immediate quotation Pentecost cites from chapter sixteen of the *Didache* contains no less than fourteen allusions to the Olivet Discourse, and the quote from *2 Clement* chapter twelve specifically appeals to the Olivet Discourse as its source of authority. Walvoord does the same, citing the same passage in the *Didache*, and also *Constitutions of the Holy Apostles* (Book VII, Section ii, Paragraph xxxi), which contains six allusions to the Olivet Discourse (John F. Walvoord, *The Rapture Question*, Zondervan Publishing House, 1957, pp.53-56). Neither Pentecost nor Walvoord comments on the illogicality of appealing to early church history, while at the same time denying the validity of the biblical basis the early church gave for their belief in imminency. How did the new pretribulationists support the contention that Matthew 24:36-25:30 refers to the second coming? Strangely, the seeds of what was to come in the new pretribulationism were sown in the old pretribulationism. Walvoord, just as Darby, took the position that Matthew 24:36-41 describes the second coming because in the illustration of Noah's day (vv.37-39) the ones the flood "took" were the unrighteous taken in judgment; hence, if one assumes a symmetrical parallelism between the ones the flood "took" away (in the Noah illustration) and those "taken" at the event described in verses 40-41, then those taken in verses 40-41 are to be taken in judgment, which could only be true if the event is the second coming. Starting from that point, Walvoord then argues that Matthew 24:45-25:30 is simply an extension of 24:36-44. Here Walvoord is correct about the connection between 24:36-44 and 24:45-25:30, but incorrect in identifying 24:36-44 as the second coming. As will be argued further along in this volume (see the commentary at 24:37-41), neither the Noah illustration nor the event described in 24:40-41 can refer to the second coming, since an appearing that is sudden, unexpected, and virtually instantaneous, and that occurs at a time when human conditions are described as being quite ordinary—a point explicitly made in the illustration (cf. 24:38-39)—cannot be the same as an appearing that is protracted, public, and predictable, and that occurs at the peek of cataclysmic global judgments at the end of the tribulation. We should also point out that Walvoord's analysis of the parallelism in the Noah illustration is seriously in error (see footnote 20 on page 162). Note that the twin analogy of Lot's day, found in Luke 17:28-29, does not support Walvoord's view that the unrighteous are the ones removed. Thus, the assertion that Matthew 24:36-44 describes the second coming is demonstrably incorrect. The view Walvoord represents also implies an imminent second coming. How does he deal with this problem? Again, working from the perspective that those taken are taken in judgment, he argues from the Noah illustration that once Noah's ark was finished and all were safely inside, the unredeemed could have known, based on Noah's prophetic proclamation, that the flood was imminent; thus in like manner, the second coming will be imminent once all of the tribulation signs have been fulfilled (*Matthew*, p.193). Hence, according to this reasoning the second coming can be viewed as imminent once all of the precursory signs are fulfilled (*i.e.*, only at the very end of the tribulation period, immediately prior to the second coming). But such an interpretation of the passage cannot be correct, since as has already been pointed out, this interpretation hinges upon 24:36-44 being a description of the second coming, which is logically impossible, and since 24:38-39 cannot be made to fit with any biblical description of earthly life immediately preceding the second coming. Thus, the new pretribulationism was simply a logical extension of the early pretribulationists' view of 24:36-44, extending that view to 24:45-25:30. Likely this entire string of failed interpretation began with the mistaken presumption on the part of early dispensationalists that prophecy concerning the Church would not likely be found in such close proximity to a discussion of the second coming. However, any fully developed answer to the disciples' question in 24:3 would have been incomplete if it had not addressed the dual nature of Christ's future appearing, necessitating a discussion of both the second coming and the rapture. Failing to see that this passage implies a dual appearing leads inevitably to the unitary view of posttribulationism. The reason is that the very concept of a dual appearing is predicated upon the fact that one aspect of Christ's future appearing is described as imminent, while the other is definitely not imminent. When we recognize that in this discourse Jesus introduced the concept of a dual appearing, then, and only then, we are able to discern a coherent theology of the rapture and the second coming.

[13] *I.e.*, by attempting to back the doctrine out of certain other observations; for example, the fact that the Bible nowhere makes the rapture contingent upon any other future event. However, such arguments are at best merely consistent with imminency, not proof.

How do we know that Jesus was describing two distinct events, not simply giving two descriptions of the same event? The answer is simple. There can be no question that the description given in verses 36-44 is a coming that is sudden (vv.36,42,44), unannounced, unexpected by the world (vv.36-39,43,44), virtually instantaneous (vv.40-41), and that it will happen at a time when life appears fairly ordinary (note the description of life before judgment fell in the days of Noah and Lot, cf. vv.37-39). Such a description is completely incompatible with the second coming, for Jesus described his regal appearing in the preceding verses as public (vv.27-28), protracted (24:30), and preceded by numerous unmistakable signs (v.30), and on the heels of cataclysmic divine judgments so severe that the human race would face certain extinction were they to continue longer than the allotted time (v.21, cf. Rev. 6:1-18:19). Consequently, these two descriptions cannot refer to the same event, or even to the same time. Recognizing that Christ taught a dual appearing is essential to the interpretation of this section of the discourse (i.e., 24:31-25:30), and it is of crucial importance to rapture theology, since it is Christ's first mention and principal explication of that truth.[14]

Jesus' statement that he did not know the time of this event is at first perplexing. If he were truly God, how could he not have known the answer to this question? Here, for the only time in the New Testament, we see that Jesus' human conscience was not aware of all that his divine consciousness knew. Whether the supernatural knowledge Jesus exhibited throughout his ministry was revealed by the Holy Spirit or by his own divine consciousness we cannot say.[15] When we think about it, it hardly seems to matter which of these is the case. All the things that Jesus knew beyond normal human intelligence were revealed to him by God, and God had not revealed this information. But why is it that this, of all questions, God chose to keep a closely guarded secret, even from the highest of his holy angels and the human consciousness of his Son? If we see this as a casual admission of ignorance we miss an important point, for how could Jesus possibly have known that none of the angels of Heaven knew when he would appear, except by divine revelation? This leads us to an important observation: Jesus' statement was not simply a passing remark; it was a divine revelation. In other words, Jesus and the angels of Heaven not only did not know the exact time of his sudden, unexpected

---

[14] Jesus' teaching concerning the dual nature of his appearing is the backdrop for Paul's description of the rapture in 1 Thessalonians 4:13-17 and 1 Corinthians 15:51-52, and explains why Paul did not need to address the issue of the imminency of the rapture, for that matter had been definitively established by Christ.

[15] It is tempting to link this discussion to Christ's *kenosis* in Philippians 2:7. However, it is unclear whether such emptying of himself involved anything other than his manifest form (cf. Philp. 2:6). Some have held that the *kenosis* (i.e., the "emptying") involved the surrender of the independent exercise of his divine attributes, or prerogatives; however, it seems doubtful that any member of the Godhead ever acts independently, making such a distinction meaningless.

appearing, but they did not know it for a divinely intended reason. One possible reason is discussed at 24:43.

[37] "For just as the days of Noah, so will be the appearing of the Son of Man."

———

Exegetical and Textual Notes

v.37   Mark does not include this. Matthew (24:37) and Luke (17:26) are roughly equivalent, but Matthew reads, οὕτως ἔσται ἡ παρουσία τοῦ υἱοῦ τοῦ ἀνθρώπου ("so will be the appearing of the Son of Man"), whereas Luke reads, οὕτως ἔσται καὶ ἐν ταῖς ἡμέραις τοῦ υἱοῦ τοῦ ἀνθρώπου ("so will it be also in the day of the Son of Man"). Note that Matthew explicitly mentions the "appearing," which is only implied in Luke.

———

With this statement, Jesus begins the first of two illustrations he will give to describe the time during which the rapture will take place. It is important to recognize that in both illustrations he emphasizes the suddenness and unexpectedness of the onset of divine judgment that will accompany his appearing. Virtually all of the commentators interpret this section as referring to the second coming, but that cannot be correct. The second coming will not occur unexpectedly; neither will it signal the commencement of divine judgment. Rather, the second coming will be well announced, having been preceded by numerous signs, and it will bring to a culmination divine judgment having begun earlier in the period.[16] It is simply impossible that these verses could pertain to the second coming.

[38] "For as in the days before the flood they were eating and drinking, and marrying and being given in marriage, until the day Noah entered into the ark,

[39] and knew not until the flood came and destroyed them all."

———

[16] The illustration of Lot's day is inserted from Luke 17:28-30. Only Luke's account mentions Lot and Lot's wife, and it is likely that the reference to Lot's wife and the accompanying material (all of 17:31-33) was moved (post-compositionally) from a position earlier in the discourse to follow 17:30 on the incorrect assumption that the reference to Lot and his wife should go together. However, the reference to Lot and the reference to his wife were made in two entirely different contexts. Lot's wife is used to illustrate an event closely associated with the abomination in the temple at the midpoint of the tribulation period, whereas the reference to Lot illustrates the imminency of the Lord's appearing at the rapture. Because the material in Luke 17:32-33 (the reference to Lot's wife and the accompanying statement) is out of sequence, it has been moved to follow Matthew 24:18 and Mark 13:16. [Note that Luke 17:31 is parallel to Matthew 24:17-18 and Mark 13:15-16. See the parallel texts. Also see the discussion of Luke 17:26-37 in this volume under, "The Structure of the Discourse" beginning on page 21.]

"Likewise it was the same in the days of Lot; they were eating, drinking, buying, selling, planting, and building; but the day Lot went out from Sodom, it rained fire and brimstone from heaven and destroyed them all.

It will be the same when the Son of man appears."

———

Exegetical and Textual Notes

v.38   Mark omits both the Noah and the Lot illustrations. Only Matthew has the introductory clause, ὡς γὰρ ἦσαν ἐν ταῖς ἡμέραις [ἐκείναις] ταῖς πρὸ τοῦ κατακλυσμοῦ ("for as in the days before the flood").

         Matthew (24:38) has γαμίζοντες ("giving in marriage," active voice) and Luke (17:27) has ἐγαμίζοντο ("being given in marriage," passive voice). Perhaps Matthew and Luke each condensed the longer statement differently—one leaving out the active, and the other leaving out the passive.

         The last clause of Matthew 24:38 (beginning with the word, "until") and the corresponding clause in Luke 17:27a are identical.

v.39a   Luke (17:27) reads: καὶ ἀπώλεσεν πάντας ("and destroyed {them} all"); and since ἦρεν (in Matthew) can mean either "to take away" or "to destroy," it is apparent that the intended meaning in Matthew, which is somewhat ambiguous, is that the unrighteous were destroyed, not simply "taken away" (or "took") as the English translations have it.

v.39b   The illustration of Lot's day is found only in Luke (17:28-29); however, it is there carefully woven together with the Noah illustration. The introductory phrase, ὁμοίως καθὼς ἐγένετο ("likewise it was the same"), which in Luke (17:27b) joins the two illustrations, establishes that these are twin illustrations—not in all details, but in the analogical elements.

v.39c   The sentence, "It will be the same when the Son of Man appears," concludes the single illustration in Matthew (24:37-39) and the double illustration in Luke (17:26-30), demonstrating the tight integration of these two analogies. Possibly Matthew dropped the Lot illustration for brevity's sake.

         The illustration of Lot's wife, which follows the Lot illustration in Luke's text (as we have it, cf. 17:31-33), is certainly dislocated. Perhaps the dislocation occurred because an early copyist thought the two illustrations should go together. However, the two illustrations were clearly spoken in different contexts and illustrate different ideas. The illustration of Lot's wife (Luke 17:32-33) falls immediately after Matthew 24:18 (since Luke 17:31 matches to Matthew 24:17-18); and in the reconstructed text Luke 17:32-33 is appended to 24:18.

———

     Jesus gives two parallel illustrations of the deliverance of the righteous in conjunction with sudden, unexpected judgment on the unrighteous. In both cases those to be judged were unaware of their impending judgment until it actually happened.[17] We are told of people who were going about the normal, mundane activities of life, eating, drinking, marrying, planting, and building, when suddenly, unexpectedly, catastrophic judgment fell upon them. It is important to see that the Noah illustration and the Lot illustration are parallel (*i.e.*, they illustrate the same truth).[18] A common shortfall is attempting to interpret the Noah illustration (usually from Matthew) without the benefit of the parallel Lot illustration, found only in Luke 17:26-30.[19]

The meaning of these two illustrations is to be found in their common theme: sudden, unexpected, catastrophic judgment. Immediately prior to the appearing of the Lord at the rapture life will seem normal, with people marrying in anticipation of having families, planting crops in anticipation of harvesting, and building in anticipation of occupying. Then immediately in connection with the removal of the righteous (*i.e.*, those righteous by faith in Christ) out from among the unrighteous, divine judgment will fall unexpectedly. It should be apparent that the appearing referenced here cannot be the second coming, for the period immediately preceding the second coming will not be "normal" in any respect. In fact, only a few verses earlier Jesus stated that the time immediately preceding the second coming will be a time of trouble such as the world has never before seen (24:20-22), and will never see again. Also, the second coming will not be unexpected; it will be preceded by many events and even a special sign (vv.29-30), such that "all the peoples of the earth will mourn." That the world will witness the approach of the second coming is, of course, the whole point of Matthew 24:23-35.

---

[17] This is not to say that they had not been warned prophetically, but they obviously put no stock in such warnings, and thus saw no reason to believe they were in danger until judgment suddenly came upon them.

[18] That the Noah and the Lot illustrations are intended to be understood together can be seen from Luke 17:26-30, where they not only appear together, but the Lot illustration is woven between the two clauses forming Matthew 24:39, which can best be observed from the parallel texts. We should also note that the connection between the two illustrations is clearly indicated by the introduction of the Lot illustration, which begins with: ὁμοίως καθὼς ἐγένετο ἐν ταῖς ἡμέραις Λώτ ("Likewise it was the same in the days of Lot"). Failure to see these illustrations as parallel has resulted in considerable misinterpretation—primarily of the Noah illustration. Jesus' introductory clause to the Lot illustration (quoted above) makes it plain that the Lot illustration is used to illustrate the same truth as the Noah illustration. Thus, it is the points of convergence in these two illustrations that are salient.

[19] Walvoord (*Matthew*, p.193) provides an example of such interpretation. He builds an elaborate argument that Noah and the ark illustrate how the second coming will be imminent once the signs are completed (just as the flood was imminent once the ark was completed). However, this interpretation is not borne out by the parallel illustration of Lot—which is possibly why Walvoord does not mention the Lot illustration.

It should be noted that while most English translations read "…and *took* them all away" in verse 39, the translation given here reads, "…and *destroyed* them all." In another context either translation might be acceptable; however, Luke (17:27b) makes it clear that destruction is the principal idea.[20]

> **"I tell you, in that night there will be two men in one bed and one will be taken and the other left.**
>
> **[40] Then there will be two men in the field, one will be taken and one left;**
>
> **[41] two women will be grinding at the mill, one will be taken and one left."**

———

Exegetical and Textual Notes

v.39d   This statement is found only in Luke (17:34).

The reference to the time of day is important to the interpretation of these examples. In the first example (v.39d), the event is specifically stated to occur at night (in the middle of the night when men sleep). The other two examples are activities associated only with daytime work.

vv.39d-40 In the first two examples "men" is implied from the masculine verb.

v.41   The feminine verb implies "women."

———

This portion of the discourse (verses 39b-41) is almost universally misunderstood because of a failure to reconstruct the text, and most especially to see that Matthew 24:28, as it appears in Matthew's gospel, is dislocated and should appear at the end of 24:41.[21] Once we have the text properly reconstructed, it is possible to see that Matthew

---

[20] Matthew reads: καὶ ἦρεν ἅπαντας, (using ἦρε, aorist of αἴρω, which means, somewhat ambiguously, "to take up," "rid," or "destroy") and Luke reads, καὶ ἀπώλεσεν πάντας (using ἀπώλεσεν from ἀπόλλῡμι, meaning "to destroy"), thus it is clear that ἦρεν is used in the sense of "destruction," rather than the simple idea of removal. Walvoord draws an incorrect parallelism between those the flood "took" (v. 39a, AV, NASB) and those "taken" in verses 39d-41. However, no such parallelism exists since verses 39d-41 cannot describe the second coming. In both illustrations after the righteous were selectively removed from the sphere of judgment, the judgment fell upon all the unrighteous alike. (The unrighteous were not "taken" anywhere; they were simply destroyed, *in situ*.)

[21] Here Luke's order is preferable because the answer (Lk. 17:37b) immediately follows the question (Lk. 17:37a). The reason Jesus' statement in Matthew 24:28 is almost universally misunderstood is due to the failure to 1) properly reconstruct the discourse, merging Luke

24:28 (cf. Lk. 17:37b) is the answer to the question that appears in Luke 17:37a. Understanding the answer is dependent upon understanding the question.

We must not draw a false parallel between those the flood "took" (*i.e.*, destroyed) and those "taken" in verses 39d-41, as is common among some modern pretribulationists (Walvoord, *et al*). Those the flood "took" (destroyed) cannot be analogically parallel to those taken in verses 39d-41 for the following reason. According to the illustration, at the flood there was first a separation of the righteous out from among the unrighteous, not the reverse. The world was not taken out and judged; Noah was sent into the ark, and the door was closed by God, sealing Noah and his family in, and the unrighteous and divine judgment out. After the separation of the righteous from the unrighteous, judgment fell upon the unrighteous destroying all of them.[22] The same was true in Lot's day. First, Lot and his family were separated out from among the unrighteous, and then judgment fell destroying the unrighteous. We should note that in both illustrations God moved the righteous out of the path of judgment; he did not move the unrighteous into the path of judgment. Verses 39d-41 clearly describe such a separation. Thus the implication, insofar as one can be drawn from the illustrations, is that those removed from among the mixed group in verses 39d-41 are the righteous being removed from the path of the judgment to follow.[23] It is amazing that this passage is so universally misconstrued, since it could not be more clear that the picture is of the removal of the righteous from the sphere of impending judgment. To suggest that this passage refers to the removal of the unrighteous at the second coming requires that one ignore the central idea of both of these illustrations (*i.e.*, that the judgment will come suddenly and unexpectedly at a time when life is proceeding as normal); and it requires an interpretation of the Noah illustration that is completely incongruous with the Lot illustration—even though the text of Luke's gospel makes it abundantly clear that these are twin illustrations (Lk. 17:26-30).

In verse 39 (of the reconstructed text) Jesus made an emphatic observation. That observation has to do with both the scope and the particularity of the "taking," or "catching away." He said that in the night the catching away happens there will be two men in one bed, one will be taken and the other left.[24] There will be two men working in one field, one will be taken and one left.[25] Two women will be grinding at one mill, one

---

17:26-37 in the proper place with the Luke 21 account; and 2) failing to align Matthew 24:28 to the Luke account, since it is undoubtedly dislocated as it appears in Matthew.

[22] Note that in both illustrations the point is specifically made that "all" (*i.e.*, all those not removed from the sphere of judgment) were destroyed (v.39).

[23] That judgment is the wrath to come at the day of the LORD.

[24] Jesus specifically refers to this event as occurring in the night (ταύτῃ τῇ νυκτὶ = "in that night"), a fact the significance of which will become apparent as all three illustrations unfold.

[25] The text reads, ἐν τῷ ἀγρῷ ("in the field"); thus both men were in the same field.

will be taken and one left. Jesus had specifically stated in the first description (the two men in one bed) that the catching away would happen "in the night," at the time that men are ordinarily asleep (*i.e.*, not at twilight, but in the middle of the night); then he added that at the same time two men will be working in a cultivated field (*i.e.*, working crops), which the disciples knew was not work suited to the middle of the night.[26] Finally, he added a third description: two women will be grinding at the mill; again, a description of work not done in the middle of the night.

> **And answering they said: "Where, Lord?" And he said to them: "Where the carcass is, there the eagles will be gathered."**

———

Exegetical and Textual Notes

v.41b   Only Luke (17:37) records the question. Both the question and the answer are inserted from Luke 17:37 (see the parallel texts). The parallel statement in Matthew (24:28) is dislocated from its actual position in the discourse. Thus, the material in Matthew 24:28 should be placed immediately after 24:41 to match with Luke 17:37. Note the fact that this statement (Mt. 24:28 and Luke 17:37b) is the answer to the question posed by the disciples in Luke 17:37a— "Where, Lord?"

καὶ ἀποκριθέντες λέγουσιν αὐτῷ ("and answering they said to him") indicates that the question was from the group.

Luke (17:37b) reads, σῶμα ("body"), whereas Matthew 24:28 reads, πτῶμα ("carcass"). The terms here are indistinguishable.

There seems to be no special significance to the term eagles (ἀετοὶ), which can be translated "vultures." There are about a dozen varieties of such birds native to Israel, most of which will eat carrion.

———

The disciples, as a group, immediately responded: "Where, Lord?" In order to understand Jesus' answer, we must first understand the disciples' question. The question was not, "Where will the ones caught away be taken?" They asked no such question regarding those taken by the angels in 24:31. Their question was not about where these will be taken; rather, they wanted to know where it was that Jesus was speaking about that it would be both the middle of the night and daylight at the same time! Being practical men, they immediately recognized the apparent enigma of what Jesus had said. It is only in the light of this question that Jesus' answer, "Where the carcass is, there the eagles will be gathered," makes sense. What does Jesus' answer mean? The question the disciples asked was not about "when," or "how," or "what," but about "where"; and so the answer pertains to "where" *i.e.*, where this sudden,

———

[26] ἀγρῷ is the dative of ἀγρός, which implies a cultivated field, especially since the field is being worked.

unannounced and unexpected catching away of the righteous prior to judgment will occur that it could be both night and day simultaneously. We must excuse the disciples for not knowing what we hope every school child today knows, that at any given moment it is both day and night on this planet. If one speaks of any global event, it cannot help but happen at day and night, and at every increment of time in between; for at any given moment every time of the day and night can be found somewhere on earth. If Jesus were speaking of a worldwide simultaneous event, he, as God, would know this, and we should not be surprised to see some hint of this in his description. However, Jesus was not about to break new ground in physical geography with the disciples. He simply said, in essence, You don't have to worry about being in the right place; just as vultures have no difficulty finding carrion, believers will be found wherever they happen to be.[27]

---

[27] The interpretations of this passage (especially Matthew 24:28, cf. Luke 17:37b) are varied. However, the commentators almost universally regard the event in question as the second coming, at which the unrighteous will be removed. Lange provides a summary of the views of the older commentators. His own view is that moral corruption attracts divine judgment just as carrion attracts birds (J.P. Lange, *Matthew*, in Lange's Commentary on the Holy Scriptures, Zondervan Publishing House in an undated reprint, pp.426-427). Among more recent covenantalists, Boice in his extensive commentary on Matthew does not comment on this passage; in fact, his entire discussion of Matthew 24 occupies less than 4 of the 676 pages of his Matthew commentary (James Montgomery Boice, *The Gospel of Matthew,* vol.2, Baker Book House, 2001). In Lenski's discussion of Matthew 24:28 he notes Luke 17:37 as a comparison, but not parallel text, suggesting that the two identical statements have two distinct origins. (This is a common fault among the commentators, due to the fact that, contrary to the evidence, most do not view Luke 17:22-37 as part of the Olivet Discourse.) In his discussion of Matthew 24:28, Lenski identifies the eagles as the false christs and false prophets referred to in the earlier context, and the carcass as Israel (*Matthew*, pp.945-946). In his treatment of Luke 17:37, Lenski comes very close to the correct meaning, except that he applies it to the second coming instead of the rapture. He says, "the eagles are bound to gather where the body is," and, "The reply of Jesus means: 'Neither here, nor there, nor in any particular place, but where there are men ripe for judgment'" (Lenski, *Luke,* p.891). Lenski clearly saw in the Luke account that Jesus' answer (17:37b) concerned the particularity of the disciples' "where" question (*i.e.*, that the event in question will happen at "no place in particular," meaning it will happen wherever believers happen to be). Evans in commenting on Luke 17:37 takes the position that the point of Luke 17:37 is that, "the appearance of the Son of Man 'will be as unmistakable in its revelation as carrion is to the bird of prey'" (citing J. A. Fitzmyer in, *The Gospel According to Luke*, p.1168, Craig A. Evans *Luke,* in the New International Biblical Commentary, Hendrickson, 1995, p.263). Of course this view completely ignores the fact that the question the disciples asked was not "how" Jesus would return, but "where" the phenomena he described (the "catching away") would occur. Among dispensational interpreters, Ironside views apostate Judaism, centered in Jerusalem, as the carcass and the eagles as the nations gathered against Jerusalem, as foretold in Zechariah 14

"But take heed to yourselves lest your hearts be weighted down in stupor and intoxication, and the anxieties of this life, and that day should slip up on you unexpectedly like a trap; for it will come upon all those upon the whole face of the earth."

———

Exegetical and Textual Notes

v.41c   Luke's more extended version (Lk. 21:34-36) is inserted for Matthew 24:41-42.

———

(H.A. Ironside, *Matthew*, Liozeaux Brothers, 1994, p.186). Walvoord, though dispensational, adopts the classic view found among amillennialists. He says: "Just as when an animal dies, the vultures gather, so when there is moral corruption, there must be divine judgment." (Walvoord, *Matthew*, p.190). Bock, applying this to the second coming, says that Christ's coming will be "as visible as vultures pointing out dead bodies" (Bock, *Luke*, vol.2, pp.1439-1441). All of these interpretations fall short on several counts. First, they fail to recognize that the description given in 24:36-41 cannot be the regal appearing (see the discussion beginning with verse 36). Second, they fail to interpret Matthew 24:28 as the answer to the disciples' question in Luke 17:37a, (usually because they fail to see that these are the same discourse, and thus fail to reconstruct the text, putting Matthew 24:28 where it belongs—after verse 41). Third, they tend to view the individual elements of Jesus' answer as analogical (*i.e.*, the carcass represents spiritual corruption, the eagles represent divine judgment, etc.), rather than that the statement of Matthew 24:28 (Luke 17:37b) as a whole merely illustrates a point—that this event is not unique to a certain location, but that it is truly a universal event. This raises a point that must be addressed. It might be objected that such an explanation would be inappropriate, since carrion would hardly be an appropriate analogy for the Church. However, such an objection would not be valid because the carrion is not analogical at all; the carrion does not represent anything but carrion; the carrion and the birds together (as a whole) illustrate a truth regarding "where" the event is to occur. (If one were to consider Matthew 24:28 and Luke 17:37b as analogical, then Calvin's view that Christ is the food, *i.e.*, the carrion upon which the believers feed, would be highly problematic!) The question of what event is in view here and who is taken and who is left must be deduced by comparison of the particulars in 24:41-42 that precede this statement with the particulars of the regal appearing. When we do that, we see that this event could not be the regal appearing and therefore must refer to another event. That such a sudden and unexpected catching away is clearly described in subsequent scripture makes the identification straightforward, since there are only two possibilities, and one, the second coming proper, has been ruled out. The catching away mentioned here by Jesus can only be the event later described in more detail by Paul in 1 Corinthians 15:51-52 and 1 Thessalonians 4:13-18—*i.e.*, the rapture of the Church. One additional comment is in order. While Luke 17:36 does not appear in the Greek text (it was apparently copied from Matthew 24:40), it is nevertheless true that Matthew 24:39b-41 must be merged with Luke 17:34-37 (which requires Matthew 24:28 to be moved to the end of verse 41) to get the complete text of this illustration (as complete as can be), for neither Matthew nor Luke has the complete text, and Mark is not helpful since it omits the entire pericope (verses 36-44).

πάντας τοὺς καθημένους ἐπὶ πρόσωπον πάσης τῆς γῆς ("all those dwelling upon the whole face of the earth") would be difficult to apply to a purely local view of the tribulation, as do many covenantalists. The tribulation is a global event (Isa. 13:6-14; 24:1-5; 34:1-4). See also the footnote on page 144 concerning the scope of the tribulation.

———

Again, we see that the description can apply only to the rapture. The regal appearing of Christ will not come suddenly and unexpectedly. Although Jesus' remarks were addressed to the disciples, the ultimate audience is all those who will be living in view of the imminent rapture. The trap—the judgment that will follow the rapture—will spring, and there will be a generation that will be caught in this trap. At that time, the unredeemed will be left to endure the terrible time of tribulation on earth.[28] Jesus reminded his disciples that the tribulation is to be a global event—so there will be no place of safety.[29]

> **[42] "Watch therefore, always petitioning that you might be qualified to escape all these things that are about to happen, and stand before the Son of Man, because you do not know which day your Lord is coming."**

———

Exegetical and Textual Notes

v.42   Matthew and Mark only summarize this warning. Luke's more extended version (Lk. 21:34-36) is inserted for Matthew 24:41-42, with the following exceptions: Matthew's introduction to verse 42 (γρηγορεῖτε οὖν, "Watch therefore"), and his last nine words in verse 42 (ὅτι οὐκ οἴδατε ποίᾳ ἡμέρᾳ ὁ κύριος ὑμῶν ἔρχεται, "because you do not know in what day your Lord is coming") were retained. Note that Luke 12:39-46 is parallel to Matthew 24:43-51a. Therefore, Luke's summary of the parables of the virgins and the stewards (12:35-38) places those parables as falling between Matthew 24:42 and verse 43 (see the parallel texts). Alternatively, it is possible that Luke's summary of the two parables was moved to an earlier point; however, in either case the indication is that those two parables were intended to illustrate the event just described in verses 36-41 (*i.e.*, the rapture). It seems more likely that Matthew simply moved these parables to a later point in the discourse where he could report

———

[28] Those left at the rapture may still be saved. There is a common misperception among some that those who hear the gospel prior to the rapture but do not exercise faith may not be saved after the rapture. This is a completely erroneous idea based upon a misinterpretation of 2 Thessalonians 2:7-12, which makes no mention of the rapture. 2 Thessalonians 2:7-12 refers to a delusion that will be sent during the second half of the tribulation upon those who have blatantly refused to accept the truth. Those individuals will be deceived into believing "the lie," *i.e.*, that the Antichrist is God (v.11 cf. v.4).

[29] ἐπὶ πρόσωπον πάσης τῆς γῆς ("upon the whole face of the earth") should dispel any false notion that the tribulation is to be a local event confined to the environs of the holy land, an error common among covenantal interpreters.

them in greater detail, whereas Luke chose to report them in their original sequence, but in a highly condensed form.

κατισχύσητε (aorist, subjunctive, passive, of καταξιόω –"to reckon worthy"). Personal merit is not necessarily in view. The term can mean, "to be qualified" by virtue of meeting some criteria—faith, in this case (cf. Lk. 20:35).

ἐκφυγεῖν from ἐκφεύγω (ἐκ = "out," and φεύγω = "to take flight") meaning "to escape from," or "to make a getaway," hence by inference, "to avoid" some adverse circumstance, cf. Acts 16:27 and 19:16. The idea conveyed is not that one might survive the tribulation, but that they might make an escape and thus avoid the events entirely (κατισχύσητε ἐκφυγεῖν ταῦτα πάντα = "qualified to escape all these things"—i.e., "all the things" previously mentioned). This argues strongly that the rapture is in view, for this could not be applicable to the second coming. Also, the previous verse makes it clear that the things to which Jesus referred will come upon "all those dwelling upon the whole face of the earth" (ἐπεισελεύσεται γὰρ ἐπὶ πάντας τοὺς καθημένους ἐπὶ πρόσωπον πάσης τῆς γῆς). The only way one could avoid such a circumstance would be removal from the earth prior to these events taking place. Although Jesus was speaking to the disciples, it is apparent that they were not the ultimate audience, for they did not survive to the rapture. Apparently Jesus had in mind a mixed audience at the end of the Church age. Thus the idea is that those professing faith should be sure that they possess faith, and are thus qualified to participate in escaping the wrath to come (via the rapture), which would make this warning similar to the many other warnings against personal apostasy in the New Testament (cf. 1 Tim. 4:1-3; 2 Pet. 2:1-22; Heb. 3:1-14; 6:4-12; 10:26-31; 12:14-29, I John 1-3, etc.). The fact that the parables of the virgins and stewards, which pictures a mixed group of those prepared and those unprepared at the sudden appearing of the master (Mt. 25:1-30) immediately follows 24:42, confirms that this is what Jesus had in mind. [By comparison of Matthew 25:1-30 with Luke 12:35-46, it is apparent that Matthew 25:1-30 was spoken between verses 42 and 43 of Matthew 24 (see the parallel texts).]

ταῦτα πάντα τὰ μέλλοντα γίνευθαι ("all these things about to happen") signifies things that are "impending" and will certainly happen, not necessarily what will happen shortly. The last reference to "all these things" (v.33) was to events at, or very near the end of the tribulation period.

Here Luke is quite independent. Matthew and Mark state only: "Watch therefore, because you do not know which day your Lord is coming."

———

Jesus said they are to be "watchful, always petitioning." [30] How does one become qualified to escape the coming day of the LORD by means of the rapture? The answer is, "by faith." Those who are of faith will be qualified to escape and to stand before the Son of Man. Sadly, not all who hear the gospel act upon it in sincerity, and many, even within the visible church will be caught in this trap when the rapture occurs. Matthew's statement, "because you do not know which day your Lord is coming" (Mt. 24:42) and

———

[30] δεόμενοι is the present participle (middle voice) of δέομαι ("to beg," or "to beseech"); hence, the idea is to entreat God continually for one's own benefit.

Mark's similar statement (Mk. 13:33) is yet additional evidence that the rapture is in view, since by the time the second coming becomes imminent, everyone on earth will be aware of what is about to happen, and thus, such a warning to believers would be pointless if applied to the second coming.

———

Special Note:

The similitudes of the virgins (25:1-13) and the stewards (25:15-30) fit here (between 24:42 and 24:43); however, Matthew's order of presentation has been retained (keeping them in chapter 25) to make it easier for the reader to locate the material, and to preserve Matthew's versification of 25:1-30. For the justification for locating these illustrations here, see the commentary and notes on 25:1-30.

———

[43] "But you know that if the master of the house knew in which watch the thief was coming, he would have been vigilant and would not have allowed his house to be broken through."

———

Exegetical and Textual Notes

v.43   Verse 43 parallels Luke 12:39, and since Luke 12:35-38 summarizes the two similitudes in Matthew 25:1-30 (the virgins and the stewards), Matthew 24:43 was spoken after those parables. We must bear in mind that all three of the accounts of this discourse are condensed. It appears that Matthew moved these similitudes to a later point in the discourse where he could report them in greater detail. Luke instead simply chose to report them in their original sequence in greatly abbreviated form.

       Mark does not include the material found in Matthew 24:43-44 (cf. Lk. 12:39-40), but he alone includes the answer to Peter's question recorded in Luke 12:41, which further illustrates that the synoptics were condensed from a longer account.

       Matthew and Luke (12:39) are similar except that Matthew reads, ποίᾳ φυλακῇ ("in which"), whereas Luke (12:39) reads, ποίᾳ ὥρᾳ ("in which hour"); and Matthew reads, ἐγρηγόρησεν ἂν καὶ οὐκ ἂν εἴασεν διορυχθῆναι τὴν οἰκίαν αὐτοῦ, ("he would have been vigilant and {would} not have allowed his house to be broken through"), whereas Luke omits, ἐγρηγόρησεν ἂν καὶ ("he {would} have been vigilant and…").

       οἰκοδεσπότης signifies the "ruler" or, "master of the house," not the incorrect extrapolation "goodman" as in the AV.

———

Jesus introduced the rapture in verses 36-42 and gave two parables illustrating the rapture in 25:1-30. In commenting on verse 36 we asked why Jesus made a point of saying that no one but the Father knows the day and hour, *i.e.* the precise time of the rapture. We must see Jesus' statement in verse 36 as more than a simple curiosity that he as God incarnate would not know this. It is rather that Jesus made a point of stating this fact, and even drew upon divine omniscience, either directly or indirectly, in proclaiming that none of the angels in Heaven knew either. Clearly Jesus was saying more than that he simply did not know this information; he was indicating that it is a secret. Thus, it is apparent that by divine intent, the precise time of the rapture is so secret that God chose not to reveal it to any creature, including the human consciousness of his Son. This is a deep mystery, but here in verse 43 Jesus pulls back the veil of that mystery.

Most interpreters take verse 43 to mean that believers are to be alert for the coming of Christ, just as the head of a house should ever be alert for the thief.[31] But if the head of the house represents the believer, and Christ is the thief, the whole illustration is awry. Why would the believer need to remain alert in order to prevent Christ from breaking into his house? And if this refers to the regal appearing as many interpreters insist, does a thief appear unexpectedly in the night, clean the house, set all in order, settle accounts, judge the unrighteous, reward the faithful, and remain to rule over the house as Christ will do at regal appearing? Certainly not! This illustration simply is not suitable to the regal appearing. At his second coming Jesus will not come as a thief, but as a conquering king in great glory (24:30-31 cf. Zech. 14:1-8; Rev. 19:11-20:3). A thief comes suddenly, unexpectedly, at a time when the master of the house is not expecting, and takes something of value and flees before his plan can be thwarted.[32] It is probably no coincidence that the word Paul chose in 1 Thessalonians 4:17 to denote the rapture is related to the word for "robbery."[33] Thieves do not come to set things right, they come to plunder. In this analogy, the thief represents Christ, and Satan is the head of the house.[34] Thus it is the sudden, unannounced, and unexpected coming of Christ at the rapture that is in view—not the regal appearing.

The question may be asked why Jesus would use such an analogy. If Jesus is the thief and Satan the ruler of the house, how could it be within Satan's power to thwart the rapture, necessitating such a sudden and unexpected, and virtually instantaneous event? The answer is not stated, but we may surmise at least one possibility. It is

---

[31] For example see: Walvoord, *Matthew*, p.194.

[32] This parallels the description of the appearing given in verses 36-41 of a sudden and unexpected, and virtually instantaneous appearing—not at all the way the regal appearing will occur.

[33] ἁρπαγησόμεθα (1 Thess. 4:17, translated, "caught up" in both the AV and the NASB) is the future, passive of ἁρπάζω ("to seize," or "to snatch away"), one cognate of which is ἁρπαγμός ("robbery"), and another is ἁρπαγή ("plunder," or "booty").

[34] The word translated "goodman" (AV) and "the head of the house" (NASB) is ὁ οἰκοδεσπότης, meaning, "the despot," or "the ruler of the house"—there is no implication of uprightness as implied in the AV. In Matthew 12:29, Jesus implied that this world is (presently) Satan's house— i.e., "the house of the strong man" (εἰς τὴν οἰκίαν τοῦ ἰσχυροῦ).

mentioned in this very discourse that angels will be actively involved in gathering both the elect and the non-elect at the regal appearing of Christ (Mt. 24:31 cf. 13:41, 49-50). It is also true that angels will be involved in some capacity at the rapture (1 Thess. 4:16). Therefore, it would not be unreasonable to assume that angels might play some critical role in the rapture of believers from the earth, similar to the gathering of the righteous at the second coming. We do not know why God would choose to employ angels for such a purpose when he could accomplish the task entirely without their help. But God often chooses to use intermediate means, and there is no reason why he could not use angels to effectuate the rapture. If indeed that is to be the case, the rapture would need to be sudden, unexpected, and virtually instantaneous, and imminent (prior to any prophesied signs) so as not to allow Satan and his host to interfere.[35] Unlike the regal appearing, the rapture is not an invasion "in main force," but a hostage rescue mission. Satan is aware of the promise made to the Church (1 Thess 4:13-5:11, esp. vv.9-10) that it will be spared from God's wrath *via* the rapture, and that the day of the LORD cannot begin until the Church is caught away.[36] We may assume that makes the Church on earth a hostage, and that Satan would do anything within his power to prevent the

---

[35] The fallen angelic powers have the capacity to obstruct the work of God's holy angels (Dan. 10:1-21, esp. v.13; Rev. 12:7-10). While they might not be able to prevent the rapture entirely or permanently, they might have the capacity to obstruct it sufficiently to make such an operation unfeasible unless conducted surreptitiously. This still does not answer the question of why Jesus, in his human consciousness, was not aware of when the rapture will take place. We cannot give a definitive answer to this question, but it seems to be implied that such knowledge is kept secret ultimately to keep it from the ruler of this world. How Satan might obtain this knowledge from either the holy angels or the human consciousness of Christ we cannot say, but he is a powerful adversary.

[36] 1 Thessalonians 4:13-5:11 is the principal passage delineating the necessity of a pre-wrath rapture (*i.e.*, that the Church must be raptured prior to the outpouring of divine wrath at the day of the LORD). [Note that the term "pre-wrath" as used here does not represent a particular view of the timing of the rapture, only that the rapture must occur before the beginning of divine wrath. Accordingly, pretribulationism, midtribulationism, Rosenthal's pre-wrath view, and imminent pre-wrath rapturism are all classified as pre-wrath views.] Paul said in 1 Thessalonians 5:9-10, "For God did not appoint us to suffer wrath but to receive salvation through our Lord Jesus Christ. He died for us so that whether we are awake or asleep, we may live together with him." This statement is clearly intended to convey that the rapture of the Church (described in 4:13-17) will occur prior to the outpouring of the divine wrath associated with the day of the LORD (described in 5:1-3). Paul's reference in 5:10 to those who are "awake" (alive) and those who are "asleep" (dead) clearly reflects back to 4:15-18, which describes the two states of believers at the time of the rapture. The contextual identification is quite clear. Thus, Paul explicitly states that the saints, both the living and the dead, will be caught up before the beginning of God's wrath at the day of the LORD. In other words, the extreme terminal point at which the rapture could occur is the moment prior to the outpouring of God's wrath at the day of the LORD. (For a discussion of rapture views, see "Rapture Theology" in the Appendices.)

rapture, which will clear the way for the day of the LORD leading to the end of Satan's rule. Thus, it is critically important that Satan not know the time when Christ will suddenly appear to take his Church, and for the same reason, neither can the Church know. Therefore, the only way for believers to be prepared for such an imminent event is to be ready at all times.[37]

---

[37] Imminency does not mean that the rapture is near, only that it could occur at any moment; that is to say that no signs are designated as preceding the event, hence it is "imminent" at all times prior to its occurrence. The description given by Christ in 24:36-25:30 is the principal basis for belief in the imminency of the rapture (which explains why the reassignment of this passage to the second coming by Thieseen and Chafer in the mid-1900s has thrown pretribulationism into a tailspin, since the argument from imminency was the principal argument for pretribulationism). Generally, dispensational theologians have mistakenly assumed that belief in the imminency of the rapture is compatible only with pretribulationism. However, that is an error that has resulted from thinking of the rapture only in sequential terms. Naturally, if an event is sequential to other events—none of which has yet transpired—it cannot be imminent unless it is the first event. To illustrate the difference between sequential and random views of the rapture, we could imagine a stack of cards where a tribulation event has been written on each card, and the cards have been sorted according to the order of the events. Now let us imagine another card representing the rapture. If we place the rapture card in the middle of the sorted stack (sequencing it with the tribulation events), and begin to turn the cards over one by one, simulating the passage of each event, the rapture could not be imminent from the present perspective, since we could not turn that card over until we had first turned over all the preceding cards. Under such circumstances, the turning of the rapture card could only be imminent if it were the first card in the stack. That's the sequential conception of the rapture. Now let us consider a random conception of the rapture—not that it is random from God's perspective, but simply that it is not tied to the tribulation sequence of events. Here we could use the same stack of cards, but instead of placing the rapture card with the stack of tribulation cards, we put it off to the side, with the provision that it can be turned over at any time, randomly, with respect to all but some of the cards near the bottom of the stack. Even before the first card is turned over, the rapture is imminent. (Recall that it is random, it can be turned over at any time prior to the last few cards.) If the rapture card is not turned over first, it remains imminent until it is finally turned over. Of course, the rapture must occur prior to the beginning of the day of the LORD, i.e., divine wrath (1 Thess. 4:13-5:11); the problem here is that no one knows for certain how many of the cards extending from the bottom of the stack are associated with the day of the LORD. [Pretribulationists assume that all of the tribulation cards are associated with the day of the LORD, but there is neither biblical proof, nor an effective theological argument to prove this; and there seems to be strong evidence to the contrary. (See the footnote at 24:10-12 regarding 2 Thessalonians 2:1-12.)] Applying this analogy, if one thinks of the rapture only in sequential terms, imminency could be considered a proof of pretribulationism. (Indeed, this is the classic argument for pretribulationism.) On the other hand, if even the possibility exists that the rapture might be random with respect to some tribulation events, imminency cannot be used as proof of pretribulationism. In such a case, this would not mean that the rapture could not occur pretribulationally; it would mean only that there is no

[44] "Because of this you also be ready, because the Son of Man will come at an hour you do not anticipate."

But Peter said, "Lord, are you speaking this parable only to us, or to everyone?" {And the Lord said}, "What I say to you, I say to all: Watch!"

————

Exegetical and Textual Notes

v.44a   Matthew and Luke (12:40) are nearly identical, except that Matthew begins with διὰ τοῦτο ("on account of this").

v.44b   The question by Peter is inserted from Luke 12:41, and the answer from Mark 13:37. (See the parallel text.) Mark 13:37 is the last verse in Mark's account. (Note that Mark omits the material about the master of the house and the thief.)

————

Verse 44 is the implication that flows from verse 43. Because Jesus' appearance at the rapture is to be sudden and unexpected, *i.e.* imminent—that is, without signs, it is necessary for his followers to be in a state of readiness always. Again, this could not be applicable to the second coming. At no time since the beginning of the Church age has the regal appearing been imminent, nor will it ever be as long as the Church is on earth.[38] Thus, the application of this statement to the second coming entirely misconstrues the warning. In attempting to repel this objection, some who apply this to the second coming argue that it is the precise moment (*i.e.*, "the hour", rather than "the day") that Jesus was concerned about believers missing; but such a view trivializes the warning.[39] Are we to believe that Jesus' concern in this warning was simply that his

theological necessity for the rapture to be pretribulational. [To say that the rapture "may" occur pretribulationally, is not the same as saying that it "must" occur pretribulationally—which is the position of pretribulationism—neither is the burden of proof the same for these two assertions. Pretribulationists must not only prove that the rapture could occur pretribulationally, but that it could not occur at any other time; therefore the burden of proving pretribulationism is far greater than for proving the possibility of a pretribulational rapture. So far, pretribulationists have failed to meet this burden of proof (see "Rapture Theology" in the Appendices).]

[38] If one accepts the dual nature of Christ's appearing, they must acknowledge that the second coming could never be imminent for the Church, since the Church will be removed before the second coming occurs. The only appearing that could be imminent for the Church is the rapture. Thus, unless this passage has no direct applicability to the Church, which would be quite odd, it cannot refer to the second coming. That the passage has applicability to the Church seems to be addressed in Mark 13:37, where in response to Peter's question (found in Lk. 12:41) Jesus indicated the general applicability of this warning to the group that included the disciples (prospectively)—*i.e.*, the Church.

[39] For an example of this position see, John F. Walvoord, *The Prophecy Knowledge Handbook*, Victor Books, 1990, pp.392-398. The position Walvoord advocates there was popularized in the late

disciples might not be watching at the exact moment of the regal appearing? If that were the issue, wouldn't the catastrophic bowl judgments, the gathering of nations for the battle of Armageddon, and finally the sign in the sky to be seen by the whole world (24:29-30) make such a concern moot? For who on earth will fail to know when the second coming is about to happen? Is not the principal teaching of Matthew 24:23-31 that the regal appearing is going to be unmistakable when it happens? The relegation of this warning to the second coming is simply untenable, for it makes no sense whatsoever.

Now that it has been established that the rapture is in view rather than the regal appearing, we might ask what Jesus meant by, "you also be ready." This is often taken to be a warning to true believers, which results in a somewhat ambiguous interpretation.[40] What does a believer do to get ready? This is not a statement addressed to believers, but to the professing body, *i.e.,* the visible church (prospectively, for its inception was only about seven weeks away). There were in Jesus' day many "hangers on." They followed Jesus, heard his teaching, outwardly acknowledged him as Lord and his teaching as truth, and were in the eyes of men, indistinguishable from genuine believers; but because Jesus knew men's hearts, he knew that not everyone who called him "Lord" knew him as Savior (Mt. 7:21-23). And he prophesied that this problem would only continue to grow as the kingdom of Heaven progressed through the course of the Church age (Mt. 13). Thus it is that Jesus issued this sober warning to the greater body of those who profess to know him: "You also be ready." How does a person get ready for the rapture? The answer is that they must exercise faith in Christ. While godly works ought to follow true faith, it is the nature of the faith that is of critical importance, for works only evidence the quality of faith. It is here that we see most clearly the connection of the parables of Matthew 25:1-30 to this section (24:36-51), for the virgins without extra oil and the unfaithful steward represent those who are not ready at the rapture, *i.e.,* those professing, but not possessing Christ. What will be the cost of such failure? They will be left behind, though they may yet be saved if they eventually exercise saving faith. Undoubtedly many of the first to come to know Christ after the rapture will be those who heard the gospel previously but failed to make a firm decision; though they may have been a student of the Bible, a church member, an officer in a church, or a pastor or missionary, they will be left behind in an instant. It is incredibly sad to think that in the face of so many warnings, both by Jesus, and others, that so many who have heard the truth of the gospel and even the truth of the rapture

---

1800's by posttributionist Nathaniel West in his book, *Daniel's Great Prophecy* (1898), a summary of which can be found in George Eldon Ladd's, *The Blessed Hope,* William B. Eerdmans Publishing, 1956, p.46.

[40] The error of "partial rapturism," that only those believers who are "watching" will be raptured, is based on the false assumption that Jesus' warning here is directed to believers.

will be left behind at his appearing. While they will still have opportunity to respond to the gospel and be saved, there will be no second chance to escape the day of the LORD. In an instant, the Church will be taken, and the door of escape from the tribulation will be shut (Mt. 25:10).

Jesus stated that the rapture will occur at a time when it is not anticipated. He had already told the disciples that it will be like Noah's time, and Lot's time, in which people were carrying on their routine activities, completely unaware of the impending deliverance of the righteous and subsequent judgment on the unrighteous. Even so, in the days leading up to the rapture, people will be going about their ordinary activities. No one but God knows when the rapture is going to happen; all that can be done is to be ready at all times. Failure to do so is to court sudden disaster.

Peter's question, "Lord, are you speaking this parable only to us, or to everyone," is found only in Luke 12:41. Jesus' answer, "What I say to you, I say to all: Watch," is found only in Mark 13:37. Peter was perplexed by Jesus' warning, and he wanted to know to whom this warning pertained. Jesus' answer leaves no doubt that his warning applied to the disciples and to all those who would come after them until the time the event takes place. That being the case, this warning could not pertain to the second coming, since the second coming cannot be imminent during the Church age. It is apparent that this verse cannot pertain to the second coming, for how could anyone fail to know when the second coming is about to happen—especially the saved who will be longing for their deliverance? Those who ascribe verse 44 to the second coming fail to consider the conditions of the late tribulation period. Much of the world's population will have perished and life will be extremely difficult for those that remain. In addition, believers will have to contend not only with the dire conditions brought about by global judgment, but also with extreme persecution. It would not be unreasonable to think that near the end of the period, the hope of Christ's soon return and deliverance will be the foremost thought on the mind of every believer. To apply this passage (vv. 36-51) and the parables of the virgins and the stewards (25:1-30) to the regal appearing is completely inconsistent with a normal/objective interpretation of tribulation prophecy. These words could only have been spoken in reference to an event having the potential to catch those professing belief by surprise, if they should become spiritually or theologically careless—which could only be true of the rapture. If the rapture were to happen today, no one would be more surprised than those Christians who are not anticipating an imminent rapture, which sadly, is the bulk of the professing church. Such will not be the case at the second coming when the professing body will have been purified, and the believers' very survival will depend upon the swift return of Christ. Thus, it should be clear that the warning in verse 44 was spoken in regard to the rapture, not the second coming.

[45] And the Lord said, "Who then is the faithful and prudent servant whom the Lord appointed over his household to give them food at the proper time?

[46] Blessed is the servant whom his lord at his coming finds so doing.

[47] Truly I say to you that he will appoint him over all his possessions."

———

Exegetical and Textual Notes

v.45   Matthew 24:45-51a and Luke 12:42-46 are nearly identical. Mark does not include this section.

The introductory phrase: καὶ εἶπεν ὁ κύριος ("and the Lord said") is found only in Luke 12:42.

Matthew uses the term δοῦλος ("servant," or "slave"), and Luke (12:42) uses οἰκονόμος, referring to a household steward. The terms are interchangeable here (note Luke 12:43 where Luke substitutes δοῦλος for the previous οἰκονόμος).

Matthew reads, ἐπὶ τῆς οἰκετείας ("over the household"), and Luke (12:42) reads ἐπὶ τῆς θεραπείας ("over the attendants").

Matthew reads, τοῦ δοῦναι αὐτοῖς τὴν τροφὴν ἐν καιρῷ ("to give them their food in {due} season"), Luke 12:42 reads, τοῦ διδόναι ἐν καιρῷ [τὸ] σιτομέτριον ("to give in {due} season the allotment").

v.46   Matthew and Luke (12:43) are identical except for the order of the last two words.

v.47   Matthew and Luke (12:44) are nearly identical except that Matthew uses, ἀμὴν ("truly")—a transliteration of the Hebrew particle אמן ["amen"]; whereas Luke (12:44) uses the adverb ἀληθῶς ("truly").

———

Verses 45-51 conclude the discussion of the rapture that began in 24:36 and includes the two parables of 25:1-30 (which fall between 24:42 and verse 43). Thus in the progression of the discourse, when we come to the end of 24:51 the next pericope is 25:31-46. Jesus had already spoken the parables of the virgins and the stewards found in 25:1-30 (though it is out of sequence in Matthew), and briefly mentioned the reason for the secrecy concerning the time of the rapture (vv.43-44). He now makes an appeal that harkens back to the parables of the virgins and the stewards. All who enter into the faith are appointed to tasks and provisioned for the work to which they have been appointed. It should be the goal of all such servants to be "faithful" and "prudent." These are not redundant terms; a servant's faithfulness describes his attitude toward his master who assigned the task, and prudence describes the servant's attitude toward the task itself. Our Lord calls us to be both faithful to him and prudent in the way we discharge our stewardship. To do so is great gain; and it is particularly important that Christ's servants be in the process of doing his work when he comes. Verse 47 clearly indicates that one's future position of opportunity in the kingdom will be determined by present faithfulness to the Lord and prudence in the tasks to which one has been assigned. While all of the redeemed can expect an inheritance in the kingdom, rewards will be given on the basis of merit; and there will be some who will have much, some who will have little, and some who will have none (1 Cor. 3:10-15).[41]

[48] "But if that wicked servant says in his heart: 'My lord delays,'

[49] and begins to abuse his fellow servants, and eats and drinks with drunkards,

[50] the lord of that servant will come on a day in which he does not expect and at an hour he does not know,

[51] and will severely punish him, and relegate him his lot with the hypocrites; there will be wailing and gnashing of teeth."

---

[41] There are several misconceptions concerning the nature of eternal rewards. 1) Rewards in the kingdom are commonly thought of as tokens (*e.g.*, crowns, *etc.*). Jesus dispelled this myth in Matthew 19:27-29 and 25:14-30, as well as here in 24:35-47. The reward Jesus mentioned most is responsibility and authority in the kingdom. 2) It is commonly thought that rewards in Heaven have only temporary significance because the redeemed will return their rewards by casting them at Jesus' feet. This erroneous teaching is based on a misinterpretation of Revelation 4:1-11. The picture in Revelation 4:1-11 is of worship in Heaven. The four living creatures repeatedly give glory to God, and as often as they do that the twenty-four elders fall down and worship, placing their crowns before the throne. This pattern is repeated continually in Heaven. The idea that these elders represent the Church in Heaven is possible, though highly uncertain; and even if so, it does not say that they give back their crowns. How would this pattern of worship be continually repeated if such were the case? 3) Another misconception is that all believers will have equal status in Christ's kingdom. Unfortunately, many Christians think of salvation as a conclusion rather than a beginning. They reason that salvation is all that matters, and since everyone in Heaven will be saved, they assume that everyone in Heaven will have equal status; but that is not what the Scriptures indicate. Jesus said that some would be honored over others in his kingdom, and that privilege, authority, and honor in the kingdom will be given to those who serve him faithfully in this life. In Matthew 20:17-23 we read that James and John and their mother came and requested that in the kingdom one son would sit on Jesus' right and one on his left. The gist of this request was that these two be given positions of honor and authority in the kingdom. Jesus did not deny that such positions exist; in fact, he affirmed it to be true when he said that such positions are "for those for whom it has been prepared by my Father." Not everyone in the kingdom will be seated in the first seat; some will be first and some will be last, and some will be arranged in the middle. But the important thing to recognize is that rewards do matter, and that although eternal inheritance is based upon grace, rewards are based on how well one does at their assigned tasks with what he, or she is given.

Exegetical and Textual Notes

v.48   As noted at verse 45, Matthew 24:45-51a and Luke 12:42-46 are nearly identical. Mark does not include this section.

Matthew reads, ὁ κακὸς δοῦλος ("wicked servant"), whereas Luke (12:45) simply reads "servant."

ἔρχεσθαι ("to come") is explicit in Luke (12:45), but implied in Matthew.

v.49   Matthew reads: τοὺς συνδούλους αὐτοῦ ("his fellow servants"), and Luke 21:45 reads: τοὺς παῖδας καὶ τὰς παιδίσκας ("the menservants and the maidservants").

Matthew reads: ἐσθίῃ δὲ καὶ πίνῃ μετὰ τῶν μεθυόντων ("and eats and drinks with drunkards"), whereas Luke (21:45) reads: ἐσθίειν τε καὶ πίνειν καὶ μεθύσκεσθαι ("to eat and to drink and to become drunk"). Perhaps both are slight abridgements of a longer statement, such as: "and eats and drinks and becomes drunk along with drunkards."

v.50   Matthew and Luke (12:46a) are identical.

v.51   διχοτομήσει, from διχοτομέω, meaning literally, "to cut in two"; or metaphorically, "to punish severely." In the New Testament this term appears only in Matthew 24:51 and Luke 12:46, further supporting the case that Luke 12:39-46 is a displaced section of the discourse.

Matthew reads: μετὰ τῶν ὑποκριτῶν ("with the hypocrites"); Luke 12:46b reads: μετὰ τῶν ἀπίστων ("with the unbelievers"). This ruling servant represents one who is not a true believer; thus the context is established that Jesus is here referring to the mixed body, *i.e.*, the visible church, which is composed of both saved and lost. This is the same body referred to (prospectively) in the parables of the kingdom of Heaven in Matthew 13 (though the kingdom of Heaven extends beyond the Church age).

v.51b   ἐκεῖ ἔσται ὁ κλαυθμὸς καὶ ὁ βρυγμὸς τῶν ὀδόντων ("there will be wailing and gnashing of teeth") is found only in Matthew.

Here, in contrast to the faithful and prudent servant of verses 45-47 whom the master will reward by entrusting to him all of his possessions, we find the wicked servant who will be severely punished. Both have been entrusted with stewardships within the visible church, but one is not a genuine believer; he is a hypocrite as evidenced by his wickedness and his complete failure in the task assigned to him. He occupies a position of responsibility within the kingdom of Heaven (as broadly constituted, *i.e.*, in the visible church), but his heart is the heart of an unbeliever, as evidenced both by his behavior and by the judgment pronounced upon him. Such servants will be judged, and that judgment will begin when Christ comes and suddenly and unexpectedly removes his true Church, and leaves these hypocrites to go through the tribulation and ultimately to be judged at his regal appearing (Mt. 25:31-46) and eventually at the great white throne (Rev. 20:11-15) if they fail to repent and exercise genuine saving faith. The place of "wailing and gnashing of teeth" is further described in Matthew 8:12 as a place of "outer darkness" and undoubtedly finds its ultimate fulfillment in the Lake of Fire (*i.e.*, Hell).[42]

---

[42] Jesus is the source of virtually everything revealed in the New Testament about eternal punishment (Mt. 5:22,29-30; 10:28; 18:9; 23:15,33). "Hell" and "the Lake of Fire" are two names for the place of eternal punishment, and should be distinguished from "Hades" (or, "Sheol"), the interim abode of the dead, which prior to Christ's death and ascension was the temporary abode of both the righteous and the unrighteous dead (cf. Lk. 16:23), but which now contains only the unrighteous dead, since believers ascended with Christ to Heaven. (Hence, "paradise," the location of the righteous dead, which was once in Hades, now refers to Heaven.) [While this view, often referred to as the "two compartment view," is beyond the scope of the present discussion, it does seem to be the best explanation of the biblical data, in spite of the fact that it is widely rejected by covenantalists and even some dispensationalists. For further discussion see, "Regeneration and Indwelling in the Old Testament," by the author (Internet paper: www.biblicalreader.com/btr), 2009.]

25:1-30 Commentary

The two similitudes found in Matthew 25:1-30 were likely spoken between verses 42 and 43 of chapter 24, but in Matthew they are placed after the discussion of the rapture (24:36-51), perhaps due to the fact that Matthew wanted to report them in less condensed form. The evidence for the placement of these two illustrations between 24:42 and verse 43 is as follows: Luke 12:39-46 is virtually identical to Matthew 24:43-51a, and since Luke 12:35-38, which appears to summarize the two similitudes, precedes Luke 12:39-46, it seems likely that the material in Matthew 25:1-30 was spoken between Matthew 24:42 and verse 43.[1]

---

[1] Luke (12:46) does not record the last clause found in Matthew 24:51. Luke 12:35-38 mentions keeping one's loins girded (figurative for remaining alert) and keeping one's lamp burning. Also, verse 36 mentions the lord of the house returning from a wedding celebration. While not identical to the details of Matthew 25:1-13, this appears to be a gross summarization of the similitude of the ten virgins. We must bear in mind that similitudes are broad analogies having a central point with some elements having no significance other than to complete the illustration. Obviously, a summary of a similitude is apt to be a gross restatement of the main point, which here is unabated readiness. If we took the accounts to be transcripts of Jesus' statements this would be problematic, but clearly they are not transcripts and the reporters exercised considerable leeway, under the inspiration of the Holy Spirit, in how they summarized the source material. Thus, Luke 12:35-38 appears to loosely summarize Matthew 25:1-13. Since the Luke 12:35-38 material falls between Matthew 24:42 and verse 43 this likely indicates the location in the discourse at which these similitudes were given. As to the placement of the similitudes prior to 24:43, note that Luke 12:39-46 is virtually identical to Matthew 24:43-51; thus, Luke 12:35-38 (the summary of the similitude of the virgins) comes before Matthew 24:43. The location of the similitude of the stewards can also be seen from Mark. Mark 13:34, which summarizes the similitude of the stewards, occurs prior to the material in Luke 12:38, which as has been established falls prior to Matthew 24:43; and in no case could Mark 13:34 fall later than Matthew 24:45, since the material in Matthew 24:45 follows the material in Mark 13:37 (*i.e.*, Mark 13:37 is

[1] "Then will the kingdom of the heavens be likened to ten virgins, who taking their lamps went forth to meet the bridegroom,

[2] but five of them were foolish and five prudent.

[3] For the foolish taking their lamps did not take oil with them,

[4] but the prudent took oil in vessels along with their lamps.

[5] And while the bridegroom was delaying they all grew weary and slept.

[6] But in the middle of the night there was a cry, 'See, the bridegroom, come out to meet him.'

[7] Then all those virgins were awakened and trimmed their lamps.

[8] And the foolish said to the prudent, 'Give us some of your oil, because our lamps are going out.'

[9] But the prudent answered saying, 'No, lest we not have enough for us and you; rather go to the merchants and buy for yourselves.'

[10] But as they were going away to buy, the bridegroom came, and those ready went in with him to the wedding celebration, and the door was shut.

[11] Then later the remaining virgins came also saying, 'Lord, Lord, open {the door} for us.'

[12] But answering he said, 'Truly I say to you, I do not know you.'

[13] Watch therefore, because you do not know the day or the hour."

———

Exegetical and Textual Notes

v.1 ἡ βασιλεία τῶν οὐρανῶν ("the kingdom of the heavens") is the same as in the parables of Matthew 13—the corporate body of those believing in Christ, which extends from the first proclamation of the gospel to the second coming. According to the parables of Matthew 13 the visible expression of the kingdom of Heaven is a mixed company of saved and lost, though only the saved are truly part of the kingdom of Heaven. As the kingdom of Heaven advances, there will be many who will outwardly associate themselves with the kingdom but are not genuinely saved; according to the parables, they are: seeds sown in unproductive soil, tares, birds in the tree, and inedible fish caught in the net. The fact that in Matthew 13 the kingdom

———

the answer to the question asked in Luke 12:41 that precedes the material in Matthew 24:45-51). Thus, Luke places the similitude of the virgins prior to 24:43 and Mark places the similitude of the stewards prior to 24:43. These complex relationships are best observed from the parallel texts.

of Heaven culminates at the second coming is not an argument for posttribulationism since there is to be a dual appearing, which was not revealed prior to the Olivet Discourse.

ὁμοιωθήσεται ("likened") indicates this is a similitude.

Some manuscripts (among which are: D, f¹, 1195, it[a, aur, b, d, q, r1], vg, syr[s, p, h], arm, Diatessaron, Origen, and others) read: τοῦ νυμφίου καὶ τῆς νυμφῆς ("the bridegroom and the bride"). The original reading is uncertain; however, even if this were the original reading, it would not contravene the interpretation that this illustrates the rapture, since this is not a description of the rapture event, but a similitude regarding how the Church is to wait—with watchfulness. (See the comment on the nature of similitudes in the main body discussion.)

v.4   αἱ δὲ φρόνιμοι ἔλαβον ἔλαιον ἐν τοῖς ἀγγείοις μετὰ τῶν λαμπάδων ἑαυτῶν ("but the prudent took oil in vessels {along} with their lamps"). All ten initially took lamps with oil, as can be seen from the fact that when they were awakened, the foolish found their lamps were going out (v.8, ὅτι αἱ λαμπάδες ἡμῶν σβέννυνται – "because our lamps are being quenched"). The difference between the prudent and the foolish was that the prudent took extra oil in vessels, whereas the foolish did not.

v.5   χρονίζοντος ("delaying") indicates that the bridegroom did not arrive at the time anticipated by the virgins.

ἐνύσταξαν πᾶσαι καὶ ἐκάθευδον ("they all grew weary and slept"). All of the virgins, not just the foolish, grew weary and began to sleep.

v.6   The statement here does not fit with the second coming, for at that time the righteous will not be called out, rather the unrighteous will be removed (Mt. 13:30,41-43,49-50).

vv.7-8   All of the virgins were awakened and all trimmed their lamps, but the lamps of the foolish were going out because they had not anticipated the delay and the need for extra oil. Various identifications have been offered for the oil (the Holy Spirit, salvation, etc.). However, in the illustration oil seems to represent endurance in salvation, not in the personal sense (Arminianism), but in the broader historical sense, meaning that during Christ's unexpectedly long delay in coming, the light of the gospel has gone out in some elements of the professing church.

v.9   The prudent could not share their oil, not because they were selfish, but because it was impractical. They said, Μήποτε οὐ μὴ ἀρκέσῃ ἡμῖν καὶ ὑμῖν ("No, lest we not have enough for us and you"). They were provisioned only for their own personal need. Indeed one cannot provision another with respect to salvation; it must always be obtained from the source.

v.10   Note that the prudent (representing the redeemed) are taken, and the foolish (representing the unredeemed) are left, which is not compatible with the second coming.

v.11-12   This should not be confused with Matthew 7:22-23, which although similar, refers to the regal appearing. (As of the saying in Matthew 7:23 Jesus had not yet revealed the truth of the dual appearing; it was revealed for the first time in this discourse.)

This passage has occasioned much discussion as to the identity of the virgins. However, as is the case with most similitudes, the basic interpretation is not difficult.[2] The similitude concerns the kingdom of Heaven. In Matthew 13, Jesus had taught the disciples that the kingdom of Heaven would coexist with an ever-growing body of people professing, but not possessing genuine faith; this latter group is represented figuratively by seeds that do not bear fruit, tares, and bad fish. He also taught that the kingdom of Heaven would extend to his second coming at the end of the age, at which time the unrighteous would be gathered out so that the righteous could inherit the kingdom (Mt. 13:37-43,49-50). In this discourse, Jesus revealed for the first time that there is also to be a removal of the righteous prior to the regal appearing, in fact, prior to the judgment at the day of the LORD (24:36-51). This event is commonly referred to as, "the rapture."[3] Jesus will mention the rapture again, two days hence, on Thursday at the Last Supper (Jn. 14:1-3); and Paul further develops this truth, primarily in 1 Corinthians 15:51-52 and 1 Thessalonians 4:13-18.

That this similitude pertains to the rapture, rather than the regal appearing, is evident from a number of observations. First, the position of the similitude in the discourse (between 24:42 and 43) places it in the middle of the discussion of the rapture, which occurs in 24:36-51.[4] Second, the picture of a mixed Christianity (believers and unbelievers visibly united in the profession of a common faith) while fitting well with the visible church at the end of the Church age, does not fit at all with the latter part of the tribulation, when believers will face great persecution and martyrdom (Rev. 6:9-11), and after those who merely professed faith have fallen away (24:10) and the non-elect have come under a powerful delusion to worship and serve the Antichrist (2 Thess. 2:11). Third, the picture of all the virgins growing sleepy and beginning to sleep could hardly describe believers during the latter part of the tribulation period whose lives are being spiritually refined (Dan. 12:2; Zech. 13:8-9), and who from the midpoint of the period will be in constant peril because of their testimony (Mt. 24:15-20; Rev. 6:9-11). To

---

[2] Amillennialists view this as a description of the second coming. Even many pretribulationists view it as a picture of Christ returning at his regal appearing after already having claimed his bride, the Church, earlier (see, Walvoord, *Matthew*, pp.196-197). The fog surrounding the interpretation of this passage is not due to any ambiguity in the passage itself, but mostly to a rejection of the clear implications of the passage by those who do not wish to see the rapture here, and who thus feel compelled to wrestle the passage into the context of the second coming.

[3] The term "rapture" does not appear in any of the standard English translations, though the idea is present in the Greek text of 1 Thessalonians 4:13-17. The term itself is derived from the Latin translation of 1 Thessalonians 4:17, in which the Greek word ἁρπαγησόμεθα (future passive of ἁρπάζω {harpazō}, meaning "to snatch away") is translated *"rapiemur,"* (1st person, future of *"rapiō," meaning* " seize," or "carry off"). Hence, the sudden catching away of believers described in 1 Thessalonians 4:13-17 (cf. 1 Corinthians 15:51-52) is termed, "the rapture."

[4] See the arguments beginning at 24:36 in the previous chapter.

suggest that the body of believers present on earth during the latter tribulation period could be fairly characterized as "asleep" (v.5) fails to recognize what the Scriptures say about the nature, purpose, and some events of the tribulation period. The tribulation saints, more than any other generation of believers, will be the ones who owing to their great faithfulness and testimony, will pay the ultimate price for holding forth the truth and maintaining a pure testimony amid the most difficult persecution history has ever, or will ever see (Rev. 6:9; Mt. 24:15-22). Given what we know of the tribulation, it seems far more likely that the tribulation saints will be more anxious for the appearing of Christ than any generation in history, and more so every passing day, for it is their only hope of physical survival. Fourth, the admonition given in verse 13 clearly connects this event to what was described earlier in 24:36-42, especially verses 36,41, and 42 (in the reconstructed text), which as has been pointed out, can only pertain to the rapture, not the regal appearing.[5]

We must be careful not to confuse the similitude with what it illustrates, which is a common error. According to the text this is a similitude.[6] Some interpreters blur the distinction between metaphor and reality by interpreting the similitude as a description of the event itself.[7] While the similitude does tell us something about the nature of Christ's appearing at the rapture, it is not a description.[8] It is true that Christ will return

---

[5] Since the time of Henry C. Thiessen and Lewis Sperry Chafer it has been popular for pretribulationists to interpret the similitude of the ten virgins as referring to the second coming. (See the previous discussion at 24:36.) According to this view, the similitude of the ten virgins describes Christ returning, having previously claimed his bride at the rapture, and calling redeemed Israel (represented by the virgins with oil) into the wedding feast in the millennium; but some of Israel will not be ready (redeemed) and will be left out (as represented by the virgins without oil for their lamps). Although it is true that Christ will return with his bride at his regal appearing, and saved Jews and Gentiles will enter the kingdom with him, reading that into this similitude is highly problematic since we are told in verse 1 that this similitude pertains to "the kingdom of Heaven," and when we look at the other passages dealing with the kingdom of Heaven, not one is limited in scope to the Jewish nation during the tribulation period as this interpretation requires. In every other mention of the kingdom of Heaven the entire interadvent age (which includes the Church age) is in view. Thus, applying this similitude to Israel in the tribulation does not fit the stated scope of the passage, (i.e., the kingdom of Heaven). Also, the delay during which the virgins await the bridegroom is best identified with the interregnal period up to the rapture, not the relatively brief seven-year tribulation period. This is seen even more clearly in the following similitude of the stewards, since their stewardship begins with the departure of the master and extends to his return "after a long time."

[6] Some aspect of the kingdom of Heaven (i.e., the appearing of Christ) is "likened" (ὁμοιωθήσεται) to what is illustrated here (25:1).

[7] This error is particularly prevalent among pretribulational interpreters.

[8] Consistent with the law of non-contradiction, a thing cannot be compared to (i.e., "similar to") itself; thus this cannot be both a similitude and a description of the event itself. Interpreting this

with his bride, the Church, at his regal appearing, but that truth is not in view here.[9] This similitude is simply an illustration of how the rapture event (described in 24:36-51) will occur; it will happen suddenly at an unsuspected time, and some will not be prepared and will be left behind.

Here, the bridegroom represents Christ and the ten virgins represent the kingdom of Heaven (in its larger visible aspect, including all who profess faith in Christ—largely composed of the visible church). During the unexpectedly long delay (v.5), that body grows tired and its lamps grow dim (v.7).[10] When the cry comes to go out to meet the bridegroom, some of the virgins are unable to do so, for they have run out of oil and must first go to the suppliers of oil. These unprepared virgins represent the unsaved of the visible church. They cannot go out to meet Christ on the basis of the preparation of others; they must see to their own preparation (salvation). In the meantime the bridegroom came and those who were ready went in with him to the celebration and the door was shut. Afterward, the remaining virgins came and called out to be admitted, but it was too late; the door had been shut and entrance was then impossible.[11, 12] We are not told if the virgins who returned later were successful in obtaining oil; apparently that was not germane to the point of the illustration.

---

section as a description has led many pretribulationists to connect this with the second coming proper when Christ will return with his bride; but that is not at all what is in view.

[9] It was Paul, not Christ, who first revealed the truth that the Church is to be the bride of Christ, cf. 2 Corinthians 11:2 and Ephesians 5:22-30.

[10] There are several indications in this discourse that the interregnal period is to be unexpectedly long: 1) the comment by the servant in Matthew 24:49, "My lord delays"; 2) the slumber of the virgins as a result of the delay of the bridegroom in Matthew 25:5; and, 3) the long absence of the master in 25:19.

[11] This does not mean that salvation is not possible, only that entrance into Heaven *via* the rapture is impossible. The rapture will occur suddenly, and there will be no further opportunity of escape for those left behind; they will be left to go though the tribulation. If they subsequently place their faith in Christ unto salvation, they will be delivered at the second coming; or if they do not survive, they will be resurrected at the beginning of the millennium (Rev. 20:4).

[12] Here we see a great inconsistency among those who view this parable as pertaining to the second coming, for in the parable it is clearly the righteous that are removed, leaving the unrighteous *in situ*; however, the same interpreters generally regard 24:36-41 as well as the parables of Matthew 13 (cf. vv.30,41, and 49-50) as teaching that at the second coming the unrighteous will be removed, leaving the righteous to inherit the kingdom (see, Walvoord, *Matthew*, pp.193-194). Walvoord waffles on this issue in his treatment of Matthew 13, suggesting that while it is the unrighteous that will be removed, the ingathering of the righteous will occur simultaneously (Walvoord, p.101); interestingly, he fails to even mention this issue in his treatment of 24:36-41 and 25:1-31. How could the unrighteous be taken out from among the righteous (cf., 13:30,41,49-50; 24:36-41) if the righteous are not present? Of course, this problem

There are a number of objections that could be raised against this interpretation, all of which have simple solutions. First, we must ask: If Christ is the bridegroom, would it not be analogically incorrect for the prudent virgins to represent the Church (the bride of Christ), since in this illustration the virgins are not brides but part of the bridegroom's entourage. If we think about it, what this question really asks is whether the relationships in a similitude must exactly mirror the reality illustrated, and the answer is obviously, "No"—that's not the purpose of a similitude. Similitudes are not complete pictures (*i.e.,* descriptions), which is why they are said to be "like," or "similar" to something in some respect. Similitudes focus on only a limited number of ideas or relationships. Here Jesus said that his appearing will be "like" a bridegroom arriving late to receive his entourage into the wedding feast. Yes, Christ is the bridegroom of the Church, but that is not what is being illustrated in this similitude; in fact, that truth isn't even taught in the gospels at all. Here the illustration is about being ready and the consequences of not being ready, and the similitude is limited to that idea. The second objection is that if having oil represents preparedness (*i.e.,* spiritual regeneration) would it not be inappropriate that the unprepared virgins are told to go and "buy" oil, since salvation cannot be purchased by the sinner. Here the answer is similar to that above. The similitude illustrates the need for preparedness in view of Christ's imminent appearing (cf. 1 Thess. 5:4-6). The similitude is not constructed to take into account every dimension of soteriological truth. Third, if oil represents spiritual regeneration, why did the master later say to the five left behind that he did not know them (v.12) after they returned from their search for oil? We are not told whether these five were successful in obtaining oil or not, and it is apparently not germane to the illustration, which is focused on the initial appearing and taking of those prepared. The point of the illustration is that some were not ready when the bridegroom came, and nothing could be done to remedy the situation so that they might enter the feast. This is a sad truth. Undoubtedly in the minutes, hours, and days after the rapture, many will be faced with the fact that family, friends, and associates have been taken and they have been left. In view of this it is incumbent upon those who know Christ to challenge all who profess faith to diligently examine themselves, and to make certain they are truly saved (cf. 2 Pt. 1:10). When the rapture happens, all of the unsaved of the visible church will be left; some will later be saved and some will not, but that is not the point of the illustration. Apparently the statement "I do not know you" (v.12) signifies the eternal destiny of those left who never respond to the gospel.

The similitude closes with this admonition: "Watch therefore, because you do not know the day or the hour." This corresponds to the admonitions in 24:41 and 42 (in the reconstructed text), and twice in 24:44 (in the reconstructed text), which in each case

---

results entirely from the misidentification of 24:36-25:30 as the second coming, when in fact, it is the rapture.

pertain to the rapture. Obviously such an admonition could not be applicable to the second coming, because according to 24:23-27 everyone will know when the second coming is about to happen.

[14] "For it is like a man going on a journey who called his own servants and entrusted his possessions to them,

[15] and to one he gave five talents, and to another, two, and to another, one, to each according to his own ability, and he departed.

[16] The one receiving the five talents immediately went and traded with them and earned another five.

[17] Similarly the one receiving two talents earned another two.

[18] But the one receiving one talent went and dug into the ground and hid his master's money.

[19] Then after a long time the lord of those servants came and settled with each of them.

[20] And approaching him the one who had received the five talents brought another five talents saying, 'Lord, you entrusted five talents to me; see, I have earned another five talents.'

[21] His lord said to him, 'Well done, good and faithful servant; you were faithful over a few things, I will appoint you over many things; enter into the joy of your lord.'

[22] Also approaching, the one having received the two talents said, 'You entrusted to me two talents; see I have earned another two talents.'

[23] His lord said to him, 'Well done, good and faithful servant; you were faithful over a few things, I will appoint you over many things; enter into the joy of your lord.'

[24] And also approaching, the one having received the one talent said, 'Lord, I knew that you are a demanding man, reaping where you did not sow, and gathering where you did not scatter;

[25] And departing in fear I hid your talent in the ground; see, you have what is yours.'

[26] And answering, his lord said to him: '{So,} you wicked and lazy servant, you knew that I reap where I do not sow, and I gather where I do not scatter?

[27] Therefore, you ought to have deposited my money with the bankers, and at my coming I would have received it with interest.

[28] Therefore take the talent from him and give it to the one having the ten talents;

[29] for to everyone who has more will be given, and he will have an abundance; but from the one who does not have even what he has will be taken from him.

[30] And cast out the useless servant into the outer darkness; where there will be wailing and gnashing of teeth.'"

———

Exegetical Textual Notes

v.14   Here we have a slightly more complex analogy than before. It begins with ὥσπερ γὰρ ("for as") rather than the previous ὁμοιωθήσεται ("likened"); thus this analogy is a companion to the previous similitude. *GP* (sec. 228) shows Luke 19:12-37 as parallel to Matthew 25:14-30; however, the context in Luke is two days earlier (on Sunday, two days prior to the Olivet Discourse). That fact, and the numerous differences in the details of the two stories indicate that Luke 19:12-37 was not spoken on the occasion of the Olivet Discourse—though the stories are similar and undoubtedly make the same point.

v.19   μετὰ δὲ πολὺν χρόνον ("and after much time"). Here, as in the previous analogy, there is a considerable amount of delay in the master's return.

vv.24-25   The irresponsible servant is the only one to offer an excuse. The master's assessment is that this slave is "wicked" (πονηρὲ) and "lazy" (ὀκνηρέ).

v.30   τὸ σκότος τὸ ἐξώτερον: ἐκεῖ ἔσται ὁ κλαυθμὸς καὶ ὁ βρυγμὸς τῶν ὀδόντων ("outer darkness, {where} there will be wailing and gnashing of teeth") does not speak simply to being left behind at the rapture, but to eternal punishment (cf. Mt. 8:12).

———

This illustrates the same truth as the previous similitude—that lack of diligence in matters of faith will have enormous consequences. Here a master entrusted to each of three servants an amount of money commiserate with each servant's ability. The master then departed on a journey and left the servants to manage the resources with which they had been entrusted. This arrangement allowed considerable freedom and responsibility as to how the assets would be managed. Two servants were very diligent and produced a substantial gain in accordance with their respective abilities, but the third servant refused to accept the responsibility and hid the money, producing no gain at all. As in the previous illustration, the master was long in coming (v.19). Upon his return, he settled accounts with each servant. The first two, having doubled their master's money were extolled and admitted into the joy of their master (vv.20-23), while the third servant, the one who hid his master's money, was excoriated for his wickedness and laziness (vv.24-30), and his talent was taken from him and given to the servant who had the ten talents, and he himself was cast into outer darkness— undoubtedly an allusion to eternal damnation. The question arises as to how such an illustration could pertain to the rapture, since no such judgment takes place at the rapture. The answer is that the illustration focuses on faithfulness in view of the imminent appearing of Christ. This, and the previous similitude pertain to the kingdom of Heaven (v.1), and the kingdom of Heaven extends from the initial proclamation of the gospel by Christ to the regal appearing. To illustrate how the rapture and the second coming relate to the kingdom of Heaven, we could think of a train with two stops. The train represents the kingdom of Heaven in its broader visible aspect (which includes those truly redeemed and those who merely profess faith but are not redeemed, as in the visible church); of course only the redeemed are actually part of the kingdom. As the train moves forward, the rapture is the first stop, and all who are truly redeemed are taken, the rest are left. The second coming is the second stop; at this stop the unrighteous are removed to eventually face eternal judgment, and the righteous are left to inherit the kingdom. Thus, those who associate themselves with the visible expression of the kingdom of Heaven but are not genuinely saved will be unprepared for the rapture, and those who persist in their unbelief will eventually experience eternal damnation, even though their condemnation will occur at a later judgment, the particulars of which are not developed in this parable.

25:31-46 Commentary

Outline

We now begin the final portion of the discourse. This section, which picks up where 24:51 leaves off, principally describes the judgment at the end of the age after the second coming. However, it also serves another important purpose: that of establishing that the millennial aspect of the messianic kingdom follows the second coming. In the history of the church there have been three basic conceptions of the messianic kingdom: premillennialism, amillennialism (or "realized eschatology"), and postmillennialism.[1] These distinct views of the messianic kingdom not only present different views of the prophetic future, but they also have broad implications for biblical interpretation in general. When the Bible is understood in accordance with its plain uninterpolated statements, apart from extra-biblical assumptions, it clearly teaches a premillennial messianic kingdom.[2] This is most clearly seen in the major passages describing the second coming. Of the three major passages that give detailed descriptions of Christ's second coming (Zech. 14:1-11; Mt. 24:30-31, cf. 25:31-46; and Rev. 19.11-20:6), all three explicitly place the beginning of the messianic kingdom immediately following the Lord's return.[3] Premillennialism takes these descriptions normally in accordance with a

---

[1] Amillennialism is not appropriately named, since amillennialists do not deny that there is a millennium; they simply believe that the millennium is occurring now, with Christ reigning over the messianic kingdom from Heaven. Amillennialism is more appropriately called "realized eschatology"—a view that seems to have arisen as a result of the influence of anti-cosmic Platonism and Christian gnosticism in the second and third centuries.

[2] This can be seen from the fact that those who deny premillennialism both use and defend the allegorization of scriptures where a normal/objective interpretation would lead to a premillennial understanding of the messianic kingdom.

[3] It is often asserted that Matthew 16:27-28 indicates that the messianic kingdom began within the lifetime of some of Jesus' disciples, and that is partly true. Matthew 16:27-28 does indeed pertain to the messianic kingdom, but only to its redemptive aspect, *i.e.*, the inauguration of the new covenant (Heb. 9:15-17, cf. Mt. 26:28). Covenantalists confuse this limited initial aspect of the

conventional and objective understanding of the passages.[4] Amillennialism does not take these descriptions normally/objectively but instead interpolates them (*via* allegorization) to refer to things in the spiritual realm.[5] Postmillennialism, a more biblically conservative view that grew out of amillennialism, accepts a more literal view of the millennium, while retaining the amillennial conception of Christ's rule from Heaven. Both amillennialism and postmillennialism subscribe to a postmillennial second coming.[6]

If the uninterpolated statements of scripture present a premillennial picture of the messianic kingdom, how did amillennialism and postmillennialism arise? Historically, there can be no serious doubt that the early church understood the prophecies of the millennium in a premillennial sense.[7] Justin Martyr provides an excellent example of premillennialism in the early to mid-second century.[8] However, gnosticism, with its allegorization of the Old Testament and anti-Semitism and replacement theology, was likely the source of amillennialism in the second century

---

kingdom with the messianic rule of Christ on earth that will be manifested in the millennium and beyond; thus, they confuse "the part" for "the whole." This is not a benign error, for in so doing they distort many scriptures in their attempt to bring order to the chaos created by their own defective view of the kingdom.

[4] By "conventional" is meant, "in accordance with the usual conventions of language," *i.e.*, such that the message is interpreted using the same conventions of language that were used in its composition (*i.e.*, grammatical-historical interpretation).

[5] "Interpolation" is a process by which an interpretation is made based on assumptions about what the text says, rather than by what the text actually says. Amillennial interpolation often involves the allegorization of passages in order to avoid their normal/objective meaning (see, "Hermeneutics," beginning on page 17).

[6] In time past both amillennialism and postmillennialism were referred to simply as "postmillennialism," with one view holding to realized eschatology and the other to a futurist view of the kingdom, but with Christ ruling from Heaven. Today, amillennialism is often a blending of both the realized view and the futurist view of the kingdom.

[7] The Jewish expectation (except for the Sadducees and others who rejected much of the OT) was that Messiah would come and personally establish his kingdom. This view, which was based on a normal/objective understanding of OT prophecy, was carried over into the NT. From the very beginning, NT eschatology was merely an extension of OT eschatology as is demonstrated by the fact that in this very discourse Jesus stated that the key to understanding his teaching is to understand the book of Daniel (cf. Mt. 24:15). Additionally, it is clear that the very early church was premillennial. In fact, while the eastern church converted to amillennialism in the second century, most likely due to the influence of the dominant Greek culture and philosophy and the influence of gnosticism, premillennialism remained the dominant view in the western church through the fifth century.

[8] Cf. *Dialogue With Trypho* (chapters LXXX-LXXXI).

church.[9] Postmillennialism, which only developed in the post-reformation era, was simply a derivative of amillennialism, and has since been largely reabsorbed back into amillennialism, though currently there seems to be some revival of the view.

How do amillennialists justify their view of the kingdom? Generally, they point out that Christ's kingdom was present spiritually during his earthly ministry, as evidenced by his authority over the powers of darkness, and that he explicitly stated that his kingdom was "not of this world" (Jn. 18:36). This is then used to support the idea that the kingdom is essentially spiritual (*i.e.*, not physical), and thus to justify the interpolation of all other biblical prophecy in such a way as to conform to a spiritual (non-material) view of the kingdom. Of course such interpolations are not compatible with the normal, conventional meaning of the biblical statements, and this process requires a normal/objective system of hermeneutics for prophecy already fulfilled (such as the prophecies of the first advent) and a non-conventional (subjective, allegorical) system of hermeneutics for those yet to be fulfilled—except for those prophecies the amillennialist wishes to view literally. From a strictly logical standpoint, such a view is an epistemological nightmare leading inexorably to the conclusion that such prophetic material has no objective meaning at all (which sadly, is reflected in the state of many amillennial institutions). To some degree dispensationalists have exacerbated this problem by failing to acknowledge that the kingdom of God has been present from the time of Christ's initial proclamation of the gospel, or at the very least from the time of his crucifixion (Mt. 16:28). Undoubtedly the dispensational reluctance to acknowledge this is due to concern that such an acknowledgment might be misinterpreted to agree with amillennialism, since amillennialists characteristically confuse the initial spiritual aspect of the kingdom (the proclamation of the gospel and the inauguration of the new covenant) with the entirety of the kingdom program, including the messianic reign in the millennium and beyond. Nevertheless, dispensationalists are wrong in failing to acknowledge that at least one aspect of the kingdom—its redemptive aspect—has been active throughout the Church age. Without any basis in logical or theological necessity,

---

[9] Gnosticism was a blending of Christianity with Greek philosophy and mythology (Platonism and stoicism). The result of this fusion was an allegorical view of Christian themes that was decidedly anti-cosmic and anti-Semitic. Gnosticism was widespread in the church in the second and third centuries. Valentinus, a leading gnostic, was nominated to be the Bishop of Rome (c.143) and was only narrowly defeated. While most of the distinctly gnostic doctrines were eventually condemned, some ideas persisted, particularly the allegorization of the Old Testament, cosmic dualism, anti-Semitism, replacement theology, and realized eschatology. Pétrement says that both Origen and Augustine were "profoundly influenced by gnosticism and to a large extent incorporated it into their doctrines" (Simone Pétrement, *A Separate God: the Origins and Teachings of Gnosticism*, HarperSanFrancisco, 1990, p.24). The gnostic worldview is the most likely source of amillennialism in the church, though amillennialism was not codified in the western church until after Augustine.

amillennialists portray the spiritual aspect of the kingdom as incompatible with a material aspect. It seems inconceivable to them that the kingdom could encompass both the spiritual and the material realms. Perhaps this is due to amillennialism's roots, and hence its interpretive history in anti-cosmic dualism.[10] If one assumes that redemption will extend to the physical creation, a doctrine plainly taught in the New Testament (Rm. 8:20-21), what logic decrees that the kingdom could not be manifested in the material realm—just as taught in the Old Testament and in Revelation? Indeed, since Adam's sin affected not only his spiritual condition, but also the material world, why would we not expect redemption to extend to both the spiritual and the material world? Is redemption only a "patch" designed to fix part of the problem brought about by sin? Apparently, amillennialists do not see that in calling into question the redemption of the material creation, they call into question the entire redemption program; for how can man, who is both spiritual and material, be redeemed if the redemption does not extend to the material realm? [11] Of course, the denial of the redemption of the physical creation calls into question the significance of Christ's bodily resurrection, which is no doubt why some amillennialists prefer to view the resurrection as a purely spiritual event.[12]

The thing to keep in mind is that both the Old and New Testaments unequivocally present a premillennial view of the kingdom, and that fact was clearly recognized by the early church prior to the Hellenization of the church in the second century. Attempts by amillennialists to re-characterize the Old Testament and the book of Revelation after the pattern of realized eschatology greatly misrepresents the biblical facts.[13]

---

[10] Amillennialism, like gnosticism, is fundamentally dualistic. For a discussion of the anticosmic character of amillennialism and its gnostic roots see, "The Non-Christian Anticosmic Roots of Amillennialism," by the author (Internet paper available at: www.biblicalreader.com/btr), 2006.

[11] This is the argument Paul made in Romans 8:18-25 and also in 1 Corinthians 15:12-19.

[12] This is the view held by full preterism.

[13] As an example of how far amillennialists have gone to read amillennialism into the Bible, consider "progressive parallelism," or what is sometimes referred to as "the recapitulation theory." The prototype of this view originated in the forth century with Tychonius (Tichonius), a North African Donatist, and was popularized by Augustine. Progressive parallelism is a scheme for reversing the order of events in Revelation 19 and 20 (second coming [chp. 19] > millennium [chp. 20]) so that they can be made to fit with amillennialism (millennium [chp. 20] > second coming [chp. 19]). This scheme proposes that Revelation gives the history of the Church from the first coming to the second coming in seven parallel accounts, or "recapitulation cycles" (chapters 1-3, 4-7, 8-11, 12-14, 15-16, 17-19, and 20-22). According to this view, Revelation gives the history of the Church seven times in different ways. By breaking the text between chapters 19 and 20, between the description of the second coming and the description of the millennium, amillennialists claim that the second coming occurs at the end of Church history, whereas the millennium occurs at the beginning of Church history, and thus the millennium described in

[31] "But when the Son of Man comes in his glory and all the angels with him, then he will sit on his glorious throne;

[32] And all the nations will be gathered before him, and he will separate them from one another, as the shepherd separates the sheep from the goats;

[33] and he will set the sheep on his right, but the goats on the left."

Exegetical and Textual Notes

v.31   The relationship established by ὅταν // τότε ("when" // "then") clearly establishes the second coming as the time at which Christ will take his seat on the throne of his kingdom. [Roberson discusses the use of ὅταν in temporal clauses only generally, *RGGNT*, p.971-974. Bauer cites Matthew 25:31 as an example in sec. 1b, *BAGD*, p.587. According to Bauer, ὅταν establishes the condition that is to be met before a specified action occurs. In this case, the time at which Christ will sit on his glorious throne is specified in the adjectival clause, *"when* he comes in his glory and all the angels with him," *i.e.*, at his second coming.] If the throne mentioned here is not the throne of Christ's kingdom, then what throne is it? Although θρόνου ("throne") appears without the article, it is nonetheless definite since it is qualified as "his glorious throne," of which there could be no other.

v.32   πάντα τὰ ἔθνη ("all nations") indicates the scope of this judgment. It will include all of those who are alive and remain until the second coming. Whereas ἔθνη ("nations") is neuter, the pronoun αὐτούς ("them") in ἀφορίσει αὐτούς ("separate *them*") is masculine. This reflects that while the nations will be gathered, the judgment is not on a national basis. According to a comparison of Matthew 13:41-43 and 49-50 with 24:31, the angels will gather both the righteous and the unrighteous at the end of the age. Thus, the nations will be present, but they will not be grouped as nations, rather, the individuals of all nations will be gathered and then separated according to the status of each person, whether righteous (on the basis of faith) or unrighteous. It is these two groups to which αὐτούς refers.[14] These two groups will then be

---

chapter 20 actually occurs (in time) before the second coming described in chapter 19. Of course this structure is completely alien to the book of Revelation, for there is nothing in the book to suggest such a structure, and much to preclude it. It would be completely unnatural to split Revelation in the manner proposed by this scheme since the section from 19:11 to 21:8 comprises one long series of copulative statements, each of which begins with καὶ εἶδον ("and I saw," cf. 19:11,17,19; 21:1,4). It is almost as if the text were structured in such a way as to prevent the insertion of a break anywhere between 19:11 to 20:8. We should remember too that both Zechariah 14 and Matthew 24-25 present the same sequence (second coming > millennium) found in Revelation 19:11-20:8; thus, all three accounts are uniform in presenting the second coming as premillennial.

[14] Mounce assumes that the change of gender between ἔθνη ("nations" –neuter) and αὐτούς ("them" –masculine) indicates an individual judgment (see, Robert H. Mounce, *Matthew*, in the

judged summarily (as groups). The individual judgment of the unrighteous will occur later, before the great white throne (Rev. 20:11-15).

———

Here as elsewhere, the error of realized eschatology is evident. Certainly Jesus was referring to the throne of the messianic kingdom—what other throne could it be?[15] And there can be no doubt that the description of his coming in glory with all of the angels harkens back to 24:30-31, referring to the second coming. It is also clear that Jesus explicitly stated that he will take his seat upon (*i.e.*, ascend to) that throne when he comes at his second coming, which is entirely consistent with the picture given in each of the other two major descriptions of the second coming (Zech. 14, and Rev. 19:11-20:3). Of course it is apparent that if he does not ascend to the throne of his kingdom until his return, he could not now be seated upon that throne in Heaven as the amillennialists claim.[16] The options here for the amillennialists are limited. Since it would be difficult to

———

New International Biblical Commentary, 1991, pp.235-236), but that is only partly correct, for the description is clearly that of a summary judgment. Apparently Christ will separate individuals into two groups and then pass judgment summarily on each group. There will be an individual judgment of the unrighteous, including their status and deeds, before the great throne of Revelation 20:11-15, but that judgment takes place after the millennium, and it is described in completely different terms. Those who appear at the judgment described here, in Matthew 25:31-46, are those who have survived the tribulation; there is no mention of the resurrection of the dead. The judgment described in Revelation 20:11-15 states that all of the dead, which at that point will include all the unrighteous, will be resurrected and then judged individually. Thus, the two descriptions pertain to two distinct judgments: the first, a summary judgment to determine who enters the millennial phase of the kingdom, and the second, a final, individual judgment of the unrighteous prior to the beginning of the eternal phase of the kingdom. Consequently, the unrighteous who survive the tribulation and are judged summarily at the judgment described in Matthew 25:31-46 will be resurrected and judged individually after the millennium and before the eternal phase of the kingdom begins.

[15] This throne and the judgment are described as being on earth, after the second coming. What throne has Christ on earth other than the throne of the messianic kingdom? This is precisely the picture given in Zechariah 14:1-21, which describes the second coming and Messiah's subsequent reign upon the earth as King (see esp. vv.9, 16-17), and in Revelation 19:11-20:4. That the Scriptures of both the Old and New Testaments explicitly teach the premillennial return of Christ to establish his kingdom is one of the most well-attested facts of the Bible.

[16] Luke 22:69 and Colossians 3:1 refer to Christ as seated at the right hand of God. Undoubtedly as God he has a heavenly throne. But the throne of Heaven is not the throne of the messianic kingdom, nor is it ever portrayed as such. The Jews of Jesus' day who accepted the prophecies of a messianic kingdom, including the disciples to whom Jesus here spoke, understood the Old Testament to teach that the messianic throne would be an earthly throne, and while Jesus never hesitated to correct their mistaken ideas, he offered no correction on this point, rather he reinforced it by this statement. The throne mentioned here could only be the messianic throne

argue that this is not the second coming, and since it is apparent that this throne could not be anything other than the throne of the messianic kingdom (for it is the earthly throne of Christ, explicitly referred to as "his glorious throne"), most amillennial interpreters choose to ignore the reference to the throne and to focus on the judgment described in the subsequent verses.[17]

When Christ returns with the angels and takes his seat on his glorious throne, all the peoples of the earth will be gathered before him. Jesus had already taught in Matthew 13:41-42 and verses 49-50 that the angels will gather the unrighteous at the second coming. And in 24:30-31 he said that the angels will gather his elect (the righteous by faith) at his return. Thus, the scene at the second coming is as follows: The angels will gather both the righteous and the unrighteous of all nations before Christ. Christ will then separate them into two groups, placing one group on his right and the other on his left. (This might seem impractical given the present world population, but the population of the earth will be greatly reduced by this point in time, and this description is certainly cursory.) The simile of the shepherd provides a mental picture, as a shepherd of sheep and goats would use his staff to direct the sheep in one direction and the goats in the other as they entered their folds. We should not make the mistake of thinking that because a simile is used to provide a mental picture that this judgment is not literal; literal truths are often illustrated by such figures.

> **[34] "Then the King will say to the ones on his right, 'Come, those blessed of my Father, inherit the kingdom prepared for you from the foundation of the world.**
>
> **[35] For I was hungry and you gave me something to eat; I was thirsty and you gave me something to drink; I was a stranger and you took me in,**

---

and no other; and it is highly significant that Jesus explicitly stated that he will take his seat on that throne when (ὅταν) he returns in glory with all the angels. (See the exegetical and textual notes section concerning verse 31.) This is precisely as pictured in Zechariah 14:1-21 and Revelation 19:11-20:4. Sadly, attention to this one very plain detail could have spared the Church almost two thousand years of replacement theology and realized eschatology, along with all of the damage that has resulted from the allegorization of the biblical text to support these corrupt theories.

[17] Among them are: Lange (*Matthew*), J.C. Ryle (*Matthew-Mark,* vol. 1 in Ryle's Expository Thoughts on the Gospels, Baker Book House, 1977), Lenski (*Matthew*), and Boice (*Matthew,* vol.2). Riddlebarger, in his defense of amillennialism, devotes twenty pages to the discussion of the Olivet Discourse, but he too fails to comment on the obvious implication of this verse (*A Case for Amillennialism*, pp.160-179). Clearly amillennialists are uncomfortable with the implication of this statement.

[36] naked and you clothed me, sick and you visited me; I was in prison and you came to me.'

[37] Then the righteous will answer him saying, 'Lord, when did we see you hungering and feed you, or thirsty and give you drink?

[38] And when did we see you a stranger and take you in, or naked and clothe you?

[39] And when did we see you sick or in prison and come to visit you?'

[40] And answering the King will say to them, 'Truly I tell you, inasmuch as you did it to one of the least of these my brethren, you did it to me.'

[41] Then he will also say to the ones on the left, 'Depart from me accursed ones into the eternal fire prepared for the Devil and his angels;

[42] For I hungered and you did not give me {anything} to eat, I thirsted and you did not give me anything to drink.

[43] I was a stranger and you did not take me in, naked and you did not clothe me, sick and in prison and you did not visit me.'

[44] Then they also will answer saying, 'Lord, when did we see you hungering or thirsting or a stranger or naked or sick or in prison and did not minister to you?'

[45] Then he will answer them saying, 'Truly I say to you, inasmuch as you did it not to one of the least of these, neither did you do it to me.'

[46] And these will go away into eternal punishment, but the righteous into eternal life."

––––––

Exegetical and Textual Notes

v.34 Here in referring to himself prior to taking his seat on the throne, Jesus uses the title "Son of Man" (v.31), but after ascending to the throne he uses the title, "the King" (ὁ βασιλεὺς).

Δεῦτε ("Come!") has the force of an imperative. By this the King bids them to join him in the kingdom, which having been prepared from the foundation of the world is now to unfold. Note the contrast with, Πορεύεσθε ἀπ' ἐμοῦ ("Depart from me") in verse 41.

Not only are they bid "Come," but to inherit (κληρονομήσατε –aorist, indicating definitive action) *i.e.*, to take possession of the kingdom.

ἡτοιμασμένην ("having been prepared") is a perfect passive participle. The idea is not that God has been preparing the kingdom since the foundation of the world, but that it has been prepared since the foundation of the world.

v.40   ἐνὶ τούτων τῶν ἀδελφῶν μου τῶν ἐλαχίστων ("to one of the least of my brothers") The King is obviously speaking to the audience on his right, and therefore must be referring to their treatment of a particular subset of believers to whom he refers as, "my brothers." This subset would have to be either persecuted Gentile believers or persecuted Jewish believers. Given that this discourse is focused primarily on the Jewish people in the tribulation, it seems likely that the King has in mind the aid and comfort that Gentile believers rendered to persecuted Jewish believers during the tribulation. The Church, having already been raptured, is not included in this judgment. This is the judgment of those saved after the rapture that survive unto the Lord's coming. The millennium was promised to believing Israel, and while these believing Gentiles are invited to share in that blessing, they do so out of the overflow of God's grace to Israel (cf. Gen. 12:1-3); this statement is a joyous reminder of that blessed relationship.

v.41   Πορεύεσθε ἀπ' ἐμοῦ ("Depart from me") is the antithesis of Δεῦτε ("Come!") in verse 34.

        εἰς τὸ πῦρ τὸ αἰώνιον τὸ ἡτοιμασμένον τῷ διαβόλῳ καὶ τοῖς ἀγγέλοις αὐτοῦ ("into the eternal fire prepared for the devil and his angels"), cf. verse 46. This presents a problem in that Revelation 20:11-15 indicates that the unrighteous will not be consigned to the Lake of Fire until the judgment at the great throne following the millennium. This problem is resolved if we understand the statements here and in verse 46 not as immediate, but as ultimate; in other words, the Lake of Fire is to be their ultimate, though not immediate destination.

———

Having made the separation, the King will bid those on his right to inherit the kingdom prepared for them from the foundation of the world. One does not inherit the fruit of their own labor, but what another bequeaths. The idea conveyed by the expression, "prepared for you from the foundation of the world," is not that the kingdom has been in a perpetual state of preparation since the foundation of the world, but that from the dawn of creation, the kingdom was already prepared, awaiting only the perfection of God's elect. In this sense, the kingdom of God is not of this world (Jn. 18:36), though it will be manifested in and through this world. In this the sovereignty of God is evident, for the kingdom has never been contingent upon man or man's actions, but only upon God. Whether they realize it or not, ultimately, men always carry out the grand purpose of God who works all things after the counsel of his own will (Eph. 1:11). This is a deep mystery, which no human mind can fully comprehend. God has worked his own will in human history since the beginning.

The description given of those on the right is not the criteria for judgment, but the characteristics of the truly righteous. They are those whose lives displayed their true spiritual nature in the practical treatment of elect Jews who will be severely persecuted during the tribulation. Note that the entire description is practical: providing water, food, clothing, and visitation of those sick and in prison.

Likewise those on the left will be commanded to depart into the eternal fire prepared for the Devil and his angels. Because Revelation 20:11-15 pictures the dead as being raised and judged individually after the millennium before being consigned to the

Lake of Fire, we may assume that the account given here was greatly condensed by the Lord. They will not be allowed to enter the kingdom; thus it seems apparent that they will perish and be raised after the millennium to face individual judgment at the great white throne described in Revelation 20:11-15.

Appendix: Daniel 9:24-27 - The Prophecy of the 70 Weeks

The prophecy of the 70 weeks of Israel was given in answer to Daniel's prayer recorded in Daniel 9:3-19. In this prophecy the angel Gabriel revealed God's program for Israel's future. Jesus referred to the prophecy in Matthew 24:15 and indicated that understanding this prophecy is essential to understanding his Olivet Discourse. Since the 70 weeks prophecy reveals the key chronological features of Israel's history from the decree to restore Jerusalem, up to the establishment of the millennial kingdom, it is the key to understanding events leading up to the second coming of Christ, most particularly the events of the tribulation period. Thus the 70 weeks prophecy provides the chronological structure for understanding both Jesus' Olivet Discourse and much of the book of Revelation. The prophecy reads as follows:

> 24"Seventy weeks have been decreed for your people and your holy city, to finish the transgression, to make an end of sin, to make atonement for iniquity, to bring in everlasting righteousness, to seal up vision and prophecy and to anoint the most holy place.

> 25"So you are to know and discern that from the issuing of a decree to restore and rebuild Jerusalem until Messiah the Prince there will be seven weeks and sixty-two weeks; it will be built again, with plaza and moat, even in times of distress.

> 26"Then after the sixty-two weeks the Messiah will be cut off and have nothing, and the people of the prince who is to come will destroy the city and the sanctuary And its end will come with a flood; even to the end there will be war; desolations are determined.

> 27"And he will make a firm covenant with the many for one week, but in the middle of the week he will put a stop to sacrifice and grain offering; and on the wing of abominations will come one who makes desolate, even until a complete destruction, one that is decreed, is poured out on the one who makes desolate." (Dan. 9:24-27, NASB)

The particulars of the prophecy

We should note that the Hebrew term *shabūa`* (translated "week") simply means "seven." We could refer to this as the prophecy of the 70 "sevens," but the term "week" is so widely used that it seems best to retain the familiar terminology. Of course, the prophecy could not refer to normal weeks of days, since the events of the prophecy could not fit into such a short span of time. While premillennialists and amillennialists disagree on the interpretation of the prophecy, there is general agreement that the first 69 weeks refer to weeks of years, at least approximately [1]

---

[1] Amillennialists generally view the last week of the prophecy as encompassing the time from the end of the 69th week to the second coming, including the entire Church age.

It is helpful to identify the particulars before trying to decipher the chronology of the prophecy. Both Daniel's prayer and the prophetic answer brought by Gabriel are dated in the first year of the reign of Darius the Mede, the son of Ahasuerus, shortly before the end of Israel's 70 years of Israel's captivity (Dan.9:1).[2] The phrase, "your people" refers to Israel, and "your holy city" refers to Jerusalem. The statement, "to make an end of sin, to make atonement for iniquity, to bring in everlasting righteousness, to seal up vision and prophecy and to anoint the most holy place," refers to a historical progression of events leading up to the establishment of the visible, earthly kingdom that had been promised. Messiah being "cut off" is a reference to Messiah's death. The destruction of the city and the sanctuary refers to the destruction of Jerusalem and the temple (fulfilled in A.D. 70), after Christ's death (fulfilled in A.D. 33). The "Prince who is to come" is a reference to the Antichrist who will come to power during the tribulation period (cf. Mt. 24:15-22; 2 Thess. 2:3-4; Rev. 13:1-9).[3] He is the same individual referred to by Paul in 2 Thessalonians as "the man of lawlessness," and by John in Revelation as the first "beast." The "covenant" (v.27) is a treaty made between Israel (the many) and the Roman Prince (the Antichrist). The last, or seventieth week (v.27) represents the tribulation period. "Desolations" refers to the horrible and destructive events to take place during the period of the prophecy. The phrase, "on the wing of abominations" is a reference to the Roman Prince seating himself in the temple and claiming to be God (2 Thess 2:3-4; Rev. 13:1-9), and likely to the setting up of an image to the Antichrist in the temple (Rev. 13:14-15). The "complete destruction, one that is decreed, is poured out on the one who makes desolate" is a reference to the destruction of the Roman Prince at Christ's return, when Christ will crush the Antichrist's kingdom and establish God's kingdom on earth (cf. Dan. 2:44-45; 7:1-27; Rev. 19:19-20).

---

[2] The precise identity of this Darius (cf. 5:31; 6:1,6,9,25,28; 11:1) is uncertain. The Darius mentioned by Daniel is not to be confused with the Persian King Darius I (also known as "Darius the Great," 521-486 B.C.) mentioned in the books of Ezra, Haggai, and Zechariah.

[3] Some amillennial interpreters identify the covenant maker in Daniel 9:27 as the Messiah, and therefore they view the covenant referenced there as the new covenant. However, such an interpretation seems highly unlikely. Given the structure of the passage, it is apparent that the antecedent to "he" in verse 27 is the Prince who will come from the people who destroy the city and the sanctuary (v.26), *i.e.*, the Roman Prince (the Antichrist). If the reference in verse 27 were to the new covenant, why is it stated that it will be made for only one week? The new covenant is an eternal covenant (Jer. 31:31-37 cf. Ezek. 37:21-28, esp. v.26; Heb. 9:12). The New Testament draws a clear connection between Christ's eternal priesthood and the new covenant (Heb. 7:17-8:13), demonstrating the eternality of the new covenant.

Structure and chronology of the seventy "weeks" prophecy

Premillennialists interpret the prophecy of the 70 weeks as a literal chronology leading up to the second coming, at which time Christ will establish the visible aspect of the kingdom of God on earth, the first phase of which is the millennium. They also regard the 70th week as the future time of tribulation described by Christ in the first half of the Olivet Discourse, and by John in Revelation (6:1-20:3). Dispensational premillennialists view the prophecy as pertaining to Israel, not the Church, in accordance with the opening statement of the prophecy (cf. v.24, "Seventy weeks have been decreed for your people and your holy city"). Accordingly, they view the present Church age as falling parenthetically between the 69th and 70th weeks—a mystery hidden in ages past (Eph. 3:1-10).[4]

Amillennialists generally view the 70 weeks as symbolic, and consequently the chronology can be viewed somewhat elastically. Typically, they view the first 69 weeks as the time from the starting decree (usually identified with the decree of Cyrus in 539-538 B.C.) to Messiah, and the 70th week as encompassing the death of Messiah, the destruction of Jerusalem and the temple, and the entire Church age (and millennium) up to the time of the second coming.[5]

While it seems likely that the structure of the 70 weeks has some symbolic significance, it cannot be denied that it is also a chronology. Israel's 70 years of captivity also likely had symbolic meaning; nevertheless, the chronology was still literal. It simply does not follow that because a particular number was chosen for its symbolism that the number is merely allegorical. In the case of the prophecy of the 70 weeks, it is clear that the structure was intended to serve as a chronology (cf. 9:25, note the "from" / "to" expression). There are several observations that lead to the conclusion that the prophecy must be understood as a chronology. First is the enumerative structure: the prophecy is clearly built on the structure of 70 x 7, and even if that structure is symbolic, the symbolism is dependent upon understanding the structure itself. To illustrate this, suppose the prophecy had been built on the structure of "60 x 6," would the interpretations given still be the same? Probably not. Thus, whether there is symbolism or not, it ought to be clear that a literal understanding of the structure is prerequisite to understanding the prophecy. Second, the enumerative structure is sequential, *i.e.*, linear. In this prophecy the first group of 7 weeks precedes the second group of 62 weeks, which precedes the 70th week. Thus, the prophecy is not simply about 70 weeks; it is

---

[4] Most dispensationalists view the Church age as ending prior to the beginning of the 70th week (pretribulationism), however, some view the Church age as ending sometime during the 70th week, thus not all dispensationalists are pretribulational.

[5] Such a view is typical of partial preterism. Full preterists view the 70th week as having been completely fulfilled by the conclusion of A.D. 70.

about 70 sequential weeks. Third, specific historical events, *e.g.*, the death of the Messiah, the destruction of Jerusalem and the temple, the making of a covenant, the cessation of daily sacrifices at the temple, the abomination that will make the temple desolate, and the final destruction of the one who makes the temple desolate, are all linked to the sequence of the 70 weeks. This evidences an underlying chronological structure. Fourth, there are good reasons to believe that the weeks are units of time. In comparing Daniel 9:27 with Matthew 24:15-22 and Revelation 12:6,14, it appears that the 70th week is 2520 days long.[6] Of course, if the length of the 70th week is 2520 days, then no amillennial interpretation thus offered could be correct, for they all require the 70th week to be much longer. Fifth, a purely symbolic interpretation of the 70 weeks lacks explanatory power. If the 70 weeks structure is not a chronology, then what is the symbolic significance of the fact that Messiah is said to be "cut off" and the city and the sanctuary destroyed after the 69th week, or that certain events, such as the making of a covenant and the cessation of the daily sacrifices in the temple are said to occur at specific points during the 70th week? Sixth, when the prophecy is understood as chronological, the portions of the prophecy that have already been fulfilled coincide with history.

    The chronology is the most challenging aspect of the prophecy. Assuming that the prophecy is chronological, the first task is to determine the starting and ending points of the first 69 weeks.[7] The prophecy specifies the starting point as "the issuing of a decree to restore and rebuild Jerusalem" (Dan. 9:24), and the end point is "until Messiah the Prince." This leaves us with two challenges: determining which of the various decrees to use as the starting point, and what point in the life of the Messiah is the correct endpoint of the 69th week. Of the decrees that have been suggested as the starting point, only one matches the criteria of the prophecy: the 444 B.C. decree of Artaxerxes, issued at the behest of Nehemiah, since it alone allowed for the rebuilding of the fortifications (walls, gates, and fortress) necessary to the eventual restoration of the

---

[6] Revelation 12:6 states that the time during which the woman (Israel) will be protected in the wilderness is 1260 days, which is also said to be 42 months (Rev. 12:14, cf. Dan. 7:25). Since the persecution of Israel begins midway through the tribulation period at the time the abomination of desolation is set up (Mt. 24:15ff, cf. Dan. 9:27), and it extends to the second coming, the length of the second half of the tribulation is likely 1260 days, making the entire week 2520 days. Why the 70 weeks prophecy employs a 360-day year is not known for certain; however, it is apparent that the Hebrew calendar, which has a variable number of days to the year (varying from 353 to 385 days), could not be used where the length of each year must be uniform, as is the case with this prophecy.

[7] The first 69 weeks are given as two groups: 7 weeks, and 62 weeks. Therefore, the last week of the 62 weeks is the 69th week (7 weeks + 62 weeks = 69 weeks). The prophecy does not specify any event for the conclusion of the first 7 weeks, though it may be more than coincidence that the last material included in the Old Testament (Ezra/Nehemiah) was likely recorded shortly after 400 B.C. (approximately 49 years {or 7 x 7 weeks} after the start of the 70 weeks).

city and its fortifications as implied in Daniel 9:25, "with plaza and moat."[8] Also, the conditions under which the restoration began, described in Nehemiah 4:1-23 and 6:1-14, match the conditions stated in the prophecy (Dan. 9:25).[9] The other decrees to which interpreters have pointed are concerned mainly with the return of the Jews and the minimal reoccupation of Jerusalem and the rebuilding of the temple, not the restoration of the city. Due to the importance of this prophecy, one would expect that the implementation of such a decree would be well documented. In fact, the book of Nehemiah, recorded a little over a hundred and thirty years after the prophecy, does just that, documenting the beginning of the restoration of Jerusalem pursuant to Artaxerxes' 444 B.C. decree, and the circumstances surrounding the initial work of restoration (Neh. 4:1-23; 6:1-14, cf. Dan. 9:25). Therefore a strong case can be made for viewing Artaxerxes' 444 B.C. decree as the starting point for the prophecy. As to what event in the life of Messiah serves as the endpoint of the 69 weeks, the prophecy does not specify.[10]

Early in the twentieth century, Sir Robert Anderson attempted to calculate the time from Artaxerxes' decree to the triumphal entry of Christ using the start date of

---

[8] Jerusalem was minimally occupied prior to this decree, but because the defensive fortifications destroyed at the time of the Babylonian invasion had not been repaired, only an unprotected village existed amidst the ruins of the once great fortress city. That village was continually subject to intimidation by hostile neighbors. Obviously any decree that did not provide for the rebuilding of the defensive structures could not have been the decree prophesied in Daniel 9:25. Although the wording of the actual decree is nowhere given, the extent of the restoration begun pursuant to the decree is evident from the book of Nehemiah (esp. 2:5-8). While previous decrees allowed Jews to return to the land and to rebuild the temple, Artaxerxes' decree in the twentieth year of his reign is the only decree that allowed for the rebuilding of the defensive fortifications that would pave the way for the eventual restoration of Jerusalem.

[9] The prophecy states that the city would be rebuilt, "even in times of distress" (Dan. 9:25). The book of Nehemiah records that pursuant to Nehemiah's request of Artaxerxes, the walls of Jerusalem were rebuilt amidst ridicule, opposition and even severe threats of force from Sanballet, the governor of Samaria, and Tobiah, the governor of Ammon, as well as others (Neh. 2:9; 4:1-7; 6:1-2). As the rebuilding of the wall progressed the threat of attack grew so intense that half the workers stood watch with swords, spears, and bows in hand, while the other half worked with their weapons at their side (Neh. 4:7-23). There was also an assassination plot against Nehemiah (Neh. 6:1-4), and when that did not succeed, the opposition set a trap to discredit him (Neh. 6:5-14); however, all of those plots failed. These difficulties certainly qualify the rebuilding of Jerusalem under Nehemiah as occurring in a time of distress as prophesied in Daniel 9:25.

[10] Except for the passion week, it is not possible to give a precise date for the events in Jesus' life. We know that he was crucified on Friday, Nisan 14th, likely in A.D. 33, and from that a timeline of the passion week can be derived. (For arguments supporting A.D. 33 as the year of the crucifixion see, Harold W. Hoehner, *Chronological Aspects of the Life of Christ*, Zondervan Publishing House, 1977, pp.65-114.)

Nisan 1, 445 B.C. and the year of Christ's crucifixion as A.D. 32.[11] Anderson used a 360-day year in his calculations and made adjustments for converting from the Hebrew calendar to the Julian calendar. However, there were numerous problems with Anderson's calculation, including both the year of Artaxerxes' decree (445 B.C.) and the year of Christ's crucifixion (A.D. 32). Both of these dates are now known to be untenable.[12] More recently Harold Hoehner provided calculations from the decree of Artaxerxes to the triumphal entry using Nisan 1, 444 B.C. as the start date and A.D. 33 as the year for the crucifixion.[13] The calculations involve the conversion of dates from the Hebrew lunisolar calendar, and there are unresolved questions as to how the calculation should be done. However, if one uses a date prior to the 5th day (*i.e.*, days 1-4) of Nisan, 444 B.C. as the start date, the 69th week terminates anywhere from March 29th (Sunday)

---

[11] Nehemiah 2:1, which refers to the decree of Artaxerxes, states that the decree was made in the month of Nisan, in the twentieth year of Artaxerxes' reign, but it does not specify the exact day. For the purpose of these calculations Anderson used Nisan 1 [which he stated was March 5], 445 B.C. Aside from the fact that the year is incorrect (see the note below), the date conversion is also incorrect (Nisan 1, 445 B.C. would have been March 13th, not March 5th in the Julian calendar). [C. F. Keil (Daniel, pp.379-380) states that Artaxerxes' action referred to in Nehemiah 2 was not a decree, but merely a "royal favor," implying that it does not meet the specification of Daniel's prophecy (Dan. 9:25). Such an assertion is misleading. That Nehemiah does not refer to Artaxerxes' action as a decree is irrelevant. The Hebrew term דבר (*dabar*, meaning a "word," or "command"), employed in Daniel 9:25, does not specify a particular form of directive. That Artaxerxes' action was some sort of decree can reasonably be inferred from the fact that in all probability nothing short of an official decree could have resulted in rebuilding of the fortifications of Jerusalem amidst the hostile opposition of the surrounding regional officials; and there is no reason why the King would send Nehemiah on such a task and fund it, at least partially, and not make his action official when it was easily within his power to do so. Note that Artaxerxes sent Nehemiah with official letters, which presumes a legal basis for the rebuilding of the city (Neh. 2:7-8).]

[12] The decree of Artaxerxes made in the month of Nisan in the twentieth year of his reign (Neh. 2:1) should be dated in the year 444 B.C., since according to the accession-year system of reckoning, the reign of Artaxerxes should be dated from the first full calendar year of his reign (444 B.C.). Also Harold Hoehner has argued that the A.D. 32 year of the crucifixion is not tenable due mainly to the fact that Christ was crucified in a year when Nisan 14th (Passover) fell on a Friday, which was not the case in A.D. 32. Hoehner presents the case that A.D. 33 is the most likely date of the crucifixion (Hoehner, *Chronological Aspects,* pp.65-114).

[13] See Hoehner, *Chronological Aspects,* pp.115-139. The March 4/5 date Hoehner gives for Nisan 1, 444 B.C. is incorrect. Nisan 1, 444 B.C. fell on April 2 . Also, Hoehner gives March 30th A.D. 33 (a Monday) as the date of Christ's triumphal entry, when the date should be Sunday, March 29th. For a discussion of some of the problems in Hoehner's chronology see: "Two Significant Problems With Harold W. Hoehner's Chronology of the Life of Christ," by the author, Biblical Reader Communications, 2012, available online.)

A.D. 33, to April 2, A.D. 33 (the day before Christ's crucifixion).[14] Assuming that Nehemiah intended the first day of the month in Nehemiah 2:1 (which does not specify a day) as the date for Artaxerxes' decree and that A.D. 33 is the correct year of the crucifixion, the conclusion of the 69th week would fall on Sunday, March 29th (Nisan 9th), A.D. 33, the day Christ road into Jerusalem and presented himself in the temple and was rejected by the leaders of Israel; he was crucified five days later on April 3 (Nisan 14th), A.D. 33.[15]

Implications for the interpretation of the Olivet Discourse

Jesus in Matthew 24, and Paul in 2 Thessalonians 2, associated the abomination in Daniel's 70th week with the future time of tribulation just prior to the establishment of the millennial aspect of the kingdom of God. It has been established from a comparison of Daniel 9:27 with Revelation 12:6,14 that the length of the 70th week is 2520 days. It is apparent from Daniel 9:27 that the 70th week begins with the making of a covenant between the Roman Prince whose people destroyed the city and the sanctuary, and that this last week is divided into two equal parts, with the abomination in the temple occurring at the midpoint and the destruction of the Roman Prince (the Antichrist) occurring at the conclusion of the 70th week. This serves as the basic chronology of the tribulation period and is therefore essential in understanding both Jesus' teaching in the first half of the Olivet Discourse and the book of Revelation from 6:1 to 20:3. While Revelation presents a sequence of events that will occur during the tribulation, it nowhere presents a chronology anchored to a timeline as found in the prophecy of the 70 weeks. Thus, understanding of the prophecy of the 70 weeks is essential to

---

[14] The dates given here are Julian.

[15] One possible calculation of the 70 weeks prophecy is as follows: (The intermediate result in each calculation is given as an integer since the least significant figure in the prophecy is an integer.) The last half of the 70th week is 1260 days; the 70th week is 2520 days, thus there are 476 solar years in the first 69 weeks (calculated as the integer result of 69x2520/365.24219); and 476 solar years is 173,855 days. When 173,855 days are added to the start date (Nisan 1, 444 B.C.—the first day of the month is chosen because Nehemiah does not specify any other day, actually any day between the first day and the fourth day would meet the requirements of the prophecy), the result is Sunday, Nisan 9 (March 29), A.D. 33, which was the date of the triumphal entry of Christ into Jerusalem five days before his crucifixion. Jesus was likely crucified on Friday, Nisan 14 (April 3), A.D. 33. [To confirm this calculation, note that the Julian day number for Nisan 1, 444 B.C. is 1,559,344; that day number plus 173,855 days (the number of days in 476 solar years) results in Julian day 1,733,199, which converts to Sunday, Nisan 9 (March 29), A.D. 33. Also, since the beginning of Hebrew months was based on visual observation of the moon, and conditions for observing the moon can at times be unfavorable, the start of a month could vary by a day, but would be compensated in subsequent months. Thus over the span of this prophecy the date should not be off more than one day, if at all.]

understanding the chronology of the tribulation events discussed in Matthew 24-25 and Revelation 6:1-20:3.

Appendix: The Biblical Basis of Premillennialism

The Bible says that Christ will personally return to establish his kingdom; that view is called "premillennialism." Every prophecy of the second coming in which a chronological relationship with the tribulation or the millennium is given places the second coming of Christ immediately at the end of the tribulation, as its concluding event, or immediately prior to the beginning of the millennial kingdom (cf. Zech. 14:1-11, Mt. 24:29-31 and Rev. 19:11-20:6). In Matthew 25:31-34 Jesus was very clear as to when the millennium will begin in relation to his coming; he said: "But *when* the Son of Man comes in His glory, and all the holy angels with Him, *then* He will sit on His glorious throne" (v.31, NASB, italics added). Also note the description of the second coming in Zechariah 14:4-9.

> In that day His feet will stand on the Mount of Olives, which is in front of Jerusalem on the east; and the Mount of Olives will be split in its middle from east to west by a very large valley, so that half of the mountain will move toward the north and the other half toward the south. You will flee by the valley of My mountains, for the valley of the mountains will reach to Azel; yes, you will flee just as you fled before the earthquake in the days of Uzziah king of Judah. Then the LORD, my God, will come, and all the holy ones with Him! In that day there will be no light; the luminaries will dwindle. For it will be a unique day which is known to the LORD, neither day nor night, but it will come about that at evening time there will be light. And in that day living waters will flow out of Jerusalem, half of them toward the eastern sea and the other half toward the western sea; it will be in summer as well as in winter. And the LORD will be king over all the earth; in that day the LORD will be the only one, and His name the only one. (Zech. 14:4-9, NASB)

Also note John's description in Revelation 19:11-20:4.

> And I saw heaven opened, and behold, a white horse, and He who sat on it is called Faithful and True, and in righteousness He judges and wages war. His eyes are a flame of fire, and on His head are many diadems; and He has a name written on Him which no one knows except Himself. He is clothed with a robe dipped in blood, and His name is called The Word of God. And the armies which are in heaven, clothed in fine linen, white and clean, were following Him on white horses. From His mouth comes a sharp sword, so that with it He may strike down the nations, and He will rule them with a rod of iron; and He treads the wine press of the fierce wrath of God, the Almighty. And on His robe and on His thigh He has a name written, "KING OF KINGS, AND LORD OF LORDS." Then I saw an angel standing in the sun, and he cried out with a loud voice, saying to all the birds which fly in midheaven, "Come, assemble for the great supper of God, so that you may eat the flesh of kings and the flesh of commanders and the flesh of mighty men and the flesh of horses and of those who sit on them and the flesh of all men, both free men and slaves, and small and great." And I saw the

> beast and the kings of the earth and their armies assembled to make war against Him who sat on the horse and against His army. And the beast was seized, and with him the false prophet who performed the signs in his presence, by which he deceived those who had received the mark of the beast and those who worshiped his image; these two were thrown alive into the Lake of Fire which burns with brimstone. And the rest were killed with the sword which came from the mouth of Him who sat on the horse, and all the birds were filled with their flesh. Then I saw an angel coming down from heaven, holding the key of the Abyss and a great chain in his hand. And he laid hold of the dragon, the serpent of old, who is the devil and Satan, and bound him for a thousand years; and he threw him into the Abyss, and shut it and sealed it over him, so that he would not deceive the nations any longer, until the thousand years were completed; after these things he must be released for a short time. Then I saw thrones, and they sat on them, and judgment was given to them And I saw the souls of those who had been beheaded because of their testimony of Jesus and because of the word of God, and those who had not worshiped the beast or his image, and had not received the mark on their forehead and on their hand; and they came to life and reigned with Christ for a thousand years. (Rev. 19:11-20:4, NASB)

We see in this description Christ returning with the armies of Heaven (a reference to the angels, cf. Rev. 19:17-18; 20:1-3 cf. Mt. 24:29-31). He will strike down his enemies and rule over the earth. Satan will be bound and sealed in the Abyss, and the saints will be resurrected from their graves to rule with Christ for a thousand years (during the millennium). Clearly this passage portrays a premillennial second advent. Notice the starting parameters of the kingdom: Christ's enemies are destroyed, Satan is bound and sealed in the Abyss, and the saints are resurrected to rule with Christ. The description given here is completely incompatible with either amillennialism or postmillennialism. If the Bible teaches amillennialism or postmillennialism, why does it employ a premillennial figure? This is really the defining truth: If premillennialism is taught in the Bible—and it is plainly taught in these passages—then all non-premillennial views are wrong.

Covenantalists characteristically confuse the various aspects of the kingdom of God, and worse, they envision the Church as replacing Israel in the earthly aspect of the kingdom. At least three distinct aspects of the kingdom of God are referenced in scripture; they are: the *universal*, the *visible*, and the *invisible* aspects. God's sovereignty over all creation is referred to as his universal kingdom. This concept appeared early in Israel's history and is a frequent theme in the Psalms (cf. 10:16; 29:10; 103:19-22; 145:10-13). The universal aspect of the kingdom of God encompasses all creation and includes even the realm of the ungodly (both human and angelic), for everything is subject to the sovereignty of God (cf. Ps. 103:19-22).

To the Hebrew mind the kingdom of God was equated with God's theocratic rule over the nation of Israel. Ultimately this rule was to have its fullest expression in the rule of God through his Messiah, at which time Israel would be vindicated and exalted, and experience the joy of profuse divine blessing and peace. This aspect can be referred to as the visible aspect of the kingdom, since it is to take a physical form. Only in the New Testament does the millennial aspect of the visible kingdom come into sharp focus. We learn from the book of Revelation that the earthly kingdom rule will occur in two phases. The first phase is to occur on the present earth before it is renewed, and is usually referred to as "the millennium" since it is indicated as lasting for approximately one thousand years (Rev. 20:4-10). The second phase of the visible kingdom occurs in eternity with the creation of the new heavens and earth, and the arrival of the New Jerusalem to rest upon the newly re-created earth (Rev. 21:1-22:5).[1]

Those who fail to recognize the differing aspects of the kingdom inevitably confuse one aspect for another. Perhaps the most significant failure is in understanding the nature of the invisible aspect of the kingdom. The invisible aspect of the kingdom of God refers to God's rule in the hearts of those yielded to him. This aspect, like the universal aspect, is a present reality. It is largely developed in the gospels (cf. Mt. 6:33; 18:1-4; Mk. 9:1; Lk. 17:20-24; Jn. 18:36), but it can be found elsewhere in the New Testament (cf. Col. 1:13). Covenantalists generally confuse the visible and invisible aspects of the kingdom and incorrectly view references to the invisible aspect as support for a spiritualized millennium (whether completely spiritualized as in amillennialism, or partially spiritualized as in postmillennialism). They do this because the "fog" of covenantal theology prevents them from seeing some of the distinctions in redemptive history; this leads to an inability to distinguish between the various aspects of the kingdom. Needless to say, this flaw results in a catastrophic failure for covenantalism.

Why must there be a future earthly kingdom built around a regenerated nation of Israel? The Old Testament concept of an earthly kingdom emerges first from the covenant made with Abraham and is then expanded in the land, Davidic, and new covenants. These four covenants shape the Old Testament concept of the visible kingdom of God, which as we will see, is inseparably tied to national Israel. Since these

---

[1] The reason for the necessity of the visible kingdom to unfold in two phases (the millennium, and then eternity) is that the eternal phase can only begin once all sin has been reconciled and the creation purified. Such will not be the case until sin is judged after the millennium (Rev. 20:7-15) and the creation is renewed in perfection (Rev. 21:1-27 cf. Rom. 8:20-21). Amillennialists (and postmillennialists) who object to such a division should recognize that their own eschatology requires the same, since in both cases the millennium, as they conceive it, occurs before the perfect eternal age. Why God has chosen to begin the visible kingdom prior to the final judgment of sin and perfection of creation is not known. Perhaps his purpose in establishing the visible kingdom prior to the final redemption of creation is to demonstrate that man's sin problem is not due to any deficiency in his knowledge or environment (as is so commonly held by humanistic thinkers today), but to his nature.

covenants define the kingdom program, it is important that we understand what they say. The principal texts of the Abrahamic covenant are: Gen. 12:6-7; 13:14-17; 15:1-21; 17:1-14; and 22:15-18. In these passages God made the following promises to Abraham: his name would be great (12:2); he would be the father of many nations (17:5); his descendants would be innumerable (13:16; 15:5; 22:17); kings would come from him (17:6); God would be his God (17:7); the one who blesses Abraham would be blessed, and the one who curses Abraham would be cursed (12:3); and the covenant would be perpetual (17:7). In addition to the promises made to Abraham, God also made the following promises to Abraham's descendants: they would become a great nation (12:2); they would come to possess the land forever (17:8); God would be their God (17:8); they would be victorious over their enemies (22:17); and God's covenant would be established with them forever (17:7). The covenant also included a blessing for the Gentiles, that they would be blessed through Abraham (12:3; 22:18). The Abrahamic covenant expressly promises that Abraham's descendants will come to possess the land that God showed to Abraham, and that they will live in that land as recipients of divine favor forever. The Abrahamic covenant is the central covenant of the Bible. The first eleven chapters of Genesis give the background leading up to this covenant, and the rest of the Bible, both Old and New Testaments, record the outworking of this covenant. Even the gospel going to the Gentiles is a provision of the Abrahamic covenant (Gen. 12:3; 22:18). The three subsequent unconditional covenants (the land, Davidic, and new covenants) simply expand upon the provisions initially established in the original set of promises made to Abraham. The Mosaic covenant is of an entirely different type; it was a temporary measure designed to bridge the gap between the emergence of national Israel and the implementation of the new covenant at the cross. The Mosaic covenant does not expand upon the original promises given to Abraham, nor is it an unconditional covenant. Grasping the meaning and significance of these covenants is crucial to an understanding of the message of the Bible, because it is through these covenants and the prophecies that illuminate them that the divine plan for man's future is revealed. Now that we have an idea of the importance of the covenant God made with Abraham, we turn our attention to its further development in the land, Davidic, and new covenants.

The land covenant, so called because it was made with Israel upon their entrance into the promised land, is recorded in Deuteronomy 29:1-30:20. Moses indicated the connection between the land and Abrahamic covenants when he said: "You are standing here in order to enter into a covenant with the LORD your God, a covenant the LORD is making with you this day and sealing with an oath, to confirm you this day as his people, that he may be your God as he promised you and as he swore to your fathers, Abraham, Isaac and Jacob" (Deut. 29:12-13, NIV). What God swore to Abraham and subsequently confirmed to Isaac and Jacob, he was prepared to implement as Abraham's children stood on the verge of their entrance into the land over four hundred years later.

The land covenant does not alter the original promises given to Abraham; rather, it elaborates them. This covenant seems to have had two immediate purposes. The first was to ensure that the people understood that their inheritance of the land was the direct result of the promises previously made to Abraham (29:12-13); and the second was to clarify the condition under which Israel could expect to enter into the enjoyment of this promise, the condition being their continued obedience to God (29:16-29). One of the most interesting features of this covenant is found in Deuteronomy 30:1-10, where God said that the children of Israel would rebel in the future and that their rebellion would cost them the enjoyment of the covenant blessings and they would be dispersed from the land, but the covenant would not be invalidated; rather, the blessing would be reserved for a generation of their descendants who would call upon him and to whom he would respond by bringing them back into the land. It is important that the distinction between the "enjoyment" and the "validity" of the covenant be understood. On this issue covenantalists are confused; they incorrectly assume that if the Jews are not presently enjoying the blessings of the covenant, such is an indication that the covenant has been invalidated. However, as indicated in Deuteronomy 29:1-30:20, nothing could be further from the truth. The promise God made was to a people, not to a particular generation. If a generation or many generations are unfaithful, that does not invalidate the covenant to the people, because the covenant is unconditional and based solely on the faithfulness of God. The land covenant should be seen as a reaffirmation and amplification of the land promises previously made to Abraham, and its perpetual validity is apparent from the language employed.

The Davidic covenant, found in 2 Samuel 7:12-16, has four key provisions. First, David would have a son who would build the house of the LORD (v.13). This provision was fulfilled in Solomon. Second, God said that while he would correct David's son, he would never take the throne from him (vv.14-15). Third, God promised that David's lineage would endure forever (v.16). Fourth, God promised that the right to the throne of Israel would perpetually remain with David's line (v.16). While the text of the covenant does not directly refer to the Abrahamic covenant, the connection is apparent since the people that David's line will perpetually have the right to rule are the people of the promise under the Abrahamic covenant. Jeremiah later made a connection between these two covenants when he prophesied: "Thus says the LORD, 'If My covenant for day and night stand not, and the fixed patterns of heaven and earth I have not established, then I would reject the descendants of Jacob and David My servant, not taking from his descendants rulers over the descendants of Abraham, Isaac and Jacob. But I will restore their fortunes and will have mercy on them'" (Jer. 33:25-26, NASB). The Davidic covenant expands upon the political aspect of the Abrahamic covenant. The New Testament makes the point of establishing that Christ is both the natural descendant of David and legal heir to the throne of Israel, and thus as "the Son of David" is qualified to rule the nation in fulfillment of God's covenant with David (cf. Lk. 1:32; Mt. 21:9).

The prophecy of the new covenant is found in Jeremiah 31:31-34. In this prophecy God promised that he would someday establish a new covenant with Israel (in contrast to the Mosaic covenant, which was only temporary) under which he would write his laws on their hearts, cf. v.33 (a reference to the giving of the Holy Spirit indicative of regeneration). The result will be that all Israel will know the LORD (v.34). In so saying, God declared the covenant of the Law to be weak, ineffectual, and soon to pass away (cf. Heb. 8:13).

It is important to recognize that the Abrahamic covenant and the three ancillary covenants (the land, the Davidic, and the new covenants) are all unconditional. This does not mean that there is no condition to be met for them to be enjoyed, for there is a condition for enjoyment; that condition is genuine faith. Rather, the unconditional nature of these covenants refers to the fact that Israel's disobedience, both past and present, cannot invalidate the promises made to them, because the validity of those promises was never linked to Israel's faithfulness; only the "enjoyment" of the blessings was conditioned upon faith. Though generations of Abraham's descendants have turned from their Messiah, yet God maintains his promises, ready to fulfill them to the elect generation in the future that will turn to Christ. When the unconditional nature of these promises is understood it becomes apparent that whatever partial and temporary benefits Israel may have enjoyed in the past, in no sense have these promises been fulfilled. Thus, if they cannot be invalidated, and they have not been fulfilled, their fulfillment must be future. The position of covenant theology, which generally sees no place for the fulfillment of these covenants to national Israel in the future, is that their validity was conditioned upon Israel's faith, and since Israel broke faith with God, manifested ultimately in the rejection of Christ, these covenants have been invalidated and the promised blessings have been transferred, or defaulted to the Church. This view is called, "replacement theology."[2]

There are three reasons for believing that God has not abandoned his covenant with Abraham. The form of the covenant given in Genesis 15:9-21 is that of an unconditional, or unilateral covenant in which all of the obligation for the fulfillment rests solely with one party; in this case, God is the sole responsible party. The scene in Genesis 15:1-21 in which Abraham divided various animals, and God, depicted by a great smoking furnace, passed between the divided pieces, is a picture of the sealing of

---

[2] Historically amillennialists have held to the idea of replacement, according to which the promises made to Israel were transferred, or defaulted to the Church in some "spiritual" sense. However, defining how these promises could be fulfilled to the Church spiritually has proved to be difficult, and highly speculative. As a result some amillennialists assert that the promises have been invalidated, while a few deny that God made any promises to Israel. Both of these positions are clearly contrary to the plain statements of Scripture (for additional discussion see, "Who is the Seed of Abraham," by the author).

the Abrahamic covenant. The fact that only God passed between the pieces is significant. Normally, in this type of covenant, known as a "suzerainty-vassal treaty," both parties would pass between the divided pieces together, indicating their mutual obligation to keep the conditions of the covenant. That the record makes the point that God alone passed between the pieces is highly significant and indicative that the covenant obligations rested solely with him. In other words, this was a unilateral covenant; it was not up to Abraham or his descendants to do anything to insure the continued validity of the covenant. Of course no one could enter into the enjoyment of the covenant apart from faith (Gen. 17:13-14). Nevertheless, faithlessness on the part of an individual or an entire generation could not invalidate the covenant itself; such would merely exclude that individual or generation from the enjoyment of the covenant blessings. The validity of the covenant, and its enjoyment, are two entirely distinct issues. God rejected those who rejected the covenant relationship, but he did not reject the covenant, which was based upon his own faithfulness. If a generation of Abraham's descendants arises that will accept the covenant relationship (by faith), they will enter into the enjoyment of the covenant blessings. Since the promises were made concerning a people, they will be fulfilled when an elect generation of Jews turns to God and accepts the Messiah whom God sent.

Even though Abraham's descendants were disobedient and fell into idolatry, subsequent statements made in Scripture indicate that their disobedience had not invalidated the covenant. For example, the Abrahamic covenant was invoked in 1 Chronicles 16:16-18, a thousand years after it was made. During much of the time since the giving of the covenant Israel had lived in idolatry, yet the covenant was not invalidated. Psalm 105:10-11 says: "Then He confirmed it to Jacob for a statute, to Israel as an everlasting covenant, saying, 'To you I will give the land of Canaan as the portion of your inheritance…'" (NASB). If disobedience or the lack of faith could invalidate the promises of God under the covenant, it surely would not have survived the first one thousand years of Israel's history.

The land, Davidic, and new covenants are also indicated as being unconditional and eternal covenants. When seen in light of their connection to the Abrahamic covenant, it becomes clear that they all share the same unconditional quality. Concerning the unconditional nature of the Davidic covenant, God said through the psalmist in Psalm 89: "I will maintain my love to him forever, and my covenant with him will never fail. I will establish his line forever, his throne as long as the heavens endure. If his sons forsake my law and do not follow my statutes, if they violate my decrees and fail to keep my commands, I will punish their sin with the rod, their iniquity with flogging; but I will not take my love from him, nor will I ever betray my faithfulness. I will not violate my covenant or alter what my lips have uttered. Once for all, I have sworn by my holiness and I will not lie to David that his line will continue forever and his throne endure before me like the sun; it will be established forever like the moon, the faithful witness in the sky" (Psa. 89:28-37, NIV). Almost four hundred years later, on the eve of Israel's expulsion from the land because of rampant idolatry, God spoke these words through the prophet Jeremiah: "Thus says the LORD, 'If you can break My covenant for the day and My covenant for the night, so that day and night will not be at their appointed time, then My covenant may also be broken with David My servant so that he will not have a son to reign on his throne, and with the Levitical priests, My ministers. As the host of heaven cannot be counted and the sand of the sea cannot be measured, so I will multiply the descendants of David My servant and the Levites who minister to Me'" (Jer. 33:20-22, NIV).

Both the nature of these covenants and subsequent biblical statements reflecting on them indicate they were made unconditionally and eternally, thus they could not have been invalidated by Israel's past unbelief; God intends to fulfill these covenants through his sovereign election of a future generation of Abraham's descendants (Jer. 31:31-37). The covenant God made with Abraham, along with the subsequent expansions and elucidations (*e.g.,* Isa. 11:4-10; 35:5-10; 60:1-22; 65:17-25; Ezek. 34:25-31; Joel 2:21-27; 3:18-21) serve as the source material for our understanding of the visible aspect of the kingdom of God. Any theology of the kingdom must reflect what is contained in these scriptures.

The land covenant repeats the land promises of the Abrahamic covenant and elaborates the basis for Israel's enjoyment of this promise, which is faith and obedience.[3] In this covenant God foresaw Israel's disobedience and dispersion (Deut. 30:1-8), and promised their restoration upon a return to faith in him. Of course, Israel's ultimate return to the Lord can only occur as a result of inward spiritual conversion. The Davidic covenant is an expansion upon the national aspect of the Abrahamic covenant in that it specifies that David's house is to have a perpetual right to the throne of Israel. The promise requires that when the kingdom prophecies are fulfilled, a member of David's line must rule over Israel. This is to be fulfilled by Christ (Isa. 9:6-7). The prophecy of the new covenant specifies how God intends to bring about the implementation of the promises he made to Abraham—by genuine spiritual renewal on the part of Abraham's descendants. Before God can fulfill his promises to Abraham, he must raise up an elect generation of Jews who will respond to his offer of salvation.

What is the millennial kingdom to be like? Scripture indicates that the millennium will be inaugurated shortly after the second coming (Zech. 14:1-9; Mt. 24-25, esp. 25:31; Rev. 9:11-20:6). Revelation 20:3-6 states that a resurrection of believers will occur at the beginning of the millennium, not at the end as postmillennialists and

---

[3] It might be objected that if obedience is a condition to the eventual enjoyment of the covenant, the covenant is not entirely a promise to be realized by faith. The answer is that the obedience is reckoned to those who exercise genuine saving faith, just as righteousness is reckoned.

amillennialists claim.[4] The millennial kingdom will be global; however, Israel, and Jerusalem in particular, will occupy the center stage during the period since it is from there that the Messiah will reign (Isa. 2:1-4), and Israel will occupy a special place of honor at the head of the nations (Isa. 60:1-22; 61:4-9; 62:1-12; Jer. 16:14-18; 30:18-22; Mic. 4:1-2; Zeph. 3:20). Naturally, this will necessitate a more complete regathering of the Jewish people (Isa. 11:12; 49:8-26; 66:1-20; Amos 9:11-15; Zech. 8:1-23).

As indicated by the name, the millennium will be approximately one thousand years in duration (Rev. 20:2,3,4,6,7) as is evidenced by the fact that Satan's confinement, which begins immediately prior to the millennium, is to last for one thousand years, after which he will be released for a short time. His release will result in a great rebellion and the deaths of those who follow him (Rev. 20:7-10).[5] It may well be that the destruction of the perverse invokes the dissolution of the present heavens and earth and prepares the way for the new heavens and earth (Rev. 20:7-21:8). Humanly, the millennium will be a period characterized by health, prosperity, and longevity (Isa. 65:18-25, cf. 35:3-7).

Governmentally the millennium will be a theocratic kingdom with Christ ruling from Jerusalem, which will serve as both the religious and political center of the world (cf. Isa. 9:6; Rev. 20:6). There will continue to be nations during the millennial period, and each nation will continue to have a significant measure of freedom in governing itself (Isa. 2:2-5). Apparently some laws will originate from Zion. The presence of people in their unglorified state, including an increasing number of unregenerate people, especially toward the end of the period, will naturally result in problems. Disputes between nations will still occur, but with less frequency and certainly with less intensity. Apparently it will be necessary on occasion for Christ to remind some nations of their spiritual obligations; in some cases he will do that by withholding blessings such as rain (Zech. 14:16-19). Clearly, the millennium is not a perfect age; indeed that is the whole point of a two-phase kingdom—that the perfect, eternal age cannot begin until all sin is finally judged and the creation is restored to perfection.

---

[4] Some amillennialists claim that the resurrection of some of the Old Testament saints at Jerusalem, which occurred after Christ's resurrection, was the fulfillment of Revelation 20:4. However, that resurrection, recorded in Matthew 27:52, was very limited in scope and could hardly qualify as the resurrection of the tribulation martyrs described as a future event from the perspective of Revelation 20:4.

[5] One might wonder why God would temporarily release Satan from his confinement near the end of the millennium. At least one reason would seem to be that God will use Satan as a catalyst for the judgment of those born during the millennium who reject God and his Son. The effect of this future release will certainly provide insight into the role that Satan has played in past human history.

Economically the millennium will represent a time of unparalleled prosperity (Joel 2:21-27; Amos 9:13-15). Amos prophesied: "Behold, days are coming," declares the LORD, when the plowman will overtake the reaper and the treader of grapes him who sows seed; when the mountains will drip sweet wine and all the hills will be dissolved" (Amos 9:13, NASB). The amelioration of many of the effects of the curse placed upon the earth after the fall of man (cf. Isa. 11:6-9; Rom. 8:18-24) will undoubtedly account for much of the prosperity; however, the presence of Christ and the influence of godliness in personal relationships, business, government, social institutions, and the sciences will certainly have great effect, not to mention the positive economic impact brought about by the elimination of armed conflict. (Isa. 2:4).

Socially the millennium will be characterized as a time of unprecedented peace, world harmony, and justice (Isa. 9:1-7). The presence of Christ and the absence of Satan's influence, at least until the end of the period, will affect the world in such a positive way that even with an ever increasing population of unredeemed people, the world will experience unparalleled harmony not seen since before the fall of man.

It should be clear that covenant theology's allegorical view of the kingdom bears little resemblance to the picture presented in the Scriptures. Contrary to the position of replacement theology, God has every intention of fulfilling his promises to elect Israel (cf. Psa. 105:8-11; Jer. 33:20-26; Rom. 11:1-36). The fact that Israel rejected their Messiah, and God from both Jew and Gentile forged a new entity, the Church, did not nullify God's program for Israel. It merely postponed it until it can be fulfilled to an elect generation of Jews. In fact, that is one of the primary purposes of the coming tribulation, to bring about that result.

It is true that Church age saints share in the distinction of being designated "children of Abraham." Abraham is, metaphorically speaking, the father of all who believe (Gal. 3:6-9,29 cf. Gen. 12:3). The blessings that the Church enjoys have their roots in the promises made to Abraham (Gal. 3:8-9). However, it would be incorrect to interpret that to mean that the blessings promised to Israel have been invalidated, or transferred to the Church. Although Galatians 6:16 is sometimes cited as an example of the Church referred to as "Israel," the Church is not mentioned there; Paul was merely drawing a distinction between those who were outwardly Israelites (by birth and tradition), and those who were "the Israel of God," by birth and faith (*i.e.,* saved Jews). In saying such, he nullified the argument of the Judaizers that one must be circumcised to be right with God—since even Jews could only be saved by faith. The presence of saved Jews in the Church (referred to as "the Israel of God") does not equate the Church with Israel; the duality of Israel and the Church is strictly maintained in the New Testament. In Romans 11:1-36 where Paul gives the analogy of the root and the branches it is significant that he maintains the distinctness of Israel and the Church.

Based upon the promises made in the Abrahamic, land, Davidic, and new covenants, we can say that God's unconditional and unalterable promise to Israel is for a literal, physical kingdom with Messiah ruling, in which the regenerated descendants of Abraham will live in fellowship with God, in a state of perpetual blessing. The blessings to the Gentile world will result from the overflow of God's blessings to Israel (Rom. 11:18). Such a picture is compatible only with a premillennial view of the return of Christ.

Appendix: The Character and Chronology of the Tribulation

The Character of the Tribulation

       Both the Old and New Testaments describe a time of unprecedented global distress immediately preceding the second coming of Christ to establish his kingdom. According to the 70 weeks prophecy given in Daniel 9:24-27 this period is to be approximately seven years long. The day of the LORD commences sometime in the second half of the tribulation period.[1] It begins as a time of divine wrath and transitions into a time of great blessing in the millennium and eternity. While most dispensationalists identify the entire seven years of tribulation as divine wrath, that view is lacking in biblical support, and regrettably, it results both in an inaccurate view of the tribulation and incorrect inferences regarding the timing of the rapture of the Church.[2] The difficulty of the tribulation period ensues from three primary sources: the

---

[1] For the arguments supporting this see the subsequent discussion of tribulation chronology in this Appendix beginning at page 242.

[2] Several approaches have been used to argue that the entire tribulation period is divine wrath. One approach is the presumed unity of the tribulation period. Pretribulationists (who believe the rapture *must* precede the start of the tribulation) generally equate the tribulation with the day of the LORD in order to establish that the entire tribulation is a time of divine wrath (and hence the necessity of a pretribulational rapture); but the basis for equating the two is the prior assumption that the tribulation is, entirely, a time of divine wrath. In other words the reasoning goes like this: the tribulation period is divine wrath because it is the day of the LORD; and it is the day of the LORD because it is entirely a time of divine wrath. This is a circular argument. The argument is sometimes expressed in abbreviated form as follows: Whenever the Old Testament discusses the coming day of the LORD, judgment is in view; thus the tribulation is a time of judgment (see, Pentecost, *Things to Come*, pp.230 and 233-237). Pentecost cites twenty passages to demonstrate that the tribulation is a time of judgment, but none of the passages cited speaks to the extent of divine wrath during the tribulation period. The fact that the tribulation includes divine wrath is beyond dispute. Pentecost demonstrates only that divine wrath will occur sometime during the tribulation—a point upon which virtually all premillennialists agree. However, none of the evidence he presents proves that the entire tribulation is divine wrath. The manifestation of divine wrath in the tribulation period, and the extent of the tribulation period that can be characterized as divine wrath are distinct issues. Pentecost states that since the judgments associated with the second coming will need to occur over a period of time, the entire tribulation period must be a time of judgment (Pentecost, p.230). That is an incredible leap. Why would the judgments directly associated with the second coming need to extend over the entire seven-year period? Pentecost offers no justification whatsoever; he also argues that if the day of the LORD did not begin until the second coming, it would be preceded by signs and could not come, as indicated in 1 Thessalonians 5:2, as "a thief in the night" (Pentecost, p.230). This overlooks the fact that if the day of the LORD were to begin on the heels of the rapture, the rapture itself would

be a sign to which the day of the LORD would be contingent. The timing of the rapture cannot be used to determine the extent of divine wrath during the tribulation period, since the timing of the rapture is itself dependent upon the question of when the wrath begins. While the day of the LORD is undoubtedly a component of the tribulation period, there simply is no good reason to assume that the entire seven-year period is to be divine wrath, or that the day of the LORD must begin when the seven-year tribulation period begins. We should note that even within pretribulationism there has been considerable disagreement as to when the day of the LORD is to begin. C.I. Scofield in the original *Scofield Reference Bible* (p.1349) stated that the day of the LORD would begin at the second coming, after the apocalyptic judgments of Revelation 11-18 (*i.e.,* after the seventh trumpet bowl judgments); and Lewis Sperry Chafer seems to have agreed with that view (Chafer, *Systematic Theology*, IV, pp.11, 383, 398; VII, p.110). (Scofield's note was changed in 1967 with the publication of *The New Scofield Reference Bible* to reflect that the day of the LORD will begin with the rapture of the Church; see the footnote on page 1363 of *The New Scofield Reference Bible*.) Another approach for equating the entirety of the tribulation period with the day of the LORD is to assert that the seals, trumpets, and bowls of Revelation 4-19 are all divine judgments; and therefore, since it is reasonable to expect that the first seal occurs early in the tribulation period, it follows that the entire seven-year tribulation period is a time of judgment. However, there is no evidence that the seals themselves represent divine wrath. Rather, the seals appear to be movements within the tribulation period. As noted, Scofield limited the apocalyptic judgments to the seventh trumpet, *i.e.,* the bowls of wrath. It is assumed by many that since Revelation pictures Christ, in Heaven, breaking the seven seals, that those seals must be divine judgments. While Christ's breaking of the seals certainly indicates his sovereignty over the tribulation events, perhaps as a reminder during those difficult times that God is still sovereign, even when evil appears to reign, it does not follow that the seals must be divine wrath. Revelation does not mention divine wrath until 6:15-17, which is after the time of the sixth seal has passed. There is an additional problem in viewing all of the seals as divine wrath. The fifth seal (Rev. 6:9-11 cf. Mt. 24:9, 15-22) involves the martyrdom of many saints living at that time during the tribulation. Pretribulationism has always been at a loss to explain how the persecution and death of these faithful saints could be attributed directly to divine wrath. If all the seals represent divine wrath, then the martyrdom of the saints under the fifth seal must be divine wrath; yet Revelation pictures it as an evil to be punished by a future, but soon, outpouring of divine wrath (6:11 cf. 8:1-6). The fact that these martyrs are pictured in Heaven under the altar making great lamentation to God (6:9-11), and asking how long he will restrain his judgment in avenging of their blood upon the world, is indicative that the deaths of these saints can in no way be attributable to God's justice in the execution of wrath. God responds that they must wait a little while for the answer to their petition (6:11). The events of the seventh seal (the sequence of trumpet and bowl judgments) are plainly indicated to be in response to the prayers of the saints from under the heavenly altar (8:1-6 cf. 16:4-7 and 19:2); they are also the only components of the tribulation period that are specifically designated as divine wrath (Rev. 15:1; 16:1). Thus, it is not without significance that the first mention of divine wrath in Revelation occurs just prior to the opening of the seventh seal (6:17). Given these observations, it is difficult to sustain the case that all of the seals represent divine wrath. And if God's wrath has not commenced by the close of the fifth seal, at most, only the last two seals could involve divine wrath. Since wrath is not activities of godless men, the activity of Satan, and divine wrath once the day of the LORD begins. The purpose of the tribulation is two-fold: it includes a time for preparing an elect people, both Jew and Gentile, and an elect nation (Israel) to enter the millennium at Christ's return; it also serves as a time of judgment upon a world in abject rebellion against God. As such, the tribulation plays a vital role in preparation for the visible (geopolitical) aspect of the kingdom of God.

The Old Testament figure of the refiner's fire is one of the metaphors employed to illustrate how God will use this time of great distress to prepare an elect people and nation for entrance into the kingdom (Dan. 12:10). It was revealed through Zechariah that only one third of the Jewish nation would survive this time of distress (Zech. 13:9-18). Both Zechariah and Ezekiel foresaw the conversion of Israel during the tribulation (Zech. 12:10-14; Ezek. 20:33-38). While the entire period will be a time of distress, sometime in the second half the day of the LORD will begin. The result will be worldwide devastation, and only a fraction of the world's population will survive to the end of the period (Isa. 13:9-13). Concerning the day of the LORD, Paul said:

> Then that lawless one will be revealed whom the Lord will slay with the breath of His mouth and bring to an end by the appearance of His coming; that is, the one whose coming is in accord with the activity of Satan, with all power and signs and false wonders, and with all the deception of wickedness for those who perish, because they did not receive the love of the truth so as to be saved. For this reason God will send upon them a deluding influence so that they will believe what is false, in order that they all may be judged who did not believe the truth, but took pleasure in wickedness. (2 Thess. 2:8-12, NASB)

Not only will the wicked refuse to repent of their sin, they will fall into a delusion, worshiping the Antichrist as God. This delusion will be God-sent. Since the world will reject the true God, God will send a delusion upon the world so they will believe "the lie," *i.e.,* that the Antichrist is God (2 Thess. 2:11 cf. 3-4).

---

mentioned until after the time of the sixth seal is past (6:17), and since there is a momentous transition between the sixth and seventh seals (8:1), the case could be made that the most likely point for the day of the LORD to begin might be with the opening of the seventh seal. There simply is no biblical support for viewing the tribulation as coextensive with the day of the LORD, and the weak deductions to which pretribulationists appeal underscore this point. Daniel does not mention the day of the LORD in relation to the 70 weeks prophecy; however, we know that the day of the LORD must fall sometime within the 70th week, since the first 69 weeks of the prophecy are past, and both the 70th week and the wrath associated with the day of the LORD end in connection with the second coming of Christ at the conclusion of the tribulation period. However, there is no sound biblical or theological reason for believing that the entire 70th week is taken up with the day of the LORD, though undoubtedly the day of the LORD must occupy some portion of the tribulation period extending to the second coming.

Biblical background of the tribulation

None of the prophets foresaw all of the features of the tribulation. It is only by comparing one prophecy with another that we are able to gather all of the details concerning the period. It is important to note that most of the Old Testament prophecies pertaining to this period are focused on the judgment to be manifested at the day of the LORD; Daniel 9:24-27 is the one notable exception. If we fail to recognize this, it presents the illusion that the entire tribulation is a time of divine wrath. Daniel was the only Old Testament prophet to whom God revealed specific chronological information about the extended seven-year period; and it is easy to confuse the part (the day of the LORD), with the whole (Daniel's seventieth week—the tribulation period).

One of the earliest mentions of the day of the LORD occurs in Psalm 110:1-7. There God speaks of judging the nations and crushing their rulers in preparation for the rule of Messiah. Other early references to the tribulation occur in Joel (c.835 B.C.), Amos (755 B.C.), and Isaiah (740-680 B.C.). Joel pictures this as a devastating military campaign (2:11), and a judgment upon the nations for their sin and rebellion against the LORD (3:1-16). Amos refers to this time as a day of darkness. The tribulation is a major theme in Isaiah, where it is the focus of several extended passages. Isaiah pictures it as a terrible time of divine judgment in which the splendor of the LORD's majesty will be revealed and the eyes of arrogant men will be humbled (2:10-11). He says it is to be a time of "wailing," all hands will "go limp," every man's heart will "melt," they will be seized by "terror," "pain," and "anguish" (13:6-8). It is significant that in Isaiah the period is viewed as a global phenomenon. Speaking to Isaiah, God said: "Therefore I will make the heavens tremble and the earth will shake from its place at the wrath of the LORD almighty, in the day of his burning anger" (Isa. 13:13). The reason for this catastrophic judgment is given in Isaiah 13:10; there God said: "I will punish the world for its evil, the wicked for their sins. I will put an end to the arrogance of the haughty and will humble the pride of the ruthless" (NIV). The language of Isaiah's prophecies reach a crescendo in chapter 24 where he says: "See, the LORD is going to lay waste the earth and devastate it, he will ruin its face and scatter its inhabitants" (v.1); "The earth will be completely laid waste and totally plundered" (v.3); "The earth's inhabitants are burned up and very few are left" (v.6, NIV). This period includes a time of cosmic judgment; Isaiah (34:4) says, "All the stars of the heavens will be dissolved and the sky rolled up like a scroll; all the starry host will fall like withered leaves from the vine, like shriveled figs from the fig tree" (NIV). Even allowing for a degree of hyperbole, the description bespeaks horrific, global judgment. What is not clear is the precise nature of the individual components of the judgments, and their chronological relationship to other events of the period.

The book of Daniel (c. 530 B.C.) provides the first and most precise chronological information concerning the extended tribulation period, and it lays the foundation for understanding the prominent role played by the one who is there referred to as, "the Prince to come" (Dan. 9:26, AV). It is only in Daniel that we learn Israel's final great time of distress in this age is to be a seven-year period (9:24-27 cf. 12:11), divided into two parts of three and one-half years each. Even the book of Revelation, which devotes fourteen chapters to the discussion of the tribulation, does not give a clue to the period's chronological superstructure other than a basic sequence of events. Daniel also yields considerable information regarding the coming Roman Prince.[3] This individual plays a central role in world political events, spiritual deception, religious apostasy, and the persecution and martyrdom of believers during the period (7:25; 9:27; 11:36-39). Likewise, it is in Daniel that we learn of the coming world alliance, a confederation of nations that will exist just prior to and during the period, and through which the coming Prince (the Antichrist, cf. 1 Jn. 2:18) will exercise his power (2:40-45; 7:19-27).[4] While numerous passages describe this period as immediately preceding the millennial kingdom (Joel 2-3; Isa. 24-25; 34-35, Dan. 9:24-27), it is Zechariah (520-518 B.C.) who informs us that the tribulation will be brought to a conclusion at the personal appearing of the LORD, bodily, to dispense judgment to his enemies and to personally establish the visible, geopolitical aspect of his kingdom on earth. Speaking through Zechariah, God said: "I will gather all the nations to Jerusalem to fight against it; the city will be captured, the houses ransacked, and the women raped. Half the city will go into exile, but the rest of the people will not be taken from the city. Then the LORD will go out and fight against those nations, as he fights in the day of battle. On that day his feet will stand on the Mount of Olives, east of Jerusalem, and the Mount of Olives will be split in two from east to west, forming a great valley, with half of the mountain moving north and half moving south" (Zech. 14:2-4). Demonstrating the close connection of this event with the beginning of the millennial kingdom, Zechariah continues: "And the LORD will be king over all the earth; in that day the LORD will be the only one, and His name the only one" (Zech.14:9, NASB).

The connection between the regal appearance of Christ (*i.e.*, "the second coming") and the conclusion of the tribulation is reinforced by Christ in the Olivet Discourse and repeated in Revelation 19:11-16. The Olivet Discourse provides additional details concerning the character of the period, some of which were not previously revealed, but most of which are further developed in the book of Revelation; these include: the persecution and martyrdom of the saints (Mt. 24:9,15-22), the great apostasy (Mt. 24:10), the spiritual degeneration and deception during the period (Mt. 24:5,12,23-

---

[3] Not to be confused with "Messiah the Prince" in verse 25. The Prince who is to come (v.26) has a connection to the people who will destroy the city and the sanctuary (*i.e.*, the Romans). Jesus had no such connection.

[4] The term "Antichrist" occurs only in 1 John 2:18,22; 4:1-3, and 2 John 7; however, it has become the universal name employed to refer to the satanically empowered dictator and false messiah, Daniel's "Prince to come" (Dan. 9:24-27), the "man of lawlessness" (2 Thess. 2:3-11), the "first beast" of Revelation (Rev. 13:1-10).

27), the public sign of Christ's regal advent (Mt. 24:29-31), and the judgment following the second coming—which occurs in the interlude between the tribulation and the millennium (Mt. 25:31-46). Another key feature of this discourse is that it provides important chronological clues that help to link the timelines of the books of Daniel and Revelation.[5] Interestingly, an analysis of the scope of the information from the various sources, both Old and New Testament, reveals that Jesus referred to more individual elements of the tribulation period than any other single source of information, and most of that material was presented in the Olivet Discourse.[6]

With the exception of the Olivet Discourse and the book of Revelation, the New Testament does not add significantly to the body of truth already revealed about the particulars of the tribulation. Paul mentions the nature of the abomination spoken of by Daniel as an act in which the man of lawlessness (the Antichrist) will enter the temple and proclaim himself God (2 Thess. 2:4 cf. Dan. 11:36-37). Paul clearly links the power of the man of lawlessness with the power of Satan (2 Thess. 2:9), and he says in 2 Thessalonians 2:9-12 that God will send a strong delusion on the followers of the Antichrist so that they will believe "the lie" of the man of lawlessness—that is, his claim to deity. Perhaps Paul's greatest contribution to the discussion of the tribulation is his statement in 2 Thessalonians 2:3-4 that the day of the LORD will not come until the man of lawlessness is revealed in the temple at the middle of the period, thus placing the beginning of the day of the LORD, and consequently the manifestation of divine wrath, sometime in the second half of the tribulation period.[7] In the Olivet Discourse the Lord gives a condensed description of the tribulation, with an overview of the entire seven-year period (vv. 4-14), and special treatment of some features of the second half of the period (vv. 15-31), including details of his regal appearing (vv.29-31); he also reveals for the first time the dual nature of his appearing (*i.e.*, that there is to be a sudden removal of the redeemed sometime in advance of the second coming).

The book of Revelation greatly advances our knowledge of the tribulation. It is there for the first time we are given a glimpse of the period from the heavenly perspective. Through John's narration of his vision we see Christ in Heaven before the throne of God breaking the seals of a book, the contents of which is a series of greatly distressing events—all of which qualify as "tribulation," but only some of which are

---

[5] For an examination of the chronologies of Daniel and Revelation in relation to the Olivet Discourse, see "The Chronology of the Tribulation" in this Appendix beginning on page 242 (esp. pp.245-246).

[6] For a breakdown by subject matter on the various sources of information about the tribulation in both the Old and the New Testament see figure 6.1 in, *What the Bible Says About the Future*, Second edition, by the author, p.97.

[7] A discussion of 2 Thessalonians 2: 1-5 can be found further along in this Appendix beginning at page 247, and also at page 262.

divine judgment. These events consist of three series. The seven seals represent the major movements of the period; seven trumpets unfold from the seventh seal, and seven bowls unfold from the seventh trumpet. Due to the unique nature of the seventh seal it seems likely that the day of the LORD begins during the time of that seal. The seventh seal has a unique and momentous introduction: Heaven is silent for the span of half an hour. The seventh seal is the only multifaceted seal; it contains two sequences of judgment, thirteen in all. The seventh seal embodies all of the elements attributed to the day of the LORD by the Old Testament prophets, and it is pictured as an answer to the prayer for vengeance (wrath) upon those on the earth who unjustly killed the saints during the time of the fifth seal (8:3-5 cf. 6:9-11). These reasons, in combination with Paul's statement in 2 Thessalonians 2:3-4 that the day of the LORD will not come until after the man of lawlessness has been revealed in the temple and the apostasy has taken place, make a strong case that the day of the LORD begins during the seventh seal, or close thereto.

Not only does John record the major movements of the period (the seals), he includes a considerable amount of information regarding other events. For instance, he records the tribulation scene as viewed from Heaven (Rev. 4:1-5:14; 15:1-8), the sealing of the 144,000 Jewish witnesses (7:1-8), the great congregation of martyrs appearing in Heaven (7:9-17), the ministry of the two prophetic witnesses on earth (11:1-14), war on earth and in heaven (12:1-17), the great persecution of the saints (13:1-10), the ministry of the false prophet (13:11-18), world evangelism (14:6-7), the final end of those who worship the Antichrist (14:9-13), the destruction of Babylon—representing Gentile political and religious domination (17:1-19:10), the regal appearing of Christ (19:11-16), and Armageddon (19:17-21). John is also a major source of information for events following the tribulation and an especially important source for events following the millennium.

Preconditions for the tribulation period

Daniel alone gives the two critical preconditions for the beginning of the tribulation period: 1) the existence of national Israel; and, 2) the re-emergence of a future form of the Roman Empire under ten leaders, through which the Antichrist, though not one of the ten, will derive his authority to rule and will emerge as a satanically empowered dictator (Dan. 9:26-27; Rev. 17:12-13). Since the period formally begins with the signing of a treaty between these two parties (Dan. 9:27), it is evident that the absence of either party would preclude the start of the period. In order for the tribulation to unfold both Israel and a modern alliance of nations with some historical connection to the ancient Roman Empire, or the people groups thereof, must be in place.

At the time Daniel wrote, Israel was in captivity and the temple, destroyed by the Babylonians in 586 B.C., had not yet been rebuilt. It would have been apparent to Daniel that in order for the prophecies given to him to be fulfilled, the nation would have to be regathered from their captivity. In fact, it would have been possible for Daniel to discern the building of a third temple based on information in the prophecy of the 70 weeks.[8] The book of Daniel is clear on this point: Israel is the focal point of the tribulation. Failure to recognize this key point has led to many false interpretations of both scripture and history. One error that must be avoided is incorrectly identifying the Church as a new, spiritual form of Israel, or a replacement for Israel. That Israel and the Church are distinct entities is a point that is well established in the New Testament (Rom. 11); [9]

---

[8] According to the prophecy the second temple would be destroyed after the 69th week (v.26) and before the beginning of the 70th week (v.27). Since the temple worship during the 70th week presupposes a temple, it is reasonable to conclude that the prophecy requires the building of a third temple.

[9] Romans 11:1-32 teaches the distinctness of Israel and the Church and indicates that God's plan includes a future for Israel. Having written the most extensive treatise on salvation contained in the New Testament, and having established the fact that Jew and Gentile have equal access to God (10:11-13), Paul anticipated what would be a logical question in the minds of his readers: If it is so that the gospel has now gone to the world, and there is now, in the post-cross era no distinction between Jew and Gentile, how does this truth fit with the promise made to Abraham and his physical seed? In other words, is the gospel going to the world to be interpreted as an indication that God no longer intends to fulfill the promises made to Abraham and his descendants? The question Paul posed is logical in light of the promises and prophecies of the Old Testament. His answer is an unequivocal, "No!" God has not rejected his people Israel (vv.11-32). Some might suggest that Paul's answer was nothing more than a summation of what he had said previously, *i.e.,* that since there is no distinction between Jew and Gentile, Jews still have equal access to God. However, that is not at all what Paul said. Why would Paul argue that individual Jews could be saved? No one in the early church questioned that fact. The very early church was composed almost exclusively of Jews, and all of the Apostles were Jews. To suggest that Paul was merely continuing an argument of equal access is patently absurd. He was not talking about the possibility of individual Jews coming to salvation; he was talking about the disposition of the nation. Let us get the question Paul anticipated, and its answer straight. The question is not: "Do Jews still have equal access to God by faith in Christ?" The question is: Has God rejected his people *i.e.,* the ones whom he foreknew (Amos 3:2)? The answer he gave is an unequivocal, "No." Having asked the question he anticipated and given its answer, Paul moved next to the explanation. His first argument was that history demonstrates Israel's disobedience and lack of faith has not invalidated the covenant (vv.2-6). As proof, he appealed to the Old Testament Scriptures. He quoted 1 Kings 19:10 in which Elijah complained to God that Israel in its spiritually degenerated state had forsaken the covenant, torn down God's altars, and killed his prophets. Nevertheless, in spite of all that, God did not abandon Israel. Why? –Because God had a remnant according to his grace. In other words, the fulfillment of the covenant made with Abraham and his seed is not based on works (*i.e.,* Israel's righteousness), but upon God's grace and his choice in election. Paul went on to develop this point further in verses 6-9. In fact, he established from the Old Testament that God himself was the source of Israel's spiritual stupor and blindness (vv.7-10). How are we to understand this? Clearly Paul was indicating that God

allowed Israel to stumble into spiritual darkness for a purpose—that he might manifest to them that their election as a nation is solely by grace. Paul then repeated his original question in a different way. He asked: "Did they (Israel) stumble (ἔπταισαν, "to stagger" or "stumble"—a recoverable misstep, or metaphorically speaking, "a blunder"), so as to fall (πέσωσιν = "to fall into ruin" {irrecoverably})? It was an acknowledged fact that Israel had stumbled; the question addressed here is: Did this stumbling result in Israel's complete and irrecoverable fall, *i.e.*, the nation's disinheritance by God? Paul's answer is a definitive, "No!" ("May it never be" [μὴ γένοιτο] is the equivalent of the English expression, "Absolutely not!") Paul's explanation of what happened, and why it happened, is that Israel's transgression had resulted in the salvation of the Gentiles (which illustrates a clear dispensational transition between the Old and New Testament economies). Secondly, Paul said that God had a purpose in allowing Israel to stumble and in the gospel going to the Gentiles; it was to provoke Israel to jealousy that they might be saved. In verse 12 Paul reflected on the blessedness of Israel coming to God in the future. If God brought salvation to the world out of Israel's spiritual failure, what will he bring out of their conversion? This theme is developed further in verse 15, where Paul said that Israel's acceptance will result in "life from the dead," likely a reference to the physical resurrection promised for the last days (cf. Dan. 12:1-3, also Rev. 20:4). Interestingly, this resurrection is said to occur at the beginning of the millennium, shortly after Israel's conversion—the literal interpretation of which is consistent only with premillennialism. How is it that Israel could have failed so miserably, and yet as a people not have forfeited their right to the promises under the Abrahamic covenant? Paul's answer is fourfold. First, because Israel's calling is according to God's grace. Just as individual sinners have no merit in which to boast of their own personal salvation, but are brought to God through his own divine election, so the fulfillment of the promise to Abraham and to his descendants is on the same basis. How could it be otherwise? This point, Paul had already established in verses 2-10. Secondly, we must expand our view of Israel to include all elect Jews from Abraham to that elect generation in the future to whom the promises will be fulfilled. Paul said in verse 16, "…if the first piece of dough be holy, the lump is also; and if the root be holy, the branches are too" (Rom. 11:16, NASB). He then gave an analogy; he said that Israel stands before God, with respect to the promises, with the same standing as Abraham, Isaac, and Jacob (Rom. 11:28). He was not talking about personal salvation; covenant relationship and salvation are two distinct issues. Those who are the descendants of the chosen line (descending from Abraham through Jacob [Israel]) are the physically elect line. Whether or not individuals within that line exercise faith unto salvation and enter into the blessings of the covenant is a matter of individual election. In order for the covenant to be fulfilled, there must be both a physically and spiritually elect people, but the fact that Israel as a nation has not responded to God in faith does not abrogate their physical election, or the validity of the promises; it merely abates the fulfillment until the condition of faith is met. Third, the right to the promises has not been forfeited, because Israel's hardening is only temporary and partial (vv.17-27). Paul warned the Roman Christians not to assume an attitude of superiority over the branches that were broken off (*i.e.*, Israel in its state of unbelief); after all, he said, the Gentiles were not the natural branches, they were engrafted wild branches from another, uncultivated tree. They may partake of the sap (*i.e.*, the life) of the root, but they are not the natural branches and should never lose sight of the fact that the root supports them, not they the root. We could say that those who deny the continued validity of God's covenant with Israel undercut their own standing. Such is the nature of covenantalism; in its arrogance that the Church has now supplanted Israel, it does precisely what Paul warned the Church not to do. Paul anticipated such a response (v.19), and again repeated his warning (v.20), "…you stand by faith. Do not be conceited (μὴ ὑψηλὰ φρόνει, "do not exalt yourselves in your own minds"), but fear; for if God did not spare the natural branches, neither will He spare you." Indeed, God can re-engraft Israel if they do not remain in unbelief (vv.23-24). How would any of this discussion in Romans 11 make sense if Israel and the Church were the same entity as covenantalists maintain? What Paul has stated as a mere possibility in verses 17-24 (*i.e.*, that Israel could be grafted back into the tree), he declared to be a future certainty in verses 25-27. He revealed a mystery in order to keep their egos in check; that mystery is that Israel's hardening is only partial (ἀπὸ μέρους = "of a part") and temporary (until such time as "the fullness of the Gentiles comes in"), cf. v.25. Once the fullness of the Gentiles comes in all Israel will be saved. Paul's assertion that Israel will undergo a national conversion in the future is consistent with many Old Testament passages (Isa. 44:1-5, 21-23; Jer. 3:15; 23:14-18; 31:1, 27-34; Ezek. 11:19-20; 20:1-44; 36:25-32; 37:11-14, 21-28; 43:6-9; Hos. 6:1-3; 14:4-8; Joel 2:12-17, 38-32; Mic. 7:18-20; Zech. 13:7-9). The truth that Paul revealed here, that God has a future planned for Israel in which the nation will come to faith and the covenant will be fulfilled to them (verse 27 specifically mentions the covenant), evidences that promises were made to Abraham's physical seed, and that those promises have not been revoked, forfeited, or transferred. Furthermore, the conception of the future given in this passage is precisely that of historic, dispensational premillennialism—not covenantalism. The fourth reason Paul gave that the right to the promises had not been forfeited is because God's gifts to and calling of Israel are irrevocable (vv.28-29). At the time this letter was written, Israel was in rejection of the gospel (v.28), but they are nonetheless, according to God's choice (ἐκλογὴν, "election," v.28), beloved for the sake of the fathers to whom the promises were made. Let us consider that. It is sometimes argued that this statement simply refers to elect Jews within the Church, but Paul cannot be referring to elect Jews within the Church, since he states that from the standpoint of the gospel "they are enemies" (v.28). Clearly, he was referring to a people (Israel) who at the time he wrote this letter were not regenerated—who, in fact, had rejected the gospel; and he states that despite their current spiritual condition, they are still, according to God's election, "beloved," because of their fathers. Finally, Paul completes his thought in verse 29 with these words: "for the gifts and the calling of God are irrevocable" (note that the opening preposition links this clause as a continuation of the previous thought concerning Israel's election). Where does this line of reasoning lead us? Simply to this: The gifts and the calling of God, once given, will not be rescinded. This does not mean that God may not discontinue temporary endowments as we see happen in the case of Saul in the Old Testament. Such endowments were not gifts, and were by nature temporary. What Paul's statement means is that God will never take back a gift; and there can be no doubt that God's promise to Abraham constituted an eternal gift, as Paul himself clearly implies here, and which is expressly stated by God in the giving of the promise (Gen. 13:15; 17:7,9,19). Paul concludes his line of argumentation by comparing the present disobedience of Israel to the former disobedience of the Gentiles, neither of which can be seen as a final disposition. God previously shut up the Gentiles in their disobedience in order to show them mercy, by bringing them to the end of themselves; and he is now doing the same with Israel (vv.30-32).

therefore, it is not possible that the Church could fulfill Israel's role in the coming tribulation and millennium.

We learn from Daniel not only that Israel must be in existence prior to the beginning of the tribulation, we also learn of an alliance of nations that will be in existence and through whose rulers the Antichrist will derive his authority. The details of the emergence of this alliance are laid out in Daniel 2:1-45 and 7:1-28. In order to understand the place this confederation of nations occupies in the prophetic program, we must understand Daniel 2:1-45, the account of Nebuchadnezzar's dream, and Daniel 7:1-28, the account of Daniel's prophetic vision.

a. Nebuchadnezzar's dream (Daniel 2:1-45)

The first information regarding the empire over which the Antichrist will rule was revealed in Daniel 2:1-45. The revelation is in two parts: a dream given by God to Nebuchadnezzar, the King of Babylon (vv.29-35), and the interpretation of that dream given through Daniel (vv.36-45). In his dream Nebuchadnezzar saw a great statue with a head of gold, chest and arms of silver, belly and thighs of bronze, legs of iron, and feet partly of iron and partly of clay. As Nebuchadnezzar continued to watch, a rock was cut out not by human hands. This rock struck the statue on its feet and toes crushing them; at the same time the statue crumbled and was swept away by the wind, but the rock that struck the statue became a great mountain, filling the whole earth. God revealed the meaning of Nebuchadnezzar's dream to Daniel, who explained it to the King (2:27-45). According to Daniel's interpretation, each of the parts of the statue represents a world empire, four in all (vv. 37-40). Nebuchadnezzar, representing Babylon, was the head of gold. Afterward there were to be three more world empires (historically, these correspond to Medo-Persia, Greece, and Rome). The fourth empire was different from the others in that it was described as having two forms: the first form being the legs of iron, and the second being the feet partly of iron and partly of clay. As one proceeds from the head to the feet, the prophecy moves forward in time; thus the form represented by the feet and toes is to be the final form of the fourth world empire, which is Rome. God also revealed through Daniel the meaning of the rock cut out not by human hands, which crushed the feet and toes and caused the entire statue to crumble and to be blown away. The rock represents the kingdom of God, which will replace all the previous world empires and which will endure forever (v.44). Several observations are to be made from this passage, all of which will be confirmed subsequently in Daniel's parallel vision (Dan. 7:1-28). First, Nebuchadnezzar's dream relates to that period of time that Jesus, in the Olivet Discourse, referred to as "the times of the Gentiles" (Lk. 21:24), that time during which Israel is to be dominated by Gentile powers, beginning with Babylon and extending through the tribulation up to the point at which Christ appears and establishes the visible kingdom of God. Second, the dream relates to the future, since it pictures the inauguration of God's eternal kingdom on earth (cf. 7:13-14, 26-27; 12:9). Third, some form of the fourth world empire (Rome) will be present at the time God sets up his eternal kingdom. It will be different from the original form in that as the feet and toes of the statue were composed of iron and clay, which do not adhere, so this kingdom will be an alliance of nations, some weak and some strong, each with its own characteristics (vv.42-44). In destroying this kingdom God will end the period of Gentile world domination pictured in Nebuchadnezzar's dream.

b. Daniel's Vision (Daniel 7:1-28)

Fifty-one years after Nebuchadnezzar's dream, God communicated a parallel revelation to Daniel in a vision (Dan. 7:1-28).[10] The main points of Daniel's vision correspond to the main points of Nebuchadnezzar's dream. In his vision Daniel saw four beasts. The first was like a lion and had the wings of an eagle. As Daniel watched, the wings were torn off and the beast was lifted from the ground so that it stood on its two feet like a man and the heart of a man was given to it. As Daniel continued to look, he saw another beast that looked like a bear. This second beast was raised up on one of its sides, and it had three ribs in its mouth (v.5). Afterwards, Daniel saw a third beast that looked like a leopard with four wings on its back. This beast had four heads, and it was given authority to rule. Finally, Daniel saw a fourth beast with iron teeth, terrifying and very powerful. It crushed and devoured its victims and trampled whatever was left of the former beasts. The fourth beast had ten horns, and another horn came up among them. The last horn uprooted three of the original horns; Daniel described it as having eyes like the eyes of a man and a mouth speaking boastfully (vv.7-8). Next Daniel saw thrones set in place, and the Ancient of Days taking his seat of judgment. As Daniel continued to look, the little horn was slain and his body was thrown into the fire. At this point Daniel saw one "like a son of man" approach the Ancient of Days. This one was given authority, glory, and sovereign power to rule; and all the people of the earth worshiped him. His kingdom is to be an everlasting kingdom. Daniel did not understand the meaning of the things he had seen, so in his vision he approached one standing nearby and asked the meaning of the vision. He was told that the four beasts represent four kingdoms that will arise on the earth, and that the saints of the Most High will receive the kingdom and possess it forever (vv.15-16). He was still concerned over the meaning of the fourth beast. As he continued to watch, this beast was waging war with the saints and overcoming them (vv. 19-21 cf. Mt. 24:9; Rev. 6:9-11). However, the

---

[10] Nebuchadnezzar's dream occurred in 604 B.C. (the second year of his reign), and Daniel's vision occurred in 553 B.C. (the first year of Belshazzar).

Ancient of Days intervened, and the kingdom was given to the saints (vv.21-22).[11] The explanation that Daniel received concerning the fourth beast was that it represented a fourth kingdom that will arise on the earth. This fourth kingdom will be worldwide, different from all the previous kingdoms, and it will crush all of the preceding kingdoms. The ten horns on the beast are representative of ten kings who will arise, and the little horn represents another king who will arise and subdue three of the ten. This one will speak against God and oppress the saints, who will be given into his hand for three and one-half (years). However, God will judge this king and turn the kingdom over to the saints who will possess it forever (vv.23-27).

c. Correlating Nebuchadnezzar's dream and Daniel's vision

Both Nebuchadnezzar's dream and Daniel's vision pertain to the period in history known as "the times of the Gentiles," the period during which Israel is under Gentile domination (Lk. 21:24). Each of the beasts in Daniel's vision corresponds to part of the statue in Nebuchadnezzar's dream. Both Nebuchadnezzar's dream and Daniel's vision deal with the successive world empires of Babylon, Medo-Persia, Greece, Rome, and the future alliance that comes out of Rome (*i.e.*, Rome's final form). Both prophetic revelations foresaw the fourth kingdom as present immediately prior to and replaced by God's eternal kingdom. Also, both revelations contain certain details about the fourth world empire and God's eternal kingdom that will follow. From a comparison of Nebuchadnezzar's dream and Daniel's vision it is possible to construct the following picture of the alliance that will be in place at the beginning of the tribulation. Both revelations indicate that the final form of the Roman Empire will be composed of an alliance of ten nations, or groups of nations; this is represented in Nebuchadnezzar's statue by the ten toes and in Daniel's vision by the ten horns.[12] Daniel 2:40-43 indicates that this final kingdom is to be a "divided kingdom" as indicated by the fact that while iron and clay can be molded together, they do not adhere. Adding to this the fact that the little horn must subdue three of the original horns (Dan. 7:24), it is apparent that this empire is a confederation built upon intrigue, coercion, and force. By comparing these two prophetic revelations with Daniel 9:24-27, we can identify the "little horn" of Daniel

---

[11] Revelation 8:1-20:6 is a detailed account of God's intervention through the outpouring of divine judgment to prepare the way for the visible (geopolitical) kingdom of God on earth.

[12] There could be more than ten nations in this alliance. The number ten refers to the number of principal leaders in the initial confederation; three of those will be overthrown by the Antichrist (the "little horn"). The Antichrist is not one of the leaders of these ten nations; he is an individual chosen by those leaders, who will give him authority to rule (Rev. 17:12-13). We may surmise that some future global disaster (possibly natural/physical, economic, or political), or the fear of some impending disaster will be the occasion for these leaders to surrender their national sovereignty to the Antichrist.

7:24-25 as the Prince (*i.e.*, the Antichrist) who will make the covenant with Israel, which will begin the seven-year period of tribulation.

The first half of the seven-year period

Daniel 9:27 indicates that the tribulation is to be divided into two equal parts; and at the midpoint the Roman Prince will break his covenant with Israel, desecrating the temple. Paul expanded on the nature of this desecration as the time when the man of lawlessness will enter the temple purveying himself as God and being worshiped as such (2 Thess. 2:4). Likely the abomination itself involves the setting up of an image of the Antichrist in the temple (Mt. 24:15 cf. Rev. 13:11-18); it is this event that marks the beginning of a time of distress so severe that it will be unequaled since the beginning of the world (Mt. 24:15-22).

The covenant that begins the tribulation period

The tribulation period formally begins with the signing of a treaty between the Antichrist and the nation of Israel (Dan. 9:27).[13] While the precise nature and provisions of this treaty are not stated, it is likely that it will be some form of security guarantee for Israel, the lesser and weaker of the two powers. It is possible this treaty will allow for the rebuilding of the temple, since the temple must be in operation by the midpoint of the period, and since the breaking of the treaty involves a desecration of the temple. Perhaps this treaty will be the occasion of great celebration and hopefulness that the Middle-East conflict is finally at an end. This may account for why Paul said, "While people are saying, 'Peace and safety,' destruction will come on them suddenly, as labor pains on a pregnant woman, and they will not escape" (1 Thess. 5:3). Paul was clearly referring to the onset of the events leading up to the day of the LORD (cf. v. 2), and it is interesting to note that "labor pains" is the metaphor used by Christ in Matthew 24:8 to describe the opening phase of the tribulation (cf. Isa. 26:17-27:1). Just as labor pains are not the main event, but merely lead up to the birth, so there will be waves of distress in the tribulation leading up to the main event, which is the day of the LORD.

The rebuilding of the Jewish temple (the third temple)

The Jewish temple must be rebuilt in order for some of the prophecies of the tribulation period to be fulfilled. The construction of this temple could begin either before or after the seven-year period begins; however, it must be sufficiently complete prior to the midpoint for sacrifices to be offered (Dan. 9:27). Since the reintroduction of the sacrificial system supposes not only the temple structure, but also a qualified and trained priesthood with all of the implements and intricate procedures for sacrificial worship, one could probably conclude the necessity for advance preparation extending

---

[13] Israel will not recognize the true character of the Antichrist until well into the tribulation period, possibly as late as the midpoint, when the abomination in the temple occurs.

back well before the beginning of the tribulation. Not only must the Jews relearn the intricacies of worship in the temple, much research and preparation will be required both for the qualification of priests and the purification of the temple, and the re-creation of its implements. In any case, the temple and sacrificial system must be in place prior to the midpoint of the period; there are several reasons for this. 1) Daniel 9:27 states that in the middle of the tribulation the Prince will put a stop to sacrifice and grain offering, even desecrating the Holy Place. 2) In Matthew 24:15, Jesus referred to Daniel 9:27 and warned that when believers living at that time see the abomination spoken of by Daniel standing in the Holy Place, they are to realize that the time of great tribulation is upon them. 3) The Apostles Paul and John both refer to the temple of the tribulation period. Paul alluded to the abomination in the temple, stating that the man of lawlessness will seat himself in God's temple displaying himself as being God (2 Thess. 2:3-4); and John in his vision of the tribulation period reported being asked to measure the temple and its altar (Rev. 11:1).

The beginning of tribulation events—seals 1-4

The most detailed account of the events of the tribulation is recorded in the book of Revelation. In John's vision he saw the tribulation events unfold from a heavenly perspective, and it is from that perspective he related his description of what he saw. In his vision John saw God seated on his throne. The scene was certainly beyond the limits of what John could easily record. It was as if he struggled for words to describe the incredible, and in some cases, horrific events. In John's vision, he saw God seated on a throne, attended by myriads of the heavenly host (Rev. 4:1-11). As John stood in awe of the scene he noticed a scroll in the right hand of God, sealed with seven seals. A proclamation was heralded: "Who is worthy to break the seals and open the scroll?" John wept because no one in Heaven, or on earth, was found who was worthy to open the scroll; but then John saw in his vision a Lamb looking as if it had been slain, standing by the throne. The Lamb reached out and took the scroll from him who sat on the throne. Suddenly, all of Heaven erupted in praise, adoration, and worship of the Lamb. As John continued to watch, the Lamb began to break the seals of the scroll (Rev. 5:1-14). Most of the events recorded in the book of Revelation are presented as the outcome of the breaking of these seven seals, which are the seven great movements of the tribulation period. It is important to recognize that the seals do not represent discrete events, but movements into which most of the events are grouped. While the book of Revelation generally proceeds sequentially, there are some parenthetical and recursive sections that interrupt the chronological flow.[14] Paul indicated in 2 Thessalonians 2:1-3 that the day of the LORD cannot begin until after the abomination in the temple, which

---

[14] For a more information on the chronology of the book of Revelation see, "The Chronology of the Tribulation" in this Appendix beginning on page 242.

occurs at the midpoint of the period; and as we will see there are reasons for suspecting that the day of the LORD may begin during the time of the seventh seal, or close thereto.

Four of the seven seals of Revelation will be broken in the first half of the tribulation period.[15] The first seal allows for the geopolitical events associated with the rise of the kingdom of the Antichrist (Rev. 6:1-2). This confederation of nations seems to be in a state of flux throughout the period, as is indicated by the constant state of conflict. The breaking of the second seal allows war (Rev. 6:3-4). Daniel indicates that the "little horn" (the Antichrist), will pull up by the roots three of the leaders of the ten-nation alliance. Likely it is this event that propels him to the place of control over this empire (Dan. 7:8). The third seal allows for large-scale famine (Rev. 6:5-6), and during the time of the fourth seal a quarter of the world's population will perish as a result of the wars, famine, and pestilence (Rev. 6:7-8), though the details are sketchy.

The invasion of Israel by many nations

In Ezekiel 38-39, Ezekiel described a great invasion that will take place involving "Gog" of the land of Magog, the prince of Rosh, Meshech, and Tubal.[16] This power, located to the east and northeast of the Black Sea, along with its allies (Persia [Iran], Ethiopia [Sudan], Put [Libya], Gomar and Beth-Togarmah [the region near Turkey]) will invade Israel and eventually experience their destruction as God intervenes to preserve his people. Not only will this invading army be destroyed, but the homeland of the principal nation (Magog) will also be destroyed (39:6). The prophecy in Ezekiel pictures this happening at a time when Israel is living in peace and safety, but prior to their national conversion (39:22-29 cf. Zech. 12:1-14). This invasion will occur in connection with the abomination at the midpoint of the period and the subsequent siege of Judea and portions of Jerusalem; it appears that this siege will last through the second half of the tribulation period until Christ returns to rescue his people.

The spiritual rebirth of Israel

Although there is to be a partial regathering of Israel to their land prior to the beginning of the period, and almost certainly additional regatherings throughout the first part of the tribulation period, Israel is regathered in unbelief, as indicated in the

---

[15] The fifth seal corresponds to the persecution that begins shortly after the abomination takes place in the temple at the midpoint of the period (cf. Mt. 24:8-13). Thus, it appears that the first four seals take place in the first half of the period.

[16] (See the footnote on page 127.) It seems best to equate Gog with the Antichrist. This is in contrast to the popular "two-invasion theory." According to the two-invasion theory, the invasion described in Ezekiel 38-38 is the first of two invasions of Israel during the tribulation, with the invasion by Gog and the invasion by the Antichrist (Mt. 24:25) being distinct. However, there are major difficulties with this theory; consequently, it seems best to view Gog and the Antichrist as the same individual.

prophecy of the "dry bones" (Ezek. 37:1-14 cf. 36:22-38). Zechariah 12:2-10 places the conversion of Israel after God defends them from the nations that have invaded the land (likely a reference to the invasion of Israel by Gog, cf. Ezek. 38-39). Precisely when this spiritual rebirth occurs is uncertain; however, it will occur sometime in the second half of the period.

The second half of the seven-year period

While the first half of the tribulation period is not without its difficulty, the most severe events, including the day of the Lord, fall into the second half of the period. The events are summarized as follows.

1. Satan and his host thrown down to the earth

Revelation describes a conflict between Michael and his angels, and Satan and his angels that seems to occur near the midpoint of the period. As a result of this conflict in the heavens, Satan and his host of fallen angels will be confined to the earth (Rev. 12:7-13). "Heaven" undoubtedly denotes the physical heavens rather than the heavenly city (note the use of the plural "heavens" in v.12, which ordinarily refers to the physical heavens, *i.e.*, the universe). This event signals the beginning of a period of great joy in the heavens (which are apparently the domain of some angels, cf. Rev. 12:12), but great distress upon the earth. As Satan sees that his time is short, he will persecute believers with great fury, both Jews and Gentiles (v.12). His anger will be particularly focused on Israel (vv. 13-17). This event is closely associated in time with the abomination in the temple. From this point forward things on earth will go from bad to worse. Nevertheless, God's wrath is yet to be poured out; all that has occurred so far is merely distress caused by human and angelic rebellion against God.

2. The abomination that makes the temple desolate

The midpoint of the period is marked by the abomination in the temple. This event is first mentioned in Daniel 9:27. Jesus warned that this will mark the beginning of the time of severe persecution (Mt. 24:15-22) for Jewish believers. But what is the abomination? Interestingly, this event is neither expanded upon by Christ, nor directly mentioned in the book of Revelation, though Revelation does mention the worship of the Antichrist (Rev. 13:1-8). It was Paul in 2 Thessalonians 2:2-4 who pulled back the curtain of mystery surrounding the nature of this event. Paul indicated that the Antichrist, whom he referred to as "the man of lawlessness," will oppose every god or object of worship, even taking his seat in the temple of God in an attempt to manifest himself as God (2 Thess. 2:7-12).

Putting together the accounts from Matthew 24:15-22 and Revelation 12:7-13:18, the sequence of events at the midpoint is as follows: Satan and his followers will be confined to the earth (Rev. 12:7-12). The Antichrist will enter the temple purveying himself as God (Rev. 13:1-18 cf. 2 Thess. 2:3-4). Those with discernment will recognize the significance of this event and immediately flee Jerusalem and Judea (Mt. 24:15-22). God will provide a place of safety for those who flee into the wilderness (Rev. 12:14). Satan and his Antichrist will attempt to destroy those who flee, but divine intervention will prevent them from doing so (Rev. 12:15-16).

3. The new world economic and religious order

Once the true character of the Antichrist is manifested through his desecration of the temple, two things will quickly fall into place. First, the false prophet (referred to in Revelation 13:11-15 as the second "beast"), will immediately begin to perform lying signs and wonders attesting to the deity of the Antichrist (Rev. 13:11-18). Secondly, Revelation 17 indicates that an apostate religious system already in place will be utilized to promote the worship of the Antichrist. As further inducement to worship the Antichrist the false prophet will provide for every person to receive a mark on his forehead or right hand, indicating acceptance of the religion of the Antichrist (Rev. 13:16-18). Unless one has this identifying mark or number they will be blocked from making financial transactions.

4. The ministry of God's two prophets

At the midpoint of the tribulation two prophets will appear on the scene and prophesy in Jerusalem for most of the remainder of the period (Rev. 11:3-13). These two prophets will testify to the true God and prophesy, and their enemies will be powerless to stop them (v.5). Not only will these prophets prophesy, they will have the power to call down plagues on the earth (v.6), which will clearly demonstrate the inferiority of the Antichrist to the real Christ. When their ministry is finished, God will allow the Antichrist to slay these two prophets. Their dead bodies will lie in the street for three and a half days while the rebellious of the earth celebrate their deaths. However, the celebration will be cut short when these two prophets are raised from the dead and ascend into heaven in plain sight of their enemies (Rev.11:7-13).

5. The martyrdom of Christians

The fifth seal (Rev. 6:9-10) is broken shortly after the midpoint of the tribulation and allows the Antichrist to overcome and martyr many Christians. This persecution and martyrdom was foreseen in Daniel (7:25), Matthew (24:9), and Revelation (6:9-11). Jesus' survey of the tribulation in Matthew 24:9-25 is largely occupied with the description of this persecution. The sixth seal allows for a great cosmic disturbance, possibly involving an object striking the earth (Rev. 6:12-17). As terrifying as this event will be, it is only a harbinger of what is yet to come. That the event described in the sixth seal is cosmic in nature is further supported by two observations. 1) The response of those on earth will be to hide in caves and the rocks of the mountains (v.16)—not a response one would expect for an earthquake, but certainly appropriate for those seeking shelter from the falling debris of a small cosmic collision. 2) This incident immediately precedes the first four trumpets (Rev. 8:7-13) which are all clearly described as cosmic in nature. It is the sixth seal that will signal the great day of God's wrath is imminent (cf. Rev. 6:16-17).

6. The 144,000 Jews sealed

Although the distress of the first six seals will be difficult, it will pale in comparison to the divine judgments that are to come afterward. It will be well into the second half of the period when God seals 144,000 virgin Jewish men (Rev. 7:1-8 cf. 14:4); this sealing appears to protect them from certain aspects of the judgments to follow (v.3 cf. 9:4) and signifies their election to a unique body of believers (Rev. 14:1-5). Beyond these few statements we do not know the full significance of this sealing.[17]

7. The seventh seal

The seventh seal encompasses a series of seven judgments referred to as the trumpet judgments, and the seventh trumpet is another series of seven judgments referred to as the bowl judgments, all of which issue from the seventh trumpet. Both the frequency and intensity of these judgments increase as the end of the period approaches. So severe is the judgment of this time, Jesus said that if it were allowed to continue longer than the appointed time no one would survive, but for the sake of his elect God will not allow that to happen (Mt. 24:22). God's preservation of his elect is both merciful and necessary, since there must be elect survivors to enter the millennium in natural (unglorified) bodies in order to repopulate the earth as indicated in Isaiah 65:17-25.

In his vision as John saw the breaking of the seventh seal, he recorded that there was silence in Heaven for about half an hour. It is as if Heaven gasps at the prospect of what is about to come upon the earth. Seven angels were given seven trumpets (v.2), and another angel appeared at the golden altar with a golden censer and much incense (v.3). The smoke of this incense and the prayers of the saints ascended to God. The prayers were those made by the martyred saints from under the altar; they are prayers for retribution upon those on the earth who killed them because of their testimony of faith in Christ (Rev. 6:9-11). The angel is seen taking the censer filled with fire from the altar and hurling it to the earth (vv.4-5). This gesture would seem to indicate that God is now prepared to answer the prayers of the saints that their blood might be avenged, and that those on the earth be judged for their wickedness. It is possible that this event signals the beginning of the day of the LORD.

---

[17] The 144,000 reappear in Revelation 14:1-4 where they are pictured on Mount Zion with Christ, apparently after the tribulation is over, singing a song that only they can learn.

8. The trumpet judgments

The trumpet judgments are a seven-fold judgment. The first four of the judgments form a sequence of cosmic events unleashing enormous destruction upon the earth. The first trumpet pictures something similar to hail burning as it falls from the sky. Its mixture with blood undoubtedly indicates the terrible result it will have as it rains down upon the earth. The devastation to the earth will be catastrophic; falling debris will burn a third of the earth. Included in the destruction is a third of earth's plant life. The second trumpet judgment depicts an object falling to the earth that John could only liken to "a great mountain, burning with fire" (Rev. 8:8-9). The impact of this object will destroy a third of the earth's oceans. It is of such destructive proportions as to be rivaled only by the biblical flood. The third angel sounded his trumpet and something in appearance like a star, burning as a torch, fell from heaven. Of course, John spoke phenomenologically, describing the event the way it appeared to him. This is an object, which from John's vantage point, looked like a star. The result of this object, possibly an asteroid or comet fragment hitting the earth will be that a third of the world's fresh water will be contaminated and many people will die. The fourth trumpet is another cosmic judgment. We know only that some event will affect the visibility of the sun, moon, and stars for one-third of the day and one-third of the night. This phenomenon is probably the same as that described in Isaiah 13:9-10 (cf. 24:19-23). The events of the first four trumpet judgments will comprise the greatest catastrophe the earth has seen since the biblical flood.

After the fourth trumpet, John's attention turned to the voice of one proclaiming, "Woe, woe, woe, to those who dwell on the earth, because of the remaining blasts of the trumpet of the three angels who are about to sound" (Rev. 8:13, NASB). It is difficult to imagine judgments any more severe than those having already taken place, but that is what the angel proclaims. As the fifth angel sounded his trumpet, John saw another angel, referred to as a "star," literally, "a bright one," who had fallen (aorist participle— "fallen" at some time in the past) from heaven to the earth (Rev. 9:1-12). While the identity of this angel is not stated, it is possible that it refers to Satan, who was previously cast out of heaven and confined to earth (Rev. 12:7-13). The angel was given the key to the Abyss—a place where certain demonic creatures are imprisoned (cf. Lk. 8:31; Rev. 20:1-3; also Jude 5-7). When the angel opened the Abyss, the sun and the sky were darkened by the smoke which arose out of it, smoke like that of "a great furnace." Out of this smoke came something that from John's vantage point appeared like locusts descending out of the cloud down upon the earth (v.3). These creatures were given the power to afflict men for a period of five months. Although they do not have the power to kill, their sting is like the sting of a scorpion (v.5). During this five-month period, men will be tormented so severely they will wish to die. Only those 144,000 who have the seal of God will be exempt from this terrifying ordeal (v.4).[18] The sixth trumpet signals the release of four angels specifically prepared for this time (Rev. 9:13-19). These fallen angels will be responsible for the deaths of one-third of the world's population by provoking a great war. This passage depicts an army of immense size and destructive force. It is virtually certain that the huge number of combatants, translated "two hundred million" in the NASB (δισμυριάδες μυριά), literally "myriads of myriad{s}," is hyperbolic, meaning a vast or innumerable host. In any case, from the description this certainly ranks as one of the most destructive wars in history. John states that fire, smoke and brimstone proceeded from the mouths of the "horses" upon which this army was conveyed.[19] Again, John employed phenomenological speech in his description of this future war for which he had no appropriate vocabulary.

Finally, the seventh trumpet was sounded. John described the opening scene of this judgment in Revelation 11:15-19. After an excursus in 13:1-15:4, John resumed his discussion of the last trumpet, which unfolded into the seven bowl judgments. The first bowl caused malignant sores to break out on those who received the mark of the Antichrist (the "beast") and worshiped his image (Rev. 16:1-2). The second bowl struck the sea (oceans) such that the water was fouled, becoming like blood, and all the sea creatures in them died (v.3). The third bowl affected the fresh waters in the same way (vv.4-7). The fourth bowl resulted in men being scorched by the heat of the sun (vv.8-9, cf. Isa. 24:6). Yet even after all this, John records that men did not repent, but blasphemed God, whom they clearly recognized as the source of these plagues. Perhaps this awareness will be due to the ministry of the two prophets of God. The fifth bowl caused darkness to fall over the kingdom of the Antichrist (vv.10-11). The sixth bowl prepared the way for the military campaign that will lead up to Armageddon (Rev. 16:12-16 cf. Dan. 11:40-45, Joel 3:9-14). The seventh bowl brought large-scale destruction to the earth of the sort that might be expected from a nuclear war, or possibly another cosmic collision (Rev. 16:17-21).

9. The second coming of Christ

With the completion of the last bowl judgment and the assembling of the armies of the Antichrist in the region of the plain of Megiddo, the stage will be set for the final scene. The Antichrist will turn his attention to the final destruction of the Jewish nation.

---

[18] It is difficult to know how symbolic some of the descriptions are. However, whether symbolic or not, they depict actual events.

[19] Many interpreters point to such expressions as evidence that the book of Revelation cannot be taken at face value. However, we must consider the difficulty that John faced as he struggled to describe his vision of modern warfare. He did not have words for the implements of modern warfare, so he described them as best he could, and we must understand them as best we can. But to dismiss the description as mythic or allegorical simply because John did not have a modern vocabulary is unjustified.

It is in the midst of this desperate circumstance that Christ will descend to the earth to rescue Israel. The particulars concerning the second coming of Christ are revealed in a number of passages (Zech. 14:1-8; Mt. 24:29-31; Rev. 19:11-21), but it is John's account in Revelation that yields the sharpest detail. When the particulars of the second coming are combined from the various accounts the following picture emerges: 1) The sign of Christ will appear in the sky (Mt. 24:29). 2) The world will see Christ returning (Mt. 24:30). 3) This sight will provoke a bitter lament from the unredeemed as they see the Lord approaching in unspeakable splendor and power (Mt. 24:30). 4) Christ will descend upon the Mount of Olives (Zech. 14:4). 5) He will destroy the forces of the Antichrist (Zech. 14:1-3). 6) The Antichrist and his prophet will be thrown into the Lake of Fire (Rev. 19:19-20). 7) The armies that oppose Christ will be slain by the words of his mouth (Rev. 19:21, cf. 2 Thess. 2:8; Zech. 14:12; Isa. 11:4), and the carnage will be very great (Rev. 14:19-20). 8) The surviving saved and unsaved will be gathered for judgment (Mt. 24:31, cf. 13:40,49-50). 9) Satan will be bound and confined in the Abyss (Rev. 20:1-3), presumably along with his host of angelic followers.

The second coming of Christ and the associated events will conclude the tribulation, though some things remain to be done before the millennial phase of the visible kingdom can begin. Of those alive at the end of the period, some will be redeemed, others not. Since only the redeemed may enter the kingdom, there must be a judgment to determine who may enter; this judgment is described by Jesus in Matthew 25:31-46. At this judgment the redeemed will be admitted into the kingdom and the unredeemed will be sent into Hades to await their final judgment following the millennium (Rev. 20:11-15).

The chronology of the tribulation period

There are three areas of chronology to be addressed: 1) absolute external chronology—when the tribulation period will begin with respect to the present; 2) relative external chronology—when the tribulation period occurs in relation to other prophesied future events; and 3) internal chronology—the approximate chronology of the events within the tribulation period.[20]

Absolute external chronology

It is not possible to determine when, with respect to the present, the tribulation period will begin, other than that it will occur in the future. Neither the existence of the Church, nor the length of the Church age is discernable from the Old Testament; also the New Testament nowhere indicates the length of the Church age. Some have tried to

---

[20] Most of the following material on the chronology of the tribulation is adapted from the author's work, *What the Bible Says About the Future,* Second edition. The reader may wish to consult the many illustrations in that volume, which are not reproduced here.

determine the date of the rapture or the beginning of the tribulation period; but all such efforts are futile since the prerequisite information is not given in scripture. However, it is possible to know when the tribulation will begin with respect to other future events, and it is possible to discern a great deal about the internal chronology of the tribulation period.

Relative external chronology

By relative external chronology is meant the chronological relationship of the tribulation to other prophesied events. The Bible indicates that the period of tribulation is a prelude to the millennium. Its purpose is both to prepare Israel for the return of Christ to usher in his eternal kingdom (Zech. 13:7-9), and to judge the world for its unbelief and rejection of God and his Son, Jesus Christ (2 Thess. 2:8-11). Thus, the tribulation is a future event that will lead up to the millennial kingdom. Note the following reasons for believing that the tribulation is a future event.

a. The tribulation and the millennium are sequential phases of the day of the Lord

Scripture presents the judgment aspect of the tribulation and the blessings of the millennium as two phases of the same period called, "the day of the Lord." For this reason many passages treat the tribulation and the messianic kingdom together (Isa. 1:24-2:4; 24:1-25:12; 34:1-35:10; Joel 2:1-32; Zech. 12:1-13:9). The Old Testament knows no other relationship than that the beginning of the day of the Lord (in its judgment aspect) is the prelude to the establishment of the visible aspect of the Messianic kingdom. A study of the second coming also sheds light on the chronological relationship of the tribulation period to the millennium. Many passages that deal with the second coming picture it as the consummation of the tribulation period and the beginning of the millennium (Zech. 14:1-11; Rev. 19:11-20:6; see also Isa. 35:4-10; 61:2b-3; Joel 3:9-21; Zech. 2:6-13).

b. The prophecies concerning the tribulation could not have been fulfilled in the past.

The tribulation period must be in the future for two reasons: 1) No set of events in history matches the events of the tribulation period. 2) There are preconditions to the beginning of the tribulation that have not been met. That no set of events in history matches the prophetic description of the tribulation period, when those prophecies are understood in a normal/objective manner, is fairly obvious; therefore, let us focus on the preconditions.

There are preconditions both to the beginning of the tribulation, and to some of the events pertaining to the midpoint, and those preconditions have not been met. One prerequisite to the beginning of the period is that subsequent to the destruction of Jerusalem and the second temple in A.D. 70, Israel must come back into existence as a nation at a time when some form of the Roman Empire exists. Daniel 9:24-27 pictures the tribulation as beginning when the Roman Prince (the Antichrist) makes a covenant with

Israel. This necessitates the existence of both parties to this covenant. Note also that the nation of Israel is at the center of many tribulation prophecies (Jer. 30:4-7; Dan. 9:27; Joel 2:1-11; 3:1-16; Zeph. 1:2-3:11; Mt. 24:4-31; Rev. 7:1-8; 11:1-2), and one of the descriptions applied to the tribulation period in the Old Testament is, "a time of trouble for Jacob" (Jer. 30:7). Since Israel ceased to exist nationally in A.D. 70 and did not come back into existence until 1948, it is impossible that any events between A.D. 70 and 1948 could qualify as the fulfillment of the tribulation prophecies. That no events prior to A.D. 70 qualify as the fulfillment of the tribulation prophecies is evident from Daniel 9:24-27, which clearly indicates that the tribulation will not begin until sometime after the destruction of Jerusalem and the second temple, which occurred in A.D. 70. Another precondition is that the abomination in the temple, which takes place at the midpoint of the tribulation, cannot occur until the tribulation temple (Israel's third temple) is in operation (cf. Dan. 9:27; Mt. 24:15 and 2 Thess. 2:3-4). The necessity of a third temple can be deduced from the prophecy of Daniel's 70 weeks (9:24-27). The 70 weeks prophecy pictures the tribulation (the 70th week) beginning after the destruction of the second temple (v.26), which occurred in A.D. 70. This prophecy requires that a third temple be built sometime after the destruction of the second temple in order for the abomination referred to in verse 27 to take place. Since the third temple has not been built, the tribulation events pertaining to the third temple must be future.

Internal chronology

The internal chronology of the tribulation period presents the most challenges to the student of prophecy, because the chronology of the period is not laid out in a single passage, or even in a single book of the Bible. Our examination of internal chronology will focus on four areas: 1) the length of the period; 2) the major divisions; and, 3) an approximate timeline for major events; and 4) the beginning of the day of the LORD.

a. The length of the tribulation

The length of the tribulation period can be derived from a comparison of Daniel, Matthew, and Revelation. Daniel 9:27, which describes the 70th week of the 70 weeks prophecy, indicates that the abomination in the temple will occur at the midpoint of the period. Matthew 24:4-22 describes the time of Israel's persecution during the tribulation period as beginning when the abomination is set up in the temple, and Revelation 12:6 states that Israel, having fled to the wilderness, will be nourished there for 1260 days. Thus, half of the tribulation period is 1260 days (or approximately 3½ years, cf. Rev. 12:14). That being the case, the total length of the tribulation is approximately 7 years.[21] It is possible to confirm this figure from within the book of Daniel. Daniel 7:25 refers to the fact that the saints living in the tribulation period will be given over to the Roman Prince for "a time, times, and half a time"; this expression is equivalent to three and one half ("a

---

[21] See the previous discussion of the 70 weeks prophecy in the Appendices (p.199).

time" = 1, "times" [Heb. dual] = 2, and "half a time" = ½) [years]. This is confirmed in Revelation 13:5-7, where we read that the authority of the Antichrist to overcome the saints and to compel the inhabitants of the earth to worship him (beginning at the midpoint) is said to extend for 42 months (v.5), or 3½ years. Since the persecution begins at the midpoint and extends to the second coming, the total length of the tribulation period is 7 years, approximately.

b. Major divisions within the tribulation

The prophecy of the 70 weeks provides the key to the internal chronology of the tribulation. That key is the reference to the fact that the abomination in the temple marks the midpoint of the period. Several important prophecies reference this event, or are linked in some way to prophecies that do. Without this piece of information, it would be impossible to construct a useful chronology. Because the abomination in the temple occurs at the midpoint of the tribulation, and because it marks a turning point in the character of the period, the study of the tribulation is arranged according to the subdivision of two halves. This is the arrangement Jesus gave in Matthew 24:4-31, where verses 4-8 describe the first half of the period and verses 9-14 describe the second half, with a recursive section (vv.15-31) starting back in the middle with the abomination and focusing on certain events of the second half.

c. The individual chronologies of Daniel 9:24-27, Matthew 24:3-31, and Revelation 6:1-20:3

The three major tribulation prophecies that convey significant chronological information are: Daniel 9:24-27; Matthew 24:3-31; and Revelation 6:1-20:3.

The chronology of Daniel

While many details concerning the tribulation are revealed throughout the book of Daniel, the basic chronology of the period is presented in the prophecy of the 70 weeks. This prophecy identifies three key events on the tribulation timeline. Those events are: 1) the signing of a treaty between Israel and the Roman Prince that begins the period; 2) the abomination in the temple that marks the midpoint; and, 3) the close of the period, which is marked by the destruction of the one who makes the temple desolate (*i.e.*, the Roman Prince, cf. Dan. 9:27).

The chronology of Matthew 24:4-31

In the Olivet Discourse Jesus gave an overview of the tribulation including the judgment of the nations, which falls between the close of the tribulation and the beginning of the millennium. The chronological structure of 24:4-31 is of considerable importance in understanding tribulation chronology. Several schemes have been proposed for the chronology of this passage. The following are three examples. 1) One proposal suggests that verses 4-14 refer to events in the Church age, leading up to the tribulation period, which according to this scheme are described in verses 15-31. The problem with this view is that it places events clearly associated with the second half of the period into the first half, and events associated with the first half of the tribulation into the period prior to the tribulation. 2) Another proposal is that only verses 4-8 refer to the Church age. The difficulty with this view is that it would jump from the Church age (vv. 4-8) directly to the second half of the tribulation period (vv. 9-31), with no mention of the events of the first half of the tribulation. (The time of severe persecution described in verse 9 clearly falls into the second half of the period, cf. Dan. 7:25 and Rev. 13:1-18.) 3) Yet another proposal is that verses 4-14 describe the first half of the tribulation, whereas verses 15-31 describe the second half. This view faces the same difficulty as the first view, in that it places events associated with the second half of the period (vv.9-14) into the first half of the period (*e.g.*, the martyrdom of the saints, cf. Dan. 7:25). A better option is that verses 4-8 refer to the first half of the tribulation and verses 9-14 refer to the second half, with verses 15-31 representing a recursion back to the middle of the period in order to focus on certain details of the second half. Such a view reflects the transitions found between verses 8 and 9, and between verses 14 and 15.[22]

The chronology of Revelation (6:1-20:3)

The book of Revelation, from 6:1 through 20:3, is essentially in sequential order. However, there are four features to the chronology of Revelation that must be given special attention. 1) Revelation 6:1-20:3 contains three parenthetical sections (7:1-7:17; 10:1-10:11 and 14:1-15:8). These sections do not advance the timeline. 2) This portion of Revelation also contains two recursive sections (11:1-11:13 and 12:1-13:18); in both cases the recursions return to the middle of the period and continue to the end. 3) Time compression and expansion can present problems in that a relatively short section of the book may cover a much longer period of time than a more expansive section. (For instance, the first half of the tribulation period occupies only eight verses.) 4) Some events may overlap since it is not necessary for one event to completely run its course before another begins. One major difficulty with the chronology of Revelation is that it mentions only one of the three chronological markers given in the 70 weeks prophecy – that being the end of the period.[23]

d. The beginning of the day of the Lord

While we cannot be absolutely certain as to when the day of the Lord begins, a credible case can be made that it begins during the time of the seventh seal (Rev. 8:1-6).[24]

---

[22] See the illustration on page 104.

[23] The abomination described in Daniel 9:27 is alluded to in Revelation 13:1-10, but that statement is in one of the recursive sections of the book, where it is disconnected from the main timeline.

[24] The day of the Lord begins during the tribulation period and continues into eternity. The beginning phase of the day of the Lord is a time of great wrath upon the world for its rejection of God and his Son, and its treatment of the saints. The second phase of the day of the Lord is a time

Of the three major passages from which it is possible to discern any tribulation chronology (Dan. 9:27; Mt. 24:3-31; Rev. 6-19) the only passages that specifically identify elements of the tribulation as divine wrath are Revelation 6:16-17 (spoken after the events of the sixth seal) and 15:1-16:21 (in regard to the seven bowls of wrath). It is possible that the sixth seal is the final warning of the wrath to come with the opening of the seventh seal. The two witnesses will have been prophesying the coming day of the LORD before this event happens. When the cosmic event occurs during the time of the sixth seal, it will convey an unmistakable message: Time has now run out. Even those who reject Christ will be fully aware of the fact that divine judgment is imminent (Rev. 6:15-17). While it is tempting to include the sixth seal as part of the day of the LORD because of the nature of the event and the fact that it is so similar to the first four trumpets (which are clearly divine wrath), from a literary standpoint it is clear that the intended transition falls between the sixth and seventh seals, not between the fifth and sixth seals. Also there seems to be a profound qualitative shift with the opening of the seventh seal.

In Revelation 7:1-8 John records the sealing of the 144,000 male Jewish witnesses. Why are they sealed between the sixth and seventh seals? If the sealing is a form of protection from some of the effects of divine wrath (cf. Rev. 7:3), does not the time of their sealing suggest that divine wrath is yet to come? When John finally comes to the breaking of the seventh seal (Rev. 8:1ff.), our attention is immediately arrested, for here John records something of great significance that is said in relation to no other seal. He wrote: "And when He broke the seventh seal, there was silence in Heaven for about half an hour" (NASB). What sound is heard in Heaven other than the continual praise of an infinitely worthy God? Has there ever been silence in Heaven since the creation of the world? We do not know, but we do know that this event is momentous. Something is about to happen that is unlike anything else in this period, or in world history, or, so far as we know, since the beginning. As John proceeds with the description, seven angels are given seven trumpets. We also see another angel holding a golden censer with much incense, and added to it are the prayers of the saints from beneath the golden altar that is before God (Rev. 8:1-6 cf. 6:9-11). This is the same altar mentioned in Revelation 6:9, from which the saints who were martyred under the fifth seal made their petition to God for vengeance upon those who dwell upon the earth. The imagery could not be clearer. God is now ready to judge the world through the undiluted outpouring of divine wrath. Possibly what has happened up to this point is that God has allowed evil people, with the help of demons, latitude to manifest their nature as never before. They will make war, cause destruction and death, and kill the saints. Thus God will judge them by an

---

of great blessing, first in the millennium, then in eternity. The day of the LORD stands in contrast to "the times of the Gentiles" (Lk. 21:24), during which God has allowed the Gentile nations to assert themselves over his elect people.

unprecedented outpouring of wrath. To this we need to add two additional observations. First, in 2 Thessalonians 2:1-9 Paul taught that the day of the LORD will not come until sometime in the second half of the tribulation period. He said:

> Now we request you, brethren, with regard to the coming of our Lord Jesus Christ and our gathering together to Him, that you not be quickly shaken from your composure or be disturbed either by a spirit or a message or a letter as if from us, to the effect that the day of the Lord has come. Let no one in any way deceive you, for it will not come unless the apostasy comes first, and the man of lawlessness is revealed, the son of destruction, who opposes and exalts himself above every so-called god or object of worship, so that he takes his seat in the temple of God, displaying himself as being God. Do you not remember that while I was still with you, I was telling you these things? And you know what restrains him now, so that in his time he will be revealed. For the mystery of lawlessness is already at work; only he who now restrains will do so until he is taken out of the way. Then that lawless one will be revealed whom the Lord will slay with the breath of His mouth and bring to an end by the appearance of His coming; that is, the one whose coming is in accord with the activity of Satan, with all power and signs and false wonders, and with all the deception of wickedness for those who perish, because they did not receive the love of the truth so as to be saved.
> (2 Thess. 2:1-10, NASB)

Here Paul stated that the day of the LORD will not begin until after the Antichrist is revealed and "*the* apostasy" takes place. Some pretribulationists have interpreted the apostasy, or "falling away," as a reference to the rapture, and the revealing of the man of lawlessness as a reference to the appearing of the Antichrist at the beginning of the tribulation period. However, Paul clearly intended for his readers to understand that the revealing of the man of lawlessness is his revealing in the temple, which occurs at the midpoint of the tribulation. Since verses 3-5 comprise one sentence in the original and the grammatical structure requires us to understand the apostasy and the revealing as related events, the apostasy to which Paul referred must be the apostasy that will take place in conjunction with the Antichrist's revealing in the temple. In Matthew 24:3-25 Jesus outlined the events of the tribulation. In verses 4-8 he outlined the events of the first half of the period, and in verses 9-14 the events of the second half, with a recursion jumping back to the midpoint beginning with verse 15 and extending to verse 31. The particulars of the events given by Paul in 2 Thessalonians 2:3-12 are the same set of particulars given by Jesus in Matthew 24:9-25 (which describe the tribulation from the midpoint forward). Jesus said the abomination in the temple will be accompanied by false miracles and spiritual deception (v.24) and will be followed by a great persecution and martyrdom of the saints (v.9), along with a great "falling away" from the faith (vv.10-13). In 2 Thessalonians 2:3-12 Paul described the same set of events: the revealing of the Antichrist in the temple with false miracles and spiritual deception, and the associated "falling away" or apostasy. It should be apparent that both Jesus and Paul were describing the same set of events. That being the case, the clear implication is that the day of the LORD cannot begin until after the apostasy associated with the revealing of the Antichrist in the temple, which places the day of the LORD sometime in the second half of the tribulation period.[25]

We should also note that the event occurring during the time of the fifth seal—the martyrdom of believers—seems to indicate that the period of divine wrath has not begun by that point in time. The events of the fifth seal, recorded in Revelation 6:9-11 (cf. Mt. 25:10), involve the martyrdom of some of the saints living at that time. How can the suffering and death of God's faithful be attributed to an act of divine justice? If on the other hand, the martyrdom occurring at this time represents an event that God has sovereignly allowed, it is the direct causes (Satan, his agents, and evil men)—not God—who are responsible for this evil. That the martyrdom during the fifth seal represents moral evil allowed by God, rather than divine wrath executed by him, is seen from the fact that the martyred saints petition God for justice in avenging their deaths at the hands of evil men (Rev. 6:9-11). If God righteously punishes the evil committed during the time of the fifth seal (Rev. 8:1-6, esp. v.3, cf. 6:9-10), how can it be maintained that the fifth seal is God's righteous judgment upon the world? If the event that occurs during the time of the fifth seal does not represent divine wrath, then it seems likely that the day of the LORD has not yet begun by that time. Thus, we find two strong arguments (Paul's statement in 2 Thessalonians 2:1-10, and the argument from the fifth seal) indicating that the day of the LORD could not begin until sometime in the second half of the tribulation.[26]

---

[25] Also see the discussion of 2 Thessalonians 2:1-12 under, "Rapture Theology" in the following Appendix (p.262).

[26] This does not mean that the rapture could not occur prior to the beginning of the tribulation. The rapture is imminent (Mt. 24:36-44) and could occur at any time prior to the beginning of the day of the LORD. The onset of divine wrath merely serves as the terminal point of the window during which the rapture could occur.

Appendix: Rapture Theology

The rapture refers to Christ's return for his Church, when he will resurrect the dead in Christ and transform the bodies of living saints into their glorified form, instantly calling his Church out of this world and into Heaven; it is an event that is to be completely without warning or signs.[1] While the Bible does not state when the rapture will occur, it does indicate that it is imminent (*i.e.,* that it could happen at any time), and that it will occur before the day of the LORD begins. The subject of the rapture is highly relevant to an understanding of the Olivet Discourse, since this discourse is the first mention and principal explication of the dual nature of Christ's future appearing. (The first future appearing is the rapture of the Church prior to the beginning of the day of the LORD, and the second appearing is the second coming proper at which time Christ will conclude the tribulation judgments and establish his kingdom on earth.)

Since the early 1900s the most popular viewpoint on the timing of the rapture has been "pretribulationism"—the view that the rapture must occur before the tribulation period begins. Prior to the popular revival of premillennialism, which began in earnest in the late nineteenth century, most Christians simply believed that Christ would return and there would be a general judgment, with the righteous inheriting eternal life and the unrighteous inheriting eternal punishment. This is the view of both amillennialism and (with slight modification) postmillennialism. However, premillennialism with its face-value interpretation of future prophecy envisions a literal reign of Christ upon the earth in fulfillment of the promises made to Abraham and his descendants. Needless to say, premillennialism's view of the future is more complex in terms of sorting out what will happen, and when it will happen. Assuming premillennialism to be true, one must deal with the question of whether the tribulation is past or future, as this has everything to do with one's view of the rapture of the Church. If one happens to hold, as do some covenant premillenialists, that the tribulation prophecies were fulfilled in the first century destruction of Jerusalem or the early persecution of the church, then one must hold to a "posttribulational" view of the rapture (meaning that the rapture occurs after, though not immediately after, the tribulation). There are also covenant premillennialists who hold to a literal future tribulation, but believe in a posttribulational rapture.[2]

---

[1] The principal passages describing the rapture are: Matthew 24:36-25:30; 1 Corinthians 15:51-52; and 1 Thessalonians 4:13-18. [The Matthew passage is disputed by many modern pretribulationists. See the footnote concerning pretribulationism beginning on page 155.]

[2] All covenantalists, regardless of their view of the millennium, see the rapture as occurring at the time of the second coming. The reason for this has to do with their view of the Church (*i.e.,* the Body of Christ). According to covenant theology there is only one people of God; and thus, all believers of every historical era are part of the Church (including the Old Testament and the tribulation saints). Since there will be Christians on the earth during the tribulation,

However, most premillennialists believe that the Church will be raptured in advance of the second coming, prior to the outpouring of divine wrath during the tribulation period.[3] The most widely accepted of these views is "pretribulationism"—the belief that the Church must be raptured before the tribulation begins.

Two other views, partial rapturism (the view that only Christians who are watchful will be raptured) and midtribulationism (the view that places the rapture near the midpoint of the tribulation), were poorly supported and neither achieved the level of acceptance that pretribulationism attained. Prior to the 1990s, if one were dispensational, they probably subscribed to pretribulationism. Since the latter part of the twentieth century pretribulationism has become almost a test of orthodoxy in some circles, and it is not uncommon to find it in the doctrinal statements of churches and Christian organizations. It wasn't until the 1990s that pretribulationism faced its first major challenge from within. Marvin Rosenthal, a former International Director of The Friends of Israel Gospel Ministry, a conservative and pretribulational missionary organization, published *The Prewrath Rapture of the Church*.[4] The view proposed by Rosenthal is that since divine wrath is, for reasons he delineates, limited to the latter portion of the tribulation, the Church need only be spared from that portion of the period. Thus according to Rosenthal, the rapture, which is not imminent (from the present perspective), will occur approximately 18 to 24 months prior to the second coming. This book was widely read, and a few pretribulationists, as well as some midtribulationists, began to gravitate toward this view. Although Rosenthal's arguments do not hold up under scrutiny, the view appealed to some who had looked at rapture theology deeply enough to recognize that there were significant problems with pretribulationism's principal arguments.[5] It is unfortunate that Rosenthal's view has come to be identified with the term "pre-wrath," since both pretribulationism and mid-tribulationism are also pre-wrath views; they simply disagree on how much of the tribulation period is divine wrath. Because of the almost certain confusion that might otherwise result from the use of the term "pre-wrath," I will refer to Rosenthal's view as "Rosenthal's pre-wrath view" to distinguish it from pre-wrath positions in general (*i.e.,* any view that places the rapture prior to the beginning of the day of the LORD).

---

covenantalists see this as evidence that the Church will be present; such a view leads naturally to posttribulationism. [Generally, only covenant premillennialists are classified as posttribulational. Amillennialists usually spiritualize eschatology to the point that they do not see the rapture as a discrete event.]

[3] Such a view is generally characteristic of dispensational premillennialism.

[4] Marvin Rosenthal, *The Pre-wrath Rapture of the Church,* Nashville: Thomas Nelson Publishers, 1990.

[5] For an examination of Rosenthal's arguments see: *What the Bible Says About the Future*, Second edition, Chapter 8: "The Rapture of the Church," pp.175-212, by the author.

The biblical background of the rapture

The study of the rapture is of great significance to Church age believers; it represents the completion of salvation—the final and ultimate redemption—the sanctification of the body. Paul wrote in Romans:

> For we know that the whole creation groans and suffers the pains of childbirth together until now. And not only this, but also we ourselves, having the first fruits of the Spirit, even we ourselves groan within ourselves, waiting eagerly for our adoption as sons, the redemption of our body. For in hope we have been saved, but hope that is seen is not hope; for who hopes for what he already sees? But if we hope for what we do not see, with perseverance we wait eagerly for it. (Rom. 8:22-25, NASB)

The final redemption of the body is the great hope shared by every believer. It is the teaching of the New Testament that for the Church age believer, that hope will be realized in an instant, when Christ suddenly appears in the sky to resurrect the dead, and to transform the bodies of living saints into their glorified eternal form, as they are caught up in the air to be with Christ (1 Cor. 15:51-53; 1 Thess. 4:13-18).

Since the existence of the Church was not revealed in the Old Testament, and since the rapture pertains to the Church, there is no reference to the rapture in the Old Testament. Jesus was the first to mention this event (Mt. 24:36-51; Jn. 14:3), and it was he who revealed that his return would involve a dual appearing (Mt. 24:36-25:30), with the first of these appearings—the rapture—being imminent (Mt. 24:36-25:30).[6]

Paul extended the rapture theme, mentioning it in eight passages (Rom. 8:20-23; 1 Cor. 15:35-38; Eph. 1:13-14; Phil. 1:6,10; 3:10-11,20-21; 1 Thess. 1:9-10; 4:13-18; Tit. 2:11-14). From Paul's statements we can gather the following facts concerning the rapture.

1. The spirits of Church age believers who die prior to the rapture will be reunited with their resurrection bodies (1 Thess. 4:14).

2. The resurrected believers will rise first (1 Cor. 15:52-53; 1 Thess. 4:15-16).

3. Living believers will be "changed" (*i.e.*, their bodies will be transformed into a glorified state suitable for eternity) and they will be caught up to meet Christ in the air (1 Cor. 15:52-53; 1 Thess. 4:17).

Paul also mentioned that the Church is not destined to experience the wrath of God at the day of the LORD, but to the obtaining of salvation (1 Thess. 1:1-10; 5:9, cf. Rom. 5:9).

James made reference to the rapture and associated it with personal accountability before Christ, possibly alluding to the judgment seat of Christ that follows the rapture (James 5:7-9). Peter equated the rapture with the completion of the

---

[6] See the commentary in this volume beginning at 24:36.

believer's salvation (1 Pt.1:3-5). John mentioned the rapture twice and alluded to the transformation of the bodies of believers at the appearance of Christ (1 Jn. 2:28; 3:2); he also indicated that the glorified bodies received by the saints will be like Christ's glorified body (1 Jn. 3:2, cf. Phil. 3:20-21).

The only detailed descriptions of the actual event occur in three passages: Matthew 24:36-25:30, 1 Corinthians 15:51-53, and 1 Thessalonians 4:13-18. Since Matthew 24:36-25:30 is presented in the commentary, that information will not be repeated here.

In 1 Corinthians, Paul gave the following description.

> Behold, I tell you a mystery; we will not all sleep, but we will all be changed, in a moment, in the twinkling of an eye, at the last trumpet; for the trumpet will sound, and the dead will be raised imperishable, and we will be changed. For this perishable must put on the imperishable, and this mortal must put on immortality. (1 Cor. 15:51-53, NASB)

In 1 Thessalonians he said:

> But we do not want you to be uninformed, brethren, about those who are asleep, so that you will not grieve as do the rest who have no hope. For if we believe that Jesus died and rose again, even so God will bring with Him those who have fallen asleep in Jesus. For this we say to you by the word of the Lord, that we who are alive and remain until the coming of the Lord, will not precede those who have fallen asleep. For the Lord Himself will descend from heaven with a shout, with the voice of the archangel and with the trumpet of God, and the dead in Christ will rise first. Then we who are alive and remain will be caught up together with them in the clouds to meet the Lord in the air, and so we shall always be with the Lord. Therefore comfort one another with these words. (1 Thess. 4:13-18, NASB)

A number of observations flow from Matthew 24:36-25:30, and the two Pauline passages above.

1. The future appearing of Christ has an imminent aspect (the rapture), and a non-imminent aspect (the second coming), cf. Mt. 24:29-25:30.

2. The precise time of the rapture is not known (Mt. 24:42-25:30).

3. Some details of the rapture were apparently a mystery until revealed through Paul (1 Cor. 15:51).

4. At the rapture, Christ will appear in the sky (1 Thess. 4:16).

5. Christ will be accompanied by the souls of the saints who have died, returning to be reunited with their resurrection body (1 Thess. 4:14).

6. The event is to be signaled by a shout from an archangel and a trumpet call (1 Cor. 15:52; 1 Thess. 4:16).

7. The dead in Christ will be resurrected, and then those who are alive will be changed (*i.e.,* transformed into a glorified state), cf. 1 Thess. 4:15-17.

8. Christ will call believers, both the resurrected and the transformed, out of this world (1 Thess. 4:17). Note how the description of the rapture differs from that of the second coming.

9. Believers who live to the rapture will not pass through death (1 Cor. 15:51).

10. The entire event will happen almost instantly (1 Cor. 15:52).

11. The raptured saints will never be separated from Christ (1 Thess. 4:17).

Since the rapture pertains to the Church, it seems likely that the Old Testament saints, along with the tribulation saints that die before the tribulation period ends, will be raised after the second coming (Dan. 12:1-2; Rev. 20:4). In order to understand how the rapture is possible, we must grasp the unique nature of the Church and how God's program for Israel and the Church are distinct.

The nature of the Church

It is God's plan to consummate the salvation of those belonging to the Body of Christ (the Church) at the rapture, and it is the unique nature of the Church that makes the rapture possible. Every saved person in history has a place in the plan of God, but not every saved person in history is part of the Church. I am not referring to the visible, organized church that includes both saved and lost, but to the invisible Body of Christ (Col. 1:18,24), *i.e.,* those who are baptized into Christ by the Holy Spirit. The Church did not exist until the Holy Spirit began baptizing believers into the Body of Christ at Pentecost, A.D. 33 (Acts 1:5 cf. 1 Cor. 12:13). The following facts are essential in understanding who is part of the Church.

1. The Church is the Body of Christ (Col. 1:18,24), and Spirit baptism is the necessary operation of the Holy Spirit that makes one a member of the Body of Christ (1 Cor. 12:13). Since Spirit baptism began on the day of Pentecost (A.D. 33) that was the birth of the Church.

2. By their statements, it is possible to determine that the apostles recognized that Pentecost (A.D. 33) marked the beginning of the Church (Acts 11:15-16).

3. Jesus indicated the Church to be a future reality from the standpoint of his earthly ministry (cf. Mt. 16:18—note the future tense).

4. The nature of the Church age as parenthetical, distinct from God's program for Israel, is reinforced by its complete absence from Old Testament prophecy, which explains God's program for Israel in great detail. Note for example how the Church age is completely absent from the prophecy of Daniel's 70 weeks (Dan. 9:24-27), falling entirely between the 69th and 70th weeks. Likewise it is missing

entirely from the descriptions of the first and second advents of Christ as described in Isaiah 61:1-3.

Views on the timing of the rapture

While we will not go into a full discussion of the differences between dispensationalism and covenant theology, it is important to know that one's view with respect to dispensationalism and covenant theology will have a profound impact on their view of the rapture.[7] Unlike dispensationalists, covenantalists make no distinction between Israel and the Church, viewing all redeemed people as part of the same spiritual body. Since the Bible indicates that redeemed people will be present on earth throughout the tribulation, covenantal interpreters take that as evidence that the rapture does not occur until the second coming. Thus, all forms of covenant theology are posttribulational. Dispensationalists, who reject the covenantal inference that all redeemed people comprise the same spiritual body, do not view the presence of redeemed people in the tribulation as an indication of the presence of the Church, which they view as a distinct body of believers originating at Pentecost (A.D. 33) and extending to the rapture. Among dispensationalists the pretribulational view has been the dominant view of the rapture. However, there are other views associated with dispensationalism; they are: "midtribulationism," which places the rapture at the midpoint of the tribulation; "Rosenthal's pre-wrath view," which places the rapture sometime in the second half of the tribulation; "partial rapturism," which sees only those believers who are prepared as being raptured with the rest being left to go through part or all of the tribulation period; and "imminent pre-wrath rapturism," which views the rapture as imminent and possibly, but not necessarily, pretribulational.[8]

If the Scripture teaches the imminency of the rapture, as the case has been made in the commentary at 24:36-25:30, then midtribulationism, Rosenthal's pre-wrath view, and posttribulationism could not be correct, since those views are not compatible with an imminent rapture. Consequently, the question is whether the Bible does, in fact, teach the imminency of the rapture; and if so, whether imminency requires a pretribulational rapture. Since the case has already been made that the Lord taught a dual appearing, with the rapture being imminent, that point need not be re-argued.[9] Here, we will focus on whether an imminent rapture must be pretribulational, and whether there are any other arguments that might require a pretribulational rapture. It should be stated at the

---

[7] For a discussion of the differences between dispensationalism and covenant theology see, *What the Bible Says About the Future*, Second edition, Chapter 3: "How Systems of Belief Affect Our View of Future Prophecy," pp. 41-54 by the author; and, *There Really is a Difference! A Comparison of Covenant and Dispensational Theology*, by Renald Showers.

[8] For information on the imminent prewrath rapture position see, *Toward a Biblical View of the Rapture*, by the author (Biblical Reader Communications, 2011).

[9] See the discussion beginning at 24:36 in the commentary.

outset that the issue is not whether the rapture "could" be pretribulational. Obviously, if the rapture is imminent, it could happen at any moment, and thus it could occur pretribulationally. The issue is whether it can only occur pretribulationally, as is the central tenet of pretribulationism.

Does proof of the imminency of the rapture prove pretribulationism?

It has long been assumed, both by pretribulationists and by opponents of pretribulationism, that proof for the imminency of the rapture is tantamount to proof of pretribulationism. Consequently, pretribulationists have insisted that both the Scriptures and the beliefs of the early church support imminency, and opponents of pretribulationism have taken the opposite position. The case for the imminency of the rapture has already been made in the commentary, and will be presumed as fact in the following discussion. The question then is this: Does imminency prove pretribulationism? In exploring this question, it would be helpful if we knew how pretribulationism came to be associated with imminency in the first place.

Prior to the emergence of the various alternate dispensational views in the 1900s, there were only two major views of the rapture among premillennialists: pretribulationism and posttribulationism. Of these two views, only pretribulationism is compatible with an imminent rapture, and it was assumed that if imminency were true, then pretribulationism must also be true.

In time, other theories emerged: midtribulationism (1941) and Rosenthal's pre-wrath view (1990). Since both of these views are incompatible with imminency, the same line of argumentation was applied to them—pretribulationism must be the correct theory since it is the only theory compatible with imminency. Of course, this is a reductive error, since it has not been established that pretribulationism is the only possibility compatible with imminency.[10] What if pretribulationism isn't the only possible theory compatible with imminency? What if the rapture could be imminent, but not pretribulational? If so, although imminency would mean that the rapture could be pretribulational, it would not lead to the conclusion that it must be pretribulational. Imminency could not then be used as evidence of pretribulationism. Accordingly, it is critically important to know whether an imminent, non-pretribulational rapture is possible, for until we know that, we cannot answer the question of whether imminency proves pretribulationism.

---

[10] To illustrate this logic, it's like saying that since Christmas occurs in a month ending in "r" it must be in November, since January, February, March, April, May, June, July, and August do not end in "r." What's wrong with this logic? Obviously we didn't exhaust all the possibilities, because September, October, and December also end in "r." If all we knew about the timing of Christmas was that it occurs in a month ending in "r," we would have to conclude that while it might occur in November, it could just as well occur in September, October, or December.

Historically, students of rapture theology have assumed that belief in the imminency of the rapture is compatible only with pretribulationism.[11] However, that is a logical error that has resulted from thinking of the rapture as a sequent event. To think of an event sequently is to view it as part of a sequence, in this case, the sequence of tribulation events. Naturally, a sequenced event cannot be imminent (from the present perspective) unless it is the first event in a sequence of events that could begin at any time. To illustrate the difference between a sequent view of the rapture and a non-sequent (*i.e.*, random) view, let's say we have fifty cards; and on each card we write the name of a tribulation event, and we sort the cards in order. We could then make a card for the rapture. Now, if we put the rapture card in the middle of the stack and begin to turn the cards over one by one, simulating the passage of each event, the rapture would not be imminent since we could not turn the rapture card over until we had turned over all the cards that precede it in the stack. The only way the rapture could be imminent from the present perspective would be if it were the first card in the stack. Applying this analogy, according to pretribulationism the rapture is the first event and it is therefore imminent; but mid-tribulationism, Rosenthal pre-wrath rapturism, and posttribulationism do not place the rapture first, and thus, those theories do not view the rapture as imminent. That's the sequent conception of the rapture. An alternate conception would be a non-sequent, or random view.[12] To illustrate the random view we will use the same stack of imaginary cards, but instead of sorting the rapture card with the stack of tribulation events, we will set it off to the side, with the provision that it can be turned over at any time. Before we even turn the first card the rapture is imminent, because it could be turned over first. Of course, if the rapture card isn't turned over first, it would still be imminent because it could be turned over next. (Remember, the rapture card isn't subject to the sequence of the stack.) Again, if it isn't turned over next it remains imminent until it is finally turned over.

Because thinking of the rapture in sequence with tribulation events has dominated rapture theology, most students of prophecy mistakenly assume that if the rapture is imminent, it must be the first event on the prophetic calendar (hence, pretribulational); conversely, if they do not view the rapture as the first event of the prophetic future, they characteristically deny the imminency of the rapture. Clearly, these views share a common idea: they are all sequent theories. However, the Scriptures do not specify the place in the stream of future prophetic events where the rapture occurs, other than that it must occur before the beginning of divine wrath at the day of the LORD. (Of course that only establishes the terminal point of the rapture window, not a sequence.) Here is where we need to make a critical observation: If the timing of the

---

[11] For a discussion of the imminency of the rapture see the footnote beginning on page 155, and the discussion of 24:36-25:30 in the commentary.

[12] Not that it is random to God, but that it is not linked to the sequence of tribulation events.

rapture is not specified in scripture, it is imminent—not because it is the first event, but because the timing isn't specified, leaving open the possibility that it could occur at any time. This is a crucial distinction, since it allows for the possibility of a pretribulational rapture, but does not necessitate such.[13] In demonstrating that the rapture can be imminent without necessarily being pretribulational, we have shown that imminency does not prove pretribulationism. This illustrates the reductive fallacy that was referred to earlier. Imminency, while compatible with pretribulationism, is not proof. All imminency proves is that the rapture could occur at any time, which is not the same as pretribulationism.

Are there other arguments that might prove pretribulationism?

As has been stated, the argument based on the imminency of the rapture has always been the primary argument for pretribulationism, albeit defective. However, in the early 1900s key pretribulationists re-characterized Matthew 24:45-25:30 as pertaining to the second coming rather than the rapture.[14] Since Matthew 24:36-25:30 is the only biblical passage that explicitly teaches the imminency of the rapture, and since earlier pretribulationists had already relegated 24:36-44 as being a description of the second coming, the re-characterization of the remainder of the passage (24:45-25:30) left pretribulationists with no explicit biblical support for their primary argument. Because of this weakening of the biblical support for imminency, the wrath argument has taken on increased importance in the defense of pretribulationism. The wrath argument states that since the Church is not to be the object of God's wrath (1 Thess. 4:13-5:11, esp. 5:9-10), the rapture of the Church must occur before the manifestation of the divine wrath associated with the day of the LORD. Of course, in order for this argument to support pretribulationism the entire seven-year tribulation period must qualify as divine wrath. In other words, for the wrath argument to support pretribulationism the day of the LORD must begin at the beginning of the tribulation period. One approach in arguing that the entire tribulation period is divine wrath has been from the presumed unity of the period. Pretribulationists sometimes equate the tribulation period with the day of the LORD in order to establish that the entire tribulation is a time of divine wrath; but the basis for

---

[13] Pretribulationists might argue that all of this is a moot point since the rapture is the only prophesied event prior to the beginning of the day of the LORD. However, such a statement assumes the day of the LORD begins immediately at the inception of the tribulation period—an assumption for which there is no proof; indeed the weight of evidence argues strongly to the contrary (see the discussion of 2 Thessalonians 2:3-11 that follows).

[14] This re-characterization originated in the early 1900s and can be detected in the writings of Henry C. Thiessen and Lewis Sperry Chafer; it is quite prominent in the rapture theology of John F. Walvoord, and latent in the writing of J. Dwight Pentecost. The reasons for the re-characterization of Matthew 24:45-25:30 as describing the second coming rather than the rapture, are discussed at length in the footnotes of the commentary at 24:36.

equating the two is the prior assumption that the tribulation is entirely a time of divine wrath (a circular argument). This is sometimes expressed as follows: Whenever the Old Testament discusses the coming day of the Lord, judgment is in view; thus the tribulation is a time of judgment. For an example of this approach, see J. Dwight Pentecost's *Things to Come*, pages 230 and 233-237. Pentecost quotes twenty passages in an effort to prove that the tribulation is a time of judgment, but not one of those passages speaks to the extent of the divine wrath during the tribulation period. The fact that the tribulation includes divine wrath is beyond dispute. Pentecost's evidence demonstrates only that divine wrath occurs sometime during the tribulation—a point upon which virtually all premillennialists agree. However, none of his arguments are useful in proving that the entire tribulation is divine wrath. In other words, the manifestation of divine wrath in the tribulation period and the extent of the tribulation period that can be characterized as divine wrath are distinct issues; and evidence that the tribulation includes divine wrath does not argue that the entire period is divine wrath. Pentecost further states that since the judgments associated with the second coming need to occur over a period of time, the entire tribulation period must be a time of judgment.[15] Of course that is an incredible leap. Why would the judgments directly associated with the second coming need to extend over the entire tribulation period? Pentecost offers no justification whatsoever. He also argues that if the day of the Lord did not begin until the second coming it would be preceded by signs and could not come, as indicated in 1 Thessalonians 5:2, as "a thief in the night."[16] He overlooks the obvious flaw in this argument that if the day of the Lord is to begin on the heels of the rapture, then the rapture would serve as a sign.[17] Of course, the timing of the rapture cannot be used to determine the extent of divine wrath during the tribulation period, since one would have to know the extent of divine wrath to know the last point at which the rapture could occur—a circular problem. While the day of the Lord is undoubtedly a component of the tribulation period, there simply is no biblical or logical reason to assume that the entire seven-year period is to be divine wrath, or that the day of the Lord must begin at the time the tribulation period begins. We should also note that even within pretribulationism there has been considerable disagreement as to when the day of the Lord is to begin. C.I. Scofield held that the day of the Lord will begin at the

---

[15] Pentecost, *Things to Come,* p.230.

[16] Pentecost, p.230.

[17] Note that in 1 Thessalonians 5:1-11 Paul did not say the day of the Lord will take believers by surprise, only that it will take the unbelieving world by surprise, and that would be true regardless of the point at which it begins, because the unredeemed are in spiritual darkness (v.4).

second coming, after the judgments of Revelation 11-18 (*i.e.*, after the seventh trumpet); and Chafer seems to have been in general agreement with that view.[18]

Another approach in equating the entirety of the tribulation period with the day of the LORD is to assert that the seals, trumpets, and bowls of Revelation 6-19 are all divine judgments, and therefore, since it is reasonable to expect that the first seal occurs early in the tribulation period, it follows that the entire seven-year tribulation period is a time of judgment. The difficulty with this line of reasoning is that there is no evidence that the seals represent divine wrath. Rather, the seals appear to be simply movements within the tribulation period. As noted, Scofield limited the apocalyptic judgments to the seventh trumpet, *i.e.*, the bowls of wrath. It is assumed by many that since the book of Revelation pictures Christ breaking the seven seals, that the seals must be divine judgments. Certainly this indicates God's sovereignty over the tribulation events, perhaps as a reminder during those difficult times that God is still sovereign even when evil appears to reign; nevertheless it does not follow that all of the seals represent divine wrath. Revelation does not mention divine wrath until 6:15-17, which is after the events of the sixth seal have passed. And, there is a serious complication in viewing all of the seals as divine wrath. The fifth seal (Rev. 6:9-11 cf. Mt. 24:9, 15-22 and Dan. 7:25) includes the deaths of many faithful saints who maintain their testimony in the face of persecution and martyrdom. Pretribulationism has always been at a loss to explain how the persecution and death of these saints could be attributed directly to an act of divine justice. If all the seals represent divine wrath, then the fifth seal must be divine wrath also; yet Revelation pictures the major event during the time of the fifth seal as an evil to be punished by a future, but soon, outpouring of divine wrath (6:11 cf. 8:1-6). The fact that these martyrs are pictured in Heaven under the altar making lamentation to God (6:9-11) and asking for justice in avenging their blood is indicative that the deaths of these saints can in no way be attributable to God's justice in the execution of divine wrath. In answer to the prayers of these saints for justice and vengeance, God responds that they should wait for their petition to be answered (6:11); and the events of the seventh seal (the sequence of trumpet and bowl judgments) are plainly indicated to be, at least in part, in response to the prayers of the saints from under the altar (8:1-6 cf. 16:4-7 and 19:2). Interestingly, these are the only components of the tribulation that are specifically designated as divine wrath (Rev. 15:1; 16:1). Thus, it is not without significance that the first mention of divine wrath in this book occurs after the breaking of the sixth seal, just prior to the breaking of the seventh seal (6:17). Given these observations, it is difficult to sustain the case that all of the seals represent divine wrath. Of course if God's wrath has not commenced by the close of the fifth seal, at most only

---

[18] See the footnote on page 1349 in the original *Scofield Reference Bible*. (That footnote was subsequently changed in *The New Scofield Reference Bible*, p.1363.) Also see: Chafer, *Systematic Theology*, vol. IV, pp.11, 383, 398; and vol. VII, p.110.

the last two seals could include divine wrath. Since wrath is not mentioned until after the time of the sixth seal is past (6:17), and since there is a momentous transition between the sixth and seventh seals (8:1), the case could be made that the likely point for divine wrath to begin (*i.e.*, the beginning of the day of the LORD) is with the opening of the seventh seal, though it is not necessary to argue that point in order to see the problem with pretribulationism's use of the wrath argument. There simply is no biblical or theological evidence that the tribulation is coextensive with the day of the LORD. While we know that the day of the LORD must fall sometime within Daniel's 70th week, since the first 69 weeks of the prophecy are past, and both the 70th week and the wrath associated with the day of the LORD terminate at the second coming, there is simply no good argument demonstrating that the entire tribulation period represents divine wrath.[19] Thus, the wrath argument fails to prove pretribulationism, though it does require the rapture to occur before the day of the LORD begins.

A major problem with pretribulationism's central thesis: 2 Thessalonians 2:1-12

Having noted the inability to prove the claim that the entire tribulation is divine wrath, we now turn our attention to 2 Thessalonians 2:1-9, which poses a serious obstacle to pretribulationism's wrath argument in that it asserts that the day of the LORD will not begin until sometime in the second half of the tribulation, after the apostasy associated with the revealing of the Antichrist in the temple at the midpoint of the tribulation period. If it can be demonstrated that the day of the LORD does not begin until sometime in the second half of the tribulation period, then pretribulationism's claim that the entire tribulation is divine wrath is not only unproven, but disproven. Paul states in 2 Thessalonians 2:1-12:

> (1) Now we request you, brethren, with regard to the coming of our Lord Jesus Christ and our gathering together to Him, (2) that you not be quickly shaken from your composure or be disturbed either by a spirit or a message or a letter as if from us, to the effect that the day of the Lord has come. (3) Let no one in any way deceive you, for it will not come unless the apostasy comes first, and the man of lawlessness is revealed, the son of destruction, (4) who opposes and exalts himself above every so-called god or object of worship, so that he takes his seat in the temple of God, displaying himself as being God. (5) Do you not remember that while I was still with you, I was telling you these things? (6) And you know what restrains him now, so that in his time he will be revealed. (7) For the mystery of lawlessness is already at work; only he who now restrains will do so until he is taken out of the way. (8) Then that lawless one will be revealed whom the Lord will slay with the breath of His mouth and bring to an end by the appearance of His coming; (9) that is, the one whose coming is in accord with the activity of Satan, with all power and signs and false wonders, (10) and with all the

---

[19] The tribulation period and the day of the LORD are co-terminal, but not necessarily coextensive.

deception of wickedness for those who perish, because they did not receive the love of the truth so as to be saved. (11) For this reason God will send upon them a deluding influence so that they will believe what is false, (12) in order that they all may be judged who did not believe the truth, but took pleasure in wickedness. (NASB)

In this passage Paul stated that the day of the LORD will not begin until after "the apostasy" (v. 3, ἡ ἀποστασία)—not just any apostasy, but "*the* apostasy" (the one prophetically anticipated) that occurs in connection with the revealing of the man of lawlessness (καὶ, "and" is used here ascensively, meaning "even," or "indeed"). Note how much attention Paul devotes to the description of the revealing of the man of lawlessness (vv.3-9). Why? –Because the revealing of the man of lawlessness distinguishes this particular apostasy from all others. Some pretribulationists have interpreted "the falling away"(the apostasy) as a veiled reference to the rapture, and the revealing of the man of lawlessness as the appearing of the Antichrist at the beginning of the tribulation period. However, given Paul's statement as we have it, it is apparent that he intended his readers to understand the revealing of the man of lawlessness as his revealing in accordance with his true character as Antichrist, when he seats himself in the temple of God (v.4). How do we know this? 2 Thessalonians 2:3-4 comprises one sentence in the original, and it is apparent that the falling away and the "revealing" are thus related components of the same description, which is further developed in verses 5-9. This is a specific apostasy—the one in connection with Antichrist's revealing (v.4) when he takes his seat in the temple purveying himself to be God with satanic power displayed in signs and wonders deceiving those who have rejected the truth, *i.e.*, the non-elect (vv.5-9). We know from Daniel 9:27 that this event marks the midpoint of the tribulation period. As we have seen in the commentary, there is a parallel to this description in Matthew 24:4-25 in which Jesus stated that the abomination in the temple (v.15) will be accompanied by persecution and apostasy (vv.10, 15-22), spiritual deception of the non-elect (vv.11, 24-28), lawlessness (v.12), and deceptive signs and wonders (v.24). It is thus apparent that Paul had Jesus' Olivet Discourse in mind when he penned 2 Thessalonians 2:1-12, since he mentioned five of the six major aspects associated with the midpoint of the tribulation as outlined in Matthew 24:9-24.[20] The five matching characteristics in these two passages (one spoken by Christ, and the other penned by Paul) are listed together nowhere else in the New Testament. Assuming a chronology of Matthew 24:4-31 in which verses 4-8 refer to the first half of the tribulation, and verses 9-14 refer to the second half, with verses 15-31 being a recursion back to the midpoint expanding on the second half, the actual order of these events is:

---

[20] Although it is likely that the gospels were written after 2 Thessalonians, undoubtedly accounts of Christ's Olivet Discourse circulated early in the churches at Jerusalem and Antioch, and it is not likely that Paul would have been unfamiliar with this important material.

1) the revealing of the Antichrist in the temple; 2) the great persecution, martyrdom and apostasy; 3) lawlessness; 4) deceiving signs and miracles; and, 5) the deception of the non-elect. It is important to note that due to the recursive structure of Matthew 24:15-31, the apostasy mentioned in 24:10 actually occurs after the revelation of the Antichrist in the temple mentioned in 24:15.[21] The apostasy most likely occurs in connection with the great persecution that follows the Antichrist's revealing (cf. vv.16-22). Unless one is willing to argue that Paul's description of the man of lawlessness in the temple and the related spiritual deception, lawlessness, and deceiving miracles described in verses 3-9 have no direct connection to the apostasy described within the same sentence, it should be apparent that the apostasy referred to by Paul is the apostasy that will take place shortly after the midpoint of the tribulation.[22] Since it is apparent that both Jesus and Paul described the same set of events, and since these events, in both places, are unquestionably associated with the revealing of the Antichrist at the midpoint of the tribulation period, it is evident that Paul taught that the day of the LORD would not arrive until sometime in the second half of the tribulation period, after the apostasy associated with the revelation of the Antichrist in the temple. That being the case, while there is overlap between the seven-year period of tribulation and the day of the LORD, they cannot be co-extensive as required by the pretribulational version of the wrath argument.

While the New Testament does indicate that the rapture is imminent (Mt. 24:36-25:30), and that it must precede the beginning of the day of the LORD (1 Thess. 1:10; 5:9-10 cf. 4:13-5:8) it does not indicate that the rapture must occur pretribulationally. We previously ruled out midtribulationism, Rosenthal's pre-wrath view, and posttribulationism on the grounds that they are incompatible with the imminency of the rapture; and we have also ruled out pretribulationism on the grounds that it is neither required by imminency nor supported by the wrath argument. Thus, with respect to the timing of the rapture all we can say with certainty is that it is imminent, perhaps, but not necessarily, pretribulational, and that it will occur prior to the beginning of the day of the LORD. Any view of the timing of the rapture that exceeds the bounds of these statements should be viewed with caution.

---

[21] See the discussion of the chronology of Matthew 24 on page 104, and also on page 245ff.

[22] Some pretribulationists regard the apostasy in verse 3 as either a veiled reference to a pretribulational rapture, or an apostasy, or general state of apostasy occurring during the Church age prior to a pretribulational rapture of the Church. Both of these explanations fail to account for the structure of Paul's passage in 2 Thessalonians 2, and its connection to Jesus' parallel description in the Olivet Discourse.

Bibliography

Works Cited in This Volume

Aland, Kurt, ed. *Synopsis of the Four Gospels.* United Bible Societies, 1982.

Bock, Darrell L. *Luke 9:52-24:53.* Grand Rapids: Baker Academic, 1996.

Boice, James Montgomery. *The Gospel of Matthew (Volume 2): The Triumph of the King.* Grand Rapids: Baker Book House, 2001.

Calvin, John. *Institutes of the Christian Religion.* trans. by Henry Beveridge. Peabody: Hendrickson Publishers, 2008.

Chafer, Lewis Sperry. *Systematic Theology.* Volumes 4 & 5. Grand Rapids: Kregal Publications, 1993 reprint.

Evans, Craig A. *Luke,* in The New International Biblical Commentary. Peabody: Hendrickson Publishers, 1995.

Feinberg, Charles L. *The Prophecy of Ezekiel: The Glory of God.* Chicago: Moody Press, 1972.

Geldenhuys, Norval. *Commentary on the Gospel of Luke,* in The New International Commentary on the New Testament. Grand Rapids: William B. Eerdmans Publishing Co. 1951.

Hoehner, Harold W. *Chronological Aspects of the Life of Christ.* Grand Rapids: Zondervan Publishing House, 1977.

Hurtado, Larry W. *Mark,* in the New International Biblical Commentary. Peabody: Hendrickson Publishers, 2001.

Ironside, H.A. *Mark.* Baltimore: Liozeaux Brothers (1994 revision of Expository Notes on the Gospel of Mark, originally published in 1948.)

_____. *Matthew.* Baltimore: Liozeaux Brother (1994 revision of *Expository Notes on the Gospel of Matthew,* originally published in 1948.)

Josephus, Flavius. "The Wars of the Jews," in *The Works of Josephus.* (translated by William Whitson) Lynn, Massachusetts: Hendrickson Publishers, 1980.

Keil, C.F. *Biblical Commentary on the Book of Daniel,* Volume 10 in The Commentary on the Old Testament by C.F. Keil and F. Delitzsch. Grand Rapids: William B. Eerdmans Publishing Co., 1980 reprint.

Ladd, George Eldon. *The Blessed Hope.* Grand Rapids: William B. Eerdmans, 1956.

Lange J.P. *Matthew,* in Lange's Commentary on the Holy Scriptures. Grand Rapids: Zondervan Publishing House, (undated reprint, possibly 1950).

Lenski, R.C.H. *The Interpretation of St. Luke's Gospel.* Minneapolis: Augsburg Publishing House, 1961.

_____. *The Interpretation of St. Mark's Gospel.* Minneapolis: Augsburg Publishing House, 1964.

_____. *The Interpretation of St. Matthew's Gospel.* Minneapolis: Augsburg Publishing House, 1961.

McKnight, Scott. *Interpreting the Synoptic Gospels.* Grand Rapids: Baker Book House, 1988.

Mounce, Robert H. *Matthew,* in the New International Biblical Commentary. Peabody: Hendrickson Publishers, 1991.

Pentecost, J. Dwight. *Things to Come: A Study in Biblical Eschatology.* Grand Rapids: Zondervan Publishing House, 1976.

Perrin, Norman. *What is Redaction Criticism?* Philadelphia: Fortress Press, 1969.

Pétrement, Simone. *A Separate God: The Origins and Teaching of Gnosticism.* trans. by Carol Harrison. New York: HarperSanFrancisco, 1990.

Riddlebarger, Kim. *A Case for Amillennialism: Understanding the End Times.* Grand Rapids: Baker Books, 2003.

Robertson, A.T. *A Harmony of the Gospels For Students of the Life of Christ.* New York: Harper & Brothers Publishers, 1922.

Rosenthal, Marvin. *The Pre-wrath Rapture of the Church.* Nashville: Thomas Nelson Publishers, 1990.

Ryle, J.C. *Ryle's Expository Thoughts on the Gospels.* vol 1: Matthew-Mark. Grand Rapids: Baker Book House, 1977.

Scofield, C.I. *The Scofield Reference Bible.* New York: Oxford University Press, 1917.

Showers, Renald E. *The Most High God: A Commentary on the Book of Daniel.* Bellmawr: The Friends of Israel Gospel Ministry, 1989.

Smith, Sam A. "Regeneration and Indwelling in the Old Testament," [Internet paper: www.biblicalreader.com/btr], 2009.

_____. "The Biblical Doctrine of Personal Apostasy." [Internet paper: www.biblicalreader.com], 2007.

_____. "The Non-Christian Anticosmic Roots of Amillennialism." [Internet paper: www.biblicalreader.com], 2006.

_____. *Toward a Biblical View of the Rapture.* Raleigh: Biblical Reader Communications, 2011.

_____. "Two Significant Problems With Harold W. Hoehner's Chronology of the Life of Christ." [Internet paper: www.biblicalreader.com], 2012.

_____. *What the Bible Says About the Future.* (Second edition), Raleigh: Biblical Reader Communications, 2011. (Also available online at www.biblicalreader.com.)

_____. "Who is the Seed of Abraham?" [Internet paper: www.biblicalreader.com], 2005.

The New Scofield Reference Bible. (Based on *The Scofield Reference Bible*, edited by C.I. Scofield, Oxford University Press, 1917), E. Schuyler English (Chairman, Editorial Committee of the New Edition), New York: Oxford University Press, 1967.

Thiessen, Henry C., "Will the Church Pass Through the Tribulation," <u>Bibliotheca Sacra</u> vol. 92, no. 366 (1935): 187-205.

Throckmorton, Burton H., ed. *Gospel Parallels: A Synopsis of the First Three Gospels*. New York: Thomas Nelson and Son, 1957 (Reprint April, 1961).

Walvoord, John F. *Matthew: Thy Kingdom Come*. Chicago: Moody Press, 1974.

_____. *The Blessed Hope and the Tribulation: A Historical and Biblical Study of Posttribulationism*. (A volume in the Contemporary Evangelical Perspectives Series) Grand Rapids: Zondervan Publishing House, 1976.

_____. *The Prophecy Knowledge Handbook*. Wheaton: Victor Books, 1990.

_____. *The Rapture Question*. Grand Rapids: Zondervan Publishing House, 1957.

Yamauchi, Edwin M. *Persia and the Bible*. Grand Rapids: Baker Book House, 1990.

Works For Further Reading

Armerding, Carl E. and W. Ward Gasque, eds., *A Guide to Biblical Prophecy*. Peabody: Hendrickson Publishers, 1989.

Albright, W.E., and C.S. Mann. *Matthew*. Anchor Bible. vol. 26. New York: Doubleday, 1971.

Allen, W. C. *A Critical and Exegetical Commentary on the Gospel according to St. Matthew*. International Critical Commentary. 3rd ed. Edinburgh: T. & T. Clark, 1912.

Balmforth, H. *The Gospel According to Saint Luke in the Revised Version with Introduction and Commentary*. Oxford: Clarendon, 1930. Reprinted, 1958.

Baily, Keith M. *Christ's Coming & His Kingdom*. Harrisburg: Christian Publications, 1981.

Barclay, W. *The Gospel of Matthew*. Rev. ed. 2 vols. Philadelphia: Westminster, 1975.

Baron, David. *The Visions and Prophecies of Zechariah*. Grand Rapids: Kregal Publications, 1981 reprint.

Black, David Allen. *New Testament Textual Criticism: A Concise Guide*. Grand Rapids: Baker Books, 1994.

Bultmann, R. *History of the Synoptic Tradition*. Rev. ed. New York: Harper & Row, 1976.

Drury, J. *Luke*. in J. B. Philips' Commentaries. New York: Macmillan, 1973.

Erdman, C. R. *The Gospel of Luke*. Philadelphia: Westminster, 1942.

Feinberg, Charles L. *Zechariah: Israel's Comfort and Glory*. New York: American Board of Missions to the Jews, 1968.

Fitzmyer, J. A. *The Gospel According to Luke*. 2 vols. Anchor Bible. Garden City: Doubleday, 1981, 1985.

Gaebelein, A.C. *The Prophet Daniel: A Key to the Visions and Prophecies of the Book of Daniel*. Grand Rapids: Kregal Publications, 1968.

Godet, F. A. *A Commentary on the Gospel of St. Luke.* 2 vols. Edinburgh: T & T. Clark, 1888, 1889.

Gundry, R. H. *Matthew: A Commentary on His literary and Theological Art.* Grand Rapids: Eerdmans, 1982.

Hoekema, Anthony A. *The Bible and the Future.* Grand Rapids: William B. Eerdmans Publishing Co., 1989 reprint.

Johnson, S. E. *The Gospel According to St. Matthew.* Interpreter's Bible. vol. 7. Nashville: Abingdon, 1951.

Kealy, Sean. *Mark's Gospel: History of Its Interpretation.* New York: Paulist Press, 1982.

Lane, W. L. *The Gospel of Mark.* The New International Commentary on the New Testament. Grand Rapids: Eerdmans, 1974.

Lightner, Robert P. *The Last Days Handbook.* Nashville: Thomas Nelson Publishers, 1990.

Marshall, I. H. *Commentary on Luke.* New International Greek Testament Commentary. Grand Grand: Eerdmans, 1978.

Morris, L. *The Gospel According to St. Luke.* Tyndale New Testament Commentary. Grand Rapids: Eerdmans, 1974.

Pate, Daniel. *Structural Exegesis for New Testament Critics.* Minneapolis: Fortress Press, 1990.

Plummer, A. *A Critical and Exegetical Commentary on the Gospel According to S. Luke.* International Critical Commentary. Edinburgh: T. & T. Clark. 1896.

_____. *An Exegetical Commentary on the Gospel According to S Matthew.* 5th ed. London: E. Stock 1920.

Robertson, A. T. *A Translation of Luke's Gospel with Grammatical Notes.* New York: Doran, 1923.

Smith, Sam A. "Chronological-topical Index to Future Prophecy." [Index of eschatological prophecy available through the Internet at: www.biblicalreader.com], 2005.

_____. "Daniel 9:24-27 –The Prophecy of Daniel's 70 Weeks." [Internet paper: www.biblicalreader.com], 2007.

_____. "How the Amillennial Conception of the Kingdom is Developed." [Internet paper: www.biblicalreader.com], 2005.

Tan, Paul Lee. *The Interpretation of Prophecy.* Rockville: Assurance Publishers, 1981 reprint.

Tasker, R. V. G. *The Gospel According to St. Matthew.* Tyndale Bible Commentaries. vol. 1. Grand Rapids: Eerdmans, 1961.

Walvoord, John F. *Daniel: The Key to Prophetic Revelation.* Chicago: Moody Press, 1971.

_____. *The Millennial Kingdom.* Grand Rapids: Zondervan Publishing House, 1959.

_____. *The Return of the Lord.* Grand Rapids: Zondervan Publishing House, 1955.

Whitcomb, John C. *Daniel.* Chicago: Moody Press, 1985.